New Perspectives on Middle East Politics

Economy, Society, and International Relations

**Edited by
Robert Mason**

The American University in Cairo Press
Cairo New York

First published in 2021 by
The American University in Cairo Press
113 Sharia Kasr el Aini, Cairo, Egypt
One Rockefeller Plaza, 10th Floor, New York, NY 10020
www.aucpress.com

ISBN 978 1 617 97990 3

Library of Congress Cataloging-in-Publication Data

Names: Mason, Robert
Title: New perspectives on Middle East politics: economy, society, and
    international relations
Identifiers: LCCN 2020037111 (print) | LCCN 2020037112 (ebook) |
    ISBN 9781617979903 (hardback) | ISBN 9781649030610 (epub) |
    ISBN 9781649030627 (pdf)
Subjects: LCSH: Middle East—Politics and government—21st century. |
    Middle East—Economic conditions—21st century. | Middle East—Foreign
    Relations—21st century.
Classification: LCC DS63.123 .N49 2021 (print) | LCC DS63.123 (ebook) |
    DDC 320.956—dc23

1 2 3 4 5   25 24 23 22 21

Designed by Newgen India
Printed in the United States of America

Robert Mason is a fellow of the Sectarianism, Proxies and De-sectarianisation project at Lancaster University, non-resident fellow with the Arab Gulf States Institute in Washington, and currently sits on the International Studies Association (ISA) Foreign Policy Analysis Section Executive Board. He was associate professor of Middle East Studies at the American University in Cairo (2016–2019), visiting scholar in the Department of Near Eastern Studies at Princeton University in 2019, and visiting research fellow at the University of Oxford in 2016. His research focuses mainly on the international relations of the Middle East, including Gulf politics, Euro-Med and Middle East–Asia relations. Dr. Mason is the author or editor of numerous books, including *Reassessing Order and Disorder in the Middle East: Regional Imbalance or Disintegration?* (2017), *Egypt and the Gulf: A Renewed Regional Policy Alliance* (2016), *Muslim Minority-State Relations: Violence, Integration, and Policy* (2016), *International Politics of the Arab Spring: Popular Unrest and Foreign Policy* (2014), and *Foreign Policy in Iran and Saudi Arabia: Economics and Diplomacy in the Middle East* (2014).

Political Economy and International Relations of the Middle East

Robert Mason, Simon Mabon, and Ishac Diwan, series editors

Contents

Preface

I am an international relations and Middle East politics scholar by training, focusing primarily on the foreign policies of Saudi Arabia and Iran as well as some of the smaller Gulf states such as the UAE, Oman, and Qatar. However, since moving to Cairo in 2013 and having directed the Middle East Studies Center at the American University in Cairo (AUC) for three years, I have become increasingly interested in the history, society, and political economy of the wider Middle East. This book is inspired by a core postgraduate course I taught at AUC entitled "Introduction to Middle East Studies," which provided an overview of the region and dealt with concepts from the wider literature on Middle East studies, including the forces and cleavages that shape the region today.

The rapidly changing political and (in)security landscape in the Middle East since the Arab Uprisings began has meant that questions about governance, conflict, reconstruction, and economic development have become increasingly relevant and important in discussions about the region. So too the impact of powers such as Russia, China, and India and questions regarding the future orientation of US and EU Middle East policy. All these aspects are explored in this introductory volume, which highlights key social, political, and economic concepts.

I am grateful to all the contributors who have participated in this volume and brought their research and insights to their respective chapters. Any omissions remain my responsibility alone. I am grateful to Nadia Naqib and Nigel Fletcher-Jones at AUC Press for their unstinting support during the production of this text, and to Ola Seif from the AUC

Rare Books Library, who helped produce the map of the Middle East and North Africa region. Finally, this book is dedicated to my son, Omar, who continues to sustain and inspire me.

Robert Mason
Cairo/France
February 2020

Glossary, Actors, and Abbreviations

International Relations and Political Theory

Alliance: When major and minor powers work together allocating contributions according to their means.

Authoritarian upgrading: 'Involves reconfiguring authoritarian governance to accommodate and manage changing political, economic, and social conditions.'[1] Strategies may include minor changes to or consolidation of governance, shifting social bases to maintain or enhance political legitimacy, some economic liberalization, as well as the more standard aspects such as divide and rule, co-optation, coercion, and repression.

Authoritarianism: A form of government that generally refers to undemocratic rule, without the institutions and procedures of political participation and competition, or fundamental rights and controls on power. Unlike totalitarian regimes, there is no legitimating of the regime through an overarching political ideology, relying instead on values such as patriotism, nationalism, order, and so on.

Bunker states: Typified by military regimes that manipulate and defend themselves against civil unrest. They fall within the bottom quadrant with regard to commercial bank credit offered to the private sector and the proportion of contract-intensive money. Although these regimes monopolize any rents, they are vulnerable to lower oil prices because their oil revenues, workers' remittances, and foreign aid barely sustain their balance of payments.

Cold War: A period of rivalry and geopolitical tension between the United States and its allies and the Soviet Union and its satellite states lasting from 1945 until the fall of the Soviet Union in 1991.

Constructivism: An international relations theory that claims many aspects of international relations are historically and socially constructed (including norms, identity, and ideational power) rather than related to human nature or other characteristics of the world system.

Core-periphery model: A concept developed by John Friedman in 1963 to show spatially how economic, political, and cultural authority is located in dominant regions, known as the core, and in the surrounding regions, known as the periphery.

Corruption: Joseph S. Nye defines corruption as "a behavior which deviates from the formal duties of a public role (elective or appointed) because of private-regarding (personal, close family, private clique) wealth or status gains [see **Crony Capitalism**]; or violates rules against the exercise of certain types of private-regarding influence."[2] However, one could envisage a broader definition that refers to unwarranted foreign meddling, objectively poor governance, and armed militia of all persuasions.

Coup d'état: The overthrow of an existing government by nondemocratic means. It is typically unconstitutional and illegal.

Critical approaches to international relations: These include Marxist, feminist, postcolonial, and ecological perspectives that critique major theories on international relations and state behavior.

Crony capitalism: An economic system in which family members and friends of government officials and business leaders are given unfair advantages (government decisions, business opportunities, jobs, loans, etc.) compared with the rest of society. The political market shifts emphasis away from innovation, competition, and free-market principles.

Dependency theory: A strand of political-economic thought that developed out of the UN Economic Commission for Latin America and Caribbean after the Second World War. It argues that underdevelopment is the result of capital intervention, rather than 'lacking' development or investment.

Dutch disease: Coined by the *Economist* magazine in 1977 to describe the Dutch economy at the time, the term refers to commodity booms (a single economic sector) that generate macroeconomic problems from high foreign currency incomes. When the income is changed into local currency, it leads to inflation and makes other parts of the economy less competitive in international markets. Commodities such as oil and gas extraction generate few jobs and the fluctuation of prices in international markets also creates economic uncertainty. Without diversification and other backup industries to stabilize the economy and fill any contribution gaps in the government's budget, economic conditions can worsen over time.

Economic nationalism: A set of policies that favors state interventionism through domestic control of the economy, labor, and capital formation, over market forces.

Economic statecraft: The application of economic means in pursuit of foreign policy goals, including specific objectives, through the use of economic tools such as sanctions or broader objectives such as promoting free trade and open markets through a mix of incentives (see also **Soft power**).

The English School: An approach that favors detailed observation and interpretative methods over theoretically testable cases. Historical understandings, domestic politics, and the primacy of international law and institutions (according to Hedley Bull, a leading English School scholar) are key to understanding major contemporary and possible future trends, including threats, in world politics.

Exclusive economic zone (EEZ): A concept adopted at the Third UN Conference on the Law of the Sea (1982). A coastal state assumes jurisdiction over the exploration and exploitation of marine resources extending two hundred miles from the shore.

Foreign policy analysis (FPA): A branch of political science that focuses on the determinants of foreign policies and by extension state policy orientations, behavior, and international relations.

Globalization: The process by which the world's economies, cultures, and populations become more interdependent due to increasing cross-border trade, flows of investment, people, and information, and through greater intergovernmental cooperation.

Green economy: An economy that aims to reduce environmental risks and ecological scarcity while promoting sustainable development practices.

Idealism: Also known as liberalism, it is an international relations theory that stresses cooperation above all else.

Institutionalism: This theory shares Realist assumptions about the international system, but by emphasizing microeconomic and game theory, it comes to different conclusions about the potential for cooperation between nations.

International community: The states and people of the world considered in collective form.

Less developed countries (LDCs): A list of countries that, according to the UN, exhibits the lowest indictors of socioeconomic development in the world.

Military-industrial complex: An informal alliance between the military and the defense industry that supplies it, including coalitions of military and civilian government figures and corporate managers that can act as a vested-interest group. These complexes have a role in the global environment through international arms sales and other forms of military contracting. The warnings about the growing power of the military-industrial complex were outlined by President Eisenhower in his farewell speech in 1961.

More developed countries (MDCs): Also known as a developed country or industrialized country, it is a state that has a developed economy or advanced technological infrastructure relative to less developed countries.

Multipolarity: A distribution of international power in which more than two states have near equal amounts of military, cultural, economic, and political influence.

Neo-patrimonial politics: Builds on a foundation of traditional and personalized reciprocities and loyalties (see **Patrimonialism**).

Neorealism: Also known as structural realism, it asserts that power is the most important factor in international relations. First proposed by Kenneth Waltz in his 1979 book *Theory of International Politics*.

Nonstate actor: An individual, group, or organization that has social, economic, or political influence.

Omnibalancing: A theory put forward by Steven David in 1991 to explain state behavior and alliances as a result of not only 'balance of power' theory but also overall balance of political forces at the domestic, regional, and international levels and generally in favor of elite security needs.

Pariah state: A state that faces international isolation, sanctions, or possible invasion by other states that find its policies or actions unacceptable.

Patrimonialism: Defined by Max Weber as meaning a specific form of legitimation that included reciprocal exchanges between rulers and groups.

Penetrated political system: The politics of the system exists in continuous confrontation with a dominant outside political system. In the case of the Middle East, the outside system is the Western system (including Russia). The politics of a penetrated society cannot be explained without reference to the intrusive outside system.

Political repression/violence: The act of subduing individuals or parts of the population through institutional or physical force to achieve political goals. They often involve violations of human rights amounting to human rights abuses.

Realism: Also known as political realism, it is a view of international relations that stresses competition and conflict as overriding factors. Usually contrasted with Idealism. Classical realists such as Reinhold Niebuhr and Hans Morgenthau emphasize the national interest and political realities but it is not Machiavellian.

Rentier state theory (RST): Seeks to explain the impacts of external payments from rents of indigenous resources to external clients on state-society relations and governance.

Resource curse: Refers to the paradox that countries with an abundance of natural resources, such as fossil fuels, tend to have lower economic growth and worse development outcomes than countries with fewer natural resources.

Self-determination: The principle and right of a people to determine their own destiny, with particular focus on political status to control economic, cultural, and social development. It is embodied in Article I of the Charter of the United Nations and was earlier embraced by US president Woodrow Wilson and by the first leader of the USSR, Vladimir Lenin.

Social exclusion: This occurs when people cannot fully participate in or contribute to society because of denied civil, political, social, economic, or cultural rights. It is usually linked to unemployment, poverty, poor skills, poor housing, poor health, or family breakdown.

Soft power: Coined by Joseph S. Nye Jr. in the late 1980s, it is the ability to attract and persuade without resorting to force (a function of military or economic weight in global affairs) or hard power. It is usually the result of culture, political ideas, and policies.

Sovereignty: Supreme decision-making and enforcement authority with regard to a territory and population. The absence of a supreme international authority and state independence gives rise to an anarchic international system.

Sphere of influence: A territory or region over which an outside state claims control, influence, or preferential status in military, political, or economic terms, thereby limiting the autonomy of local actors and restricting the rights of other external powers.

Ungoverned spaces: Zones that lie beyond the reach of central government, often with more geographically remote areas being more susceptible to violent radicalization and extremism.

Unipolar: Refers to the distribution of power in which one state exercises most of the military, cultural, economic, and political influence.

Vassal state: A state with varying degrees of independence in its internal affairs, but dominated by another in its foreign affairs and potentially wholly subject to the dominating state.

Weak state: Generally defines a state with low or stagnant economic growth and weak governing institutions that are unable to implement policies or maintain autonomy due to corruption or conflict.

Westphalian state system: A term arising from Treaties of Westphalia in 1648 that ended the Thirty Years' War in Central Europe. It generally refers to a system of states or international society possessing a monopoly on the use of force within recognized territories.

Since relations between states are conducted through diplomatic ties, and formal treaties constituting international law, the term implies a separation of domestic and international spheres making intervention in the domestic affairs of another state illegitimate and unlawful (see **Responsibility to Protect**).

War and Conflict

Cold Peace (Israel-Egypt): A state of relative peace marked by the enforcement of a peace treaty signed by the United States, Egypt, and Israel on March 26, 1979. It is characterized by the exchange of ambassadors and coordination on security and borders, but full normalization of relations has never occurred.

Conflict spillover: The spread of violent conflict and its ramifications, including external military support, large numbers of refugees, and fragility of neighboring states.

Extraordinary rendition: The extrajudicial transfer of a detainee to the custody of a foreign government for the purposes of interrogation, detention, and oftentimes treatment amounting to torture.

Extra-regional actors: State or nonstate entities that are located outside a particular region but nevertheless have interests or obligations that drive their engagement (security, political, economic) within a region.

Failed state: A state whose political, economic, and security systems have become so weakened that it is no longer in control or where the sovereign government is no longer able to function properly.

Global War on Terror (GWOT): An international military campaign launched by the United States after 9/11 primarily focused on Afghanistan and Iraq, but also including territories in Central and Southeast Asia, the Middle East, and Africa.

Hybrid conflict: A military strategy that employs elements of state-to-state conflict and nonstate actors. While it includes aspects such as political warfare, irregular warfare, and influencing methods such as fake news, diplomacy, and foreign electoral intervention, only cyber warfare is relatively new.

Internally displaced persons (IDPs): Someone who is forced to flee their home but who remains within a country's territorial borders. They do not fall within the legal definition of 'refugee.'

International Criminal Court (ICC): Investigates and, where warranted, tries individuals charged with the gravest crimes of concern to the international community, including crimes of genocide, crimes against humanity, war crimes, and crimes of aggression.

International Humanitarian Law (IHL): Also known as the law of armed conflict, it seeks to regulate and limit the effects of armed conflict to protect civilians and others not taking part in hostilities. Promoting respect for IHL remains an urgent challenge for the international community.

Militarized state: The process by which a state organizes itself for military conflict or violence against ordinary citizens. In the Middle East, this is often in a process of 'regime remaking.'[3]

Militia: A military force that is raised from the civil population to supplement the regular army in an emergency and/or a military force that engages in rebel or terrorist activities.

North Atlantic Treaty Organization (NATO): Also called the North Atlantic Alliance, it is an intergovernmental military alliance between twenty-nine North American and European countries. The North Atlantic Treaty, which established the organization, was signed on April 4, 1949.

Post conflict economic reconstruction: The process by which peace and security or measures designed to deliver sustainable economic development are implemented in war-torn economy.

Proxy war: Occurs when a major power instigates or plays an important role in supporting (through weapons, training, or funding, for example) or directing a party to a conflict.

Radicalization: The action(s) or process of causing someone to adopt radical positions on social, religious, or political issues. Such individuals may go on to become terrorists or support terrorism.

Refugee: A displaced person who is forced to cross national boundaries and cannot return home safely. According to the United Nations, an unprecedented 70.8 million people around the world have been forced from home by conflict and persecution by the end of 2018.

Regime change: The replacement of one administration or government by another, including through the use of military force.

Regional security complex theory (RSCT): Barry Buzan and Ole Waever assert that regional patterns of security are important in international politics and even global power interests are often regional in nature.[4]

Responsibility to protect (R2P): A global political commitment made by all member states of the United Nations at the 2005 World Summit to address four concerns: genocide, war crimes, crimes against humanity, and ethnic cleansing.

Threat perception: Originally linked to theories of war, deterrence, alliances, and conflict resolution, threat perception became a distinct strand of IR scholarship as 'rationalist' models of deterrence and war included greater reference to signaling and credibility, and as political psychology became more concerned with perception and misperception of intention and military capabilities.

Weapons of mass destruction (WMDs): A nuclear, chemical, biological, or any other weapon that can kill or bring significant harm to humans and/or cause severe damage to infrastructure.

Society

Waithood: A period of stagnation whereby following the youth life stage, adult male lives stall due to an inability to find stable and salaried employment, which leaves them and young women, most of whom do not enter the labor market, unable to marry.

Youth bulge: A stage of development when a country has succeeded in reducing infant mortality but mothers still have a high fertility rate.

Select States and Subregions (in Alphabetical Order)
Egypt

Abdel Fattah El-Sisi: Egyptian politician, sixth president of Egypt since 2014 (although in control since the removal of President Morsi in July 2013) and former director of military intelligence, minister of defense and general. From February 2019, he began a one-year term as chairperson of the African Union.

Amr Moussa: Former Egyptian politician and diplomat who served as Egypt's foreign minister from 1991 to 2001 and secretary general of the Arab League from 2001 to 2011. On September 8, 2013, he was elected president of the Committee of 50 to amend the Egyptian constitution.

Anwar Sadat: Third president of Egypt from October 1970 until his assassination by fundamentalist army officers on October 6, 1981, during a military parade commemorating the 1973 Yom Kippur/Ramadan War. Sadat strengthened relations with the United States at the expense of relations with the USSR and signed a peace deal with Israel in Washington, DC, on March 26, 1979. It was proof for some Egyptian fundamentalists, along with Sadat's opposition to Sharia law, Islamic movements, and dissolution of the people's assembly, that Sadat must be removed.

Free Officers Movement: A group of Egyptian nationalist officers in the armed forces of Egypt and Sudan that instigated the Egyptian revolution of 1952.

Gamal Abdel Nasser: A leader of the Free Officers Movement and second president of Egypt from 1954 until his death in 1970. His presidency coincided with the end of British influence in Egypt, Cold War divisions caused by pan-Arabism versus pan-Islamism from Saudi Arabia, and Egypt's participation as a third partner in the Non-Aligned Movement (NAM).

Hassan al-Banna: An Egyptian school teacher and imam, known for founding the Muslim Brotherhood.

Hosni Mubarak: Fourth president of Egypt after the assassination of Anwar Sadat in 1981 until he was deposed by a popular uprising in 2011. Former career officer in the Egyptian Air Force.

King Farouk: Tenth ruler from the Muhammad Ali Dynasty, who ruled from 1936 to 1952.

Kirat El Shater: Egyptian engineer, businessman, and Islamist political activist. A leading member of the Muslim Brotherhood as deputy supreme guide and initial candidate of Freedom and Justice Party during the 2012 Egyptian presidential election before being disqualified by the election commission.

Mohamed Hussein Tantawi: Former Egyptian field marshal and politician. He was commander-in-chief of the Egyptian Armed Forces and chairman of the Supreme Council of the Armed Forces (SCAF) until he was forced to retire by then president Morsi in August 2012.

Mohamed Morsi: Egyptian engineer and Muslim Brotherhood politician who served as the fifth president of Egypt from June 30, 2012, to July 3, 2013, when he was removed by Abdel Fatah El-Sisi, then head of the army, after the June protests. He died on June 17, 2019, during a court trial in Cairo where he faced espionage charges.

Mohamed Naguib: One of the leaders of the Egyptian revolution in 1952 and first president of Egypt from 1953 when Egypt was declared a republic.

Suez Crisis: The invasion of Egypt in late 1956 by Israel, United Kingdom, and France following President Nasser's decision to nationalize the strategic waterway that connects the Mediterranean and Red Seas.

United Arab Republic (UAR): A sovereign state in the Middle East from 1958 to 1961, formed by a political union between Egypt and Syria.

Gulf States

Gulf States: Includes the Arab states of the Gulf Cooperation Council (Bahrain, Kuwait, Oman, Qatar, the UAE, and Saudi Arabia) plus Iran and Iraq.

Kafala system: Refers to the 'sponsorship system' set up in the 1950s to legally bond a migrant worker to an individual employer or sponsor (Kafeel) making the former completely dependent on the latter for their livelihood and residency. The system is used to monitor and regulate migrant laborers working in the construction and domestic sectors in the Gulf and surrounding countries such as Jordan and Lebanon.

Sectarianism: A form of prejudice, discrimination, or hatred arising from attaching superiority or inferiority to a group or party, especially in religion. In the Middle East, the drivers of conflict between Sunni and Shia are mostly within political and social contexts and operate domestically (internal sectarianism) and at the interstate level (external sectarianism).

Iran

Ayatollah Sayyid Ali Hosseini Khamenei: Twelver Shia Marja', second and current supreme leader of Iran.

Bonyad: Charitable trusts, in part created from the confiscated properties of the shah and royal family, that continue to play a major role in Iran's non-petroleum economy. Run by clerics, they provide various social services to support low-income groups. Rather than assisting in the political consolidation process after the 1979 revolution, they have continued to work in parallel to other government ministries.

Hassan Rouhani: Iranian president since August 3, 2013.

Iran-Contra Affair: In 1985 during the Iran-Iraq War (1980–1988), Iran made a secret request to buy weapons from the United States. President Reagan, in breach of a US arms embargo to Iran and paying ransoms of any sort, approved the sale of weapons. He was cognizant that Iran could help secure the release of US hostages in Lebanon while others in the administration believed it may also increase US influence in the Middle East. The proceeds of the sale were used to fund the Nicaraguan contras, a group engaged in fighting the Soviet-backed Sandinista government, which was also illegal and above the limit set by Congress.

Islamic Revolutionary Guards Corps (IRGC): A branch of the Iranian Armed Forces, founded on April 22, 1979, and answerable only to the clerical elite. It is tasked with preserving the Islamic Republic of Iran and exporting the ideals of the 1979 revolution. Also known as 'Pasdaran' (Guards) or 'Sepah' (Corps).

Joint Comprehensive Plan of Action (JCPOA): The 2015 agreement with the five permanent members of the UN Security Council plus Germany to ensure Iran's compliance on nuclear-related provisions, to be verified by the International Atomic Energy Agency (IAEA). President Trump unilaterally withdrew from the JCPOA on May 8, 2018.

Mohammad Javid Zarif: Iranian minister of foreign affairs.

Mohammad Mosaddegh: Democratically elected prime minister of Iran, 1951–1953, when his government was overthrown by a CIA-sponsored coup, also supported by the British, in favor of reestablishing the pro-Western shah as leader.

Qasem Soleimani: Major general and commander of the Iranian Revolutionary Guards Corps (IRGC) and commander of the Quds Force since 1998. Assassinated January 3, 2020.

Quds Force: A unit of the Iranian Revolutionary Guards Corps (IRGC) directed to carry out unconventional warfare, intelligence activities, and extraterritorial operations.

Velayat-e faqih: The 'Guardianship of the Jurisconsult' system of governance based on the assertion that the Muslim jurist *(faqih)* has absolute political power. Ulama (guardians, transmitters, and interpreters of religious knowledge in Islam) who support the concept disagree over how encompassing the guardianship should be.

Iraq

Abu Ghraib prison: A maximum-security Iraqi prison in operation since the 1950s. It was used as a US army detention center from 2003 to 2006. Graphic pictures of prisoner abuse, which came to light in 2003, led to an internal US military investigation in 2004. This investigation found systemic and illegal abuse by several members of the military police working there. Eleven US soldiers were convicted of crimes relating to the Abu Ghraib scandal.

Adil Abdul-Mahdi al-Muntafiki: Prime minister of Iraq from October 2018 to February 2020. Vice president of Iraq from 2005 to 2011.

Al-Qaeda (AQ): A militant Sunni Islamist multinational organization founded in 1988 by Osama Bin Laden, Abdullah Azzam, and others, during the Soviet-Afghan War.

Al-Qaeda in Iraq (AQI): Active from 2004 to 2006, it preceded Islamic State of Iraq and Syria (ISIS).

Coalition Provisional Authority (CPA): A transitional government established by a US-led multinational force following the invasion of the country and the fall of the Ba'athist government. It lasted from March 19, 2003, to June 28, 2004.

De-Ba'athification: The policy undertaken by the Coalition Provisional Authority (CPA) and subsequent Iraqi governments to remove former Ba'ath party officials under Saddam Hussein from any role in the new Iraqi political system.

Haider al-Abadi: Prime minister of Iraq from 2014 to 2018.

Islamic State in Iraq and Sham (Greater Syria) (ISIS): Also known as Islamic State (IS), Islamic State of Iraq and the Levant (ISIL),

Islamic State in Iraq (ISI) from 2006 to 2013, and Da'ash from 2013.

Kurdistan Regional Government (KRG): Exercises executive power according to Kurdistan region's laws, enacted by the Kurdistan parliament. Based in Erbil, the capital of Kurdish region, it administers governorates of Erbil, Slemani, and Duhok. Authority lies in areas such as regional budget, policing and security, education and health policies, natural resources, and infrastructure development.

Masoud Barzani: A Kurdish politician and leader of the Kurdistan Democratic Party since 1979. President of the Iraqi Kurdish Region from 2005 to 2017.

Mustafa Al-Kadhimi: Prime minister of Iraq since May 7, 2020

Nechirvan Barzani: Current president of Iraqi Kurdistan since June 1, 2019.

Nouri al-Maliki: Prime minister of Iraq from 2006 to 2014.

Peshmerger: Kurdish fighting force.

Saddam Hussein: President of Iraq from July 16, 1979, to April 9, 2003.

Status of Forces Agreement (SOFA): An agreement signed by President G. W. Bush and Iraqi prime minister Nouri al-Maliki in 2008 and ratified by the Iraqi Parliament for US forces to withdraw from Iraqi cities by June 30, 2009, and all combat forces to withdraw from Iraq by December 31, 2011.

Israel and Palestine

Balfour Declaration: A public statement issued by the British government in 1917 during the First World War announcing support for the establishment of a 'national home for the Jewish people' in Palestine

Begin Doctrine: The Israeli government's counter-proliferation policy of striking a potential enemy's capacity to possess weapons of mass destruction (WMDs).

Benjamin Netanyahu: Israeli politician, chairman of the Likud party, and prime minister of Israel since 2009.

Hamas: A Palestinian Sunni-Islamic fundamentalist militant organization. Hamas won legislative elections on January 25, 2006, and governed Gaza from 2007 to 2014, and then from 2016. Attempts have been made to establish a national unity government with Fatah (the principal political party in the West Bank), but Hamas remains entrenched in Gaza and regularly launches rocket attacks against Israel.

Intifada: Meaning 'tremor' or 'shake' in Arabic, it refers to the First Intifada, a Palestinian uprising against Israeli occupation of the West

Bank and Gaza from December 1987 until the Madrid Conference in September 1991 or the signing of the Oslo Accords in 1993. The Second Intifada or Al-Aqsa Intifada occurred from September 2000 to February 2005 following the Israeli prime minister Ariel Sharon's visit to the Temple Mount/Al-Haram Al-Sharif, the third holiest site in Islam.

Israeli settlements: Civilian communities inhabited by Israeli citizens, almost exclusively Jewish, built on lands occupied by Israel since the 1967 Six-Day War. These have been termed 'illegal' by an International Court of Justice advisory opinion (2004) and are often cited as an impediment in the peace process.

Jerusalem: One of the world's oldest cities and home of holy sites for Islam, Judaism, and Christianity. It is also one of the most contentious aspects of the Middle East peace process and is claimed by Israel and Palestine (East Jerusalem) for their capital city, but it remains controlled by Israel. Tension remains high in the Old City where religious, ethnic, and nationalist differences exist in close proximity.

Mahmoud Abbas: Also known as Abu Mazen, he is president of the state of Palestine and Palestinian National Authority (PNA). He has been chairman of the Palestine Liberation Organization (PLO) since November 2004.

Oslo Accords: A set of agreements between the government of Israel and the Palestine Liberation Organization (PLO). Oslo I was signed in Washington, DC, in 1993 and Oslo II in Taba, Egypt, in 1995.

Palestinian National Authority (PNA): The interim self-government body established in 1994 following the Gaza-Jericho Agreement to govern the Gaza Strip and Areas A and B of the West Bank, which formed part of the 1993 Oslo Accords.

Road map: A plan to resolve the Israeli-Palestinian conflict, as proposed by the Quartet on the Middle East (the United States, the European Union, Russia, and the United Nations).

Shimon Peres: Ninth president of Israel from 2007 to 2014 and one of Israel's longest serving politicians. As director general of the Defence Ministry, he established Israel's defense industry and nuclear program. In 1956, he masterminded the Sinai campaign (the Suez Crisis) and was instrumental in forming the Labor Party in 1967. He won a Nobel Peace Prize in 1994 with Rabin and Yasser Arafat for signing the Declaration of Principles with the Palestine Liberation Organization (PLO) in September 1993 regarding Palestinian self-rule (Oslo I).

United Nations Relief and Works Agency (UNRWA): The United

Nation's main agency serving Palestinians, established after the 1948 Arab-Israeli War when more than 750,000 people were displaced and more than 500 villages destroyed. It has come under pressure from the Trump administration, which has withdrawn US funding for it, as well as Israeli hostility.

Yasser Arafat: Chairman of the Palestinian Liberation Organization (PLO) from 1969 to 2004, when he became president of the Palestinian National Authority from 1994 until his death in 2004.

Yitzhak Rabin: Fifth prime minister of Israel from 1974 to 1977 and from 1992, when he embraced the peace process, including the signing of the Oslo Accords and a peace treaty with Jordan in 1994, until he was assassinated in 1995.

Lebanon

Cedar Revolution: Peaceful demonstrations and civil disobedience in Lebanon with the goal of forcing the withdrawal of Syrian troops from Lebanon and the replacement of a government suspected to be heavily influenced by Syrian interests.

Democratic Union Party (PYD, Partiya Yekîtiya Demokrat): A Kurdish Syrian affiliate of the Partiya Karkerên Kurdistanê (PKK).

Hassan Diab: Prime minister of Lebanon since January 21, 2020.

Hassan Nasrallah: Current secretary general of Hezbollah since his predecessor, Abbas al-Musawi, was assassinated by Israeli Defence Forces in 1992.

Hezbollah: A Shia Islamist political party (standing for parliament in 1992, taking ministerial positions from 2005) and militant group based in Lebanon. Established in 1982 in response to the Israeli invasion of Lebanon, it is supported by Iran in its resistance agenda against Israel.

Kurdistan Workers Party (PKK, Partiya Karkerên Kurdistanê): Turkish Kurdish militant group.

Michel Aoun: President of Lebanon since 31 October 2016.

Rafic Hariri: Prime minister of Lebanon from 1992 to 1998 and from 2000 until his resignation in 2004. He was assassinated on February 14, 2005, triggering the Cedar Revolution.

Saad Hariri: Former prime minister of Lebanon from 2016 to 2020.

Syrian Democratic Forces (SDF): Mixed Arab/Kurdish fighters, aligned with the Partiya Yekîtiya Demokrat (PYD).

Libya

Abdel Hakim Belhaj: Leader of the Tripoli Military Council and former head of the Libyan Islamic Fighting Group (LIFG), a militant

Islamist group allied with al-Qaeda. Rendered by Mi6 and the CIA back to Libya from Bangkok and tortured by the Libyan authorities in 2004.

Abdul Fattah Younis: Former minister of interior and chief of the rebel army up to his assassination on July 24, 2011.

Abdullah al-Senussi: Former intelligence chief.

Abdurrahim El-Keib: Interim prime minister of Libya, from November 24, 2011, to November 14, 2012.

Ali Zeidan: Prime minister from November 2012 to March 2014, when he was ousted by parliament.

Government of National Accord: Interim government for Libya based in Tripoli, formed under the terms of the UN-led Libyan Political Agreement signed on December 17, 2015.

Great Socialist People's Libyan Arab Jamahiriya: The name for Libya from 1986 to 2011.

The Green Book: A short book setting out the political philosophy of Muammar Gaddafi, first published in 1975.

Khalifa Belqasim Haftar: Military officer and head of the Libyan National Army (LNA).

Mahmoud Jibril: Former head of the National Economic Development Board and prime minister of the National Transitional Council (NTC) until he resigned following the death of Gaddafi on October 24, 2011.

Muammar Gaddafi: Former revolutionary, politician, political theorist, and Libyan leader who governed as revolutionary chairman from 1969 to 1977, then as 'brotherly leader' from 1977 until his death in Sirte on October 20, 2011.

Mustafa Abdul Jalil: Former minister of justice and the de facto head of state during the transitional period after the fall of Muammar Gaddafi.

National Transitional Council (NTC): De facto government of Libya after the Libyan civil war began in mid-February 2011 until it was dissolved on August 8, 2012.

Saif al-Islam Gaddafi: Second son of the former Libyan leader Muammar Gaddafi.

Qatar

Abdullah bin Nasser bin Khalifa Al Thani: Qatari prime minister since June 26, 2013.

Al Jazeera: A Qatari TV channel owned by Emir Al Thani, which has proven divisive in its coverage and broadcast content across the Middle East and internationally (see **Diplomatic crisis**).

Al Udeid: An air base for the Qatari air force and an expanding forward-operating base for the US Central Command (CENTCOM).

Diplomatic crisis: The Qatar diplomatic crisis began in June 2017 when Saudi Arabia, the UAE, Bahrain, and Egypt launched an economic boycott and cut diplomatic relations with Qatar to try to force it to change behavior, including closing down *Al Jazeera* and cutting relations with pro-Islamist Iran and Turkey.

Hamad bin Jassim bin Jaber Al Thani: Influential prime minister of Qatar from April 3, 2007, to June 26, 2013.

Sheikh Hamad bin Khalifa Al Thani: Emir of Qatar from 1995 to 2013. Responsible for state branding and internationalization/hub strategy, including winning the bid for World Cup 2022 on December 2, 2010.

Sheikh Tamim bin Hamad Al Thani: Born June 3, 1980, Sheikh Tamim is the current emir of Qatar. He replaced his father Sheikh Hamad bin Khalifa Al Thani, who stepped down on June 25, 2013.

Russia/Soviet Union

Astana: The former name of the capital city of Kazakhstan (since March 2019: Nur-Sultan). Astana became the host city of various rounds of talks between the Syrian Assad regime and segments of the Syrian opposition. The 'Astana format' was launched in 2017 and sponsored by Iran, Russia, and Turkey.

Color Revolutions: A series of revolutionary events that affected states in the former Soviet Union and the Balkans during the early 2000s, including Georgia's Rose Revolution (2003) and Ukraine's Orange Revolution (2004). Russia has attributed these events to Western influence and led its leadership to hardening its position in foreign and domestic policies.

Comintern: The Communist International (Comintern) was an international body created to achieve world communism, active between 1919 and 1943. Many left-wing parties from around the world were members of the Comintern. Some functions and personnel were transferred to the International Department of the Communist Party of the Soviet Union. Its longtime head, Boris Ponomarev, played an active role in shaping party policies toward communist movements worldwide.

Glasnost: Meaning 'openness' in Russian, it is one of the policies pursued by Gorbachev. Its aim was to achieve a higher degree of transparency in Soviet political life and encourage criticism by citizens in order to uncover deficiencies in the system.

Mikhail Gorbachev: General secretary of the Communist Party of the Soviet Union from 1985 until 1991 and the first Soviet president. He implemented the policies of Glasnost and Perestroika, which liberalized the Soviet political system. He devised a 'new political thinking' in foreign policy, aimed at defusing the Cold War rivalry and stressing the interdependence in international security. He and his aides pushed for a Soviet retreat from Afghanistan (achieved in 1989) and for a detachment from Middle Eastern allies.

Nikita Khrushchev: Prime minister of the Soviet Union from 1958 to 1964. Under his tenure ('Thaw'), the USSR experienced political and cultural liberalization. In foreign policy, the Soviet Union started to entertain a close relationship with the Middle East, particularly with Egypt, which Moscow supported even during the Suez Crisis in 1956.

Perestroika: Meaning 'restructuring' in Russian, it was one of the policies pursued by Gorbachev. It aimed at reforming the Soviet political and economic system.

Yevgeny Primakov: An influential Soviet/Russian expert in Middle Eastern Affairs. Trained in Oriental studies, he widely traveled the Middle East as a correspondent for the Soviet newspaper *Pravda*. He also acted as unofficial intermediary and entertained contacts with the KGB. Later, he headed various Soviet research institutions. He served as Russian intelligence chief from 1991 to 1996, as minister of foreign affairs from 1996 to 1998, and as prime minister from 1998 to 1999. He has advocated a return of Russia to superpower status in order to reestablish a balance with the West, including stronger ties with non-Western states.

Saudi Arabia

Abdullah bin Abdulaziz Al Saud: King of Saudi Arabia from 2005 until his death in 2015.

Mohammed bin Salman (MBS): Saudi crown prince and first deputy prime minister (since June 2017) and defense minister (since January 2015). As chairman of the Council for Economic and Development Affairs, he is the minister responsible for Saudi Vision 2030, launched in March 2018.

Salman bin Abdulaziz Al Saud: King of Saudi Arabia and custodian of the Two Holy Mosques since January 23, 2015.

Saudi Aramco: The Saudi Arabian Oil Company. Based in Dhahran, it is one of the largest companies in the world by revenue, valued possibly up to $2 trillion (there is a divergence of the upcoming market capitalization), and one of the most profitable.

Vision 2030: A plan to reduce Saudi dependence on oil and diversify its economy through various new and existing sectors such as infrastructure, tourism, and entertainment.

Syria

Bashar al-Assad: Syrian politician and president of Syria since July 17, 2000.

Free Syrian Army (FSA): Originally formed as a national resistance organization to protect Syrian protestors and initiate military operations against the Assad regime in August 2011. It has since become decentralized due to uneven international support but still represents a moderate opposition in a field dominated by extremist organizations.

Hafez al-Assad: Former Syrian politician and president of Syria from 1971 till his death on June 10, 2000.

Khaled Bagdash: Leader of the Syrian Communist Party from 1936 until 1995 and the first communist party member to be elected into an Arab parliament.

Rami Maklouf: Maternal cousin of Bashar al-Assad, with interests in many sectors of the Syrian economy, from oil and gas to telecommunications (including SyriaTel), and estimated to have controlled up to 60 percent of Syria's pre war economy. In the context of taxes/fines imposed on some of his companies, he appeared in videos in April 2020 directly appealing for President Assad to intervene.

Syrian Democratic Forces (SDF): A Kurdish-led alliance including Arab, Assyrian, and some Armenian, Turkmen, and Chechen militias. With US support, it helped defeat ISIS in Syria in 2019.

Tunisia

Abdelfatah Morou: Interim Speaker of parliament and Ennahda's first presidential candidate in 2019.

Ali Laarayedh: Prime minister of Tunisia from 2013 to 2014 following the resignation of Hamadi Jebali. Former minister of interior from 2011 to 2013.

Beji Caid Essebsi: President of Tunisia from 2014 until his death on July 25, 2019. Former minister of foreign affairs from 1981 to 1986, and prime minister from February to December 2011.

Ennahda Movement: Also known as Renaissance Party and originally called the Islamic Tendency Movement (MTI), it is a Tunisian Islamist movement with a political agenda; it emerged victorious in the country's first democratic elections in 2014. It survived two decades of repression and social exclusion to adopt a new strategy of pragmatism and reform during the political transition following the Arab Uprisings.

Harqa: Youth who were active participants in the 2011 revolution.

Kais Saied: President of Tunisia since October 23, 2019.

Mohamed Ghannouchi: Prime minister of Tunisia from 1999 to 2011, regarded as a technocrat under the Ben Ali government.

National Dialogue Quartet: A group of human rights activists, labor union leaders, and lawyers, who helped warring political parties achieve consensus in 2015, winning the 2015 Nobel Peace Prize.

Youssef Chahed: Head of the government of Tunisia since 2016 and head of Tahya Tounes secular party.

Zine El Abine Ben Ali: Known simply as Ben Ali, he was a Tunisian politician and president of Tunisia from 1987 till his fall in 2011. He died in Jeddah, Saudi Arabia, on September 19, 2019.

Turkey

Ahmet Davutoglu: Turkish academic, politician, and former diplomat. Prime minister of Turkey and leader of the Justice and Development Party (AKP) from 2014 to 2016.

Justice and Development Party (AKP): A conservative political party in Turkey with roots in its Ottoman past and Islamic identity.

Muhammed Fethullah Gulen: A Turkish Islamic scholar, preacher, and influential Ottomanist. He founded the Gulen Islamic movement, or FETO, Hizmet, in the 1970s when an imam. The movement has interests and influence across think tanks, businesses, schools, and publications globally with unknown but possible support from up to 10 percent of the Turkish population. In 2002, it formed a tactical alliance with the Justice and Development Party (AKP) against the military-dominated Turkish secular state. Since the attempted coup in 2016, the Gulen movement has been classified as a terrorist organization and experienced a clampdown in all its spheres of operation. Muhammed Gulen has since led the movement from Pennsylvania in the United States.

Recep Tayyip Erdoğan: President of Turkey since 2014, Turkish politician, and former prime minister (2003–2014). He coestablished the Justice and Development Party (AKP).

'Zero Problems with Neighbors' policy: Ahmet Davutoglu developed this policy during his term as foreign minister from 2009 to 2014, based on his book *Strategic Depth*.[5] It reconceptualized and reset relations with former Ottoman lands, including Syria, facilitated nuclear negotiations with Iran, and engaged in trade relations with the Gulf states and North Africa. The de-securitization policy lasted until the onset of the Arab Uprisings in 2011.

Yemen

Abed Rabbo Mansour Al-Hadi: Yemeni politician, vice president from 1994 to 2012, and president from February 27, 2012, to January 22, 2015, when his government was overthrown by Houthi forces.

Ali Abdullah Saleh: Yemeni politician who served as the first president of Yemen from unification on May 22, 1990, to his resignation on February 25, 2012. He was assassinated on December 4, 2017.

Houthis: Named after the family it is associated with, emerged from Yemen's northern Saada province. The Shia Zaidi revisionists have been engaged in local insurrections since 2004, but came to challenge the Saleh government directly in 2015.

National dialogue: The national dialogue concluded on January 24, 2014, with the adoption of a road map toward a full transition of Yemen to a state that upholds democracy, the rule of law, and good governance.

National Dialogue Conference: Under President Hadi and with UN support, the conference took place on March 18, 2013, and included groups of southern Hirak, Houthis, women, youth, and civil society.

People's Democratic Republic of Yemen (PDRY): The name for South Yemen after a radical wing of the Marxist National Liberation Front (NFL) came to power in 1970. PDRY existed until reunification in 1990 and had formed close ties with the Soviet Union, China, Cuba, and some Palestinian groups.

People's Republic of South Yemen (PRSY): Also known as South Yemen (which included the island of Socotra), existed from 1967 to 1970.

Notes

1. Steven Heydemann, "Upgrading Authoritarianism," *Upgrading Authoritarianism in the Arab World*, Analysis Paper 13 (Washington, DC: Saban Center for Middle East Policy at the Brookings Institution, 2007), 1.

2. Joseph S. Nye, "Corruption and Development: A Cost-Benefit Analysis," *American Political Science Review* 61 (June 1967): 419.

3. See Joshua Stacher, "Fragmenting States, New Regimes: Militarized State Violence and Transition in the Middle East," *Democratization* 22, no. 2 (2015): 259–275.

4. See *Regions and Powers: The Structures of International Security* (Cambridge: Cambridge University Press, 2003).

5. Ahmet Davutoğlu, *Strategic Depth* (Istanbul: Küre Yayınları, 2001).

Contributors

Mohamed Abdelraouf leads the Gulf Research Centre's research program on sustainability and environmental issues. He was the lead author for the UN Environment Programme (UNEP) GEO 5 and 6 reports, West Asia chapter, in the Environmental Governance section. He has published various policy papers on different environmental issues in the MENA region and authored five books. Abdelraouf is a part-time lecturer of environmental economics and accounting at various universities in the MENA region. Since 2010, he has been representing the Science and Technology Major Group at the UN Environment Programme (UNEP) and is currently serving as cochair of the UNEP Major Groups Facilitating Committee (MGFC).

Eyad AlRefai is a PhD student at Lancaster University, United Kingdom, and a teaching assistant and instructor at the Department of Political Science, King Abdulaziz University, Saudi Arabia. In his PhD research, he looks at the development of the Middle Eastern regional system by exploring the historical interaction between identities (pan-Arabism and pan-Islamism) and states, and the struggle for hegemony in the region. AlRefai is a PhD fellow with the Sectarianism, Proxies and De-sectarianisation (SEPAD) project at Lancaster University.

Dina Arakji is a research assistant at the Civil-Military Relations in the Arab States (CMRAS) program at Carnegie Middle East Center, Lebanon. She holds a master's degree in international security from Sciences Po, Paris, with a focus on the Middle East region.

Philipp Casula holds a PhD in sociology from the University of Basel, Switzerland. His PhD thesis analyzed the dynamics of domestic politics of contemporary Russia in terms of hegemony and populism. Casula's current research interest includes the cultural history of postcolonial Russia, especially the relations of the USSR and the Middle East and their cultural representation in Soviet media and academia. Among his publications are: "The Soviet Afro-Asian Solidarity Committee and Soviet Perceptions of the Middle East during Late Socialism," in *Cahiers du monde russe* 59, no. 4 (2018): 499–520; "Russia's Foreign Policy from the Crimean Crisis to the Middle East: Great Power Gamble or Biopolitics?," in *Rising Powers Quarterly* 2, no. 1 (2017): 27–51; and "Between 'Ethnocide' and 'Genocide': Violence and Otherness in the Coverage of the Afghanistan and Chechnya Wars," in *Nationalities Papers* 43, no. 5 (2015): 700–718.

Ishac Diwan is professor of economics at Paris Sciences et Lettres (a consortium of Parisian universities) where he holds the chair of the Economy of the Arab World and teaches at the École Normale Supérieure. He has held recent teaching positions at Columbia University, School of International and Public Affairs, and at the Harvard Kennedy School. He directs the political economy program of the Economic Research Forum, where he runs two projects on the study of crony capitalism and the analysis of opinion surveys. Diwan's current research interests focus on the political economy of the Middle East, in addition to broader development issues. His recent books include *A Political Economy of the Middle East* (coauthored with Melani Cammett; 2015) and *Crony Capitalism in the Middle East* (coedited with Adeel Malik and Izak Atiyas; 2019). He is widely published in top journals on issues of global finance, macroeconomic and development strategies, and Middle East political economy (see https://scholar.harvard.edu/idiwan/home). Diwan is a frequent consultant with governments and international organizations, having worked recently on policy issues in Sudan, Algeria, Lebanon, and Egypt. Previously, he worked at the World Bank—in the Research Complex, the World Bank Institute, and in Operations. He has lived in Addis Ababa (2002–2007) and Accra (2007–2011) as the World Bank's country director in East and then West Africa.

Seif Hendy holds an MA in political science from the American University in Cairo (AUC), Egypt. He has worked as a teaching assistant at AUC and as a politics reporter for *Daily News Egypt* and has completed military service in Egypt. He has also spent time teaching English to refugees in Cairo and interned at Shell Oil in 2015.

Simon Mabon is senior lecturer in international relations at Lancaster University, United Kingdom, where he directs the Richardson Institute. He holds a PhD in international relations from the University of Leeds and is the director of the SEPAD Project, funded by Carnegie Corporation, which looks at the impact of the rivalry between Saudi Arabia and Iran on the contemporary Middle East (www.sepad.org.uk).

Robert Mason is a Fellow of the Sectarianism, Proxies and De-sectarianisation project at Lancaster University, Non-Resident Fellow with the Arab Gulf States Institute in Washington, and currently sits on the International Studies Association (ISA) Foreign Policy Analysis Section Executive Board. His research focuses on international relations, with a geographical emphasis on the Gulf, European Union, United States, and rising powers. He is author or editor of numerous books, including *Reassessing Order and Disorder in the Middle East: Regional Imbalance or Disintegration?* (2017), *Egypt and the Gulf: A Renewed Regional Policy Alliance* (2016), *Muslim Minority–State Relations: Violence, Integration and Policy* (2016), *International Politics of the Arab Spring: Popular Unrest and Foreign Policy* (2014), and *Foreign Policy in Iran and Saudi Arabia: Economics and Diplomacy in the Middle East* (2014).

Neil Partrick first became interested in the Middle East when he visited the occupied Syrian Golan Heights in 1986. He has worked in Jerusalem as an editor, headed the Middle East program at a Whitehall think tank (RUSI), analyzed Saudi Arabia and Iraq for the Economist Group (EIU), and lectured in the UAE (American University of Sharjah, Sharjah). Since 2009, he has been a freelance consultant at www.neilpartrick.com. In 2018, the second edition of *Saudi Arabian Foreign Policy: Conflict & Cooperation*, for which he was the lead contributor, was published.

Introduction

Robert Mason

This book is designed to be a companion textbook for the study of the politics in the modern Middle East, including reference to the domestic, regional, and international levels. It is aimed at the interested casual reader and those taking a course or degree at the undergraduate or graduate level with a major Middle East studies or Middle East politics component. The volume provides details on the most pressing and significant emerging threats in the Middle East, as well as shaping forces to regional interactions and (lack of) cooperation with extra-regional actors.

The focus of the volume is the period post the Arab Uprisings (also known as 'Arab revolutions' but since so much blood has been spilt and due to the uncertainty and expected longevity of the transitions involved, rarely referred to as the Arab Spring any more). However, there is a keen sense that these issues are constantly evolving, as can be seen by references from 2019 up to the point of publication in 2020. By combining different disciplinary approaches, the book contributes to a growing literature on the nexus between political science, Middle East politics, and area studies. Above all, it aims to highlight key international relations and Middle East concepts, themes and issues that will continue to impact socioeconomic, sociosecurity, and sociopolitical dynamics in the Middle East. These are discussed in detail in each chapter and are clearly explained in the 'Glossary, Actors, and Abbreviations' section.

In Chapter 1, Mason and Hendy discuss the political economy of the Middle East in broad terms, zeroing in on specific issues such as demography and youth issues. Next, in Chapter 2, Mason and Arakji outline the significance of the military in many of the governance structures dominating Middle East politics and economics, how civil-military relations have

1

evolved over time, and the prospects for reform. Mabon and AlRefai argue in Chapter 3 that soft power and geopolitical competition have once again come to threaten cohesion, consensus, and permeability in the Middle East, especially after the Arab Uprisings, where weak and failed states have become new battlegrounds for regional influence. They employ the cases of Saudi Arabia and Iran as well as Qatar and the UAE in illustrating the resonance of political competition through religious and sports perspectives.

In Chapter 4, Mason and Partrick go on to explore the dual phenomena of regionalized and internationalized conflict, looking specifically at the cases of Iraq, Libya, Syria, and Yemen. Diwan, in Chapter 5, builds nicely on the previous chapter by discussing how middle oil per capita countries such as Algeria, Iran, Iraq, Libya, Sudan, Syria, and Yemen have experienced a dual curse: using oil rents for greater social repression and also distrusting autonomy in the economy, representing repression of the market. He finds, among other conclusions, that regional and international rivalry does not contribute to the preconditions for a political settlement. In Chapter 6, Mason and Casula provide historical, contemporary, and forward-looking perspectives on the international community, including the effects of decades of US policies in the Middle East, and challenges and opportunities presented by the EU, Russia, and China in the region, also through alliance choices. In Chapter 7, Mason and Abdelraouf explore the environment as an emerging and potentially major challenge to governments and societies across the region with reference to climate change, water politics, governance issues, and food security. They focus on the cases of Lebanon, Syria, Iraq, Yemen, and Egypt. In so doing, they highlight how environmental politics will form an increasingly important and urgent element of national development plans. Should they fail to be taken into proper consideration, the risks could become exponential, particularly for vulnerable communities. In Chapter 8, Mason discusses the Israel-Palestine conflict as an ongoing shaping factor in Middle East politics and how its persistence highlights the importance of political will, sovereignty, alliance patterns, and asymmetric warfare as decisive concepts in the region's governance, politics, and security.

Defining the Middle East

The term 'Middle East' was first coined by Admiral Alfred Thayer Mahan in 1901 and made popular in speeches by Sir Mark Sykes of Sykes-Picot fame or, rather, notoriety. Indeed, the secret Sykes-Picot agreement signed in 1916 for the partition of the Ottoman Empire after the First World War, along with the Balfour Declaration in 1917 in which the British government announced support for the establishment of a national home for the Jewish people in Palestine, is a key, contentious, and enduring feature of the Middle East.[1] 'Near East' was a term used in the British and American policy communities up until the Second World War, and beyond for many Americans. Both terms have become synonymous with great power relationships and core-periphery relations from dependency theory, including Western engagement and intervention, predominantly in the twentieth century.

The Middle East is generally considered to include the Arab states (i.e., those that form the League of Arab States) from Morocco in the east to Oman in the west, plus Iran, Israel, and Turkey, as Map I.1 illustrates. Although these states are diverse in their histories and traditions, they are also generally similar in their linguistic, ethnic, and/or religious composition. Hence, the Levant (including Jordan, Palestine, Israel, and Cyprus but with special emphasis on the former French mandates of Lebanon and Syria) and North Africa (including the Maghreb states of Morocco, Mauritania, Algeria, Tunisia, and Libya) can be considered to form part of a contiguous region. At times, due to geostrategic expediency, such as the G. W. Bush administration's Global War on Terror, regional definitions have shifted to include states such as Afghanistan and Pakistan. Whether scholars and policymakers should focus on geographic areas or issue-specific 'communities' in their study of Middle East politics and international affairs is an ongoing area for debate.

What is known as the Middle East in the United States and Europe is often known as West Asia in other parts of Asia, especially in states such as India and China. As these states become more prominent in international affairs, also through studies pertaining to the region in the twenty-first century, so too will their definitions and discourses. Infrastructure projects such as those in the China-Pakistan Economic Corridor (CPEC), part of China's Belt and Road Initiative (BRI), will do much to determine the future location of Pakistan in specific or various spheres of influence. Interestingly, West Asia often includes the Caucasus and excludes Egypt in favor of locating it in Africa. Changes may be evident over time as growing awareness, new regional studies, or further transnational connections blur or shift conceptual parameters.

Problematizing the Study of the Middle East

There are a number of pitfalls in the study of the Middle East, which generally fall into the following categories. First, studies can be superficial in nature, focusing on outcomes such as conflicts, terrorism, or refugees, rather than the multifaceted history and societies that make up the context for the dynamics being played out on the ground. Second, and related

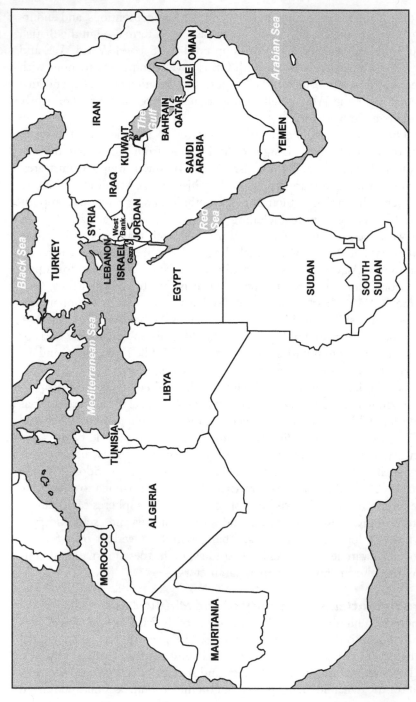

Map I.1 Map of the Middle East.

to the first, is the lack of connectivity between area studies scholars in the global south and international relations scholars in the West who are often unable to explain Middle East politics. There are some notable exceptions that have managed to locate the Middle East as a subsystem of international relations.[2] Historical awareness plays a vital part in explaining the interactions (or lack thereof) between the newly created states of the Middle East and the rest of the world. This includes awareness about the expansion of the early Islamic Caliphates through to European colonialism, the legacies of which include the Israel-Palestine conflict, Iran's hostility toward the West, and the fraught relationship between Turkey and Europe and between France and Algeria.[3]

Third, the Middle East and international actors have experienced a number of social, economic, political, and security trends, events, and inconsistent policies over the past forty years, which make generalizations about Middle East politics appear quite unconvincing. At the international level, the region has experienced a transition from a Cold War to a post–Cold War order whereby US hegemony has been exercised from the end of 1991. Approximately a decade later, the second intifada and the Arab Peace Plan put the Israel-Palestine conflict back on international foreign policy agendas but to little effect. The United States responded to the 9/11 attacks with huge US military resources deployed in Afghanistan and Iraq, using bases such as Diego Garcia and Al Udeid in Qatar to project power. The G. W. Bush administration's Greater Middle East Initiative (GMEI) focused on addressing the denial of public freedoms in the region and proposed direct funding to nongovernmental organizations (NGOs) and the formation of a body to monitor progress. It was short on realistic assessment as to the nature and pace of reform in the region and apparently oblivious to the role that US Middle East policy has had in maintaining deadlock in the Middle East peace process. The United States was simultaneously a revolutionary actor in pushing for and achieving regime change in Iraq from 2003 onward. President Obama inherited the cost from these missions in conjunction with the fallout from the 2008–2009 financial crisis and adjusted US policy accordingly. He instead focused on a military drawdown in Afghanistan and Iraq accompanied by diplomatic engagement with European allies, Russia, China, and Iran, which culminated in the Joint Comprehensive Plan of Action (JCPOA) in 2015. A military and economic pivot to Asia, the latter through engagement in the Trans-Pacific Partnership (TPP), was also made in an attempt to leverage 40 percent of the global economy toward US interests, not least in countering the rising power of China. Both the JCPOA and the TPP have been rolled back by the Trump administration, leaving a legacy of US retrenchment in its wake. A largely discredited Deal of the Century (amid the relocation of the US embassy from Tel Aviv to Jerusalem) has been promoted by President Trump to end the Israel-Palestine conflict.

At the regional level, one need only look at the Arab Uprisings to see diversity in the drivers for reform, transition, or democracy and the state response in turn, partly due to different notions of statehood. Although state sovereignty is a relatively clear concept that demarcates the Arab states, Israel, Turkey, and Iran, Roger Owen notes that the state concept also implies a functioning set of institutions and practices, which include administrative, judicial, legislative, and coercive power. It can also vary from a regime or government, a regime masquerading as a state, or part of a binary definition such as state/society, all of which can be problematic. These states came into being in different historical circumstances than many other states around the world and have formed a different relationship with their citizens.[4] There are a growing number of cases where the state system has deteriorated, particularly after the Arab Uprisings began in late 2010. We have come to talk more frequently about weak, fragile, and even failed states as a result.

The old order has disintegrated and gaps have emerged in a new regional order due to uncertainties surrounding governance and a new social contract. In this space, violent Islamist groups have prospered. While the Tunisian model in accommodating transition and power sharing has been exceptional thus far, there is also the Egyptian model of re-authoritarianism based on the heavy involvement of the military in state affairs, the Bahraini model of repression, the Syrian model of outright conflict, and the Algerian model of hitherto peaceful public-state negotiation. Oftentimes, these models are supported by Arab Gulf economic interventionism, particularly focused on Sunni monarchical regimes in Morocco and Jordan, but also pivotal regional and subregional actors such as Egypt and Sudan.

A Brief History of the Middle East

A history of contemporary Middle East politics need only go as far back as the emergence of Middle East states from the Ottoman and Persian Empires at the end of the nineteenth and beginning of the twentieth centuries. Oman is the exception, which by the eighteenth century had an empire that stretched to the east coast of Africa until Zanzibar became independent in 1964. Before decolonization and for approximately four hundred years, the Middle East was governed according to Ottoman practice and culture by rulers who owed their allegiance to Istanbul (including modern-day Syria, Iraq, Lebanon, Jordan, northern Yemen,

Israel and Palestine, and around Tripoli and Bengazi in Libya). Ottoman reforms and an encroaching European presence led to some nationalist movements gaining a foothold, such as the Armenians in Anatolia and Maronite Christians of Mount Lebanon. The Balkan Wars signified a diminishing Ottoman capacity for control in Europe prior to 1914, when the First World War facilitated its demise.

After the war, the British and French divided territories into proto-states consisting of mandates and protectorates according to their imperial interests. Middle East states then gained independence in two waves. The first wave occurred between the two world wars and led to independence for Iraq, Saudi Arabia, and Turkey. Abulaziz Ibn Saud conquered much of the Arabian Peninsula and consolidated the tribal nation under a new kingdom in 1932. The Turkish War of Independence from 1919 to 1923 fought against proxies of Armenia, France, and Greece. The victory led by Mustafa Kemal Atatürk caused the abolition of the Ottoman sultanate and the establishment of the Republic of Turkey in October 1923. Iran was already independent under the Pahlavi Dynasty by 1925 and had enjoyed centuries of Persian Empire, including the Safavid Dynasty from 1501. Egypt was granted conditional independence by the British in 1922 and full independence from British control in the revolution led by the Free Officers Movement in 1952.

The second wave came during the period of decolonization following the end of the Second World War from the mid-1940s to the 1970s. Morocco, Algeria, Tunisia, Lebanon, and Syria gained independence from France, and Spain relinquished its territorial control over parts of Morocco. The UAE, Qatar, Bahrain, Kuwait, Israel, and Jordan gained their independence from Britain. Aden, Algeria, and Libya were direct colonies of Britain, France, and Italy, respectively. Libya was occupied by allied forces and gained independence in 1947 while Aden became part of South Yemen in 1967, then Yemen during unification in 1990. The state system since the period of decolonization up to 2010 has proved relatively stable, due largely to great power intervention in favor of strongmen and the status quo.

Contemporary Issues and Challenges

Although a common Arab identity has built up over centuries and was used divisively but briefly in the pan-Arab rhetoric and actions of Egyptian president Gamal Nasser, there have been persistently poor efforts at regional integration. The reasons are many. There is competition, fragmentation, and regional competition that have resulted in an absence of regional security structure beyond the weak efforts of the Arab League.[5] The result is a contemporary identity crisis, social trauma, and democratic and capacity deficits that have disempowered society writ large and favored violent nonstate actors such as Islamic State of Iraq and Syria (ISIS), which disengage from any type of political engagement.[6] Incidents such as the Iraq ferry disaster in March 2019 where 128 civilians drowned in the Mosul River highlight the lack of capacity in Middle East states. In this case, the Mosul River police had one broken boat, no ropes, no life jackets, and no training for such an eventuality.[7]

There is also a lack of integration in the global economy due in large part to protectionist trade policies that favor business elites engaged in a patron-client relationship. Middle East merchandise trade with the rest of the world actually dropped by 2.2 percent in 2017, the only region to experience a fall.[8] There is also a lack of national competition that could benefit from economies of scale at the regional level. National governments generally want to keep control of hydrocarbon production rather than privatize, diversify, and enhance the role of the private sector. Rentier economies remain dominated by hydrocarbon revenues and high public expenditures (which are becoming increasingly difficult to maintain post 2014) while more diversified economies remain dependent on rentier states for economic benefits ranging from labor remittances to economic aid and investment.

If one were to envisage an imaginary train journey from Morocco to Turkey, it would involve traversing the sealed Morocco-Algeria border (closed in 1976, opened in 1988, and closed again in 1994). The border now includes barbed wire over 1,600 kilometers of shared border and on Algeria's other borders to fight transnational terrorism.[9] The two states have clashed over the issue of the Western Sahara and in particular Algeria's support of the Polisario Front, the national liberation movement in a region where Morocco has declared its sovereignty.

From Algeria, the train would then head toward a conflict zone in Libya, where ISIS and other militia are active and thousands of refugees have set out to Italy across the Mediterranean often with disastrous consequences. At the time of writing Field Marshal Khalifa Haftar, backed by Russia and Egypt, the UAE, and in part by France, has been wrong-footed by UN-backed Libyan forces having been able to gain control of al-Watiya airbase, south of Tripoli.

The train would then wend its way through northern Egypt, across the Suez Canal and into the Sinai Peninsula where government forces are actively engaged in a military operation against multiple armed groups, including Islamic State fighters. From there it would cross into Palestine through the Rafah crossing, which is only occasionally opened for humanitarian supplies to enter/exit Gaza. Should the Palestinian Economic

Plan launched by Jared Kushner become a reality, and a land connection built to link Gaza and the West Bank by train or road, one could envisage traveling to the West Bank and through northern Israel to the closed border of Lebanon. The alternative route might take you to the fortified border with Syria. Traveling any further through either of these countries would require a political solution on the Israel-Palestine conflict to include a normalization of relations and a ceasefire/end to the Syria conflict. The alternative might be the more circuitous route through Jordan and Iraq to the Ibrahim Khalil border crossing with Turkey. This simple exercise identifies at least five or six major security issues to overcome before a basic pan-regional infrastructure could be contemplated.

It shows unresolved political tensions that prohibit good neighborliness and the requisite cooperation for regional integration. It also shows that poorly managed conflicts and violent Islamist groups and militia of various descriptions are posing a persistent obstacle to state and national security. A renewed emphasis on good governance remains vital to normalizing economies that are focused on charting a route to broad-based growth and economic inclusion. However, continued inadequacy or failure of governance will lead to dissatisfaction and disaffection, especially among the youth, which will no doubt fuel further social unrest and risk upending the existing regional order. While authoritarian upgrading and re-authoritarianism is a common response, it is important to consider the long span of history and the relatively new state institutionalization processes at play as well as the ongoing potential for reform in the region.

One of the most persistent challenges has been great and regional power competition in the Middle East, leading to it being known as a penetrated region. US interests continue to favor an 'Israel first' policy, which puts any resolution of the Israel-Palestine conflict into question. The conflicts in Libya and Syria in particular have morphed from civil wars into proxy battles for influence and the pursuit of diverse national interests, including acting as gateways for enhanced Russian influence in the region. The lack of restraint of state and nonstate actors continues to make political resolutions difficult to achieve, Yemen being the prime example.

At the regional level, the escalating tensions between Saudi Arabia and Iran have morphed into a dangerous standoff during the Trump presidency. The need for indigenous participation in dialogue and potentially a new regional security structure is clear to see. The Westphalia project at Cambridge University identifies that regional and external actors may have a role to play as guarantors to an agreement.[10] But I argue that Saudi and Iranian de-escalation measures targeting their geo-sectarian conflict require broader measures. These include moving away from exclusively theocratic principles for their political legitimacy, respecting minority groups, and contributing to socioeconomic resilience among internal and external groups most susceptible to a sectarian recruitment agenda.

Notes

1. See James Barr, *A Line in the Sand: Britain, France and the Struggle That Shaped the Middle East* (London: Simon and Schuster, 2012).
2. These include L. Carl Brown, *International Politics and the Middle East: Old Rules, Dangerous Game* (Princeton, NJ Princeton University Press, 1984); Bahgat Korany and Ali E. Hillal Dessouki, *The Foreign Policies of Arab States: The Challenge of Change* (Cairo: American University in Cairo Press, 1984); Fawaz Gerges, *The Superpowers and the Middle East: Regional and International Politics, 1955–1967* (Boulder, CO: Westview, 1994); Michael Hudson, ed., *The Middle East Dilemma: The Politics and Economics of Arab Integration* (New York: Columbia University Press, 1998); F. Gregory Gause III, "Systemic Approaches to Middle East International Relations," *International Studies Review* 1, no. 1 (1999): 11–31; Bassel Salloukh and Rex Brynen, eds., *Persistent Permeability? Regionalism, Localism, and Globalisation in the Middle East* (Aldershot: Ashgate, 2004); and Fred Halliday, *The Middle East in International Relations: Power, Politics and Ideology* (Cambridge: Cambridge University Press, 2005).
3. See Roger Hardy, *The Poisoned Well: Empire and Its Legacy in the Middle East* (Oxford: Oxford University Press, 2016).
4. Roger Owen, "Introduction," in *State, Power and Politics in the Making of the Modern Middle East* (Abingdon: Routledge, 2004), 1–4.
5. For more on this, see Anoushiravan Ehteshami, Amjad Rasheed, and Juline Beaujouan, "Transnational Language, Transient Identities, and the Crisis of the State in the Arab Region," Project Narrative, https://www.dur.ac.uk/ owri/subprojects/transientidentities/.
6. Ibid.
7. Ghaith Abdul-Ahad, "'I've Seen Death in This City, but Nothing as Sad as This': How a Ferry Disaster Exposed the Corruption Devastating Iraq," *Guardian*, December 5, 2019, https://www.theguardian.com/world/2019/ dec/05/mosul-iraq-ferry-disaster-corruption-protests.
8. World Trade Organization, "World Trade Statistical Review 2018," 10, https://www.wto.org/english/res_e/statis_e/wts2018_e/wts2018_e.pdf.
9. The North Africa Post, "Algeria Seals Land Borders with Morocco," November 29, 2018, http://northafricapost.com/26507-algeria-seals-land -borders-with-morocco.html.
10. Korber Foundation International Affairs, "A 'Westphalia' for the Middle East?," 163RD Bergdorf Round Table, Berlin, November 11–13, 2016,

https://www.koerber-stiftung.de/fileadmin/user_upload/koerber-stiftung/
redaktion/bergedorfer-gespraechskreis/pdf/2017/Conference-Report_BG
-163.pdf.

Bibliography

Abdul-Ahad, Ghaith. "'I've Seen Death in This City, but Nothing as Sad as This':
How a Ferry Disaster Exposed the Corruption Devastating Iraq." *Guardian*, December 5, 2019. https://www.theguardian.com/world/2019/dec/05/
mosul-iraq-ferry-disaster-corruption-protests.

Barr, James. *A Line in the Sand: Britain, France and the Struggle That Shaped the
Middle East*. London: Simon and Schuster, 2012.

Brown, L. Carl. *International Politics and the Middle East: Old Rules, Dangerous
Game*. Princeton, NJ: Princeton University Press, 1984.

Ehteshami, Anoushiravan, Amjad Rasheed, and Juline Beaujouan. "Transnational
Language, Transient Identities, and the Crisis of the State in the Arab Region."
Project Narrative. https://www.dur.ac.uk/owri/subprojects/transientidentities/.

Gause III, F. Gregory. "Systemic Approaches to Middle East International Relations." *International Studies Review* 1, no. 1 (1999): 11–31.

Gerges, Fawaz. *The Superpowers and the Middle East: Regional and International Politics, 1955–1967*. Boulder, CO: Westview, 1994.

Halliday, Fred. *The Middle East in International Relations: Power, Politics and Ideology*.
Cambridge: Cambridge University Press, 2005.

Hardy, Roger. *The Poisoned Well: Empire and Its Legacy in the Middle East*. Oxford:
Oxford University Press, 2016.

Hudson, Michael, ed. *The Middle East Dilemma: The Politics and Economics of Arab
Integration*. New York: Columbia University Press, 1998.

Korany, Bahgat, and Ali E. Hillal Dessouki. *The Foreign Policies of Arab States: The
Challenge of Change*. Cairo: American University in Cairo Press, 1984.

Korber Foundation International Affairs. "A 'Westphalia' for the Middle East?"
163rd Bergdorf Round Table, Berlin, November 11–13, 2016. https://www
.koerber-stiftung.de/fileadmin/user_upload/koerber-stiftung/redaktion/
bergedorfer-gespraechskreis/pdf/2017/Conference-Report_BG-163.pdf.

The North Africa Post. "Algeria Seals Land Borders with Morocco." November
29, 2018. http://northafricapost.com/26507-algeria-seals-land-borders-with
-morocco.html.

Owen, Roger. "Introduction." In *State, Power and Politics in the Making of the Modern Middle East*, 1–4. Abingdon: Routledge, 2004.

Salloukh, Bassel, and Rex Brynen, eds. *Persistent Permeability? Regionalism, Localism,
and Globalisation in the Middle East*. Aldershot: Ashgate, 2004.

World Trade Organization. "World Trade Statistical Review 2018." https://www
.wto.org/english/res_e/statis_e/wts2018_e/wts2018_e.pdf.

1

Political Economy in the Middle East: The Cases of Demography and Youth

Robert Mason and Seif Hendy

Introduction

This chapter discusses political economy in the Middle East, complementing the chapter on civil-military relations and providing some background information on the regional economy pertinent to Diwan's chapter on middle oil countries and reconstruction. It starts with an introductory note on the regional economic situation and goes on to explore what are arguably two of the leading social drivers of the political economy of the MENA region: demography and the specific demands of youth. It includes a study of related aspects such as health, education, unemployment, lack of civil participation, radicalization, and emigration. In the context of the *Arab Human Development Report 2016*, the chapter argues for a more adaptable and scalable approach, targeting key concerns such as health, education, and jobs, which better meet the needs of today's youth. The importance of reestablishing human security and stability for many young people is vital in order to avoid a cycle of violence and squandered human capital. This is especially the case for those affected by armed conflict in places such as Syria, affected by occupation in places such as Palestine, as well as those affected more generally by a lack of governance in so-called bunker states that continually fail to prioritize socioeconomic development objectives.[1]

The Regional Economy

GDP growth in the Middle East, one of the key indicators for economic performance, has stood at an average of 4.9 percent per year between 1960 and 2010, which is in fact slightly higher than the average for middle-income and low-income countries.[2] The oil boom and rapid population growth have both contributed to a higher rate of growth when compared with less developed countries (LDCs). However, when population growth is compared with economic growth, it looks much less convincing. Taking into consideration that labor market growth was faster than population growth from the 1980s to 1990s (ending in the oil boom from 1998 to 2014), it becomes clear that economic output did not match labor force growth.[3] GDP growth should be considered across time, to account for any periods of boom and bust, and across the region, taking into consideration disparity between states.[4] Of course the resource-rich labor-importing (Gulf Cooperation Council or GCC) countries of Bahrain, Kuwait, Oman, Qatar, Saudi Arabia, and UAE did well. But, ironically, the resource-poor labor-abundant (RPLA) countries, including Egypt, Jordan, Lebanon, Morocco, and Tunisia, did better than resource-rich labor abundant (RRLA) countries, including Algeria, Iran, Iraq, Libya, Syria, and Yemen. This is perplexing as these latter countries generally have resources and labor to use for development but have not benefited significantly from labor remittances (accounting for around 10 percent of GDP in Egypt and Morocco) and not attracted high amounts of aid from oil-rich countries in the way Egypt and Tunisia have done, for example. But being even somewhat reliant on oil-rich states forces RPLA states into similar cycles of boom and bust. Furthermore, all the RRLA states have been mired in conflicts that have undermined their performance. Diwan discusses the situation of these states in more detail in Chapter 5.

In more developmental states with stronger state intervention, regulation, and planning, the economy increases incomes and a middle class, leading to multifarious changes across society (particularly through education improvements and the creation of skilled labor) as well as changes to government and governance. East Asian 'miracle' states or Tigers (Hong Kong, Singapore, South Korea, and Taiwan) all underwent rapid industrialization from the early 1960s to 1990s and maintained high growth rates through interventions in the control of credit, foreign exchange, tax policies, and investment incentives. Although the 1997 Asian financial crisis was blamed to some extent on crony capitalism but also on speculation, the banking systems, and other structural problems, there has been a considerable change in policy direction, including an expansionary policy.[5] In contrast, many states in the MENA region used import substitution industrialization (ISI) to industrialize on the back of internal demand and insulate local industry from international competition. Only through globalization of the world economy from the 1980s onward did sustained attempts at export-led growth take place. With the onset and development of global capital, markets, and agencies, the core gained new forms of leverage over the policies and strategies of LDCs. The IMF, World Bank, aid agencies, and oil-rich states continue to dominate the economic landscape of the Middle East.

Demography

From 1950 to 2000, the Middle East experienced massive population growth, from 92 million to 349 million. The main reason for annual growth of more than 2 percent was a sharp decline in mortality rates.[6] For Israel, Libya, and the Arab Gulf states, immigration was also a factor. Population growth of this magnitude has put existing state resources under pressure, sometimes with harsh economic consequences. It has thus become the most acute socioeconomic problem in non-oil-producing Arab states.[7] As of 2010, immediately prior to the uprisings, people aged 15–24 formed around 20 percent of the total population in Tunisia, Egypt, and Morocco. By and large, this can be attributed to the high birth rates and population growth that were characteristic of the entire region throughout the 1980s. In Tunisia and Morocco, the population growth has since stabilized in a way that is convergent with global averages, although it remains high in Egypt (2 percent in 2018 in contrast to the global average of 1.1 percent).

There is extensive literature covering the 'youth bulge'[8] that characterizes the demography of the MENA region. Almost two-thirds of the MENA population is under the age of 30, slightly less than half of which is between the ages of 15 and 29.[9] Yet in spite of the fact that this demographic comprises such a substantial stratum of the population, there is a notable disempowerment with regard to their economic opportunity, social mobility, and political participation.

Health

One of the primary reasons for the massive population increase in the MENA region over the past few decades, and in turn the creation of a youth bulge, is the massive reduction in both childhood mortality and maternal mortality rates. Though it may seem less obvious than childhood mortality, maternal mortality rates are highly correlated to the increase in the youth population since marriage in the Middle East tends to take place at a very early age for women. Over the past twenty-five years, maternal mortality rates have plummeted throughout the region with countries such as Kuwait, the UAE, and Libya all currently exhibiting single-digit figures for mortality per 100,000 people (4, 6, and 9, respectively).[10] There is a substantial disparity, however, as problems regarding maternal mortality continue to linger in Yemen, Algeria, and Morocco. Yemen in particular has a glaring problem with a rate of 385 per 100,000 people. But even there, there has been a 30 percent reduction since 1990. Countries such as Iran and Saudi Arabia have managed reductions of upward of 70 percent.[11]

Childhood mortality has followed a similar trend, although the reduction rates have been even higher than those of maternal mortality rates. Only in Algeria has there been a percentage decrease in childhood mortality per 1,000 live births that is less than 50 percent since 1990. The effects of childhood mortality reduction have been amplified in the MENA region due to the abnormally high fertility rates over most of the second half of the twentieth century. These fertility rates have been declining quite steeply since then, with only three countries now having a fertility rate higher than 3 children per woman (Egypt, Jordan, and Yemen).[12] To place this in context, fertility rates in Jordan between 1975 and 1980 were about 7.38 and have now reached 3.26, only slightly higher than the global average of around 2.5.[13]

Nutrition is another major health issue, especially as it impacts education and learning by affecting brain development. Food security can affect nutritional balance and diet. Supply chain management issues, economic and political decision-making all impact nutrition, as does education and public awareness. The World Food Program has reported that in very rural areas and particularly among the most vulnerable group, very young children, the risk of poor nutrition can be high.[14] A 2019 study in the *Lancet* states that poor countries are facing both obesity and malnutrition.[15] Heart disease was the leading cause of mortality across the region between 1990 and 2010 (up 44 percent), ahead of respiratory infections (up 47 percent) and stroke (up 35 percent).[16] The leading risk factors were diet (up 64 percent), high blood pressure (up 59 percent), high body mass index (up 138 percent), and smoking (up 10 percent).[17]

Looking ahead, diabetes cases in the Middle East are set to rise 110 percent by 2045, which amounts to the total population of Turkey.[18] The epidemic is due to altered eating patterns, where only 38 percent of the population eats fresh fruits and vegetables, and increased income and urbanization in the Gulf.[19] Nutritional guidelines and policies for enhanced nutritional choices appear to be very thin on the ground. In Yemen, Iraq, and Sudan, undernourishment is seen in more than 25 percent of the population.[20] There is also a causal linkage between food, work, and income/health. Since anemia (the condition in which the number of red blood cells or their oxygen-carrying capacity is insufficient to meet physiological needs) is common, it means people are less able to work and therefore less able to afford food.[21] Having a sedentary lifestyle is another cause and while this may first appear to replicate concerns in other societies, it also reflects a lack of public space and accessible medical and sports facilities for the majority of the population. Urban planning has thus far taken very little consideration of these trends or redressed the outcomes that they lead to. Thus, while the health changes in the MENA region may appear to be congruent with those of the United States and western Europe, the reasons may be somewhat different.

Clearly poverty and armed conflict can have an effect on young people's health too. They can also have pronounced effects on mental health and lead to illicit drug use, tobacco consumption, and obesity. Mental health has been an underlying, though insufficiently researched, issue regionally with the epidemics of loneliness and depression becoming more prevalent. Tunisia registers regional highs for both feelings of loneliness and suicidal consideration, with respective figures of 17.2 percent and 19.8 percent among young people in 2008.[22] Even more concerning is the prevalence of post-traumatic stress disorder across the region, no doubt highly correlated to the frequency of political violence, which ranges from 24 percent among young people in Lebanon to 69 percent in Gaza.[23]

Illicit drug use has been on the rise among 15- to-24-year-olds according to World Health Organization reports. Yemen has a particular problem with the production of the drug khat, which is used by around 90 percent of men and is legally distributed throughout the country. Morocco has a major problem with regard to hashish. The country is one of the world's leading producers of cannabis resin. The most commonly abused drugs in the region are alcohol, sedatives, stimulants, tranquilizers, and hypnotics, many of which are frequently used by secondary school and university students to cope with external pressures. The implementation of the Global School-Based Student Health Survey (GSHS) modules for alcohol and drugs has been lacking, with only four of eleven Arab countries adopting the GSHS and teaching those modules. Tobacco consumption is also quite prevalent with more than 30 percent of 13- to 15-year-olds in the Palestinian Territories, Iraq, Saudi Arabia, and Jordan all having at least tried cigarettes.

Secondary tobacco consumption is also high in many public places, including shopping malls and hotels, although tobacco-free policies have been rolled out in Djibouti, Jordan, and the UAE, and health warnings have been introduced on 50 percent of tobacco packaging in Djibouti, Egypt, Iran, and Jordan.[24] The other issue with regard to tobacco is the consumption of alternative forms such as the shisha; 61 percent of Lebanese students stated that they consumed such tobacco though only 10 percent smoked cigarettes.[25] When weighted against air quality in general (see Chapter 7), education opportunities, political will, culture, and the stress associated with the lives of contemporary youth, one can see that antismoking policies may only get so far in the short term. The lack of public information campaigns covering everything from driving to nutrition, while taken for granted in the West, are rarely matched in Middle East media.

Education

There has been increased primary, secondary, and tertiary education enrolment across the MENA region over the past decade. Yet, the region has been unable to absorb an increasingly educated populace into limited national labor markets. The problems youth face in finding employment will be discussed more specifically in the next section but they are definitely intertwined with the increase of mass public education and an economic infrastructure that does not prioritize or fully utilize the knowledge pool created by higher education. Educational choices are linked to parental preferences, realistic employment options (including entering the family business), but also aspirations such as further study (often abroad) and prestigious places to work, including multinational companies or international organizations.

In terms of expenditure on primary education as a percentage of GDP per capita: Egypt spent 10 percent in 2017, Saudi Arabia 17.7 percent in 2007, Iran 11.2 percent in 2017, Algeria 11.5 percent in 2003, Israel 21.5 percent in 2016, Oman 31.4 percent in 2016, and Morocco 19.6 percent in 2013.[26] In terms of expenditure on secondary education as a percentage of GDP per capita: Lebanon spent 5.8 percent in 2013 (latest figures), Egypt 14 percent in 2017, Saudi Arabia 17.6 percent in 2007, Iran 17.7 percent in 2017, Algeria 17.9 percent in 2003, Israel 18.7 percent in 2016, Oman 35.8 percent in 2017, and Morocco 36.5 percent.[27] Although these figures are high by OECD standards and represent absolute progress, they do not translate into significant human resource development relative to other parts of the world. Possible reasons for this include:

1. Per capital expenditure in states with small budgets and large populations is modest. Public schools and universities are notoriously underfunded, with focus on buildings rather than human resources resulting in understaffing

2. An informal economy exists between private tutors and students to circumvent the limitations of public education, which is particularly important in conflict zones where refugees lack access to formal forms of education
3. Inefficient spending
4. Market distortions in the economy
5. Underinvestment in females[28]
6. In the era of the Arab Uprisings, formal tertiary education is also competing for students' attention along with civic engagement, spurred by tech-savvy and organized youth often in clubs that can hold more sway over the institution than faculty[29]

Literacy rates in the Middle East are 95 percent in Lebanon, 71 percent in Egypt, 95 percent in Saudi Arabia, 86 percent in Iran, 81 percent in Algeria, 92 percent in Israel, 96 percent in Oman, and 74 percent in Morocco. Illiteracy is primarily concentrated among women and could be improved with a small additional investment in education aimed at closing the gender gap.[30] Here culture combined with cost appears to play a role. A report by the Population Reference Bureau on the Middle East and North Africa showed that a majority of families believed that if they could send only one child out of a son and a daughter, they would choose the son.[31] This is accurately reflected in enrolment, though there is a positive trend toward gender parity. Overall enrolment also requires improvement and remains affected by perceptions about institutional effectiveness, priorities of the family within the context of the overall political economy, and compulsory military service, which has the potential to disrupt degree programs. Since 2014, three monarchies have (re)introduced conscription: Kuwait, Qatar, and the UAE. They join Tunisia, Egypt, Syria, Iraq, Algeria, Libya, Mauritania, and Sudan.[32]

There are mixed styles of education on display in the Middle East with states choosing multiple hybrids instead of committing to a single vision. A form of balancing between states and keeping good relations with many, it can include schools and universities from Europe, China, Japan, Australia, and the United States, each with their own teaching styles (pedagogy), institutional priorities, and cultures. Furthermore with different MENA states at different levels of development and with different national priorities and political will to engage in reform there is likely to be diversity in the education systems for some time to come. As Wilson notes, development goals, such as education, need to be more closely linked to Islamic values than has so far been the case in most

Muslim-majority states in order for them to be more successfully implemented.[33] Education is yet to be the platform on which traditional values and religious practices can be reconciled with modern life, although it is beginning in some of the GCC states. Overall, though, it is Jordan, Kuwait, Tunisia, and Lebanon that have been most effective at creating mass educational opportunities, at least up to 2003, with the challenge now being the integration of their education systems with opportunities in the global economy.[34] Even in suboptimal trends such as relying on private enterprise to deliver education programming, the negative aspects of this can be at least partially mitigated through better regulation and a focus on equitable student-centered solutions.[35]

Unemployment

The most notable distinction when considering unemployment in the MENA region is that between rentier and non-rentier states, or those states with the economic resources to contemplate structural changes and those without. In weak or failed states such as Libya, Syria, and Yemen, wartime economies have become consolidated under shifting patronage networks[36] or affected by violent nonstate actors such as Islamic State of Iraq and Syria (ISIS). Employment in states such as Jordan, Lebanon, and Turkey has been affected by refugees, but evidence suggests they could boost, rather than hinder, their new host economy.[37]

While the issues of youth unemployment and labor market exclusion are of a general nature in the Middle East, women's unemployment is 80 percent higher than that of men.[38] Discrimination and conservative social norms are part of the reason for such high rates, along with general issues of mismatched skills for the labor force, lack of career-planning resources, and a limited number of more prestigious jobs. Unemployment drives rural-urban migration, putting more strain on cities, and also immigration to other states, notably the Gulf states. The Arab Uprisings illustrate that youth unemployment is a major driver of regional instability and upheaval. Addressing it more comprehensively could have significant impacts but will require some space in the political system for debate and action. In many cases, a youth strategy does not exist, is present only in draft form, or has expired.

Only Lebanon, Morocco, and Yemen have active strategies through their respective ministries of youth and sport, and these are not explicitly linked to employment.[39] Up to the Arab Uprisings, nongovernmental organizations (NGOs) were involved in youth programs in Egypt, but their activities have been scaled down. In terms of youth employment, changes to the business climate are likely to help, including job creation, access to finance, better regulation, and reduced corruption. MENA states appear to have fallen at the implementation stage and in getting the policy mix right. Low female labor force participation is also a problem, although Jordan, for example, has instituted maternity leave benefits, which raised women's participation in the labor force to 31 percent.[40] There is little point to improving graduate enrolment if employment opportunities do not follow suit, which is what appears to have happened in Tunisia in 2013 and in Saudi Arabia. More creativity is certainly needed, along with more pilot projects and a range of measures in the political economy that enhance youth futures.

Non-rentier States

In both Tunisia and Egypt, where the Arab Uprisings initially took root, thousands of young people took to the streets to demand change. There were two particularly prominent chants that rang across Tunis and Tahrir: "The people demand the fall of the regime" and "bread, freedom, social justice," which perfectly captured the grievances of these protestors. Seeking to put an end to economic insecurity, repression, corruption, and the leaderships that were deemed responsible for these things, youth in Tunisia and Egypt were the first to instigate major movements of social unrest. Both of these countries share similarities, crucially being non-rentier states,[41] and they do not currently face major civil wars. Unemployment rates of people aged 15–24 are particularly informative as to why dissatisfaction with the regime was so intense, with Tunisia at 29.4 percent and Egypt at 24.4 percent in 2010—a substantial contrast to the global average of 12.3 percent.[42] The transition of leadership was also relatively quick in contrast to the mismanaged transition process in Syria.[43]

The protests in Morocco, although quite prolonged, were less intense (unemployment was also lower at 17.7 percent) and were effectively put to an end with political concessions that did not involve the wholesale uprooting of the monarchy. What is slightly more surprising is that all three countries, despite taking divergent paths in the aftermath of the protests, have not been able to effectively combat youth unemployment. Morocco has faced a gradual increase over the eight years following 2010 (21.9 percent as of 2018) whereas Tunisia and Egypt both encountered skyrocketing figures in 2011 (the year of the unrest) before some stabilization took place, though not at the pre-2011 figures (34.8 percent and 32.6 percent, respectively, as of 2018).

Rentier States

There is a common misconception of the economic situation of oil and gas exporting countries that the extravagant and affluent sheikh is the norm. However there remain significant employment challenges facing the GCC states. The spillover effects of the Arab Uprisings did reach GCC states, who responded with both economic largesse and repression. For example, Saudi Arabia spent a large part of a $150 billion package for the kingdom and GCC neighbors on social welfare spending.[44] Youth unemployment in 2014 stood at 27.8 percent in Saudi Arabia, 27.5 percent in Bahrain, 20.6 percent in Oman, 11 percent in the UAE, and 9.2 percent in Kuwait.[45] The reasons for this lingering problem are largely structural and have only recently been addressed through national economic plans such as Saudi Vision 2030, which was launched in 2016. Primarily, there is a vast preference for public sector jobs in these countries due to the pay differential and conditions with the private sector. Public sector jobs are seen as very stable, lifetime positions. The benefits of these positions are substantial, with provisions such as healthcare or pensions being afforded and governments addressing socioeconomic concerns sometimes through salary increases.

By contrast, private sector jobs are by their nature less stable, with performance expectations in line with international standards, and open to the pressures of the global economy. This colors the way young people in the Gulf approach their employment prospects, frequently favoring to wait for a public sector opening rather than entering the private labor market. Moreover, labor laws are quite protective of Gulf citizens, and thus private employers have an overt preference for migrant workers who arrive in the Gulf in exceedingly precarious positions through the Kafala system. This is not the only way in which an apparent benefit can also turn into a detriment. The primary source of wealth in the Gulf, oil and gas and their derivatives, tends to hinder the absorption of young people looking for work as these fields are not particularly labor intensive. The lack of diversification of the Gulf economies leaves many young people either unable to find work in the oil sector or underqualified to find work elsewhere. It is thus no surprise that the two countries with the highest non-oil GDP per capita, Qatar and the UAE, have less drastic problems when it comes to youth unemployment in comparison with many of their neighbors.[46]

Additionally, though frequently disregarded, Algeria is also an oil-exporting country and is impacted by many of the very same problems that exist in all rentier societies. Initially resilient to the Arab Uprising pressures due to fears of another civil conflict such as the one that marred the country from 1991 to 2002, protests or the so-called Revolution of Smiles began in February 2019 after the ailing president Bouteflika announced his candidacy for a fifth consecutive presidential term. When looking at the demographics alone civil unrest was to be expected. Almost

70 percent of the Algerian population is under the age of 30, and 30 percent of the population is aged between 15 and 24 and face unemployment.

Diversification is particularly important in rentier states that often suffer from Dutch disease by having back-up industries to fall back on in times of economic instability but also to provide much needed jobs. The 2019 protests in Lebanon, violence and corruption in Iraq, and sanctions against Iran continue to draw scholarly attention to an employment crisis with deep roots. Subsidy reform and taxation are at least bringing in more diverse streams of income, which could soon be channeled in building more competitive companies in new industries. Nonreligious tourism in Saudi Arabia opened for business in September 2019 and promises to boost jobs further.

Unemployment Summary

Youth unemployment in the MENA region was 30 percent in 2017, the highest in twenty-five years.[47] In general, youth unemployment in the MENA region affects Palestine, Saudi Arabia, Jordan, and Tunisia the worst. Only Qatar, an energy-rich state with a small population, is able to absorb a large proportion of nationals into public sector jobs to weaken the socioeconomic pressure. The consequences of employment delays or low-level employment (either in hours worked or in low-wage jobs) for marriage, home ownership, and civic participation have led to what Singerman calls 'waithood'—the extended period between childhood and full adulthood.[48] The resentment such waiting and social dislocation has caused could, according to some academics, lead to further social unrest in future.[49] Certainly, there is evidence of dissatisfaction with the status quo judging from recent surveys carried out across the region.[50]

The 2008 financial crisis, eruptions of political violence associated with the Arab Uprisings from 2011, and the fall in the international oil price from 2014 have affected all youth in the region, as income from energy sales, labor remittances, diversification measures, and migration to the Gulf states have all become constrained. Some Arab states such as Egypt, Jordan, Lebanon, and Tunisia have good levels of diversification, which could theoretically contribute to further job creation in future and macro-economic stability overall. But the current level of economic growth is generally not enough to sustain growing populations and, importantly, growing expectations from graduates.

Human Security, Radicalization, and Emigration

Youth bulges are not directly correlated with episodes of internal political violence, but there is some evidence to suggest that they are conducive to them according to Jack Goldstone's revolution theory.[51] The revolts of 2011 have been theorized as a rupture in this social contract, a natural conclusion to what happens when the provision of basic social services is neglected by the commanding regimes.[52] This took the form of failing to absorb new entrants into the labor market as well as rising food prices due to inflation and mismanagement. Problematically, most MENA states, especially non-rentier ones, have not been able to quell the very same issues that existed before 2010. Whether because of authoritarian upgrading and/or the socioeconomic pain caused by partial economic reforms that followed, social tensions remain high. The looming issue of radicalization persists with Islamic State–affiliated group insurgencies still a risk in northern Algeria.[53] The insurgent and violent jihadi trend has been similar in Tunisia after its uprising in 2011, even if the mechanics are different.[54] It remains to be seen whether the young protesters in Algeria can combat and win over the regime and whether social order will be reinstated or disintegrate along the lines of Libya, Iraq, Syria, or Yemen.

Beyond radicalization, there is another route that plenty of young people in these countries consider—that of emigration. What is termed 'the brain drain' is very much alive in the Middle East wherein gifted young people opt to leave their nations and immigrate to areas they deem more conducive to the realization of their capabilities. In Tunisia, there has been a drastic rise in these sentiments, with 31 percent of Tunisian youth considering illegal migration in 2016.[55] By the end of 2018, an estimated 3,811 undocumented migrants reached Italy and that was after the Tunisian authorities stopped a further 6,369 Tunisians from leaving illegally in 2018.[56] Another 1,721 perished at sea in 2017.[57] With a lack of sufficient growth of formal sector jobs (indeed *harqa* youth are actively excluded from public life) and serious systemic obstacles to the employment prospects to recent graduates, it remains unlikely that such actions will abate in the near future.

The Middle East is of course notorious as one of the world's most war-torn regions. Iraq, Libya, Syria, and Yemen are all currently plagued by civil conflicts, in addition to the Israel-Palestine conflict. It is of course much more difficult to evaluate the challenges facing the youth in those countries by utilizing the conventional measures as the immediate threat to most citizens will not be an abstract version of 'human development' or 'insecurity' but a very concrete physical threat to their lives. Moreover, the radically altering demographic nature of countries at war makes the issue even more problematic. Likewise, the two neighboring countries of Lebanon and Jordan have faced serious demographic shifts due to refugees entering from Israel and Syria. The emphasis of foreign actors such as the EU is therefore often focused on issues such as shoring up stability.

As the United States Institute for Peace notes, the difficulty of working for change in the Middle East has led many young changemakers to burn out.[58] In addition to attempts to promote more inclusive societies, the Arab Uprisings from 2010 facilitated the more diffuse phenomenon of radical insurgency across the region. It is sometimes framed through the lens of youth disempowerment or poverty within each state or context in question.[59] The United Nations Development Program (UNDP) identifies eleven building blocks to preventing violent extremism, with just one aimed at providing effective socioeconomic alternatives to violence for groups at risk.[60] The drivers of radicalization are varied and can range from pan-Islamic nationalism, being inspired by friends or family who have volunteered for violent jihad, to exposure to professional recruiters and recruiters being sought out by self-radicalizers. In the case of the fifteen hundred Saudis fighting in Iraq in 2004, there was a perception that Iraqi resistance was legitimate and therefore justifiable according to Islamic belief.[61]

Conclusion: Prospects for Civil and Political Participation

World attention has been drawn to personalities such as Mohammed Bouazizi, the young street vendor who set himself ablaze in Tunisia in late 2010 and sparked the Arab Uprisings. Prominent and deliberate youth activists include Wael Ghonim, one of the organizers of a social media campaign that played a vital role in spurring mass demonstrations against Hosni Mubarak in Egypt; Raif Badawi, a Saudi writer, dissident, and activist; and Manal al-Sharif, who spearheaded Saudi women's right to drive. Others include Tawakkol Karman, who established "Women Journalists Without Chains" in Yemen in 2005 and is the youngest Nobel Peace laureate to date, and Razan Ghazzawi, a Syrian American blogger, campaigner, and activist. There are countless millions sharing information through social media platforms such as Facebook, WhatsApp, and Twitter.

Many activists have been associated with 'terrorism' and arrested often after amendments have been made to existing antiterror legislation. If not, state pressure has sometimes been brought to bear on relatives in order to reign in an activist's social influence. There are, increasingly, punitive measures against freedom of expression and assembly aimed at shoring up regime autonomy and survival. The prospects for youth activism, civic association, and participation are therefore limited. As youth has taken to online chat rooms and social media to vent frustrations and discuss and debate issues, so too has the state closed down online avenues and pursued participants internally and across state borders. But, as the *Arab Human Development Report 2016* notes, momentum in the youth bulge will be there in the region for the next two decades and this offers a historic opportunity to enhance the foundations for social, economic, and political stability, participation, and prosperity. It remains to be seen just how the pendulum will swing. A combination of governance conducive to fostering the creative and innovative capacities of youth and a pronounced effort by the youth to step up to the forefront of the political landscape without incurring exceptional costs to their safety and security will be essential prerequisites for a stable state-society dynamic.

It would be erroneous to assume that the pathway to economic development runs smooth or is trouble free anywhere. In Algeria, amid protests, there is a growing 'delinquency' crisis where drug use, urban riots, and crime are all on the rise. This appears to be a general feature of disorder in authoritarian states. However changes to the way economic policy is formulated are being trailed in Iceland, Scotland, and New Zealand, for example, where more balanced economic growth is being planned to cover social inclusion and green and family-friendly policies.[62] This kind of approach could pay dividends in the MENA region should there be a reconceptualization or reformulation of governance away from bunker states and authoritarian upgrading in favor of establishing new bases of political legitimacy that support developmental priorities, especially for the next generation.

Notes

1. See Clement M. Henry and Robert Springborg, "Bunker States," in *Globalization and the Politics of Development in the Middle East* (Cambridge: Cambridge University Press, 2010), 113–161.

2. Melani Cammett, Ishac Diwan, Alan Richards, and John Waterbury, "Economic Performance and Social Outcomes," in *A Political Economy of the Middle East* (Boulder, CO: Westview, 2015), 38.

3. Ibid., 40.

4. Ibid.

5. Robert Wade, "Gestalt Shift: From 'Miracle' to 'Cronyism' in the Asian Crisis," LSE Development Studies Institute Working Paper nos. 2–25, February 2002, http://www.lse.ac.uk/internationalDevelopment/pdf/WP/WP25.pdf.

6. Patrick Clawson, "Demography in the Middle East," The Washington Institute for Middle East Policy, March 2009, https://www.washingtonin stitute.org/policy-analysis/view/demography-in-the-middle-east-popula tion-growth-slowing-womens-situation-un.

7. Onn Winkler, *Arab Political Demography Vol. 1: Population Growth, Labor Migration and Natalist Policies* (EastBourne: Sussex Academic Press, 2005).

8. There is some divergence within the literature as to what age range adequately constitutes the label of 'youth' with the International Labour Organization using the 15–24 range whereas the Organisation for Economic Co-operation and Development preferring 15–29. For the sake of this analysis, both will be used with clarifications expressed for why one was preferred where relevant. https://www.wdaforum.org/fileadmin/ablage/ wdaforum/publications/dp2011-08.pdf.

9. United Nations Development Program, *Arab Human Development Report 2016*, 2016, 5, http://www.arab-hdr.org/reports/2016/english/AHDR 2016En.pdf.

10. Ken Sagynbekov, "Child and Maternal Health in the Middle East and North Africa," Milken Institute, February 2018, https://www.milkeninsti tute.org/sites/default/files/reports-pdf/Childhood-and-Maternal-Health -in-MENA.pdf.

11. Ibid.

12. Marcia C. Inhorn, "The Arab World's 'Quiet' Reproductive Revolution," *Brown Journal of World Affairs* 24, no. 2 (Spring/Summer 2018): 147–159.

13. Ibid.

14. Presentation by the World Food Program, American University in Cairo, September 18, 2018.

15. BBC News, "Poorest Countries Facing Both Obesity and Malnutrition," December 16, 2019, https://www.bbc.co.uk/news/health-50784281.

16. The World Bank, "In Middle East and North Africa, Health Challenges are Becoming Similar to Those in Western Countries," September 4, 2013, https://www.worldbank.org/en/news/press-release/2013/09/04/ middle-east-north-Africa-health-challenges-similar-western-countries.

17. Ibid.

18. Gulf News, "Diabetes Cases in Middle East to Rise 110% by 2045," December 19, 2018.

19. Ibid.

20. Editorial, "Food Security in the Middle East and North Africa," *Lancet*, July 14, 2018, https://www.thelancet.com/journals/lancet/article/ PIIS0140-6736(18)31563-0/fulltext.

21. Ibid.

22. Rima Afifi, Jocelyn DeJong, Krishna Bose, Tanya Salem, Amr A. Awad, and Manal Benkirane, "The Health of Young People: Challenges and Opportunities," in *Public Health in the Arab World*, ed. Samer Jabbour, Rita Giacaman, Marwan Khawaja, and Iman Nuwayhid (Cambridge: Cambridge University Press, 2012), 241.

23. Ibid., 499, 178–187.

24. James Reinl, "UAE Leads Region in Ban on Smoking," *National*, December 17, 2009, https://www.thenational.ae/world/mena/uae-leads-region-in -ban-on-smoking-1.632559.

25. Rabih K, "Lebanese Youth Heaviest Hookah Users in the World," *Lebanese Examiner*, March 5, 2019, https://www.lebaneseexaminer.com/2019/03/05/ lebanese-people-highest-hookah-usage-world-study-shows/.

26. The World Bank, "Government Expenditure per Student, Primary (Percent of GDP per Capita), https://data.worldbank.org/indicator/SE.XPD .PRIM.PC.ZS.

27. The World Bank, "Government Expenditure per Student, Secondary (Percent of GDP per Capita), https://data.worldbank.org/indicator/SE.XPD .SECO.PC.ZS?view=chart.

28. Nemat Shafik, "Big Spending, Small Returns: The Paradox of Human Resource Development in the Middle East," Egyptian Center for Economic Studies Working Paper no. 2, 1996, http://www.eces.org.eg/MediaFiles/ Uploaded_Files/percent7B185111A4-07D2-4160-A434-753DCBD78D5A percent7D_ECESWP2e.pdf.

29. From personal experience teaching in Egypt; also see: Linda Herrera, ed., *Wired Citizenship: Youth Learning and Activism in the Middle East* (Abingdon: Routledge, 2014).

30. Shafik, "Big Spending, Small Returns," 5.

31. The Borgen Project, "Improving Education Levels for Women in the Middle East," September 9, 2015, https://borgenproject.org/women-in -the-middle-east/.

32. Habib Toumi, "Kuwait Becomes 11th Arab State to Have Mandatory Military Service," *Gulf News*, July 11, 2017, https://gulfnews.com/world/gulf/ kuwait/kuwait-becomes-11th-arab-state-to-have-mandatory-military -service-1.2056483.

33. Rodney Wilson, *Economic Development in the Middle East* (Abingdon: Routledge, 2012).

34. The World Bank, "Why Some MENA Countries Did Better than Others," *MENA Development Report: The Road Not Travelled—Education Reform in the Middle East and Africa* (Washington, DC: World Bank, 2008), 203, http:// siteresources.worldbank.org/INTMENA/Resources/EDU_Flagship_Full _ENG.pdf.

35. Ibid.

36. "The Men Making a Fortune from Syria's War," *Financial Times*, October 3, 2019, https://www.ft.com/content/525ec4e4-e4a3-11e9-9743-db5a370 481bc.

37. Shelly Culbertson and Krishna B. Kumar, "Jobs Can Improve the Lives of Syrian Refugees and Their Host Communities—and Support Stability in the Middle East', *RAND*, March 2019, https://www.rand.org/blog/2019/03/ jobs-can-improve-the-lives-of-syrian-refugees-and-their.html.

38. Nader Kabbani, "Youth Employment in the Middle East and North Africa: Revisiting and Reframing the Challenge," *Brookings*, February 26, 2019. https://www.brookings.edu/research/youth-employment-in-the-middle -east-and-north-africa-revisiting-and-reframing-the-challenge/.

39. Ibid.

40. World Economic Forum and the World Bank Group, *Arab World Competitiveness Report 2018* (Geneva: World Economic Forum, 2018), 51.

41. Although both gain from tourism based on natural features such as Mediterranean and Red Sea shorelines and Egypt also gains from the Suez Canal receipts, which could be considered a rentier income.

42. World Economic Forum and the World Bank Group, *Arab World Competitiveness Report 2018*.

43. See Raymond Hinnebusch, "Authoritarian Upgrading in the Arab Uprising: Syria in Comparative Perspective," BRISMES conference paper, March 2012, https://brismes2012.files.wordpress.com/2012/02/raymond -hinnebusch-syria-authoritarian-upgrading.pdf.

44. Elizabeth Broomhall, "Arab Spring Has Cost Gulf Arab States $150bn," *Arabian Business*, September 8, 2017, https://www.arabianbusiness.com/ arab-spring-has-cost-gulf-arab-states-150bn-419429.html.

45. World Economic Forum, *Rethinking Arab Employment: A Systemic Approach for Resource-Endowed Economies*, October 2014, 6, http://www3.weforum .org/docs/WEF_MENA14_RethinkingArabEmployment.pdf.

46. International Monetary Fund, "Economic Diversification in Oil-Exporting Arab Countries," April 2016, 12, https://www.imf.org/external/np/pp/eng/ 2016/042916.pdf.

47. Kabbani, "Youth Employment in the Middle East and North Africa: Revisiting and Reframing the Challenge."

48. Diane Singerman, "The Economic Imperatives of Marriage: Emerging Practices and Identities among Youth in the Middle East," Middle East Youth Initiative, September 2007, https://www.meyi.org/publication-the -economic-imperatives-of-marriage-emerging-practices-and-identities -among-youth-in-the-middle-east.html.

49. M. Chloe Mulderig, "An Uncertain Future: Youth Frustration and the

Arab Spring," The Pardee Papers, no. 16, 2013, http://www.bu.edu/pardee/files/2013/04/Pardee-Paper-16.pdf.

50. See, for example, Jorg Gertel, "Youth in the MENA Region," in *Coping with Uncertainty: Youth in the Middle East and North Africa*, ed. Jorg Gertel and Ralf Hexel (London: Saqi, 2018), 9.

51. Shingo Hamanaka, "Demographic Change and Its Social and Political Implications in the Middle East," *Asian Journal of Comparative Politics* 2, no. 1 (May 13, 2016): 74.

52. For more on this issue, see Mehran Kamrava, ed., *Beyond the Arab Spring: The Evolving Ruling Bargain in the Middle East* (Oxford: Oxford University Press, 2014).

53. Daniel Samet, "In Algeria an Islamist Threat Still Looms over Domestic Politics," Freedom House, August 22, 2018, https://freedomhouse.org/blog/algeria-islamist-threat-still-looms-over-domestic-politics.

54. Aaron Y. Zelin, "Tunisian Foreign Fighters in Iraq and Syria," Washington Institute for Near East Policy, Policy Notes PN55, 2018, https://www.washingtoninstitute.org/uploads/Documents/pubs/PolicyNote55-Zelin.pdf.

55. Observertoire Maghrebin des Migrations, "Rapport: Migration non Reglementaire," Tunisia, 2017, 5, https://ftdes.net/rapports/fr.omm3.2017.pdf.

56. Larbi Sadiki, "Tunisia's Migration to the North," *Brookings*, January 17, 2019, https://www.brookings.edu/blog/order-from-chaos/2019/01/17/tunisias-migration-to-the-north/.

57. Ibid.

58. United States Institute for Peace, "Connecting Young Activists across the Middle East and Africa: Generation Change," April 1, 2015, https://www.usip.org/publications/2015/04/connecting-young-activists-across-middle-east-and-africa-generation-change.

59. See, for example: Atle Mesoy, "Poverty and Radicalisation into Violent Extremism: A Causal Link?," Noref Expert Analysis, January 2013, https://www.files.ethz.ch/isn/158431/e60a8a679f48427d592a1906daf569d4.pdf.

60. United Nations Development Program, "Preventing Violent Extremism through Promoting Inclusive Development, Tolerance and Respect for Diversity," 2016, 5, https://www.undp.org/content/dam/norway/undp-ogc/documents/Discussionpercent20Paperpercent20-percent20Preventing percent20Violentpercent20Extremismpercent20bypercent20Promoting percent20Inclusivepercent20percent20Development.pdf.

61. Thomas Hegghammer, "Saudis in Iraq: Patterns of Radicalization and Recruitment," *Cultures and Conflicts*, June 12, 2008, https://journals.openedition.org/conflits/10042.

62. BBC News, "Iceland Puts Well-Being Ahead of GDP in Budget," December 3, 2019, https://www.bbc.com/news/world-europe-50650155.

Bibliography

Afifi, Rima, Jocelyn DeJong, Krishna Bose, Tanya Salem, Amr A. Awad, and Manal Benkirane. "The Health of Young People: Challenges and Opportunities." In *Public Health in the Arab World*, edited by Samer Jabbour, Rita Giacaman, Marwan Khawaja, and Iman Nuwayhid, 236–249. Cambridge: Cambridge University Press, 2012.

BBC News. "Iceland Puts Well-Being Ahead of GDP in Budget." December 3, 2019. https://www.bbc.com/news/world-europe-50650155.

———. "Poorest Countries Facing Both Obesity and Malnutrition." December 16, 2019. https://www.bbc.co.uk/news/health-50784281.

The Borgen Project. "Improving Education Levels for Women in the Middle East." September 9, 2015. https://borgenproject.org/women-in-the-middle-east/.

Broomhall, Elizabeth. "Arab Spring Has Cost Gulf Arab States $150bn." *Arabian Business*, September 8, 2017. https://www.arabianbusiness.com/arab-spring-has-cost-gulf-arab-states-150bn-419429.html.

Cammett, Melani, Ishac Diwan, Alan Richards, and John Waterbury. "Economic Performance and Social Outcomes." In *A Political Economy of the Middle East*. Boulder, CO: Westview, 2015.

Clawson, Patrick. "Demography in the Middle East." The Washington Institute for Middle East Policy, March 2009. https://www.washingtoninstitute.org/policy-analysis/view/demography-in-the-middle-east-population-growth-slowing-womens-situation-un.

Cornish, Chloe. "The Men Making a Fortune from Syria's War." *Financial Times*, October 3, 2019. https://www.ft.com/content/525ec4e4-e4a3-11e9-9743-db5a370481bc.

Culbertson, Shelly, and Krishna B. Kumar. "Jobs Can Improve the Lives of Syrian Refugees and Their Host Communities—and Support Stability in the Middle East." *RAND*, March 2019. https://www.rand.org/blog/2019/03/jobs-can-improve-the-lives-of-syrian-refugees-and-their.html.

Gertel, Jorg. "Youth in the MENA Region." In *Coping with Uncertainty: Youth in the Middle East and North Africa*, edited by Jorg Gertel and Ralf Hexel, 1–23. London: Saqi, 2018.

Hamanaka, Shingo. "Demographic Change and Its Social and Political Implications in the Middle East." *Asian Journal of Comparative Politics* 2, no. 1 (May 13, 2016): 70–86.

Hegghammer, Thomas. "Saudis in Iraq: Patterns of Radicalization and

Recruitment." *Cultures and Conflicts*, June 12, 2008. https://journals.openedi
tion.org/conflits/10042.

Herrera, Linda, ed. *Wired Citizenship: Youth Learning and Activism in the Middle East*. Abingdon: Routledge, 2014.

Hinnebusch, Raymond. "Authoritarian Upgrading in the Arab Uprising: Syria in Comparative Perspective." BRISMES conference paper, March 2012. https://brismes2012.files.wordpress.com/2012/02/raymond-hinnebusch -syria-authoritarian-upgrading.pdf.

Inhorn, Marcia C. "The Arab World's "Quiet" Reproductive Revolution." *Brown Journal of World Affairs* 24, no. 2 (Spring/Summer 2018): 147–159.

International Monetary Fund. "Economic Diversification in Oil-Exporting Arab Countries." April 2016. https://www.imf.org/external/np/pp/eng/2016/ 042916.pdf.

Kabbani, Nader. "Youth Employment in the Middle East and North Africa: Re-visiting and Reframing the Challenge." *Brookings*, February 26, 2019. https:// www.brookings.edu/research/youth-employment-in-the-middle-east-and -north-africa-revisiting-and-reframing-the-challenge/.

Kamrava, Mehran, ed. *Beyond the Arab Spring: The Evolving Ruling Bargain in the Middle East*. Oxford: Oxford University Press, 2014.

Kronfol, Nabil M. *The Youth Bulge and the Changing Demographics in the MENA Region: Challenges and Opportunities*. The WDA-HSG Discussion Paper Series, no. 2011/8, University of St. Gallen. https://www.wdaforum.org/ fileadmin/ablage/wdaforum/publications/dp2011-08.pdf.

Mesoy, Atle. "Poverty and Radicalisation into Violent Extremism: A Causal Link?" Noref Expert Analysis, January 2013. https://www.files.ethz.ch/ isn/158431/e60a8a679f48427d592a1906daf569d4.pdf.

Mulderig, M. Chloe. "An Uncertain Future: Youth Frustration and the Arab Spring." The Pardee Papers, no. 16, 2013. http://www.bu.edu/pardee/ files/2013/04/Pardee-Paper-16.pdf.

Observertoire Maghrebin des Migrations. "Rapport: Migration non Reglemen-taire." Tunisia, 2017. https://ftdes.net/rapports/fr.omm3.2017.pdf.

Rabih, K. "Lebanese Youth Heaviest Hookah Users in the World." *Lebanese Examiner*, March 5, 2019. https://www.lebaneseexaminer.com/2019/03/05/ lebanese-people-highest-hookah-usage-world-study-shows/.

Reinl, James. "UAE Leads Region in Ban on Smoking." *National*, December 17, 2009. https://www.thenational.ae/world/mena/uae-leads-region-in-ban-on -smoking-1.632559.

Sadiki, Larbi. "Tunisia's Migration to the North." *Brookings*, January 17, 2019. https://www.brookings.edu/blog/order-from-chaos/2019/01/17/tunisias -migration-to-the-north/.

Sagynbekov, Ken. "Child and Maternal Health in the Middle East and North

Africa." Milken Institute, February 2018. https://www.milkeninstitute.org/
sites/default/files/reports-pdf/Childhood-and-Maternal-Health-in-MENA
.pdf.

Samet, Daniel. "In Algeria an Islamist Threat Still Looms Over Domestic
Politics.", Freedom House, August 22, 2018. https://freedomhouse.org/blog/
algeria-islamist-threat-still-looms-over-domestic-politics.

Shafik, Nemat. "Big Spending, Small Returns: The Paradox of Human Resource
Development in the Middle East." Egyptian Center for Economic Studies
Working Paper no. 2, 1996. http://www.eces.org.eg/MediaFiles/Uploaded
_Files/percent7B185111A4-07D2-4160-A434-753DCBD78D5Apercent
7D_ECESWP2e.pdf.

Singerman, Diane. "The Economic Imperatives of Marriage: Emerging Practices and Identities among Youth in the Middle East." Middle East Youth
Initiative, September 2007. https://www.meyi.org/publication-the-economic
-imperatives-of-marriage-emerging-practices-and-identities-among-youth
-in-the-middle-east.html.

Toumi, Habib. "Kuwait Becomes 11th Arab State to Have Mandatory Military
Service." *Gulf News*, July 11, 2017. https://gulfnews.com/world/gulf/kuwait/
kuwait-becomes-11th-arab-state-to-have-mandatory-military-service
-1.2056483.

United Nations Development Program. *Arab Human Development Report 2016*,
2016. http://www.arab-hdr.org/reports/2016/english/AHDR2016En.pdf.

———. "Preventing Violent Extremism through Promoting Inclusive Development, Tolerance and Respect for Diversity." 2016. https://www.undp.org/
content/dam/norway/undp-ogc/documents/Discussionpercent20Paper
percent20-percent20Preventingpercent20Violentpercent20Extremism
percent20bypercent20Promotingpercent20Inclusivepercent20percent20
Development.pdf.

United States Institute for Peace. "Connecting Young Activists across the
Middle East and Africa: Generation Change." April 1, 2015. https://www
.usip.org/publications/2015/04/connecting-young-activists-across-middle
-east-and-africa-generation-change.

Wade, Robert. "Gestalt Shift: From 'Miracle' to 'Cronyism' in the Asian Crisis."
LSE Development Studies Institute Working Paper nos. 2–25, February
2002. http://www.lse.ac.uk/internationalDevelopment/pdf/WP/WP25.pdf.

Wilson, Rodney. *Economic Development in the Middle East*. Abingdon: Routledge,
2012.

Winkler, Onn. *Arab Political Demography Vol. 1: Population Growth, Labor Migration and Natalist Policies*. EastBourne: Sussex Academic Press, 2005.

World Bank. "Government Expenditure per Student, Primary (Percent of GDP
per Capita)." https://data.worldbank.org/indicator/SE.XPD.PRIM.PC.ZS.

———. "Government Expenditure per Student, Secondary (Percent of GDP per Capita)." https://data.worldbank.org/indicator/SE.XPD.SECO. PC.ZS?view=chart.

———. "Why Some MENA Countries Did Better than Others." In *MENA Development Report: The Road Not Travelled—Education Reform in the Middle East and Africa*. Washington, DC: World Bank, 2008. http://siteresources .worldbank.org/INTMENA/Resources/EDU_Flagship_Full_ENG.pdf.

World Economic Forum. *Rethinking Arab Employment: A Systemic Approach for Resource-Endowed Economies*. October 2014. http://www3.weforum.org/docs/ WEF_MENA14_RethinkingArabEmployment.pdf.

World Economic Forum and the World Bank Group. *Arab World Competitiveness Report 2018*. Geneva: World Economic Forum, 2018.

Zelin, Aaron Y. "Tunisian Foreign Fighters in Iraq and Syria." Washington Institute for Near East Policy, Policy Notes PN55, 2018. https://www.washing toninstitute.org/uploads/Documents/pubs/PolicyNote55-Zelin.pdf.

2

Comparative Civil-Military Relations in the Middle East

Robert Mason and Dina Arakji

Introduction

This chapter discusses the role played by the military in the political economy of Middle East states, with special reference to Egypt, Lebanon, and Iran. Egypt and Iran are regarded as a 'military dictatorships' or 'praetorian republics' as they do not rule from bunker like Algeria, Libya, Syria, Yemen, Iraq, and Sudan have done, or continue to do. They are not beholden to clans, tribes, or other similar social groups.[1] Even the removal of some of their political leaders such as Muammar Gaddafi or Saddam Hussein does not necessarily alter the political structures that govern the state, as the United States learned in Iraq after 2003. Iran briefly made it into Henry and Springborg's 'conditional democracy' category after President Mohammad Khatami won the 1997 election but slid back to dictatorship under Ayatollah Ali Khamenei's reassertion of power during his second term.[2] Lebanon has been labeled as a 'conditional democracy' or 'flawed democracy.'[3] The divergent political and military structures of the cases under study will be most appropriate to broadening out the theoretical framework concerning this dynamic and will be especially relevant to informing our views on other MENA states in the same categories. Tunisia and the Palestinian Authority (post 2005) are regarded as praetorian states; Israel, Turkey, and possibly Kuwait (which holds parliamentary elections) are precarious or imperfect democracies. If Pakistan was in the MENA region, it would share the praetorian banner since its civil-military relations are often compared to those of Egypt.

Monarchies of the region are not included in this chapter since they tend to be better placed than most MENA states to engage in a globalized system.[4] Nevertheless, they do exhibit their own special features such as more active private sectors, which sometimes have joint ventures and good relations with multinational defense and security companies, especially in many of the oil-rich states of the Gulf Cooperation Council (GCC) with histories of British imperialism and US engagement. Political legitimacy continues to be dominated by security concerns, particularly about political Islam, which often represents an existential threat to monarchs who draw legitimacy from religious sources. Due to their small populations, active foreign policies, and fears of instability and coups, the use of contract soldiers in the Gulf, although a long-standing phenomenon, is becoming increasingly common.[5]

The civil-military dynamic has changed over time as conflict, welfare provision for veterans, and jobs have all loomed large in government decision-making. More recently, reform-minded government policies, particularly the trend toward economic liberalization in the 1990s, created social unrest and in some cases threatened established patrimonial networks. Regional uncertainty and disorder associated with the Arab Uprisings in 2010 has provided an incentive for the military to play an even greater socioeconomic and security role in society, particularly as states refocus on regime security and survival through authoritarian upgrading and adaptation.

Important works in this field were undertaken largely in the 1960s.[6] In the 1980s, Huntingdon published his volume covering the theory and politics of civil-military relations, which establishes that US military professionalism grew from 1789 to 1940 and that the Second World War was a turning point during which it adopted the attitudes of a liberal democracy.[7] Brooks discusses how civil-military relations impact strategic assessments and uses cases from Egypt and the US decision regarding the 2003 Iraq invasion to highlight how pathologies in civil-military relations can be catastrophic but are also quite common and hinge on the balance of power between the civilian and military leaders and the extent to which they diverge.[8] While the terminology is civil-military relations, what we find in the literature is a general domination of the military over society. Much of the literature discusses political dynamics within authoritarian contexts such as Cook's volume.[9] Indeed, in his work on the professionalization of the armed forces in the MENA region, Kamrava notes that "the very genesis of most modern MENA states can be traced back to the armed forces" and the general absence of what Huntington calls objective military control, rendering it politically sterile and neutral.[10] Grawert and Abul-Magd provide one of the few comparative studies of how militaries and other armed groups profit from their activities in the MENA region.[11] After the Arab Uprisings much attention has been focused on

Egypt.[12] Similarly, emerging scholarship has focused on coup proofing after the uprisings, particularly in Egypt and Syria, emphasizing different state strategies and a learning curve.[13]

The argument is made that in many cases the military (or Hezbollah in the case of Lebanon and the Revolutionary Guard in the case of Iran) performs an outsized economic function, but it varies according to: historical context; the national, regional, and international security environment; political vision and policies of the leadership; and internal and external threat perception and alliances. The argument complements current theories in the literature that are mostly critical of the military's deep and broadening economic role in authoritarian contexts, amid the state's constantly shifting but always invested patrimonial interests. Professionalization of armed forces is generally associated by regional leaders as being a more cohesive force with stronger national identity, making political intervention all the more likely, and therefore undesirable.[14] Thus, security sector reform (SSR) often remains a distant prospect. We note the lack of reliable data on military participation in economic domains, the multifaceted role each military plays in the national economy, and the difficulty in extrapolating purely economic calculations from strategic dimensions and vice versa.

A Brief History of Military Coups

This section identifies the patterns of governance and interventions in MENA states over the past seventy years, which in some cases are yet to resolve themselves into more stable political systems. In the 1950s and 1960s, a number of Middle East states experienced military coups, often a result of postindependence instability, out-of-touch governance, socioeconomic pressure and/or interventions, or reactions to foreign powers. Many of these cases are mentioned herein: In 1952, the Egyptian military overthrew the monarchy, and in 1953 a joint US-UK-sponsored coup (Operation Ajax) overthrew nationalist prime minister Mohammed Mosaddeq after he nationalized the Anglo-Iranian oil company. In 1958, the coup in Iraq, pan-Arab in character and anti-imperialist, especially after the Baghdad Pact was signed in 1955 and after the Suez Crisis in 1956, resulted in the overthrow of the Hashemite monarchy and a failed coup by Iraqi nationalists in 1959. In 1960, there was a military coup in Turkey in the context of diminished US aid after the Second World War and prospect that ties with the USSR might provide new lines of financial credit. After a new constitution was drawn up and elections held, the military continued to play a dual role—protect the country from external attack and safeguard the Kemalist order from internal threats, including through secessionism or Islamic revivalism.[15] This was apparent in 1997 when the Turkish military memorandum followed protests in Sincan province in Ankara against alleged Israeli human rights violations on "Al Quds night" and led to the resignation of Islamist prime minister Necmettin Erbakan. In 1993, amid instability and violence caused by the Kurdish-Turkish conflict, an alleged military coup took place involving the assassination President Turgut Özal as well as prominent journalists, mayors, and generals. In 2016, the attempted, but ultimately unsuccessful, coup led by a military faction in Turkey drew attention to the erosion of secularism and democratic rule under President Erdoğan. This time the military was unable to play an effective counterbalancing role. Pro-Nasserists and pro-political unionists facilitated the United Arab Republic (UAR), which lasted from 1958 until the Syrian conservative elite was removed by the army in 1961. In February 1963 (although it had been planned since 1962), Ba'athists carried out another coup in Iraq, known as the Ramadan Revolution, removing Prime Minister Abd al-Karim Qasim, who had taken power in 1958.

In 1961 the Algiers Putsch was a failed attempt to force President Charles De Gaulle not to abandon French Algeria. In March 1963, there was another military coup in Syria brought about by the military committee of the Syrian branch of the Arab Socialist Ba'ath Party. The failure of the 1948 Arab-Israeli War for Syria compromised the traditional elite and enhanced the influence of the military in politics. Since the electoral process was seen as corrupt, the Ba'ath Party was predisposed to the coup option. The coup also had agrarian and ethnic roots (since ethnic minorities often belonged to the same social class), postcolonial antipathies, and an anti-Israeli component. The 1965 Algerian coup brought Colonial Houari Boumédiène to power as chairman of the Revolutionary Council. Syria experienced another coup in 1966 caused by tensions between the old guard of the Ba'ath Party represented by Michel Aflaq and the younger faction represented by ultra-left-wing leader Salah Jadid. This caused a split between the Ba'ath parties of Syria and Iraq until 1970.

The British-led Trucial Oman Scouts helped Zayed bin Sultan Al Nahyan secure a peaceful transition in 1966 from his brother Sheikh Shahkbut bin Sultan Al Nahyan, who had ruled Abu Dhabi from 1926. There was a failed coup in Saudi Arabia in 1966 and again in 1969 possibly by those in the Royal Saudi Air Force. The key demand during this period was for a written constitution, not one based solely on the Qur'an. King Faisal was eventually assassinated in 1975 by his nephew with a history of mental illness. Muammar Gaddafi read Nasser's book *Philosophy of the Revolution* and became a committed Arab nationalist early in life. He set up a revolutionary group that deposed the Senussi monarchy of Idris in

1969. The same year Colonel Gaafar Nimeiry came to power in Sudan, deposing the democratic regime that had failed to end the fourteen-year-old First Sudanese Civil War (ended in 1972) and pursued radical leftist and Arab nationalist policies for the next sixteen years. Hafez al-Assad came to power through a coup ('corrective revolution') in Syria in 1970, and Sultan Qaboos ousted his father in a bloodless coup in Oman, supported by the British the same year and in the midst of the Dhofar Rebellion. Albrecht finds that no matter how much coup-proofing incumbent rulers engage in, data from 1950–2013 suggests that the prevalence of coups might be lower but that the risk will remain, especially during periods of transition or excessively long periods of rule.[16]

In the following sections, we examine the historical background, key features, arms trade, and political, social, and economic impact of the military in Egypt, Lebanon, and Iran.

Egypt

On July 23, 1952, the Free Officers Movement, a group of Egyptian nationalists including Mohammed Naguib and Gammal Abdel Nasser, led a revolution aimed at overthrowing King Farouk. Lesser known is that by 1954 Naguib attempted to restore civilian rule but his attempts were aborted by Nasser.[17] The Suez Crisis in 1956 effectively saved Nasser's presidency by providing an early success for Arab nationalism.[18] Egypt has become a case of exceptionally durable military rule, one that turned into a police state by the 1970s. This was partly addressed by Sadat's 'Corrective Revolution' in 1971 along with the imprisonment of leftists and Islamists, thereby dispersing political Islam across the Middle East and into Europe. Sadat also expelled Soviet military advisers, and in March 1976 the Egyptian-Soviet friendship treaty was abrogated. Intercultural problems played their part, with Soviet indifference and rudeness becoming a major factor in the Egyptian decision to expel them.[19]

Presidents Nasser, Sadat, Mubarak, and Al-Sisi were all officers in the military before becoming president. The embedded semiautonomous military in Egypt managed to withstand socialist, Islamist, neoliberal, and revolutionary transition ever since.[20] One could argue they have even prospered under every president, except perhaps Sadat. During the 1950s and 1960s, the military aligned itself with the middle and lower classes to form a state-led economy. In the context of the Cold War, the military was viewed as a force for modernity with socialism at its core. Order and unity, confronting foreign (colonial) enemies, or socioeconomic progress drove military interventions.[21]

The Egyptian political leadership under Sadat made sure not to depend excessively on local companies or foreign suppliers as neither could be deemed reliable after the 1967 and 1973 wars. Readiness and self-sufficiency were the hallmarks on this and future military planners. In the 1970s, following the 1973 October War, Sadat implemented an *Infitah* or 'openness' policy that paved the way for private investment to enter Egypt. It also paved the way for the newly created National Service Products Organization (NSPO) to sell in the domestic market at a profit. The military moved into food production by establishing and operating farms and factories and by construction of infrastructure such as roads, schools, and hospitals, usually focusing on price, welfare, and 'food security' as justifications.

Based on the International Monetary Fund's recommendation at the time to reduce government spending, the Egyptian government revealed that it would slash subsidies on essential commodities. As soon as this announcement was made, demonstrations and riots broke out in Cairo and other cities in what came to be known as the Bread Riots of 1977. As police resources became strained, Sadat asked the armed forces to intervene. To reduce any possibility for future coups, Sadat and then Mubarak were very careful to exhibit and exercise their civilian control as presidents over the military institution as an arm of the state. In return, however, starting in 1975, the AOI was established for military production with funds from the Arab Gulf States, and by 1979, the economic activities of the NSPO began.

Sadat's attempt to demilitarize the state by appointing civilians in the civil service instead of military officers did not last. Mubarak reversed this demilitarization of the state when he came to power. He adopted neoliberal policies that reinforced crony capitalism as part of his attempts at coup proofing. Military businesses then became more prominent from the 1990s onward. Under Field Marshall Tantawi, military agricultural activity spread to reclaim parts of the desert, including farms at Sharq al-'Uwaynat and Nubariyya.[22] New companies dealing in chemicals, plastics, mineral water, mining, petroleum, and so on were created. Each would have a joint purpose; for example, pharmaceutical companies would ensure medical care for soldiers and cement plants could produce cement for both buildings and bunkers. Any excess could be sold on the local market at prices attractive to ordinary consumers. The Arab Organization for Industrialization (AOI) became a more prominent manufacturer of jeeps, pipes, and fertilizers.

Even during the short presidency of Mohamed Morsi, the military expanded its business interests and appointed ex-generals to vital government positions. This is in line with Abul-Magd's findings that Egypt was built on the military, but that it would adapt to conditions to ensure expanding wealth and influence without the same attention to the poorer classes as Nasser had given.[23] In the meantime, the Muslim Brotherhood was accused of governing only for the 1 percent rather than the rest of the country.[24] The subsequent economic crisis hit hard. But this period is described as just another episode of power struggle between the military, security forces, and political apparatus,[25] one in which Sisi benefited from Morsi ousting Minister of Defense Tantawi, being placed in his boss's position, then distancing himself from the unpopular decisions of President Morsi. President Sisi's crackdown against the Muslim Brotherhood began in 2013, including raiding protestor camps at al-Nahda Square and Rabaa al-Adawiya Square (what would become known as the Rabaa massacre) and the proscription of the Muslim Brotherhood as a terrorist organization.

It should be noted that Egypt is not the only state to outlaw the Muslim Brotherhood. Hamas, a Palestinian militant offshoot, is already banned by Israel, the United States, and the European Union. Other states also consider the Muslim Brotherhood a terrorist organization, including Syria, where it challenged Hafez al-Assad and was banned in 1980; Saudi Arabia, from where Muslim Brotherhood figures escaped after Nasser's clampdown in the 1960s; and the UAE in 2014, where al-Islah shares some of its ideology. In states such as Jordan and Kuwait, the Muslim Brotherhood has done better at adapting to the prevailing political environment and winning seats in parliament. In Tunisia, the Ennahda Movement formed a coalition with the largest secular party in the 2014 parliamentary election.[26] Doha's decision to host and support the Muslim Brotherhood is one of the major points of contention between Egypt and its Gulf allies, including Saudi Arabia, the UAE, and Bahrain, known as the 'Qatar Crisis' since 2017.

Foreign Assistance
US foreign assistance to Egypt has been second only to Israel in the amounts spent. Egypt has since the 1990s been building up its production of US main battle tanks (MBTs). Although the Obama administration briefly suspended $195 million in 2017 over human rights concerns, the release of funds took place in August 2018 after enhanced bilateral relations and counterterrorism efforts were made. Cash flow financing (CFF), which enables Egypt to repay arms purchases over a longer term, is yet to be eliminated. The foreign military financing (FMF) that Egypt receives has reduced by 90 percent since the 1980s, due to the funding not having been fully utilized.[27] Even then, in the 1990s, the United States concluded

that only 24 percent of the end items produced in the Ministry of Military Production factories were actually military in nature.[28] Unlike some other states, Egypt has not utilized its youth to enhance scientific and technical innovation in its defense industry.

Only after the onset of the Arab Uprisings did Egypt relaunch the Mubarak Complex for the Defense Industry, having previously lacked technical, physical, and capital resources.[29] External assistance, particularly from Arab Gulf states, has helped in this regard, and they have become even more close as Egypt expresses concerns about Iranian influence in the Red Sea and Suez Canal. The UAE has also played a critical role in arming the Egyptian military, especially after Morsi was deposed and Sisi took power. Dubai-based Minerva Special Purpose Vehicles (MSPV) delivered an estimated fifty Panthera T6 armored vehicles to the Egyptian military in 2015.[30] In 2017, the UAE transferred an $11 million surveillance system to Egypt, although it is not clear who the intended end user is. In 2018, it was confirmed that Egypt had received dozens of AT-802 counterinsurgency aircraft from the UAE.[31] This could be deemed necessary in the context of an insurgency in Sinai by Islamic State and previous attacks by al-Qaeda throughout the 1990s. The year 2018 also heralded Egypt's first security and defense expo, including contributors from forty countries. Apart from political cooperation, Egypt and the UAE are also working closely on security issues in Libya, with Egyptian airbases reportedly having been used for UAE raids against militia in Tripoli in August 2014. Joint military drills have been conducted with Russia, and in November 2019, Egypt was warned by the United States not to buy Russian Su-35 warplanes on the basis that any new arms deals with Russia would complicate future deals with the United States.[32] China began exporting 120 kits of the K-8E *Karakorum* jet trainer in 2008 and further R&D deals are likely. A 'comprehensive strategic partnership' was signed in 2014, and China will remain vital in Egypt's international balancing strategy. Small arms and particularly surveillance technology in the new capital could have significant bearings on civil-military relations.

The Military and Society

The constitution omits any reference to civilian oversight of the Egyptian Armed Forces (EAF) or its activities, including with reference to selling land and assets. Indeed, Law No. 313 of 1956 prohibits the publication of any news about the military, shielding it from both public and political scrutiny. Arguably, the greatest social effect of the military is the extent of its business interests. Scholars suggest the Egyptian military controls anywhere between 5 and 50 percent of the GDP.[33] Even if the military penetration in the economy is on the lower end of these estimates, the commander-in-chief is well placed to realize military aspirations concerning the economy. By expanding military-associated production, partly through competitive advantages such as paying 0 percent VAT and through state contracts, military participation in industry is growing. The Egyptian military is engaged in constructing schools and roads, leading to an outsized influence on society. It represents an opportunity cost for the private sector, which could have enhanced its status as national economic player through better participation and regulation.

One of the main issues with the growth of military companies is the securitized nature of labor relations. Workers were long dominated by the state through the Egyptian Trade Union Federation (ETUF). However, by the late 1990s, workers were adding to the protest movement that led to a culture of protest in the 2000s and a legitimacy issue for President Mubarak.[34] They remain the strongest nationally organized socioeconomic force. But by 2017, 26 workers from the Alexandria Shipyard were on military trial for inciting fellow workers to strike for better safety and wages.[35] In 2017, Egypt also passed the Trade Unions Law No. 213, which keeps new independent trade unions under the authority of the state-controlled ETUF.[36] By May 2019, the Egyptian government amended Law No. 213, approved by Parliament, and is waiting for the Cabinet to review. It could allow trade unions to determine their own structure and by-laws, proposes to remove the control of the ETUF, and might end restrictions on trade union elections.[37] Punishment could be by fines and not imprisonment.[38]

When it comes to potentially restructuring the Egyptian economy, there has been some public articulation of possible changes. In 2012, former prime minister Ahmed Shafik said he would change the way the army is treated and it would pay taxes from its wide range of businesses.[39] Whether this would be enough to address redistributive deficiencies in the system remains to be seen. Certainly, manufacturing baby milk and setting up family parks appears to be incongruent with the military's core task as well as putting financial strain on importers of higher priced products. Operating some schools also raises questions about the learning rights of students and the physical security of children, especially during a period of armed conflict or insurgency. What these activities do provide is soft power, which translates into approval ratings in excess of 80 percent.[40] It is possible that if the economy recovers over a period of time and the state is reorientated toward a more reformed system, Egypt could see a phased withdrawal of the military industries. Given continuous population growth, recent economic changes such as subsidy reform, and the generation of persistent vested interests, this outcome is highly unlikely. The prospects for implementing SSR also remain low due to the legacy of the conflict with Israel, the affordability of national-security bodies, and the clearly negative legacy of the US invasion of Iraq, civil war in Iraq, conflicts in Syria and Libya, and an insurgency in Sinai. As long as Egypt's international partners are putting security, counterterrorism cooperation, trade, arms sales, and competition with emerging illiberal states ahead of encouraging SSR, the prospects for exogenous induced change look dim.

Security matters are most likely to be discussed in the National Defense Committee (NDC), which is dominated by military representatives (nine military versus five civilians), in the Supreme Council of Armed Forces (SCAF), or directly in the office of the president. However, at the local level, the greatest effect of the military is likely to be in local leadership. Out of twenty-seven governors, eighteen were retired army generals in 2012.[41] These governors usually covet key strategy areas such as Cairo and tourist regions in Upper Egypt, Suez Canal provinces, Sinai, Nile Delta, and Alexandria. Ministries have thus been hallowed out and all decisions are concentrated in the military elite. Even parliamentary elections were aided by Military Intelligence, which helped to organize two political parties, For the Love of Egypt (FLE) and Nation's Future Party, with the latter winning a substantial majority in 2016.[42] Beyond governance, the impact of international actors through nongovernmental organizations (NGOs) in Egypt had been severely curtailed by the introduction of Law No. 70 in 2017, which had, in effect, regulated and criminalized activities. By 2019, Law No. 149 had been ratified, which remedied these aspects; however NGOs are only expected to engage in 'societal development' activities, which limits the legality of many activities beyond this definition.[43]

Poverty has risen in Egypt by 5 percent from 2016 to 2019, and it has doubled since the early 1990s.[44] The official poverty rate was 32.5 percent in 2019.[45] Still mega-projects have proceeded, including the Suez Canal extension that opened in 2015 after just one year of construction. The New Administrative Capital was announced in March 2015, but its 2020 completion date has been delayed after some investors pulled out.[46] The primary concern of both unemployed low-skilled workers and graduates is jobs. Thus, through conscription, military enterprises, and a bloated public sector, the government provides about two in every five jobs.[47] While this gives significant leverage over the population, the combination of austerity, top-down economic planning, and alleged government mismanagement or corruption could be the biggest political threat. For example, in September 2019, Friday protests began again due in part to accusations by agitators such as Mohamed Ali, a building contractor turned whistleblower after the military allegedly failed to pay him $13 million.[48] Nevertheless, a combination of socialization, repression, and real support for the military endures. Thus, the EAF remains the preeminent security guarantor and socioeconomic force in the country.

Lebanon

During the French mandate from 1920 to 1943, France created auxiliary forces to manage internal security over Lebanon and Syria. Between 1920 and 1930, the auxiliary forces, which consisted of local troops known by different names, underwent a restructuring and fell under 'Les Troupes Speciales du Levant' with a new statute. This change enabled personnel from the French mandate in Lebanon to move up the ranks and occupy commanding posts originally reserved for French officers.[49]

In 1945, two years after France had transferred the Troupes Special du Levant's authority to the government of Lebanon, the Lebanese Armed Forces (LAF) was established under the command of Fouad Chehab. With a small force of three thousand troops, Chehab strengthened the military's national position and laid the foundation for professionalizing the force. By the end of the 1958 short-lived civil war, the military acted as an arbiter and eventually played a role in neutralizing the sectarian imbalance in the political sphere.[50] In 1958, Fouad Chehab was elected as a consensus candidate to be the fourth president of Lebanon.[51]

Following the eruption of the civil war (1975–1990), the LAF suffered a number of cases of disintegration along confessional lines. Hundreds deserted their ranks, and the number of attempts to reorganize the military failed in the 1970s and 1980s.[52] In parallel, Syria gained military and security influence in Lebanon after its troops entered Lebanon under the Arab League's deterrent force in 1976.[53]

After the 1989 Taif Agreement[54] ended fifteen years of fighting and Syria gained control over Lebanon in 1990, the military was reorganized to become a cohesive confessionally all-inclusive force. Following the withdrawal of Syrian forces in 2005, the LAF's capabilities have expanded with the support of the international community. This has generally involved training and equipping the military to strengthen Lebanon's ability to maintain stability and security.

Sectarian Features of the Lebanese Military

Lebanon's sectarian system has penetrated state institutions, including the military. The country's civil-military relations are a by-product of this system. The LAF emerged in 1990 from a fifteen-year civil war with many major units confessionally homogenous. Under the Syrian presence and postwar command of General Emile Lahoud, the country's military was restructured. Larger units were reorganized to be more cross-confessionally representative. Also, units were rotated to local sociodemographic improve.[55]

While establishing a 50:50 Christian-Muslim balance in the postwar LAF was challenging, the officer corps, including senior flagstaff appointments, maintained the parity. For instance, the LAF commander is a Maronite and the chief of staff is a Druze major general. The LAF's four deputy chiefs of staff (DCoSs) are also subject to confessional allocations. For example, DCoS for personnel is nominally Sunni, the DCoS for operations is nominally Shi'a, and DCoSs for logistics and planning are nominally Christians. Command posts of major LAF formations follow the same principle, and second-order positions' sectarian allocation is also taken into account. Usually, officers from a sect different from their seniors will fill those positions. For example, while the DCoS for operation is Shi'a, the critical position of director of military operations is nominally held by a senior Christian officer.[56]

Another example of the sectarian allocation is embodied in the military council. It is a microcosm of the six main sects in the country. While the council operates outside the chain of command and reports to the minister of defense, it allows members to inspect decisions that may appear sensitive from a sectarian perspective. The council is composed of the commander (Maronite), the general director of administration (nominally reserved for Muslim Shi'a), the inspector general (nominally Christian Greek Orthodox), general secretary of the higher defense council (nominally Muslim Sunni), and permanent member of a rank of colonel (Christian Greek Catholic).[57]

Besides the officer corps, the LAF at large does not have a strict designated sectarian apportionment. Based on figures from 2014, the sectarian composition for some 64,600 military personnel included around 71 percent Muslims, 24 percent Christians, and 5 percent registered as 'other.'[58] Nerguizian further adds that "snapshots of the LAF's sectarian make-up at any given point in time shed light on which sectarian community or communities are vying for service in the military more broadly."[59]

Political, Economic, and Social Impacts
POLITICAL
Politics has had a significant impact on the military's evolution. Between 1958 and 1970, following the election of President Chehab, the military

was a support to the president, a Maronite Christian, mainly through its intelligence branch, the Deuxième Bureau.[60] In light of the election of Suleiman Frangieh as president in 1970, the LAF's powers were reduced and restricted, effectively dismantling the Deuxième Bureau. In parallel, the rise of sociopolitical forces associated with pan-Arab and Palestinian groups and the military's sidelining paralyzed and destituted the LAF of its needed legitimacy to protect the country from the eruption of the 1975 civil war.[61]

The military degraded during the civil war, which created a security vacuum. Subsequently, Syria exploited the situation gaining the upper hand over the country's foreign and security strategy.[62] This further amplified after the 1990s, with regional and international support, enabling Syria to expand its influence. It limited the LAF's role to maintaining internal security rather than defending the country.[63] Syria also penetrated and controlled the military and security apparatus. For instance, the Syrian military and intelligence network managed appointments of leadership-level sensitive positions in the LAF.[64]

In light of the 2005 assassination of former prime minister Rafic Hariri, Syrian troops and intelligence personnel were pressured to withdraw from Lebanon.[65] Subsequently, the Lebanese political leaders developed sectarian patronage networks in an attempt to replace Syria's former influence over the military.[66] Despite the end of Pax-Syriana, the sectarian political leadership lacked consensus over a clear, cohesive foreign policy as a result of "the idiosyncratic and ideological predilections" over its regional and international orientation.[67] In parallel, a national defense strategy fell behind. This disrupted the country from having a unified defense vision.[68] Instead, the LAF developed two Capability Development Plans (CDPs)[69] with limited coordination between the executive branch of government and the military command.[70]

Economic

Lebanon's civil-military relations suffer from poor budgeting for the military. Between all the ministries, the defense budget constitutes one of the largest shares in the national state budget. However, recurrent costs, such as wages, often constitute around 80 percent of the defense budget. The military spends the rest of some 20 percent on necessary expenditures, such as current forces and facilities maintenance.[71] After the end of the civil war, military expenditure soared between 1990 and 1995 from $200 million to $700 million. From 1995 till 2008, military expenditure was more stable, ranging between $600 and $700 million.[72] While defense spending appears to have increased between 2005 and 2013, it has generally remained flat when adjusted for inflation.[73]

The lack of resources and contentious politics also hampered the country's ability to develop its military. As a result, the LAF had to rely on international assistance for its development. On November 24, 2015, in an attempt to offset the centrality of foreign assistance and reaffirm the country's burden-sharing for military development, the Lebanese Parliament issued Expedited Law No. 30. The legal document instructed the government to commit around $895 million from the state budget to modernization and improve the military over five years starting 2016. However, the law was flawed. It allowed the government of Lebanon to decrease future annual allocation in line with foreign assistance and grants.[74]

Since 2006, the international community has supported the training and equipping of the LAF, with the United States being a main contributor, to build up Lebanon's military force. However, it was in part to "gradually take on an increasingly important national security role, largely at the expense of Iran's main non-state regional ally Hezbollah."[75] Between 2010 and early 2019, the United States supported the LAF with over $1.8 billion in security assistance.[76] Other countries, such as France[77] and Italy,[78] have also supported and assisted the LAF.

SOCIAL

Lebanon's military is a highly popular institution. According to the Arab Barometer's public trust perception poll, the LAF has maintained a high level of trust between 2011 and 2018, compared with other government institutions such as the Parliament, judiciary, and the security forces, including Internal Security Forces and the General Security.[79] While public opinion polling is not "a perfect measure of national sentiment in a confessional society like Lebanon, polling evidence does provide valuable anecdotal data to frame Lebanese public opinion concerning the LAF better."[80]

The LAF's popularity can be attributed to its cross-confessional representativeness and attitude in a country heavily divided along confessional lines. It is a melting pot composed of ethno-religious groups and distinct socioeconomic backgrounds.[81]

In 1952 and 1958, under General Fouad Chehab's command, the LAF dismissed the intervention against Lebanese citizens.[82] In 2005, back then, LAF Commander Michel Suleiman refused Prime Minister Omar Karami's order to quell the citizens protesting against the Syrian presence in the country.[83]

In 2008, clashes erupted between Hezbollah, a Shia political party and an asymmetric armed group, and an embryonic militia of the Future

Movement.[84] However, the LAF did not engage. Some military officers perceived the operation as a reaffirmation of military neutrality. At the same time, others perceived it as a 'missed opportunity' for the LAF to express dissent for any competing militant entity.[85]

More recently, the LAF has had to take on a significant role. From October 17, 2019, the LAF has had to take on a significant role due to the unprecedented wave of protests against the Lebanese political establishment and established sectarian order. These were a result of growing dissent against the political leadership and an overlapping mix of socioeconomic problems and grievances.[86] Subsequently, the military was placed in the middle of these events, standing between the government and the people.[87]

Iran

Since the Iranian Revolution in 1979, there has been a wide literature on Iranian politics and governance, largely concerning *Velayat-e faqih*, in which the supreme leader, the Ayatollah, holds custodianship over the people. Much of the focus has been on questions such as what role the clerics should play in politics, but more often with regard to Iranian leadership and identity vis-à-vis foreign policy.[88] There is also a literature on the subject of Iranian civil-military relations,[89] but like studies in other parts of the MENA region, it is affected by a lack of reliable data, public opinion polls, and access to key decision-makers in the military, intelligence, and security services. Post 1979, Iranian civil-military relations have often been considered subsidiary by scholars who tend to focus on other aspects of Iranian politics and foreign policies toward Israel, the United States, and the West, including the Iranian nuclear program and related diplomacy up to and including the Joint Comprehensive Plan of Action (JCPOA) in 2015. Renewed scholarly attention has followed discontent in Iranian society, evident from the Green Revolution protesting the presidential outcome in 2009, in which hard-line Mahmoud Ahmadinejad won a second term against reformist politician Mir-Hossein Mousavi.[90] Protests were again evident in 2019–2020, caused by an increase in fuel prices.

Civil-Military Relations

The core of Iran's defense industry has roots dating back to the shah's rule, when export substitution led Iran to produce, maintain, and repair military equipment. In 1963, all military factories were to fall under the Military Industries Organization (MIO) of the Ministry of War. Plants were set up to produce ammunition, explosives, and mortar rounds, among other outputs, in recognition that self-sufficiency in defense would be desirable. The United States and the United Kingdom supplied aircraft and small arms, and from the mid-1970s Iran was manufacturing aircraft, surface-to-air missiles, and electronic equipment. The 1979 revolution disrupted MIO operations and threatened cooperation with foreign specialists. Defense cooperation shifted to states such as North Korea, Syria, and Libya out of necessity and as an extension of political support, especially important following international sanctions imposed during the Iran-Iraq War. The mainstream Iranian military and Islamic Revolutionary Guards Corps (IRGC), supported directly by the Ayatollah, have both contributed to relief operations and production, especially in the arms-related industries. The military has gone on to invest in urban infrastructure, housing projects, and banks as well as holding companies, which created new patronage networks involving smaller contractors and patronage associations.[91]

Since 1979, Iranian civil-military relations have tended to pivot around the interactions between reform-minded presidents and the IRGC. Civilians have only had a voice at junctures of economic or political crises and have been quickly suppressed by force. A further complication to the dynamic has been entities operating outside of Iran. The People's Mujahedin of Iran or Mojahedin-e Khalq (MEK), founded in September 1965, has been advocating the overthrow of the regime in favor of forming its own government and supported Saddam Hussein's Iraq during the Iran-Iraq War (1980–1988) in exchange for financial resources. Although previously listed as a terror organization by the United States, the European Union, and Canada, after a multiyear campaign to influence both Democrat and Republican politicians in Washington, DC, former directors of the CIA and FBI as well as retired generals, the Iranian group finally won approval to get delisted from the State Department's list of terror organizations in September 2012.[92]

The clerics responsible for the Islamic Revolution were almost immediately challenged by liberal nationalists and a failed coup plot, known as the Nuzhih plot, in July 1980. The plot was led by Colonel Muhammad Baqr Bani-Amiri, a retired Gendarmerie officer, and was financially and logistically supported by Shapour Bakhtiar, the shah's last prime minister, who led the National Movement of the Iranian Resistance. The plot involved several hundred active and retired Iranian paratroopers at the Nuzhih air base near the city of Hamdan.[93] The attempted coup is said to have included too many participants and was overly complex; hence, the plot was uncovered and many arrested as they arrived at the base.[94] This incident, combined with other factors, such as separatist movements in peripheral regions (e.g., Iranian Kurdistan), persuaded the incumbent

Iranian regime that the country was being undermined from different quarters and that it needed the IRGC to protect the revolution, maintain law, fight dissidence, and balance the regular armed forces.[95] The IRGC recruited ethnic Persians or Azeris (a Turkic people living mainly in the Iranian regime of Azerbaijan) from the poorer socioeconomic strata.

The Basij, which forms part of the IRGC, is the omnipresent paramilitary organization in Iran that also protects the regime and is present in institutions such as schools, universities, companies, and factories.[96] About 100,000 members of the IRGC and Basij (the Basij trained 2.4 million Iranians in the use of arms and sent 450,000 to the front line in 1983[97]), along with three armored and two infantry divisions, about 150,000 troops in total, were used during Operation Ramadan between July and November 1982 to overwhelm Iraqi defenses and in some cases clear minefields. The appalling casualty rate in Iran, in particular, strengthened its sense of martyrdom and sacrifice.[98] Iranian Shias already exhibited a fascination with death and martyrdom after the seventh-century leader Hussein was killed by the rival caliphate at the battle of Karbala in modern-day Iraq.[99] The battle is commemorated during an annual ten-day period during the first month of the Islamic calendar, Muharram, considered one of four sacred months. It continued for eight years, partly because Iran put ideology ahead of strategy, and therefore did not immediately sue for peace. Tehran also expected its troops to be welcomed as liberators when crossing into Iraq.[100]

The main turning point for the IRGC was during the Iran-Iraq War, which was initiated by Saddam Hussein to enhance his support from the Arab community concerned with Iranian expansionist policies, including interference in Iraq's social and economic affairs, make border adjustments into Iran including oil-rich areas, and reduce Iranian capacity to mount an attack in future. Iran was initially uncoordinated, and Iran's first president, Bani Sadr, wanted the regular military as the main force to fight the war. Notwithstanding any rational military reasons to do this, it was interpreted by Ayatollah Khomeini as a politization of the military and would alter the balance of power in Iran evening out revolutionary zeal with technocrat, nationalist, and liberal influences, and so Sadr was fired in 1981.[101] In the grand scheme of the war, Iraq won, supported militarily by more developed states that viewed it as the lesser of two evils. Even Israel would cooperate tacitly with Iran in what would become known as the Iran-Contra Affair.

The legacy of the war is twofold. First, it would define Iranian foreign policy for the next forty years given the heavy toll on its military and society. Various foundations were set up to support Iranian veterans and families of those killed in the war, including Bonyad Shahid va Omur-e Janbazen (Foundation of Martyrs and Veteran Affairs), which includes more than one hundred companies. Second, western Iran is still littered with millions of unexploded antipersonnel mines that have not been cleared.[102]

Ayatollah Khomeini died in 1989 and Sayyid Ali Hosseini Khamenei became the new *vali-e faqih*. President Akbar Hashemi Rafsanjani was elected in 1989 and served two terms until 1997. Both Rafsanjani and his successor, Mohammad Khatami, aimed at implementing social and economic reforms and better relations with the West, although less so easing controls over the press and political activity. Rafsanjani was later accused of supporting the Green Revolution protests in 2009 after he lost to Ahmadinejad. The IRGC felt threatened by the new civilian authority and their agenda, including restructuring the economy (and therefore Bonyads) and in the Khatami administration, addressing corruption. The army less so as Khatami did not control their budget and notwithstanding major changes, the army salaries would remain low. Since the regular military was reluctant to quell growing protests from 1994, which had formed due to the disproportionate impact that the government's socioeconomic programs were having on the lower classes, the Basij was used and became important, albeit with uncertain partisan allegiances within the political system. The Basij budget was rapidly increased during this period.[103]

Although the balance in Iranian politics favored Rafsanjani in his first term, by his second term Ayatollah Khamenei and hard-liners were able to push back. This culminated in the IRGC support for Mahmoud Ahmadinejad from 2005 until 2013. His background was as a Basij who fought in the Iran-Iraq War. He put IRGC members in important ministerial and ambassadorial positions and completely overturned the tacit rule of keeping the IRGC out of politics. In 2009, Mousavi would likely have continued Rafsanjani and Khatami's legacy of threatening IRGC economic interests and focus on attracting more foreign investment. Instead, a crackdown and house arrest for the leaders of the Green Movement ensued. In 2013, reformist Hassan Rouhani was elected president. He too attempted to negotiate with Western powers over the Iranian nuclear program in an effort to enhance economic revenues through sanctions relief and improve oil and gas exports and avoid conflict. The IRGC continued to resist such measures as an affront to their covert economy, which benefits from sanctions remaining in place. Rouhani sought to replace those veterans who obtained important positions during the Ahmadinejad era with technocrats. Restructuring IRGC companies remains fraught given the Iranian government's dependence on it in parts of the economy such as infrastructure and construction, but also for defense. Civilian protests represent a double threat in Iran—one to the legitimacy of the government and another to the socioeconomic interests of the IRGC.

A Dangerous Regional Security Environment
and Its Ongoing Effects on Society

There are multiple and often interrelated security issues apart from the above, which continue to dominate the landscape and Iranian geopolitical thinking. Hard power competition has been especially evident in the weak or failed states of Syria, Lebanon, Iraq, and Yemen. More on the regionalization of conflict can be found in Chapter 4. Soleimani was particularly effective at releasing al-Qaeda insurgents caught fleeing Afghanistan after the military campaign toppled the Taliban and released them into Iraq against US forces after 2003.[104]

The balance of power in the Gulf is one that has been particularly affected by Iran's limited access to advanced new arms sales, notably from the United States, unlike Saudi Arabia and the UAE, which continue to invest and benefit from such sales. The Arab GCC states spent $95 to $128 billion in 2017 versus $15 to $16 billion spent by Iran.[105] However, this masks the ongoing issues that many Arab Gulf states appear too willing to invest in the most advanced weaponry rather than weapons most likely to deal with the threats under study. Iran has made major advances in ballistic and cruise missiles (including naval-based capacities) and air defense systems and deploys asymmetric forces that have and could threaten shipping in the Gulf and in the Red Sea.[106] Iran's main asset continues to be manpower and use of substate actors across the region, supporting them with money, weapons, volunteers, and training programs. For a discussion on how soft power plays a role in Gulf politics, see Chapter 3.

Iranian relations with the United States have continued to slide during the Trump administration. President Trump has sought to support key regional allies such as Saudi Arabia and the UAE over advancing diplomacy with Iran. He withdrew the United States from the JCPOA on May 18, 2018, and has sought to confront Iran through the creation of a Middle East Strategic Alliance (MESA) or 'Arab NATO.'[107] A series of inflammatory comments were made by President Trump in response to President Rouhani's warning not to "play with the lion's tail."[108]

In response, President Trump tweeted:

To the Iranian President Rouhani: NEVER, EVER THREATEN THE UNITED STATES AGAIN OR YOU WILL SUFFER

CONSEQUENCES THE LIKES OF WHICH FEW THROUGH-
OUT HISTORY HAVE EVER SUFFERED BEFORE. WE ARE NO
LONGER A COUNTRY THAT WILL STAND FOR YOUR DE-
MENTED WORDS OF VIOLENCE & DEATH. BE CAUTIOUS![109]

On May 12, 2019, sabotage attacks were reported on oil tankers off
the UAE coast.[110] A drone strike was reported on two Saudi oil pumping
stations on May 14, 2019.[111] Rising tensions and a rocket attack in Iraq
led the United States to evacuate all but essential personnel in Iraq in
May 2019 while Saudi Arabia reportedly intercepted Houthi missiles over
Mecca.[112] In September 2019, two major Saudi oil installations of Abqaiq
and Khurais were targeted, although it was not clear who was responsible.
After the United States assassinated IRGC major general Qasem Soleimani in Iraq on January 3, 2020, and the IRGC accidentally shot down
a Ukrainian passenger jet in January 2020, the Iranian government has
stepped up its resistance rhetoric and repression against dissident acts.[113]
The Ukrainian jet disaster highlighted the fact that not even President
Rouhani had all the facts initially, illustrating that information was initially kept from him in a close IRGC loop.[114]

Beyond those protestors and media directly affected by repression,
most Iranians are affected by primary and secondary sanctions associated
with Iran's nuclear program and support for 'terrorism.' Inflation reached
35.7 percent in October 2019, which has affected the rural population
the most. The increases are higher for food and fuel, hence the 2019–
2020 protests. The phased reintroduction of US sanctions will likely cut
oil exports by half of their 2017/2018 levels.[115] Although a cash transfer
program has assisted the poor from 2009 to 2013, declining economic
growth is likely to have more of an impact going forward.

Prospects for Military Consolidation and Normalization in Iran
Ayatollah Khamenei is 81 in 2020 and allegedly in poor health. The process to replace him could become another juncture at which reformist
and hard-line clerics battle it out to secure their preferred candidate,
which would further undermine national unity. Discontent and protests
continue over the massacre of 1,500 protestors in November 2019, the
IRGC shooting down of a civilian plane killing 176 people, and a friendly
fire mistake in the Gulf of Oman. Incidents such as these cannot forever
be repressed so harshly, especially if innocent lives continue to be lost.
The Iranian case echoes Soviet policies of political repression and the
downing of Korean Air Lines Flight 007 in September 1983, which created widespread protests and heightened Cold War tensions. The only

solution there was the introduction of Western support for Mikhail Gorbachev, in particular for his policies of Glasnost (transparency) and Perestroika (reform). Should an Iranian political leader be able to engage and sustain in such a platform, they may succeed in shifting Iranian influence from a policy of resistance and challenging the current world order to finding mutual solutions that satisfy its religious, social, political, and economic tenets and interests. There remains the possibility that the JCPOA will be recaptured as an agreement on which to build. The IRGC is not monolithic and therefore future governments might seek to appeal to the rank-and-file members with a new program of initiatives and reconceptualize what has been a growing voice of the IRGC in politics. That will certainly be difficult so long as IRGC leadership remains hard line, and the promotion of General Esmail Qaani suggests this will continue to be the case as long as US sanctions aim to continue to affect the rural poor and destabilize the regime.

Conclusion

This chapter has illustrated that while transition from monarchies toward military-dominated 'praetorian republics' was relatively easily implemented, the reverse is less true. Policies within these systems are generally ill suited to adapt to the changing needs of society, particularly the large populations of Egypt and Iran that need and want to take advantage of opportunities presented by better integration into the global economy. In the case of Lebanon, civil-military relations have been complicated by French imperialism, alleged corruption within the sectarian system, a weak economy, and ongoing tensions between Iran-backed Hezbollah and the Western-backed Hariri government. The Syrian conflict has helped to expose these tensions somewhat.

The chapter explained how through military development or the bitter memory of conflict, self-sufficiency has become a buzzword in MENA state militaries. While the role of the military in parastatal institutions is generally accepted for reasons linked to welfare and investment, there is increasing evidence that more overt military participation in politics requires more repression and control in lieu of dialogue and socioeconomic accommodation. Trust in MENA militaries is often cited as being exceptionally high, especially when compared with other institutions. The military continues to play a major socioeconomic role through conscription, domestic security, and social welfare provision. But questions remain over how growing spheres of military activity or sectarian competition are impacting on society, especially on issues of governance, public safety, and indoctrination. Absent a public dialogue based on a military willingness to become more open and accountable, those questions will remain unanswered. In some states, street protests are likely to continue; in others, political grievances will continue to simmer.

Notes

1. Clement Moore Henry and Robert Springborg, "Bully Praetorian States," in *Globalization and the Politics of Development in the Middle East* (Cambridge: Cambridge University Press, 2010), 162.
2. See "Precarious Democracies," in *Globalization and the Politics of Development in the Middle East* (Cambridge: Cambridge University Press, 2010), 261.
3. Ibid.
4. Ibid., 213.
5. Zoltan Barany, "Foreign Contract Soldiers in the Gulf," Carnegie Middle East Center, February 5, 2020, https://carnegie-mec.org/2020/02/05/foreign-contract-soldiers-in-gulf-pub-80979; Robert Mason, "Breaking the Mold of Small State Classification? The Broadening Influence of United Arab Emirates Foreign Policy through Effective Military and Bandwagoning Strategies," *Canadian Foreign Policy Journal* (March 21, 2018): 95–112.
6. Eliezer Be'eri, *Army Officers in Arab Politics and Society* (New York: Praeger, 1970); J. C. Hurewitz, *Middle East Politics: The Military Dimension* (New York: Praeger, 1969); P. J. Vatikiotis, *Politics and the Military in Jordan: A Study of the Arab Legion, 1921–1957* (New York: Praeger, 1967).
7. Samuel P. Huntingdon, *The Soldier and the State: The Theory and Politics of Civil-Military Relations* (Cambridge, MA: Harvard University Press, 1981).
8. Risa Brooks, *Shaping Strategy: The Civil-Military Politics of Strategic Assessment* (Princeton, NJ: Princeton University Press, 2008).
9. Steven A. Cook, *Ruling but Not Governing: The Military and Political Development in Egypt, Algeria, and Turkey* (Baltimore: Johns Hopkins University Press, 2007).
10. Mehran Kamrava, "Military Professionalization and Civil-Military Relations in the Middle East," *Political Science Quarterly* 115, no. 1 (Spring 2000): 68–69.
11. Elke Grawert and Zeinab Abul-Magd, *Businessmen in Arms: How the Military and Other Armed Groups Profit in the MENA Region* (New York: Rowman & Littlefield, 2016).
12. Maha Azzam, "Egypt's Military Council and the Transition to Democracy," May 2012, https://www.chathamhouse.org/sites/default/files/public/Research/Middle%20East/bp0512_azzam.pdf; Omar Ashour, "Collusion to Crackdown: Islamist-Military Relations in Egypt," Brookings Doha Center Analysis Paper 14, March 2015, https://www.brookings.edu/wp-content/uploads/2016/06/collusion-to-crackdown-english.pdf; Zeinab Abul-Magd,

Militarizing the Nation: The Army, Business and Revolution in Egypt (New York: Columbia University Press, 2018).

13. Holger Albrecht, "Does Coup-Proofing Work? Political-Military Relations in Authoritarian Regimes Amid the Arab Uprisings," *Mediterranean Politics* 20, no. 1 (2014): 36–54; Steven Hydemann, "Upgrading Authoritarianism in the Arab World," Brookings, October 15, 2007, https://www.brookings.edu/research/upgrading-authoritarianism-in-the-arab-world/.

14. Kamrava, "Military Professionalization and Civil-Military Relations in the Middle East," 91.

15. Mohammed Ayoob, *The Many Faces of Political Islam: Religion and Politics in the Muslim World* (Ann Arbor: University of Michigan Press, 2011), 105.

16. Holger Albrecht, "The Myth of Coup-proofing: Risk and Instances of Military Coups d'état in the Middle East and North Africa, 1950–2013," *Armed Forces and Society* 41, no. 4 (2015): 659–87.

17. Robert Springborg, "The Rewards of Failure: Persisting Military Rule in Egypt," *British Journal of Middle Eastern Studies* 44, no. 4 (2017): 478.

18. Ibid.

19. E. V. Badolato, "A Clash of Cultures: The Expulsion of Soviet Military Advisers from Egypt," *Naval War College Review* 37, no. 2 (March–April 1984): 69.

20. Zeinab Abul-Magd, "Egypt's Adaptable Officers: Business, Nationalism and Discontent," in Grawert and Abul-Magd, *Businessmen in Arms*, 23.

21. Ibid., 25.

22. Ibid., 28.

23. Abul-Magd, *Militarizing the Nation*.

24. Susan Hansen, "The Economic Vision of Egypt's Muslim Brotherhood Millionaires," *Bloomberg*, April 20, 2012, https://www.bloomberg.com/news/articles/2012-04-19/the-economic-vision-of-egypts-muslim-brotherhood-millionaires.

25. Hazem Kandil, *Soldiers, Spies and Statesmen: Egypt's Road to Revolt* (New York: Verso, 2012).

26. Further details on the Muslim Brotherhood and other Islamist political groups across the region can be found here: Caroline Alexander and Sam Dodge, "Muslim Brotherhood Is at the Heart of Gulf Standoff with Qatar," *Bloomberg*, June 7, 2017, https://www.bloomberg.com/graphics/2017-muslim-brotherhood/.

27. American Chamber of Commerce in Egypt, "Egypt-US Business Data," https://www.amcham.org.eg/information-resources/trade-resources/egypt-us-relations/us-foreign-assistance-to-egypt.

28. Florence Gaub, "Defence Industries in Arab States: Players and Strategies," Chaillot Paper no. 141, March 2017, 31, https://www.iss.europa.eu/sites/default/files/EUISSFiles/CP_141_Arab_Defence.pdf.

29. Ibid., 32.

30. Frank Slijper, "Under the Radar: The United Arab Emirates, Arms Transfers and Regional Conflict," PAX, September 2017, 23.

31. Defenceweb, "Egyptian AT-802 Acquisition Confirmed," January 24, 2018, https://www.defenceweb.co.za/aerospace/aerospace-aerospace/egyptian-at-802-acquisition-confirmed/.

32. Vivian Salama, "US Threatens Egypt with Sanctions over Russian Arms Deal," *Wall Street Journal*, November 14, 2019, https://www.wsj.com/articles/u-s-threatens-egypt-with-sanctions-over-russian-arms-deal-11573769929.

33. Reuters, "From War Room to Board Room: Military Firms Flourish in Egypt," May 16, 2018, https://www.reuters.com/investigates/special-report/egypt-economy-military/.

34. Joel Beinin, "The Rise of Egypt's Workers," in *The Carnegie Papers* (Washington, DC: Carnegie Endowment for International Peace, June 2012), 1.

35. Zeinab Abul-Magd, "Workers and Officers in Egypt: The Other Failed Revolution," *Jadaliyya*, January 11, 2018, https://www.jadaliyya.com/Details/35019.

36. Ibid.

37. American Chamber of Commerce in Egypt, "Recent and Upcoming Legislation," https://www.amcham.org.eg/publications/egypt-business-climate/issue/2/Recent-and-Upcoming-Legislation.

38. Ibid.

39. Yolande Knell, "Egypt Candidate: Ahmad Shafiq, Former Prime Minister," *BBC News*, April 23, 2012, https://www.bbc.com/news/world-middle-east-17788595.

40. The Arab Democracy Barometer conducted by the Arab Reform Initiative, 2018, https://www.arabbarometer.org/survey-data/data-analysis-tool/.

41. Zeinab Abul-Magd, "The Egyptian Republic of Retired Generals," *Foreign Policy*, May 8, 2012, https://foreignpolicy.com/2012/05/08/the-egyptian-republic-of-retired-generals/.

42. Hossam Bahgat, "Anatomy of an Election," *Madamasr*, March 14, 2016, https://madamasr.com/en/2016/03/14/feature/politics/anatomy-of-an-election/.

43. The Tahrir Institute for Middle East Policy, "TIMEP Brief Law No. 149 of 2019 (NGO Law)," August 21, 2019, https://timep.org/reports-briefings/ngo-law-of-2019/.

44. Amr Adly, "Economic Growth Is Making Many Egyptians Poorer," *Bloomberg*, August 21, 2019, https://www.bloomberg.com/amp/opinion/articles/2019-08-21/how-economic-growth-is-making-many-egyptians-poorer.

45. Timothy E. Kaldas, "Egypt's Economy: Neither Collapsing nor Thriving,"

TIMEP, August 20, 2019, https://timep.org/commentary/analysis/egypts-economy-neither-collapsing-nor-thriving/.

46. Aidan Lewis and Mohamed Abdellah, "Egypt's New Desert Capital Faces Delays as It Battles for Funds," *Reuters*, May 13, 2019, https://www.reuters.com/article/us-egypt-new-capital/egypts-new-desert-capital-faces-delays-as-it-battles-for-funds-idUSKCN1SJ10I.

47. Springborg, "The Rewards of Failure: Persisting Military Rule in Egypt," 492.

48. Heba Saleh, "Egypt's Disgruntled Contractor Incites Unrest from Spain," *Financial Times*, September 25, 2019, https://amp.ft.com/content/911b9346-de23-11e9-9743-db5a370481bc.

49. Florence Gaub, "Case Study: The Lebanese Armed Forces—from Powerlessness to Integration?," *Military Integration after Civil Wars* (Abingdon: Routledge, 2010), 46–80.

50. Aram Nerguizian, "Lebanese Armed Forces Challenges and Opportunities in Post-Syria Lebanon," *CSIS*, February 10, 2009, https://bit.ly/3bchOSl.

51. The Presidency of the Republic of Lebanon, "Former Presidents of Lebanon," https://bit.ly/2Tlbikh.

52. Anne Marie Baylouny, "Building an Integrated Military in Post-conflict Societies—Lebanon," in *The Routledge Handbook of Civil-Military Relation*, ed. Thomas C. Bruneau and Florina Cristiana Matei (Abingdon: Routledge, 2013), 246–247.

53. Nerguizian, "Lebanese Armed Forces Challenges and Opportunities in Post-Syria Lebanon."

54. The Taif Agreement created the basis to end the fifteen-year Lebanese civil war. It constituted a compromise between the different factions, including "Lebanese deputies, political groups and parties, militias and leaders. It tackled many essential points pertaining to the structure of the political system and the sovereignty of the Lebanese state." See Hassan Krayem, "The Lebanese Civil War and the Taif Agreement," *AUB*, 2012, https://bit.ly/31HW8tb.

55. Baylouny, "Building an Integrated Military in Post-conflict Societies—Lebanon," 248–249.

56. Aram Nerguizian, "Between Sectarianism and Military Development: The Paradox of the Lebanese Armed Forces," in *The Politics of Sectarianism in Post War Lebanon*, ed. Basel Salloukh, Rabie Barakat, Jinan S. Al-Habbal, Lara W. Khattab, and Shoghig Mikaelian (London: Pluto, 2015), 119.

57. Ibid., 116–118.

58. 'Other' or 'unclassified' is a reference to personnel who changed religious affiliation as a result of a mixed marriage, coming from mixed sectarian family backgrounds, and/or affiliations not recognized by the state. Ibid.

59. Ibid., 120.
60. Nerguizian, "Lebanese Armed Forces Challenges and Opportunities in Post-Syria Lebanon."
61. Gaub, "Case Study: The Lebanese Armed Forces—from Powerlessness to Integration?," 50.
62. Nerguizian, "Lebanese Armed Forces Challenges and Opportunities in Post-Syria Lebanon."
63. Nicholas Blanford, "The United States-Lebanese Armed Forces Partnership Challenges, Risks, and Rewards," *Atlantic Council*, May 2018, https://bit.ly/2xGeznl.
64. Nerguizian, "Lebanese Armed Forces Challenges and Opportunities in Post-Syria Lebanon."
65. "Syrian Troops Leave Lebanon after 29-Year Occupation," *New York Times*, April 26, 2005, https://nyti.ms/3culNd0.
66. Aram Nerguizian, "The Paradoxes of Military Development in Post-Syria Lebanon Primacy of the Sectarian System," *CSIS*, May 10, 2010, https://go.aws/2VxtxUy.
67. Basel Salloukh, "The Art of the Impossible: The Foreign Policy of Lebanon," in *The Foreign Policies of Arab States: The Challenge of Globalization*, ed. Bahgat Korany and Ali E. Hillal Dessouki (Cairo: American University in Cairo Press, 2009), 300.
68. According to Article 6 of the National Defense Law, the council of ministers sets the defense and security policy and supervises implementation. See in Arabic, "Decree 102 from 1983: The National Defense Law," https://bit.ly/2Sri47y.
69. There are two CDPs. CDP1 (2013–2017) was developed for Rome 1 donor conference to support the Lebanese Armed Forces. CDP2 (2018–2022) was developed for Rome 2 donor conference to support the Lebanese Armed Forces and Internal Security Forces. Dina Arakji, "Which Kind of Armed Forces?," Carnegie Middle East Center, February 4, 2020, https://bit.ly/2ver6ww.
70. Ibid.
71. Basem Shabb, "Fiscal Reality Should Drive Lebanon's Defense Policy," *Daily Star*, September 18, 2019, https://bit.ly/375lQsn; Nerguizian, "Lebanese Armed Forces Challenges and Opportunities in Post-Syria Lebanon"; Executive Magazine, "The LAF Budget—Closed Ranks," July 3, 2012, https://bit.ly/376ecOH.
72. Nerguizian, "Lebanese Armed Forces Challenges and Opportunities in Post-Syria Lebanon."
73. Aram Nerguizian, "Addressing the Civil-Military Relations Crisis in Lebanon," *LCPS*, March 2017, https://bit.ly/3bl4z1F.

74. Ibid.
75. Aram Nerguizian, "Lebanon at a Crossroad," *CSIS*, February 25, 2014, https://go.aws/39XPHF0.
76. US Embassy in Beirut, "Fact Sheet: US-Lebanon Military Assistance and Defense Cooperation," February 13, 2019, https://bit.ly/3belhju.
77. Wassim Saif al-Din, "Lebanese Army Receives New Batch of French Arms," *Anadolu Agency*, November 11, 2018, https://bit.ly/31EQHLl.
78. Lebanese Army, "Receiving a Boat and an Amount of Military Equipment as a Donation from the Italian Authorities," October 20, 2016, https://bit.ly/2vY8O3a.
79. Arab Barometer, "Data Analysis Tool," https://bit.ly/2UrVw9e.
80. Nerguizian, "Lebanese Armed Forces Challenges and Opportunities in Post-Syria Lebanon."
81. Baylouny, "Building an Integrated Military in Post-conflict Societies— Lebanon," 249.
82. Gaub, "Case Study: The Lebanese Armed Forces—from Powerlessness to Integration?," 49.
83. Nerguizian, "Lebanese Armed Forces Challenges and Opportunities in Post-Syria Lebanon."
84. Multilayer factors triggered this crisis. The 14-March-led government headed by former prime minister Fouad Siniora aimed to dismantle Hezbollah's private fiber-optic telecommunication and dismissed the head of the security at the airport, an LAF brigadier general perceived close to Hezbollah. See Nerguizian, "Between Sectarianism and Military Development," 129.
85. Ibid., 128–129.
86. Kareem Chehayeb and Abby Sewell, "Why Protesters in Lebanon Are Taking to the Streets," *Foreign Policy*, November 2, 2019, https://bit.ly/2St4wIr.
87. Aram Nerguizian, "The Military in the Middle," Carnegie Middle East Center, October 25, 2019, https://bit.ly/37ZLMai.
88. See, for example, Ray Takeyh, *Guardians of the Revolution: Iran and the World in the Age of the Ayatollahs* (Oxford: Oxford University Press, 2011); Shireen Hunter, *Iran Divided: The Historical Roots of Iranian Debates on Identity, Culture, and Governance in the Twenty-First Century* (New York: Rowman & Littlefield, 2014).
89. See, for example, Ali Alfoneh, *Iran Unveiled: How the Revolutionary Guards Is Transforming Iran from Theocracy into Military Dictatorship* (Washington, DC: AEI, 2013); Frederic Wehrey, Jerrold D. Green, Brian Nichiporuk, Alireza Nader, Lydia Hansell, Rasool Nafisi, and S. R. Bohandy, *The Rise of the Pasdaran: Assessing the Domestic Roles of Iran's Islamic Revolutionary Guards Corps* (Santa Monica, CA: RAND, 2008); David E. Thaler et al., *Mullahs,*

Guards, and Bonyads: An Exploration of Iranian Leadership Dynamics (Santa Monica, CA: RAND, 2010); Bayram Sinkaya, *The Revolutionary Guards in Iranian Politics: Elites and Shifting Relations* (Abingdon: Routledge, 2015).

90. See, for example, Ali Ansari, *Modern Iran: Reform and Revolution* (Abingdon: Routledge, 2007); Pouya Alimagham, *Contesting the Iranian Revolution: The Green Uprisings* (Cambridge: Cambridge University Press, 2020).

91. Kevan Harris, "All the Sepah's Men: Iran's Revolutionary Guards in Theory and Practice," in Grawert and Abul-Magd, *Businessmen in Arms*, 97–118.

92. Scott Shane, "Iranian Dissidents Convince US to Drop Terror Label," *New York Times*, September 21, 2012, https://www.nytimes.com/2012/09/22/world/middleeast/iranian-opposition-group-mek-wins-removal-from-us-terrorist-list.html.

93. Mark J. Gasiorowski, "The Nuzhih Plot and Iranian Politics," *International Journal of Middle East Politics* 34, no. 4 (November 2002): 645.

94. Ahmed S. Hashim, "Civil-Military Relations in Iran: Internal and External Pressures," *Middle East Policy Journal* 25, no. 3 (Fall 2018), https://mepc.org/journal/civil-military-relations-iran-internal-and-external-pressures.

95. Ibid.

96. On a field trip to Iran in 2012, one of the contributing authors was almost arrested by the Basij in Tehran after a meeting at an embassy.

97. Dilip Hiro, "Consolidation of the Revolution," in *Iran under the Ayatollahs* (Abingdon: Routledge, 1985), 237.

98. Robert Mason, "The Shaping Factors of Regional Insecurity and Conflict in the Formulation of Contemporary Saudi and Iranian Foreign Policy," in *Foreign Policy in Iran and Saudi Arabia: Economics and Diplomacy in the Middle East* (London: I.B. Tauris, 2015), 21.

99. See Ali Shariati, *Martyrdom* (Chicago: Kazi, 2012).

100. Ray Takeyh, "The Iran-Iraq War: A Reassessment," *Middle East Journal* 64, no. 3 (Summer 2010): 365–383.

101. Hashim, "Civil-Military Relations in Iran: Internal and External Pressures."

102. Leila Alikarami, "Iran-Iraq War Continues to Claim Lives," *Al-Monitor*, April 4, 2018, https://www.al-monitor.com/pulse/originals/2018/04/iran-land-mines-iraq-war-legacy-campaign-kurdistan.html.

103. Andrew Rathmell, "Khamenei Strengthens His Grip," *Jane's Intelligence Review*, October 1995, 450.

104. Karim Sadjadpour, "The Sinister Genius of Qassem Soleimani," *Wall Street Journal*, January 10, 2020, https://www.wsj.com/articles/the-sinister-genius-of-qassem-soleimani-11578681560.

105. Anthony H. Cordesman and Nicholas Harrington, "The Arab Gulf States and Iran: Military Spending, Modernization, and the Shifting Military

Balance," Center for Strategic and International Studies, Washington, DC, Working Draft, December 12, 2018, 4, https://csis-prod.s3.amazonaws .com/s3fs-public/publication/181212_Iran_GCC_Balance.Report.pdf.

106. Ibid., 2.

107. Stephen Kalin and Jonathan Landay, "Exclusive: Egypt Withdraws from US-Led Anti-Iran Security Initiative—Sources," *Reuters*, April 11, 2019, https://www.reuters.com/article/us-usa-mesa-egypt-exclusive/exclusive -egypt-withdraws-from-us-led-anti-iran-security-initiative-sources- idUSKCN1RM2WU.

108. Islamic Republic News Agency, "Pakistani Media Widely Covers President Rouhani's Remarks," July 22, 2018, https://en.irna.ir/news/82979119/ Pakistani-media-widely-covers-President-Rouhani-s-remarks.

109. Donald Trump, "To the Iranian President Rouhani …," Twitter, July 23, 2018, https://twitter.com/realdonaldtrump/status/1021234525626609666?l ang=en.

110. Hussein Ibish, "Gulf Arabs Caught between US 'Fire and Fury' and Ira- nian 'Strategic Recklessness,'" Arab Gulf States Institute in Washington, May 21, 2019, https://agsiw.org/gulf-arabs-caught-between-u-s-fire-and -fury-and-iranian-strategic-recklessness/.

111. Ibid.

112. Ibid.

113. Nahid Siamdoust, "Silence Falls on Iran's Protest Movement," *Foreign Af- fairs*, January 6, 2020, https://www.foreignaffairs.com/articles/iraq/2020 -01-06/silence-falls-irans-protest movement; Reuters, "Opposition Web- site Says at Least 631 Killed in Iran Unrest," January 2, 2020, https://www .reuters.com/article/us-iran-protests-toll/opposition-website-says-at-least -631-killed-in-iran-unrest-idUSKBN1Z1152.

114. Farnaz Fassihi, "Anatomy of a Lie: How Iran Covered Up the Downing of an Airliner," *New York Times*, January 26, 2020, https://www.nytimes.com/ 2020/01/26/world/middleeast/iran-plane-crash-coverup.html.

115. The World Bank, "Islamic Republic of Iran," https://www.worldbank.org/ en/country/iran/overview.

Bibliography

Abul-Magd, Zeinab. "The Egyptian Republic of Retired Generals." *Foreign Policy*, May 8, 2012. https://foreignpolicy.com/2012/05/08/the-egyptian -republic-of-retired-generals/.

———. *Militarizing the Nation: The Army, Business and Revolution in Egypt*. New York: Columbia University Press, 2018.

———. "Workers and Officers in Egypt: The Other Failed Revolution." *Jadali- yya*, January 11, 2018. https://www.jadaliyya.com/Details/35019.

Adly, Amr. "Economic Growth Is Making Many Egyptians Poorer." *Bloomberg*, August 21, 2019. https://www.bloomberg.com/amp/opinion/articles/ 2019-08-21/how-economic-growth-is-making-many-egyptians-poorer.

Albrecht, Holger. "Does Coup-Proofing Work? Political-Military Relations in Authoritarian Regimes amid the Arab Uprisings." *Mediterranean Politics* 20, no. 1 (2014): 36–54.

———. "The Myth of Coup-proofing: Risk and Instances of Military Coups d'état in the Middle East and North Africa, 1950–2013," *Armed Forces and Society* 41, no. 4 (2015): 659–87.

Alexander, Caroline, and Sam Dodge. "Muslim Brotherhood Is at the Heart of Gulf Standoff with Qatar." *Bloomberg*, June 7, 2017. https://www.bloomberg .com/graphics/2017-muslim-brotherhood/.

Alfoneh, Ali. *Iran Unveiled: How the Revolutionary Guards Is Transforming Iran from Theocracy into Military Dictatorship*. Washington, DC: AEI, 2013.

Alikarami, Leila. "Iran-Iraq War Continues to Claim Lives." *Al-Monitor*, April 4, 2018. https://www.al-monitor.com/pulse/originals/2018/04/iran-land-mines -iraq-war-legacy-campaign-kurdistan.html.

Alimagham, Pouya. *Contesting the Iranian Revolution: The Green Uprisings*. Cambridge: Cambridge University Press, 2020.

Al Jazeera. "Profile: Elias al-Murr." July 12, 2005. https://bit.ly/2SqCOMN.

American Chamber of Commerce in Egypt. "Egypt-US Business Data." https://www.amcham.org.eg/information-resources/trade-resources/ egypt-us-relations/us-foreign-assistance-to-egypt.

———. "Recent and Upcoming Legislation." https://www.amcham.org.eg/ publications/egypt-business-climate/issue/2/Recent-and-Upcoming -Legislation.

Ansari, Ali. *Modern Iran: Reform and Revolution*. Abingdon: Routledge, 2007.

Arab Barometer. "Data Analysis Tool." https://bit.ly/2UrVw9e.

The Arab Democracy Barometer conducted by the Arab Reform Initiative. 2018. https://www.arabbarometer.org/survey-data/data-analysis-tool/.

Arakji, Dina. "Which Kind of Armed Forces?" Carnegie Middle East Center 4 (February 2020). https://bit.ly/2ver6ww.

Ashour, Omar. "Collusion to Crackdown: Islamist-Military Relations in Egypt." Brookings Doha Center Analysis Paper 14, March 2015. https://www.brook ings.edu/wp-content/uploads/2016/06/collusion-to-crackdown-english.pdf.

Ayoob, Mohammed. *The Many Faces of Political Islam: Religion and Politics in the Muslim World*. Ann Arbor: University of Michigan Press, 2011.

Azzam, Maha. "Egypt's Military Council and the Transition to Democracy." May 2012. https://www.chathamhouse.org/sites/default/files/public/Research/ Middle%20East/bp0512_azzam.pdf.

Badolato, E. V. "A Clash of Cultures: The Expulsion of Soviet Military

Advisers from Egypt." *Naval War College Review* 37, no. 2 (March–April 1984): 69–81.

Bahgat, Hossam. "Anatomy of an Election." *Madamasr*, March 14, 2016. https://madamasr.com/en/2016/03/14/feature/politics/anatomy-of-an-election/.

Barany, Zoltan. "Foreign Contract Soldiers in the Gulf." Carnegie Middle East Center, February 5, 2020. https://carnegie-mec.org/2020/02/05/foreign-contract-soldiers-in-gulf-pub-80979.

El-Basha, Thomas. "Mikati Forms 30-Member Lebanon Cabinet." *Daily Star*, June 13, 2011. https://bit.ly/31xomq5.

Baylouny, Anne Marie. "Building an Integrated Military in Post-conflict Societies: Lebanon." In *The Routledge Handbook of Civil-Military Relation*, edited by Thomas C. Bruneau and Florina Cristiana Matei, 242–254. Abingdon: Routledge, 2013.

Be'eri, Eliezer. *Army Officers in Arab Politics and Society*. New York: Praeger, 1970.

Beinin, Joel. *The Rise of Egypt's Workers*, The Carnegie Papers. Washington, DC: Carnegie Endowment for International Peace, June 2012.

Brooks, Risa. *Shaping Strategy: The Civil-Military Politics of Strategic Assessment*. Princeton, NJ: Princeton University Press, 2008.

Chehayeb, Kareem, and Abby Sewell. "Why Protesters in Lebanon Are Taking to the Streets." *Foreign Policy*, November 2, 2019. https://bit.ly/2St4wIr.

Cook, Steven A. *Ruling but Not Governing: The Military and Political Development in Egypt, Algeria, and Turkey*. Baltimore: Johns Hopkins University Press, 2007.

Cordesman, Anthony H., and Nicholas Harrington. "The Arab Gulf States and Iran: Military Spending, Modernization, and the Shifting Military Balance." Center for Strategic and International Studies, Washington, DC, Working Draft, December 12, 2018. https://csis-prod.s3.amazonaws.com/s3fs-public/publication/181212_Iran_GCC_Balance.Report.pdf.

Dakroub, Hussein. "'Differences' Delay Military Council Appointments." *Daily Star*, May 8, 2019. https://bit.ly/2So1SDP.

Defenceweb. "Egyptian AT-802 Acquisition Confirmed." January 24, 2018. https://www.defenceweb.co.za/aerospace/aerospace-aerospace/egyptian-at-802-acquisition-confirmed/.

Al-Din, Wassim Saif. "Lebanese Army Receives New Batch of French Arms." *Anadolu Agency*, November 11, 2018. https://bit.ly/31EQHLl.

Economist Intelligence Unit. "Lebanon—Summary: Political Structure." September 1, 2018. https://bit.ly/31tFrBz.

Executive Magazine. "The LAF Budget—Closed Ranks." July 3, 2012. https://bit.ly/376ecOH.

Fassihi, Farnaz. "Anatomy of a Lie: How Iran Covered Up the Downing of an Airliner." *New York Times*, January 26, 2020. https://www.nytimes.com/2020/01/26/world/middleeast/iran-plane-crash-coverup.html.

Gasiorowski, Mark J. "The Nuzhih Plot and Iranian Politics." *International Journal of Middle East Politics* 34, no. 4 (November 2002): 645–666.

Gaub, Florence. "Case Study: The Lebanese Armed Forces—from Powerlessness to Integration?" in *Military Integration after Civil Wars*, 46–80. Abingdon: Routledge, 2010.

Gaub, Florence. "Defence Industries in Arab States: Players and Strategies." Chaillot Paper no. 141, March 2017, 31. https://www.iss.europa.eu/sites/default/files/EUISSFiles/CP_141_Arab_Defence.pdf.

Gaub, Florence. "Postscript: The Lebanese Armed Forces in Regional Perspective." In *Civil-Military Relations in Lebanon*, edited by Are John Knudsen and Tine Gade, 145–150. New York: Springer, 2017.

Grawert, Elke, and Zeinab Abul-Magd. *Businessmen in Arms: How the Military and Other Armed Groups Profit in the MENA Region*. New York: Rowman & Littlefield, 2016.

Hansen, Susan. "The Economic Vision of Egypt's Muslim Brotherhood Millionaires." *Bloomberg*, April 20, 2012. https://www.bloomberg.com/news/articles/2012-04-19/the-economic-vision-of-egypts-muslim-brotherhood-millionaires.

Hashim, Ahmed S. "Civil-Military Relations in Iran: Internal and External Pressures." *Middle East Policy Journal* 25, no. 3 (Fall 2018): 47–66. https://mepc.org/journal/civil-military-relations-iran-internal-and-external-pressures.

Henry, Clement Moore, and Robert Springborg. *Globalization and the Politics of Development in the Middle East*. Cambridge: Cambridge University Press, 2010.

Hiro, Dilip. "Consolidation of the Revolution." In *Iran under the Ayatollahs*, 222–269. Abingdon: Routledge, 1985.

Hunter, Shireen. *Iran Divided: The Historical Roots of Iranian Debates on Identity, Culture, and Governance in the Twenty-First Century*. New York: Rowman & Littlefield, 2014.

Huntingdon, Samuel P. *The Soldier and the State: The Theory and Politics of Civil-Military Relations*. Cambridge, MA: Harvard University Press, 1981.

Hurewitz, J. C. *Middle East Politics: The Military Dimension*. New York: Praeger, 1969.

Hydemann, Steven. "Upgrading Authoritarianism in the Arab World." Brookings, October 15, 2007. https://www.brookings.edu/research/upgrading-authoritarianism-in-the-arab-world/.

Ibish, Hussein. "Gulf Arabs Caught between US 'Fire and Fury' and Iranian 'Strategic Recklessness.'" Arab Gulf States Institute in Washington, May 21, 2019. https://agsiw.org/gulf-arabs-caught-between-u-s-fire-and-fury-and-iranian-strategic-recklessness/.

Islamic Republic News Agency. "Pakistani Media Widely Covers President Rouhani's Remarks." July 22, 2018. https://en.irna.ir/news/82979119/Pakistani-media-widely-covers-President-Rouhani-s-remarks.

Kaldas, Timothy E. "Egypt's Economy: Neither Collapsing nor Thriving." TIMEP, August 20, 2019. https://timep.org/commentary/analysis/egypts-economy-neither-collapsing-nor-thriving/.

Kalin, Stephen, and Jonathan Landay. "Exclusive: Egypt Withdraws from US-Led Anti-Iran Security Initiative—Sources." *Reuters*, April 11, 2019. https://www.reuters.com/article/us-usa-mesa-egypt-exclusive/exclusive-egypt-withdraws-from-us-led-anti-iran-security-initiative-sources-idUSKCN1RM2WU.

Kamrava, Mehran. "Military Professionalization and Civil-Military Relations in the Middle East." *Political Science Quarterly* 115, no. 1 (Spring 2000): 67–92.

Kandil, Hazem. *Soldiers, Spies and Statesmen: Egypt's Road to Revolt.* New York: Verso, 2012.

Karam, Joyce. "Iran Pays Hezbollah $700 Million a Year, US Official Says." *National*, June 5, 2018. https://www.thenational.ae/world/the-americas/iran-pays-hezbollah-700-million-a-year-us-official-says-1.737347.

Knell, Yolande. "Egypt Candidate: Ahmad Shafiq, Former Prime Minister." *BBC News*, April 23, 2012. https://www.bbc.com/news/world-middle-east-17788595.

Krayem, Hassan. "The Lebanese Civil War and the Taif Agreement." *AUB*, 2012. https://bit.ly/31HW8tb.

Lebanese Army. "Historical Phases." https://bit.ly/36ZbbQ4.

———. "Receiving a Boat and an Amount of Military Equipment as a Donation from the Italian Authorities." October 20, 2016. https://bit.ly/2vY8O3a.

Lewis, Aidan, and Mohamed Abdellah. "Egypt's New Desert Capital Faces Delays as It Battles for Funds." *Reuters*, May 13, 2019. https://www.reuters.com/article/us-egypt-new-capital/egypts-new-desert-capital-faces-delays-as-it-battles-for-funds-idUSKCN1SJ10I.

Mason, Robert. "Breaking the Mold of Small State Classification? The Broadening Influence of United Arab Emirates Foreign Policy through Effective Military and Bandwagoning Strategies." *Canadian Foreign Policy Journal*, March 21, 2018, 95–112.

———. "Egypt's Future: Status Quo, Incremental Growth or Regional Leadership?" *Middle East Policy Journal* 23, no. 2 (Summer 2016): 76–94.

———. *Foreign Policy in Iran and Saudi Arabia: Economics and Diplomacy in the Middle East.* London: I.B. Tauris, 2015.

Ministry of Finance. "Citizens Budget 2018." 2018. https://bit.ly/2SoPfss.

———. "Citizens Budget 2019." 2019. https://bit.ly/2vRJ20h.

Ministry of National Defense. "Former Ministers" [Al Wuzara' Al Sabikun]. https://bit.ly/372BO6H.

The National Defense Law. https://bit.ly/2Sri47y.

Nerguizian, Aram. "Addressing the Civil-Military Relations Crisis in Lebanon." *LCPS*, March 2017. https://bit.ly/3bl4z1F.

———. "Between Sectarianism and Military Development: The Paradox of the Lebanese Armed Forces." In *The Politics of Sectarianism in Post War Lebanon*, edited by Basel Salloukh, Rabie Barakat, Jinan S. Al-Habbal, Lara W. Khattab, and Shoghig Mikaelian, 108–135. London: Pluto, 2015.

———. "Lebanese Armed Forces Challenges and Opportunities in Post-Syria Lebanon." *CSIS*, February 10, 2009. https://bit.ly/3bchOSl.

———. "The Military in the Middle." Carnegie Middle East Center, October 25, 2019. https://bit.ly/37ZLMai.

Rabil, Robert G. "Why America Should Keep Supporting the Lebanese Armed Forces." *National Interest*, December 4, 2019. https://nationalinterest.org/blog/middle-east-watch/why-america-should-keep-supporting-lebanese-armed-forces-102092.

Rathmell, Andrew. "Khamenei Strengthens His Grip." *Jane's Intelligence Review*, October 1995.

Reuters. "Explainer: Why Is Lebanon in an Economic and Political Mess?' November 6, 2019. https://www.reuters.com/article/us-lebanon-protests-causes-explainer/explainer-why-is-lebanon-in-an-economic-and-political-mess-idUSKBN1XG260.

———. "From War Room to Board Room: Military Firms Flourish in Egypt." May 16, 2018. https://www.reuters.com/investigates/special-report/egypt-economy-military/.

———. "Opposition Website Says at Least 631 Killed in Iran Unrest." January 2, 2020. https://www.reuters.com/article/us-iran-protests-toll/opposition-website-says-at-least-631-killed-in-iran-unrest-idUSKBN1Z1152.

Rose, Sunniva. "Who Is in the New Lebanese Government?" *National*, January 22, 2020. https://bit.ly/2umrwko.

Sadjadpour, Karim. "The Sinister Genius of Qassem Soleimani." *Wall Street Journal*, January 10, 2020. https://www.wsj.com/articles/the-sinister-genius-of-qassem-soleimani-11578681560.

Salama, Vivian. "US Threatens Egypt with Sanctions over Russian Arms Deal." *Wall Street Journal*, November 14, 2019. https://www.wsj.com/articles/u-s-threatens-egypt-with-sanctions-over-russian-arms-deal-11573769929.

Saleh, Heba. "Egypt's Disgruntled Contractor Incites Unrest from Spain." *Financial Times*, September 25, 2019. https://amp.ft.com/content/911b9346-de23-11e9-9743-db5a370481bc.

Salloukh, Basel. "The Art of the Impossible: The Foreign Policy of Lebanon."

In *The Foreign Policies of Arab States: The Challenge of Globalization*, edited by Bahgat Korany and Ali E. Hillal Dessouki, 283–317. Cairo: American University in Cairo Press, 2009.

Shabb, Basem. "Fiscal Reality Should Drive Lebanon's Defense Policy." *Daily Star*, September 18, 2019. https://bit.ly/375lQsn.

Shane, Scott. "Iranian Dissidents Convince US to Drop Terror Label." *New York Times*, September 21, 2012. https://www.nytimes.com/2012/09/22/world/middleeast/iranian-opposition-group-mek-wins-removal-from-us-terrorist-list.html.

Shariati, Ali. *Martyrdom*. Chicago: Kazi, 2012.

Siamdoust, Nahid. "Silence Falls on Iran's Protest Movement." *Foreign Affairs*, January 6, 2020. https://www.foreignaffairs.com/articles/iraq/2020-01-06/silence-falls-irans-protest-movement.

Sinkaya, Bayram. *The Revolutionary Guards in Iranian Politics: Elites and Shifting Relations*. Abingdon: Routledge, 2015.

SIPRI. "Sipri's Arms Transfer Database." March 11, 2019. https://www.sipri.org/databases/armstransfers.

Slijper, Frank. "Under the Radar: The United Arab Emirates, Arms Transfers and Regional Conflict." PAX, September 2017.

Springborg, Robert. "The Rewards of Failure: Persisting Military Rule in Egypt." *British Journal of Middle Eastern Studies* 44, no. 4 (2017): 478–796.

The Tahrir Institute for Middle East Policy. "TIMEP Brief Law No. 149 of 2019 (NGO Law)." August 21, 2019. https://timep.org/reports-briefings/ngo-law-of-2019/.

Takeyh, Ray. *Guardians of the Revolution: Iran and the World in the Age of the Ayatollahs*. Oxford: Oxford University Press, 2011.

———. "The Iran-Iraq War: A Reassessment." *Middle East Journal* 64, no. 3 (Summer 2010): 365–383.

Thaler, David E., Alireza Nader, Shahram Chubin, Jerrold D. Green, Charlotte Lynch, and Frederic Wehry. *Mullahs, Guards, and Bonyads: An Exploration of Iranian Leadership Dynamics*. Santa Monica, CA: RAND, 2010.

US Embassy in Beirut. "Fact Sheet: US-Lebanon Military Assistance and Defense Cooperation." February 13, 2019. https://bit.ly/3belhju.

Vatikiotis, P. J. *Politics and the Military in Jordan: A Study of the Arab Legion, 1921–1957*. New York: Praeger, 1967.

Wehrey, Frederic, et al. *The Rise of the Pasdaran: Assessing the Domestic Roles of Iran's Islamic Revolutionary Guards Corps*. Santa Monica, CA: RAND, 2008.

World Bank. "Islamic Republic of Iran." https://www.worldbank.org/en/country/iran/overview.

3

Soft Power and Geopolitical Competition in the Modern Middle East

Simon Mabon and Eyad AlRefai

In the contemporary Middle East, the pursuit of power and influence has played out in a range of complex ways with serious implications for the ordering of life. While high levels of military spending have been a common line on state budgets, competition over influence and legitimacy is manifest in a number of different ways. Joseph S. Nye Jr.'s book *Soft Power* offered a radical way of rethinking international politics through the ability to attract and persuade.[1] States across the Middle East have sought to derive legitimacy and influence through Islam in some cases, notably the king of Saudi Arabia as custodian of the Two Holy Mosques, and the Iranian government, which has sought legitimacy through its Islamic Revolution in 1979. Other states, such as the UAE and Qatar, have embedded themselves as internationally significant nodes through various policies, primarily through economic statecraft, including ambitious regional and international aid, trade and investment policies, diversification endeavors, and initiatives related to sporting events. After the events of the Arab Uprisings, where protesters posing an existential challenge to the Al Khalifa regime were crushed with excessive force, the Bahraini government also embarked on a soft power program designed to rejuvenate its image on the world stage. While the 2011 Grand Prix in Bahrain was suspended, the race in Bahrain returned to the Formula 1 calendar the following year and has remained there since.

This chapter explores efforts to derive legitimacy and exert influence over regional and international politics. It argues that regional competition has emerged in a range of different forms, with serious repercussions for political life across the Middle East. In exploring this, the chapter looks at two case studies to study the ways in which competition between rival states plays out and shapes contemporary life. The first case study considers the rivalry between Saudi Arabia and Iran over claims to Islamic legitimacy and the impact that this rivalry has had on the region. The second explores the utilization of sports as a tool of political influence and positive 'nation branding.' It studies the UAE and Qatar as two competing powers that struggle to enhance their international presence through sport. This section considers the political use of sports by engaging three sports-related aspects. First, it studies the competition over broadcasting rights of significant international sports events in the Middle East. Second, the section discusses the hosting of 'mega sporting events' as an instrument of attraction and nation branding. Third, it examines the efforts made by the UAE and Qatar in purchasing elite-level international football clubs. By studying sports as a tool of international political influence, the second section of the chapter will reflect the increasingly active role of globalization and media in shaping the image and the reputation of the Middle East states.

Religion as a Tool to Secure Political Legitimacy

For those able to lay claim to it, religion is a key source of political legitimacy for states across the Middle East. Demonstrating religious credentials plays a prominent role in the ways in which regimes improve their standing in and across both the Middle East and the wider Islamic world. As home to the two holy places of Islam, Mecca and Medina, which millions of Muslim pilgrims visit each year for hajj and umrah, Saudi Arabia is well placed to derive a great deal of Islamic legitimacy from Muslims worldwide.

While this position has helped increase the kingdom's reserves of legitimacy, it has also brought with it opportunities through which the Saudi state could be criticized. Leadership of the Muslim world contains a set of normative values that serves as a means of increasing legitimacy when adhered to, but also provides the opportunity for other actors to hold the Al Saud to account when it appears that they fail to meet these values. For example, tensions were clearly evident after the September 2015 'crush and stampede' that caused the deaths of more than two thousand pilgrims. On the first anniversary of the incident, Iran's supreme leader Ayatollah Ali Khamenei said Saudi Arabia 'murdered' the pilgrims, without any evidence to support his accusations.[2]

The rivalry between Saudi Arabia and Iran has traditionally been viewed in three ways. The first views it as a struggle for regional power, control over the Persian Gulf, and, in later years, the Middle East. The second reduces the rivalry to Islam, framing tensions between Riyadh and

Tehran as a consequence of competing claims over the leadership of the Muslim world. The third suggests that both power and religion are important and should be taken into account together in order to understand the ways in which the rivalry has played out. Building on this third approach, the following section will explore how the rivalry between Riyadh and Tehran has evolved and how this has played out in different ways contingent upon time and space.

Prior to the Islamic Revolution in Iran in 1979, relations between the two major Gulf powers had been cordial, albeit punctured by a number of instances of tension, predominantly over territorial borders. The nature of relations is perhaps best viewed through past US efforts to forge a tripartite alliance between Tehran, Riyadh, and Baghdad.

Unsurprisingly, after the toppling of the shah and the establishment of the Islamic Republic of Iran, relations across the Gulf quickly deteriorated. In the formative stages of the Islamic Republic, messages of goodwill were sent to the supreme leader, Ayatollah Ruhollah Khomeini, from King Fahd of Saudi Arabia. These messages declared support for events in Iran and were expressions of solidarity.

King Khalid welcomed the establishment of the new state:

It gives me great pleasure that the new republic is based on Islamic principles which are a powerful bulwark for Islam and Muslim peoples who aspire to prosperity, dignity, and well-being. I pray the Almighty to guide you to the forefront of those who strive for the upholding of Islam and Muslims, and I wish the Iranian people progress, prosperity, and stability.[3]

Khomeini also sought to demonstrate unity:

There is no difference between Muslims who speak different languages, for instance the Arabs and the Persians. It is very probable that such problems have been created by those who do not wish the Muslim countries to be united . . . They create the issues of nationalism, of pan-Iranianism, pan-Turkism, and such isms, which are contrary to Islamic doctrines. Their plan is to destroy Islam and Islamic philosophy.[4]

Relations quickly soured though as fears about the implications of the revolution emerged. This is perhaps best documented in Article 3.16 of the Iranian constitution, which states that foreign policy must be "based on Islamic criteria, fraternal commitment to all Muslims, and unrestrained support for the impoverished people of the world." Seeking to increase its legitimacy, the nascent Islamic Republic sought to move beyond its

Shia identity and speak to Muslims across the world, albeit in a manner inspired by Shia thought. A key target of the Islamic Republic was Gulf monarchies who were held to be impious and routinely condemned for their anti-Islamic practices. The Saudi Kingdom quickly became a prominent target for Khomeini's ire, given the system of monarchical rule and the long-standing claim to legitimacy derived from being the protectors of the two holy places of Islam. In the months and years that followed the Islamic Revolution, the Saudis and Iranians embarked on a cycle of rhetoric in an attempt to demonstrate their religious vitality and relevance.

In pursuit of this, Khomeini articulated a desire to

> export our experiences to the whole world and present the outcome of our struggles against tyrants to those who are struggling along the path of God, without expecting the slightest reward. The result of this exportation will certainly result in the blooming of the buds of victory and independence and in the implementation of Islamic teachings among the enslaved nations.[5]

As Anoushiravan Ehteshami suggests, the Islamic Revolution "disrupted the regional order and also ended the slowly emerging alliances of moderate forces in the Middle East," ending Nixon's efforts to establish a twin-pillar approach and opening space for a new form of competition along religious lines.[6]

> If we wanted to prove to the world that the Saudi Government, these vile and ungodly Saudis, are like daggers that have always pierced the heart of the Moslems from the back, we would not have been able to do it as well as has been demonstrated by these inept and spineless leaders of the Saudi Government.[7]

Khomeini would later condemn the Al Saud as "corrupt and unworthy to be the guardians of Mecca and Medina"[8] before referring to them as "traitors to the two holy shrines."[9] Unsurprisingly, this was not well received in Riyadh. King Fahd, who succeeded his brother in 1982, viewed the regime in Tehran as "hypocrites and pretenders who are using Islam to undermine and destabilize other countries."[10] The hajj became a site of competition between the two states seeking to lay claim to legitimacy across the Muslim world. Acknowledging this, Fahd argued that any efforts to demonstrate on the hajj would create an atmosphere of "chaos and upset the peace," which would not be tolerated. These fears manifested in 1987 with the deaths of four hundred pilgrims—a large number of whom were Iranian—during the hajj. Saudi framing of Khomeini would also include efforts to draw parallels with God and the Nazis.

Fearing the capacity of the Islamic Republic to erode the kingdom's legitimacy, the Al Saud sought to frame the revolution as both Shia and Persian, in an effort to reduce its appeal across the Gulf and prevent Khomeini from spreading the revolutionary goals of the revolution. In spite of this, Iranian actors were directly involved in establishing a number of groups across the Middle East, notably Hezbollah, the Lebanese 'Party of God,' and the Islamic Front for the Liberation of Bahrain (IFLB), both of which sought to advocate Khomeini's core message.

Over the following decades, the Saudis and Iranians embarked on a struggle to shape the Middle East, drawing on various strategies in pursuit of their goals, contingent upon time and space, meaning that the processes at play were shaped by local forces. Although relations between Riyadh and Tehran thawed during the 1990s as a consequence of domestic reforms, the onset of the so-called War on Terror and positioning of Iran in the 'Axis of Evil' resulted in the reemergence of fractious relations across the Gulf. The 2003 US-led invasion of Iraq opened up a new space for the two to engage in rivalry in an effort to shape the Iraqi state into their respective visions, while similar efforts occurred after the Arab Uprisings in Bahrain, Syria, and Yemen.

The presence of a number of divided societies across the Middle East gave scope for Riyadh and Tehran to exert influence across the region by cultivating relations with co-sectarian kin. In the formative years of the Islamic Republic, this was best seen in support for Hezbollah and the IFLB in the 1980s (the latter no longer exists in autonomous form), while after the 2003 invasion of Iraq, Iran cultivated links with a number of militias and political parties, many of whom had sought refuge in Iran under the regime of Saddam Hussein. In contrast, Saudi Arabia continued to provide support to their longtime ally the Al Khalifa ruling family in Bahrain across a decade of unrest on the archipelago, along with support to Sunni groups across Iraq and Lebanon.

After the Arab Uprisings, the fragmentation of political projects created opportunities for Riyadh and Tehran to maneuver in pursuit of power and influence.[11] This set of regional machinations took place through the provision of support to co-sectarian kin across the region—either to rulers or ruled—exacerbating divisions in Syria and Yemen in the process. In Yemen, the interaction of parabolic forces has had a devastating impact on politics across the state. While some have sought to reduce events in Yemen to sectarian difference, this is an inappropriate reading of the situation. Instead, the events of 2013 and onward have opened up a range of schisms across the state, along religious, tribal, economic, geographical, and secessionist lines. The Houthi movement in the north, while ostensibly Shia, possesses closer theological ties to other Sunni madhhab (school of thought within Islamic jurisprudence) than to the Twelver Shiism practiced in Iran. Moreover, the group had operated independently in the decades before the uprisings in Yemen, procuring weapons from disenchanted members of the Yemeni armed forces or on the black market.

Links between the Houthis and Iran began in earnest in the latter part of the 2010s, with the provision of weapons, finance, and training from Tehran to the movement. Over time, this support increased, although this was not without issues. Anecdotal reports suggest that members of the Houthis struggled when Iranian officials traveled to Yemen to train the group as a consequence of long-standing tensions between Arabs and Persians. Consequently, as the anecdote goes, members of Hezbollah were sent to Yemen to circumvent these tensions and provide training to the Houthis.

The presence of a Shia group on the borders of Saudi Arabia was viewed as an existential threat by many in Riyadh, prompting a military campaign to eradicate the group, seeking to prevent Iranian influence on the Arabian Peninsula. These fears were exacerbated by doubts of Iranian manipulation of events in Bahrain, where the Al Khalifa had been rocked by the emergence of a widespread protest movement explicitly rejecting sectarian affiliation. Chants of "no Sunni, no Shi'a, just Bahraini" rang out across 2011, posing an existential challenge to the future of the monarchy. What quickly followed was a process of 'sectarianization,' where protesters were framed along sect-based lines, as both Shia and Iranian fifth columnists.[12] This strategy was supported by the presence of a Gulf Cooperation Council (GCC) Peninsula Shield Force, which crossed the King Fahd Causeway in March 2011, designed to ensure the survival of the ruling family.

While there was no evidence of Iranian involvement, allegations of perfidious interference continue to be heard. Bahrain was seen as the 'epicenter' of the rivalry between Saudi Arabia and Iran, given its location and the demographic divide, where a family from the Sunni minority rules over a Shia majority. Of course, the legacy of the failed IFLB coup d'état in the early 1980s played into Al Khalifa, and Saudi, fears.

In Syria and Lebanon, there was little doubt about Iranian influence, where Tehran has spent a great deal of its foreign aid budget supporting Hezbollah and the continued rule of Bashar al-Assad. This support has played out in a range of different ways, contingent upon the peculiarities of local context, ranging from financial and political support, to overt military intervention in Syria to support Assad, who was seen as a key pillar to Iranian aspirations and security. When protests broke out across Syria, many in Saudi viewed it as an opportunity to facilitate realignment in regional politics. Although Saudi-Syrian relations have traditionally been complex, the Al Saud was keen to bring Damascus back into what Madawi Al Rasheed termed the 'Arab fold,' thereby reducing the influence of Iran in the process. Iran's initial successes prompted one senior figure to claim that it controls four Arab capitals: Beirut, Baghdad, Damascus, and Sana'a.

The formation of political projects in the Middle East, particularly those in divided societies, built in opportunities for external manipulation by regional powers. The ability of sect-based identities to resonate across state borders created conditions for Saudi Arabia and Iran to operate in pursuit of their own interests, seeking to increase their power through the mobilization and manipulation of identities and, conversely, to reduce the influence of their rivals in the process. Here, we see how religion offers the means through which power can be derived and actors can lay claim to legitimacy. Yet, the type of identity may also leave these actors open to criticism and the actions of others. As Paul Noble famously articulated, the Middle East is a vast echo chamber, meaning that events resonate across time and place.[13] This is especially pertinent concerning sectarian identities and claims to religious legitimacy, which can play out in a range of ways, with devastating consequences for the ordering of life.

Sports as an Alternative Soft Power Approach

Unlike Saudi Arabia and Iran, other states across the Gulf are unable to draw on religion as a means of increasing their legitimacy and soft power potential. Instead, these hydrocarbon-rich states have embarked on a process of rapid development, economic investments, and engagement within global narratives of prestige as a means of raising global awareness of their position in global politics. Engaging with global sporting events has provided ruling elites with a means of doing this, resulting in investments in globally prestigious sporting teams, including Barcelona, Arsenal, Paris St Germain, Manchester City, and others, while also successfully bidding to host the Football World Cup (Qatar), Formula 1 races (the UAE and Bahrain), and tennis and golf tournaments (Qatar and the UAE).

There are many answers to why and how sports can be studied as an instrument of soft power that provides political influence and leverage. Mainly, as Joseph S. Nye Jr. argues, soft power does not need 'sticks' and 'carrots' to achieve its targets; rather, it is applied by 'attraction' and 'co-opting.' Therefore, recognizing sports as a tool of universal attraction to other nations, peoples, and cultures fits Nye's definition of the concept of soft power. Moreover, hosting international sporting events (the Olympics, the World Cup, Formula 1, international boxing matches, and martial arts competitions), the acquisition of elite-level European football teams, and the 'transnational' purchase of broadcasting rights to international sports tournaments cannot be considered as a sort of hard power. However, it is power in the way that it enhances the name, image, and status of nations domestically and internationally.

Up until these cases, the function of sports as an international political/ diplomatic instrument was most visible in the 1970s, for example, the ping-pong policy/diplomacy, which, among other factors, played a significant role in achieving the historical Sino-American rapprochement. As Murray observes,

> Since the early 1970's, for example, China's re-emergence and acceptance into the international community has been closely linked to international sports. The most famous instance is—of course—the 'ping heard around the world' where an opportune series of matches between Chinese and American ping-pong players paved the way for the restoration of China's seat on the United Nations Security Council, Richard Nixon's visit to China in 1972, and the normalization of Sino-US diplomatic relations.[14]

The literature that studies the international utilization of sports as a political tool is a nascent one, but it has witnessed plenty of advancements in recent years. Scholars like Jonathan Grix, Barrie Houlihan, James Dorsey, Paul Brannagan, Richard Giulianotti, Mahfoud Amara, and Danyel Reiche shed light on specific areas of growing connections/ correlations between sport-related topics and politics, especially at the international level. Some focus on how nations project soft power by hosting 'mega sporting events,'[15] while others discuss the effects of sports on what they label as 'nation branding.'[16] They have in common the concept of soft power to understand how sports can be used as a useful tool to reorientate perception and recreate or enhance the image and the reputation of a particular country on the regional and global levels.

Due to high levels of communications, network building, and technological advancements the world has explicitly witnessed in the second half of the twentieth century, the concept of soft power is gaining more attention from scholars. This tends to be concerned about the instrumentalization of contemporary cultural and ideational phenomena and their interactions with political aspects in the disciplines of political science and international relations theory. This development created new ways of studying the growing relationships between politics and contemporary subjects in the public cultural realm such as sport, media, and the arts. Indeed, it is chiefly due to globalization, which brought an increased level of interactions between what is conceived as the internal and the external, and the possibilities of connections and communications on the individual and organizational levels around the world, that the scholarship on soft power has flourished. Sports did not become an influential political and economic tool out of a vacuum. To properly account for the political ways and means of capitalizing on international sport, we must consider recent economic developments in the global system that led states and international companies to deem sports as an effective tool in their competitions against rivals.

Satellites and broadcasting rights of sports events, and especially football, made the games more accessible to the world. As truly international events such as the Olympics and World Cup football become more global, it also makes advertising during these events and those associated with them more important. The FIFA report of the 2018 World Cup in Russia shows an estimated 3.572 billion people watched some official broadcast coverage of the event. Over half (51.3 percent) of the global population (aged 4 years and over) was captured and 76.4 percent watched for at least 30 minutes (vs. 61.1 percent in 2014).[17]

Without the telecommunication tools that globalization presented in the 1980s, such figures would not be conceivable today. Moreover, globalization revolutionized the sports viewerships and therefore enhanced the utilization of sports as a form of soft power. Increased numbers of viewers were reflected in advertisement and sponsorship figures and, following that, the reputation of a certain nation. The colossal reach and appeal that sporting teams and events have made it attractive to political actors to take their struggles into sporting arenas. Sports also offer a glittery area of attraction for nations aspiring to secure international status and reputation, but not necessarily through the cost, manpower, and risks associated with enhancing hard power capabilities alone.[18]

Sports as a Political Tool: The Cases of Qatar and the UAE

This section will analyze the global involvement of Qatar and the UAE in utilizing sports as a political tool. First, it studies the issue of broadcasting rights in the Middle East as a space of competition between Qatar and other Gulf states, but mainly the UAE. Second, the section reflects the significant utilization of 'mega sporting events' hosted in the UAE and Qatar as a tool of attraction, image building, and branding. Third, the section turns to address the case of elite international football club ownership. The competition between the UAE and Qatar has its roots within the Gulf region, and it manifests itself in multiple arenas. Sports is one aspect of this assumed struggle in which tourism and international economic investments and trade also play significant roles. As Mahfoud Amara and Borja Garcia-Garcia argue:

> The increasingly important role of Arab investors in European clubs raises questions of cultural differences, feelings of belonging and images of 'the other,' but it also brings our attention to wider issues of football governance and the distribution of power in the geopolitics of the game. With the recent (and for some, controversial) decision to award the 2022 FIFA World Cup to Qatar, it seems that a new focus of power in football governance is emerging to challenge the traditional dominance of Europe and, to a lesser extent, South America.[19]

Therefore, it is becoming relatively accurate to talk about how, why, and when states have exploited sports as a tool of attraction and influence through the process of globalization. The economic, leisure, and entertainment rivalry has shifted into the geopolitical landscape, especially in the aftermath of the Arab Uprisings. However, this study is interested in the utilization and application of sports as a soft power instrument between the UAE and Qatar, rather than in their respective roles in Yemen, Egypt, Libya, Syria, and almost the whole region, where they differ profoundly on the political and social destinies of the region and are thus more likely to use a different approach.

Sports Broadcasting Rights and Media

In the Middle East, where things are not necessarily the same as in other places around the world, to watch and hear 'the Reds' (Liverpool F.C. supporters) chanting the name of their favorite footballer, the Egyptian Mohammed Salah, Egyptians as well as fans in twenty-three Arab countries need to have a beIN Sports subscription. beIN is a Qatari network that owns the broadcasting rights of major sporting events, not only in Qatar and the Arab Gulf countries but for the entire viewership spanning Morocco to Iraq (i.e., the Arab world). By the same token, Algerians were not able to watch Khaled Mehriz, the striker who won his country its first African Cup of Nations in the summer of 2019, unless they were a beIN Sports subscriber. Mehriz plays for Manchester City, an elite football club, owned by Sheikh Mansour bin Zayed, the UAE's deputy prime minister, since 2008.

It is noteworthy to outline how the rivalry between the Gulf countries—Qatar, the UAE, and Saudi Arabia—has played a role in influencing the content of broadcast events in the region. In 2011, there was a heated discussion between Mohammed Najeeb, the general manager of Abu Dhabi Sports Network, and Nasser al-Khelaifi, the then general manager of Al Jazeera Sports and current chairman of Paris Saint-Germain (PSG) and beIN networks, on the Qatari Sport TV ALKAS. Najeeb accused Al Jazeera of breaking an agreement by which both networks divided the broadcasting rights of upcoming sporting events, including elite European football competitions and the 2014 World Cup. Al Jazeera Sports capitalized on this saga and broadcast the first year of competitions for free around MENA, which gained the channel unprecedented support and popularity in the region, along with Al Jazeera news, which had extended its influence during the Arab Uprisings. Al Jazeera, a media giant in the Middle East and around the world, is one of Qatar's key soft powers and the most successful instrument of public diplomacy and information. beIN Sports network, as Al-Jazeera sports before 2013, is the exclusive MENA broadcaster for most of the sports events regionally and globally. The network broadcasts in seven languages, including English, French, Spanish, and Arabic. beIN Sports holds the rights to broadcast UEFA Champions League in the MENA region, the United States, and France.

For media consumers in the Arab World, to watch their national teams and finest players competing at the world level, they need to pay a media company that is owned by and operated in another country, in this case Qatar. Compare this peculiar situation to that of Latin America, where people also share the same language to a large extent, but the broadcast rights for international sporting events are nationally based—a different media network has the broadcasting rights in each country. Unquestionably, the process that links regional viewership of immensely popular events to a particular television network and country comes with political strands attached, especially significant in the ever-shifting geopolitical sands of the Middle East.

For instance, after the embarrassing 5–0 opening match of the 2018 World Cup between Russia and Saudi Arabia, beIN Sports spread its coverage of the game over more than two days to tarnish not only the Saudi team and sportsmen in general but also the leadership of the country. In response, Turki Alalshikh, the head of the Saudi sports authority at the time, tweeted: "Necessary legal action will be taken in relation to

BeIN wrongdoings against KSA, its sports & officials, and for exploiting sports to achieve political goals. This proves Saudi authorities' true stance when banning this network from airing on its soil."[20] But this did not deter Saudi viewers. The 2018 World Cup witnessed high levels of media piracy:

> The statistics, which cover the entirety of the 32-day competition, reveal that 40,713 piracy links were detected by the technology-led research across all platforms. VO had partnered with content protection company LeakID in an attempt to track and fight illegal streaming sites during the competition. The results of the research highlighted the critical role played by social media in the number of pirate networks being located. 14,615 links were discovered on social media sites, with 8,462 on Facebook and a further 1,988 on YouTube. These figures represented 41,371,139 viewers, according to the VO data.[21]

The most noteworthy piracy network was beoutQ: "A pirate television network that is illegally screening the world's most popular sporting events to viewers in Saudi Arabia has become the latest flashpoint in a clash between Riyadh and Qatar that is roiling the Gulf."[22] The case of the commercial rights to broadcast sporting events in the MENA region helps to highlight the political relationships, tensions, and disagreements between states at a more official level. Furthermore, the broader issue of 'transnational broadcasting rights' in the Middle East goes back to the 1990s.

beIN Sports, Dubai Sports, and Abu Dhabi Sports channels were established to follow the footprints of, and to contest with, ART, a pan-Arab Saudi TV network (Arab Radio and TV networks owned by Sheikh Saleh Kamel, a Saudi elite figure and businessman). ART possessed the broadcasting rights of major sports events in the Middle East in the 1990s:

> AJS [Al Jazeera Sports] was established in November 2003 as part of the expansion of the Al-Jazeera network into new fields beyond the news. In its early years, AJS's main competitor was the Saudi network Arab Radio and Television (ART), until AJS purchased the six ART sports channels and all sports rights held by ART for approximately US $1 billion on November 24, 2009. As a result, AJS became the largest sports network in the Middle East and North Africa. AJS's main and almost sole competitor remains Abu-Dhabi Media, whose main assets were exclusive rights to the English Premier League and the German Bundesliga, until 2013, when AJS defeated Abu-Dhabi Media in the competition over English

Premier League rights, paying around US $300 million for the rights for three years, as well as the right to broadcast the German league matches, stripping Abu-Dhabi Media of its main assets. These new rights positioned AJS as an unbelievably strong monopoly in sports broadcasting rights in the MENA region, with exclusive rights to the French, Italian, English, Russian, German, and Spanish soccer leagues. AJS also has exclusive broadcasting rights to FIFA World Cup, UEFA European and World Championships, AFC Asian Cup, Africa Cup of Nations, and Copa America, among others.[23]

It is imperative to fully appreciate and understand the media's role, precisely TV networks in the Middle East and globally, in the facilitation of sports as an instrument of soft power. As Khalid Basyuni further clarifies:

> The Middle East's football-hungry audience has had many hosts in the past number of years to feed their football cravings. From Showtime (now OSN) and ART, to Abu Dhabi and Dubai Sports channels and BeIN Sports. But it's at this point in the journey we hit a road block in the variety of choice that is on offer to a Middle East fan and instead, we regress. Ever since BeIN Sports emerged in the market, and coupled with their acquisition of ART Sports, the channel has adopted a bullish and aggressive strategy en route to sports media dominance. With the benefit of being a cash-heavy business, BeIN engaged the strategy knowing that they would have to write cheques to rights holders far more expensive than the ones they had seen before, inflating the rights fee market in this region.[24]

Hosting 'Mega Sporting Events'
Consider the case of the UAE, which presents an interesting example to understand the relationship between politics, sports, and international image and branding. When tracing back the steps the country took, it becomes evident that since the 1990s, the UAE has embarked on domestic and international projects to transform the country into a world-leading destination for tourism, leisure, and entertainment. This dream was achieved when Dubai assumed a leading role in aspects such as economy and tourism, and Abu Dhabi was named the second-best city in the world to live and work in by 2017.[25] In the process of building world-class cities, hosting sporting events was a significant tool of UAE development plans to keep attracting international tourists.

Leveraging sporting events as a feature to serve political ends of attraction and public image enhancement can be seen clearly in 1996, when the country hosted the Asian Football Cup of Nations. Since the Saudi national team won that year, it was reflected in a growing regional appeal. Growing up in the 1990s, AlRefai was fascinated by the offshore powerboat racing contest in Dubai. We used to sit in front of the TV for almost three hours on Friday and Saturday afternoons to watch the race on the Dubai Sports channel. The Victory team, owned by Al-Maktoum, the royal family of Dubai, won 12 C1 World Championship, the equivalent of Formula 1, the highest race in the sport that is organized by the Union Internationale Motonautique, the international body for powerboat races. However insignificant this kind of sporting event might sound at the global level, by the 1990s, it had already branded the UAE, and especially Dubai, positively in the region. A range of Arab TV channels started to fill their airtime with broadcasts of these races.

This was coupled with the establishment of the Dubai Season for Tourism, the billboard to the city's infrastructure and cultural developments. Beyond building bridges with the West, in 2014, the UAE hosted the Indian Premier League (IPL) cricket, a professional-level competition played during March, April, and/or May of every year by eight squads from eight different cities in India. As Narayan Prabhu B.M. and Karan Subramanian explain, the reason for choosing the UAE was that it had hosted several events, such as golf, Formula 1, tennis, and rugby. Furthermore, sponsorship from national airlines such as Etihad and Emirates was a factor. The Abu Dhabi–based airline Etihad also sponsored several high-profile international events such as the Major League Soccer in the United States, Manchester City FC, and Harlequins RFC, thereby equating the cricket tournament with other high-profile events internationally.[26]

Liverpool FC competed in Qatar to win the 2019 FIFA Clubs World Cup, for the first time. This specific tournament was hosted four times in the UAE: in 2009, 2010, 2017, and 2018. Moreover, in 2009, the UAE became the second Arab Middle Eastern country to host the Formula 1 race after Bahrain, in an effort to boost its image, prompting more competition over prestigious sporting events across the Gulf.

Similar to the UAE, the legacy of Qatar's strategic interest in hosting mega sporting events is rooted back in the 1990s, although some would argue that the country started capitalizing on sports as a tool of attraction since 1988 when it hosted the Asian Cup. Under the leadership of Hamad bin Khalifa al Thani from 1995 until June 2013, Qatar implemented a set of progressive plans addressing many aspects of Qatari society. In the process, the country has followed a developmental path toward implementing social, educational, economic, and sports policies through the establishment of 'semigovernmental,' 'semiprivate' institutions such as Qatar Foundation.[27] Qatar Foundation is a great example to study the implementation of the country's strategy through a progressive semigovernmental bureaucracy: "The Foundation promotes a culture of excellence in Qatar and furthers its role in supporting an innovative and open society that aspires to develop sustainable human capacity, social, and economic prosperity for a knowledge-based economy."[28]

Therefore, Qatar started hosting these events as part of a bundle of transformational plans. In 2004, Qatar hosted the Gulf Cup, a regular contest that takes place between the Gulf Arab countries every two years. The one in 2004 was very special. The Iraqi national team participated for the first time since 1988. The opening ceremony was delivered by the iconic Iraqi singer Kadeem Al Saheer. That year, the Gulf Cup attracted an Arab audience beyond the Gulf region. Two years later, Qatar hosted the 2006 Asian Games. To fully comprehend how Qatar won the bid in 2010 to host the World Cup 2022, we must account for the infrastructure process and strategic planning that reflects the country's desire and seriousness in dealing with the sport as a political instrument. Corruption may have played a role in that specific bid, although Qatar's plans to capitalize on sports was not exclusively related to hosting of the 2022 World Cup even if it was a major step forward.

The World Cup 2022 is the proverbial 'jewel on the crown' for Qatar's sports development plans. "In Qatar, the sports sector is playing an increasingly prominent role in shaping national identity and progress. The achievements thus far . . . have helped change Qatar's image in the world. Success in sports has become an inspiration for the whole society and contributes to an energized, confident and modernizing nation."[29] Qatar has initiated the use of sports as an instrument of social and cultural change by establishing many semigovernmental administrations and institutions, such as the sports academy Aspire in 2004. Aspire is a sports hub that includes sports-related academic courses at different levels, from amateur to professional, and it has people of more than fifty nationalities interacting through sports.

In addition, the state widely invests in sporting leagues and infrastructure. The Aspire complex, for example, originally designed for the 2006 Asian Games, is home to the 'Aspire Academy of Sporting Excellence,' the Academy's 'Football Dreams Programme,' and 'Aspetar'—the only FIFA medical centre of excellence in the Middle East. Incorporating two five-star hotels, a 50,000 seat stadium, an Olympic swimming pool, and state-of-the-art sports science labs, the complex attempts to add to Qatar's desire to 'rise as a global player through creative focus and development of new talent infused with world-class talent.'[30]

The academy represents itself. "We are at the heart of a sporting revolution currently taking place in Qatar and around the region,"[31] and its vision is to be recognized as the world's leading sports academy by 2022, the same year in which Qatar will be hosting the World Cup finals—the exact tournament that attracted the whole world to study Qatari sports investment.

However, the case of poorly treated Asian migrant workers in Qatar has reflected negatively on its attempts at maintaining an immaculate public image and building a national brand. In order to upgrade the facilities to host World Cup 2022, Qatar is working round the clock. "Qatar is reported to be spending more than $200bn (£121bn) on a series of infrastructure projects and says the World Cup 2022 is a catalyst for a nationwide building project."[32] However, to accomplish the proposed projects, a vast number of South Asian migrant workers have arrived in Doha. The migrant workers in Qatar make up 80 percent of the population, and there is a high dependency on their presence.[33] But migrant workers face difficulties with housing and working conditions. Death rates among the workers indicate a more significant humanitarian issue facing Qatar's modernization and credibility. For example, "Nepalese migrants building the infrastructure to host the 2022 World Cup died at a rate of one every two days in 2014—despite Qatar's promises to improve their working conditions, *The Guardian* has learned."[34]

Ownership of Elite Football Clubs

Another side of private investment that is linked to Qatar's broader efforts to improve its public image and reputation through sports is the investments in international football teams, including PSG. The website of Qatar Sports Investments (QSI, funded 2004) presents the company as "a private shareholding Organization with the ambition to invest in profit-bearing sports-related projects within Qatar and also internationally, whilst becoming a globally recognized and leading sports and leisure investment company."[35]

Indeed, since 2011, PSG has dominated French football by winning six titles of Ligue 1 (the French premier league) and five trophies of Coupe de la Ligue BKT (the French professional club level). However, since acquiring the Parisian team, QSI has had the aim of securing the UEFA Champions League title. Most of the club's stunning signings of superstar footballers did not deliver the wanted goal. They paid €135 million for Kylian Mbappe and €222 million for Neymar. They have invested over €1 billion on players in the past eight years, but their record in the Champions League has been poor. In fact, "Paris Saint-Germain's Qatari owners have spent $1.17 billion on players, but the Champions League is still out of reach."[36]

If it is accurate to suggest that Qatar has won the competition over hosting mega sporting events and the purchase of MENA broadcasting rights, by the same token, it is also safe to say that the UAE won the struggle over purchasing and running international football teams. The UAE's presence in England's football stretches from Manchester City, to Ashburton Grove, London, home of Arsenal FC and the Emirates Stadium. Since 2006, it has been named after the UAE airline. The latter struck a deal with the club in 2004 to finance the delayed process of completing the stadium's infrastructure, which granted the company a long-term sponsorship of Arsenal's kit and stadium and the UAE a lasting reputation and presence.

However, unlike Qatar, the influence of the UAE investments in sponsoring and purchasing of football clubs goes beyond England and Europe. Indeed, City Football Group (CFG), the owner of Manchester City, has diversified its operation to run clubs in America as well as Australia, China, Japan, Uruguay, Spain, and India. The group also has investments in the Yokohama F. Marinos in Japan, Club Athletico Torque in Uruguay, Girona FC in Spain, and Sichuan Jiuniu in China. CFG is 87 percent owned by Abu Dhabi United Group (ADUG) and 13 percent by China Media Capital (CMC) Consortium. Until December 2015, CFG was wholly owned by ADUG, a private investment and development company belonging to His Highness Sheikh Mansour bin Zayed Al Nahyan.[37]

Furthermore, in a recent interview with Sky Sports, on November 27, 2019, Khaldoon Al Mubarak, the current group CEO of CFG and a successful UAE entrepreneur, announced that the group has started to attract investments beyond the UAE. Precisely, the American company Silver Lake, which has invested $500 million. "The sale of the 10 percent stake has just added $500m to the balance sheet and linked up with Silver Lake, business leaders in global technology investing, in the process."[38]

Given the close political relationship between the UAE and Saudi Arabia, it is little wonder that there were reports in October and November 2019 of Crown Prince Mohammed Bin Salman making a third attempt to buy Manchester United and replicate similar commercial, sports, and public relations successes for Saudi Arabia.

This section showed how the UAE and Qatar have used sports as an instrument to enhance economic and political influence and ambitions over time. It highlighted how rival states in the Middle East are able to utilize different channels and methods to gain more power, how different states are good at exploiting and expanding different niche markets, and how sports travels beyond national and regional borders to create imbedded and sometimes long-term interests and connections with states, nations, and investors. The multitude and complexity of soft power tools that rivals utilize in the region to gain competitive advantage are clearly expanding, as is the attractiveness of their model to other hydrocarbon-rich states in the Gulf.

Conclusion

This chapter discussed ideas of soft power and legitimacy by reflecting on religion and sports as mechanisms of attraction, branding, and ideational political influence. In doing so, it drew attention to the multitude of ways and means that shape the political permeability of states in the contemporary Middle East. Notwithstanding the diversity of the specific scope of each section, both studies revealed how the Middle East is connected through social, political, and cultural linkages. They illustrated how struggles across the region can take different shapes depending on their nature and the targeted audience. In the first case, religion is often the variable that Saudi Arabia and Iran are utilizing to win the minds and hearts of Muslims, not only in the region but across the globe. By providing two distinctive visions of Islam, which are mostly politicized, both countries contested the role of the leadership of the 'Ummah.' The normative aspect of the first case is apparent as it studies a cultural/religious cleavage issue.

The second case presented a modern/globalized way of competing by politizing sports and turning it into a device of attraction and nation branding. The rivalry between the UAE and Qatar is exceptionally prominent around the Middle East, especially after the Arab Uprisings. However, the deployment of sports as a political tool of influence goes beyond cultural aspects such as language, race, and religion. Hence, the struggle between the UAE and Qatar takes on a global and multilevel form. Moreover, as the rivalry between Saudi Arabia and Iran also confirms, the motives behind the contest between the UAE and Qatar are domestically and regionally driven. What both cases show is the need to appeal to broader audiences beyond domestic populations in an effort to reposition political projects within regional and international contexts. Here, a range of factors emerge, a number of which are beyond the scope of this chapter, notably the 'opening up' of states to broader comments about human rights, legal systems, and the treatment of migrant workers. Yet what both cases have shown is that states across the Gulf have sought to draw on a range of different mechanisms through which to increase their power and influence, based on both tradition and modernity, which, over time, may also lead to a range of other challenges.

Notes

1. Joseph S. Nye Jr., *Soft Power: The Means to Success in World Politics* (New York: PublicAffairs, 2005).
2. Ali Khamenei, "Imam Khamenei's Hajj Message—2016," http://english .khamenei.ir/news/4121/Hajj-hijacked-by-oppressors-Muslims-should -reconsider-management.
3. Lawrence Rubin, "Ideational Projection after the Iranian Revolution," in *Islam in the Balance: Ideational Threats in Arab Politics* (Stanford: Stanford Security Studies, 2014), 52.
4. Hooshang Amirahmadi and Nader Entessar, eds., "Iran-Arab Relations in Transition," in *Iran and the Arab World* (Basingstoke: Macmillan, 1993), 3.
5. "Excerpts from Khomeini Speeches," *New York Times*, August 4, 1987, www .nytimes.com/1987/08/04/world/excerpts-from-khomeini-speeches.html.
6. Anoushiravan Ehteshami, "The Foreign Policy of Iran," in *The Middle East in the International System*, ed. Raymond Hinnebusch and Anoushiravan Ehteshami (London: Lynne Reiner, 2002), 284.
7. "Excerpts from Khomeini Speeches," *New York Times*, August 4, 1987.
8. Con Coughlin, "The Global Brand," in *Khomeini's Ghost* (London: Macmillan, 2009), 274.
9. "Excerpts from Khomeini Speeches," *New York Times*, August 4, 1987.
10. Jacob Goldberg, "The Saudi Arabian Kingdom," in *Middle East Contemporary Survey Volume XI: 1987*, ed. Itamar Rabinovich and Haim Shaked (Boulder, CO: Westview, 1987), 589.
11. Simon Mabon, *Houses Built on Sand: Violence, Sectarianism and Revolution in the Middle East* (Manchester: Manchester University Press, 2020).
12. Simon Mabon, "The End of the Battle for Bahrain and the Securitization of Bahraini Shi'a," *Middle East Journal* 73, no. 1 (2019): 29–50.
13. Paul Noble, "The Arab System: Pressures, Constraints, and Opportunities," in *The Foreign Policies of Arab States*, ed. Bahgat Korany and Ali E. Hillal Dessouki (Boulder, CO: Westview, 1991), 57.
14. Stuart Murray, "Moving beyond the Ping-Pong Table: Sports Diplomacy in the Modern Diplomatic Environment," *Public Diplomacy Magazine* (Winter 2013): 11–38.
15. Jonathan Grix and Barrie Houlihan, "Sports Mega-Events as Part of a

Nation's Soft Power Strategy: The Cases of Germany (2006) and the UK (2012)," *British Journal of Politics and International Relations* 16, no. 4 (2014): 573–596; Michael Attali, "The 2006 Asian Games: Self-Affirmation and Soft Power," *Leisure Studies* 35, no. 4 (2016): 470–486.

16. Cornelia Zeineddine, "Employing Nation Branding in the Middle East-United Arab Emirates (UAE) and Qatar," *Management & Marketing: Challenges for the Knowledge Society* 12, no. 2 (2017): 208–221; John. S. Krzyzaniak, "The Soft Power Strategy of Soccer Sponsorships," *Soccer & Society* 19, no. 4 (2018): 498–515.

17. FIFA, "2018 FIFA World Cup Russia TM Global Broadcast and Audience Summary," 2018, https://resources.fifa.com/image/upload/2018-fifa-world -cup-russia-global-broadcast-and-audience-executive-summary.pdf?cloudi d=njqsntrvdvqv8ho1dag5.

18. In the case of Qatar and the UAE, they have successfully combined elements of soft and hard power development. See Robert Mason, "Breaking the Mold of Small State Classification? The Broadening Influence of United Arab Emirates Foreign Policy through Effective Military and Bandwagoning Strategies," *Canadian Foreign Policy Journal* 24, no. 1 (2018): 95–112.

19. Mahfoud Amara and Borja Garcia-Garcia, "Media Perceptions of Arab Investment in European Football Clubs: The Case of Málaga and Paris Saint-Germain," *Sport & EU Review* 5, no. 1 (2013): 5–20.

20. Turki Alalshikh, June 15, 2018, https://twitter.com/Turki_alalshikh/ status/1007489251641122816?ref_src=twsrc%5Etfw%7Ctwcamp%5 Etweetembed%7Ctwterm%5E1007489251641122816&ref_url=https%3A %2F%2Fwww.thenational.ae%2Fuae%2Fsaudi-considering-legal-action -against-bein-sports-for-politicising-wo.

21. Nick Friend, "'Fifa World Cup Piracy Led by Social Media' Says Report," *SportsPro*, September 10, 2018, http://www.sportspromedia.com/news/ fifa-world-cup-piracy-russia-social-media.

22. Murad Ahmed and Ahmed Al Omran, "Pirated TV Sport Emerges as New Gulf Battleground," *Financial Times*, October 1, 2018, https://www.ft.com/ content/970fc542-c173-11e8-95b1-d36dfef1b89a.

23. Tsahi Hayat, Tal Samuel-Azran, and Yair Galily, "Al-Jazeera Sport's US Twitter Followers: Sport-Politics Nexus," *Online Information Review* 40, no. 6 (2016): 785–797.

24. Khalid Basyuni, "One Broadcaster's Dominance Is Becoming a Football Fan's Dilemma," October 14, 2018, https://www.thenational.ae/business/ comment/one-broadcaster-s-dominance-is-becoming-a-football-fan-s -dilemma-1.780196.

25. The National Staff, "Abu Dhabi Named Second Best City to Live and Work In," July 16, 2017, https://www.thenational.ae/uae/abu-dhabi-named-second-best-city-to-live-and-work-in-1.609267.

26. Narayan Prabhu B. M. and Karan Subramanian, "The Impact of Sports Tourism on the UAE—a Case of the Indian Premier League (IPL)," *African Journal of Hospitality, Tourism and Leisure* 4, no. 1 (2015): 1–8.

27. Mehran Kamrava, "Royal Factionalism and Political Liberalization in Qatar," *Middle East Journal* 63, no. 3 (Summer 2009): 401–420.

28. Qatar Foundation, "About Qatar Foundation," http://www.qf.org.qa/about/about.

29. Qatar Olympic Committee, "Sports Sector Strategy (2011–2016)," Doha, Qatar, July 2011, retrieved from Aspire: http://www.aspire.qa/Documents/sports_sector_strategy_final%20-%20English.pdf.

30. Paul M. Brannagan and Richard Giulianotti, "Qatar, Global Sport, and the 2022 FIFA World Cup," in *Leveraging Legacies from Sports Mega-Events*, ed. J. Girx (New York: Palgrave, 2014), 156–165.

31. Aspire Academy, "Who We Are," http://www.aspire.qa/Aboutus/WhoWeAre/Pages/WhoWeAre.aspx.

32. BBC, "Fifa World Cup 2022: Qatar Failing Migrants—Amnesty International," November 12, 2014, https://www.bbc.com/news/world-middle-east-30016202.

33. Human Rights Watch, "Qatar: Abuse of Migrant Workers," 2015, https://www.hrw.org/node/109777.

34. Owen Gibson and Pete Pattisson, "Death Toll among Qatar's 2022 World Cup Workers Revealed," *Guardian*, December 23, 2014, http://www.theguardian.com/world/2014/dec/23/qatar-nepal-workers-world-cup-2022-death-toll-doha.

35. QSI, "Paris Saint-Germain Football Club," https://www.qsi.com.qa/investments/paris-saint-germain/.

36. Jack Kenmare, "PSG Have Spent €1.17Billion on Players and Still Haven't Got Past Champions League QF's," March 7, 2019, retrieved from Sport Bible: https://www.sportbible.com/football/news-reactions-take-a-bow-psg-have-spent-117billion-on-players-and-still-havent-past-ucl-qfs-20190307.

37. City Football Group, "Our Story," https://www.cityfootballgroup.com/our-story/.

38. Adam Craig, "Khaldoon Al Mubarak Exclusive: What Next for Man City?," *Sky Sports*, November 27, 2019, https://www.skysports.com/football/news/11679/11870920/khaldoon-al-mubarak-exclusive-what-next-for-man-city.

Bibliography

Ahmed, Murad, and Ahmed Al Omran. "Pirated TV Sport Emerges as New Gulf Battleground." *Financial Times*, October 1, 2018. https://www.ft.com/content/970fc542-c173-11e8-95b1-d36dfef1b89a.

Alalshikh, Turki. June 15, 2018. https://twitter.com/Turki_alalshikh/status/1007489251641122816?ref_src=twsrc%5Etfw%7Ctwcamp%5Etweet embed%7Ctwterm%5E1007489251641122816&ref_url=https%3A%2F%2Fwww.thenational.ae%2Fuae%2Fsaudi-considering-legal-action-against-bein-sports-for-politicising-wo.

Amara, Mahfoud, and Borja Garcia-Garcia. "Media Perceptions of Arab Investment in European Football Clubs: The Case of Málaga and Paris Saint-Germain." *Sport & EU Review* 5, no. 1 (2013): 5–20.

Amirahmadi, Hooshang, and Nader Entessar, eds. *Iran and the Arab World*. Basingstoke: Macmillan, 1993.

Aspire Academy. "About Us." https://www.aspire.qa/aboutus.aspx.

———. "Who We Are." http://www.aspire.qa/Aboutus/WhoWeAre/Pages/WhoWeAre.aspx.

Attali, Michael. "The 2006 Asian Games: Self-Affirmation and Soft Power." *Leisure Studies* 35, no. 4 (2016): 470–486.

Basyuni, Khalid. "One Broadcaster's Dominance Is Becoming a Football Fan's Dilemma." October 14, 2018. https://www.thenational.ae/business/comment/one-broadcaster-s-dominance-is-becoming-a-football-fan-s-dilemma-1.780196.

BBC. "Fifa World Cup 2022: Qatar Failing Migrants—Amnesty International." November 12, 2014. https://www.bbc.com/news/world-middle-east-30016202.

Brannagan, Paul M., and Richard Giulianotti. "Soft Power and Soft Disempowerment: Qatar, Global Sport and Football's 2022 World Cup Finals." *Leisure Studies* 34, no. 6 (2014): 703–719.

———. "Qatar, Global Sport, and the 2022 FIFA World Cup." In *Leveraging Legacies from Sports Mega-Events*, edited by J. Girx, 156–165. New York: Palgrave, 2014.

City Football Group. "Our Story." https://www.cityfootballgroup.com/our-story/.

Craig, Adam. "Khaldoon Al Mubarak Exclusive: What Next for Man City?" *Sky Sports*, November 27, 2019. https://www.skysports.com/football/news/11679/11870920/khaldoon-al-mubarak-exclusive-what-next-for-man-city.

Energy Information Administration. *Qata: Analysis: Overview*, January 30, 2014. https://www.eia.gov/beta/international/analysis.php?iso=QAT.

FIFA. "2018 FIFA World Cup Russia TM Global Broadcast and Audience

Summary." 2018. https://resources.fifa.com/image/upload/2018-fifa-world
-cup-russia-global-broadcast-and-audience-executive-summary.pdf?cloudid=
njqsntrvdvqv8ho1dag5.

Friend, Nick. "'Fifa World Cup Piracy Led by Social Media' Says Report." *SportsPro*, September 10, 2018. http://www.sportspromedia.com/news/ fifa-world-cup-piracy-russia-social-media.

Gibson, Owen, and Pete Pattisson. "Death Toll among Qatar's 2022 World Cup Workers Revealed." *Guardian*, December 23, 2014. http://www.theguardian .com/world/2014/dec/23/qatar-nepal-workers-world-cup-2022-death-toll -doha.

Grix, Jonathan, and Barrie Houlihan. "Sports Mega-Events as Part of a Nation's Soft Power Strategy: The Cases of Germany (2006) and the UK (2012)." *British Journal of Politics and International Relations* 16, no. 4 (2013): 572–596.

Hayat, Tsahi, Tal Samuel-Azran, and Yair Galily. "Al-Jazeera Sport's US Twitter Followers: Sport-Politics Nexus." *Online Information Review* 40, no. 6 (2016): 785–797.

Human Rights Watch. "Qatar: Abuse of Migrant Workers." 2015. https://www .hrw.org/node/109777.

International Monetary Fund. "Data and Statistics." 2014. http://www.imf.org/ external/pubs/ft/weo/2015/01/weodata/weorept.aspx?sy=2014&ey=2014&s sd=1&sort=country&ds=.&br=1&pr1.x=16&pr1.y=7&c=512%2C668%2C9 14%2C672%2C612%2C946%2C614%2C137%2C311%2C962%2C213% 2C674%2C911%2C676%2C193%2C548%2C122%2C556%2C912%2C6 78%2C31.

Kamrava, Mehran. "Royal Factionalism and Political Liberalization in Qatar." *Middle East Journal*, 63, no. 3 (Summer 2009): 401–420.

KantarSport. *2010 FIFA WORLD CUP SOUTH AFRICA: Television Audience Report.* 2010. http://www.fifa.com/mm/document/affederation/tv/01/47/32/7 3/2010fifaworldcupsouthafricatvaudiencereport.pdf.

Kelleher, M. "PSG and Man City Accused of 'Financial Doping' by La Liga President Javier Tebas." 2017. https://www.skysports.com/football/news/ 11095/11023034/psg-and-man-city-accused-of-financial-doping-by-la -liga-president-javier-tebas.

Kenmare, Jack. "PSG Have Spent €1.17Billion on Players and Still Haven't Got Past Champions League QF's." March 7, 2019. https://www.sportbible .com/football/news-reactions-take-a-bow-psg-have-spent-117billion-on -players-and-still-havent-past-ucl-qfs-20190307.

Khamenei, Ali. "Imam Khamenei's Hajj Message—2016." http://english .khamenei.ir/news/4121/Hajj-hijacked-by-oppressors-Muslims-should -reconsider-management.

Krauss, Werner. "Football, Nation and Identity: German Miracles in the

Post-War Era." In *Sport, Dance and Embodied Identities*, edited by N. Dyck and E. Archetti, 197–216. New York: Oxford, 2003.

Krzyzaniak, John. S. "The Soft Power Strategy of Soccer Sponsorships." *Soccer & Society* 19, no. 4 (2018): 498–515.

Mason, Robert. "Breaking the Mold of Small State Classification? The Broadening Influence of United Arab Emirates Foreign Policy through Effective Military and Bandwagoning Strategies." *Canadian Foreign Policy Journal* 24, no. 1 (2018): 95–112.

———. "The End of the Battle for Bahrain and the Securitization of Bahraini Shi'a." *Middle East Journal* 73, no. 1 (2019): 29–50.

———. *Houses Built on Sand: Violence, Sectarianism and Revolution in the Middle East*. Manchester: Manchester University Press, 2020.

Murray, Stuart. "Moving beyond the Ping-Pong Table: Sports Diplomacy in the Modern Diplomatic Environment." *Public Diplomacy Magazine* (Winter 2013): 11–38.

Noble, Paul. "The Arab System: Pressures, Constraints, and Opportunities." In *The Foreign Policies of Arab States*, edited by Bahgat Korany and Ali E. Hillal Dessouki, 57. Boulder, CO: Westview, 1991.

Prabhu B. M., Narayan, and Karan Subramanian. "The Impact of Sports Tourism on the UAE—a Case of the Indian Premier League (IPL)." *African Journal of Hospitality, Tourism and Leisure* 4, no. 1 (2015): 1–8.

Qatar Foundation. "About Qatar Foundation." http://www.qf.org.qa/about/about.

Qatar General Secretariat for Development Planning. *Qatar National Development Strategy 2011–2016*. Doha, Qatar, 2011.

Qatar Olympic Committee. "Sports Sector Strategy (2011–2016)." Doha, Qatar, July 2011. http://www.aspire.qa/Documents/sports_sector_strategy_final%20-%20English.pdf.

QSI. "Paris Saint-Germain Football Club." https://www.qsi.com.qa/investments/paris-saint-germain/.

Rubin, Lawrence. *Islam in the Balance: Ideational Threats in Arab Politics*. Stanford: Stanford Security Studies, 2014.

Silver Lake. "Overview." 2019. https://www.silverlake.com.

The National. "Abu Dhabi Named Second Best City to Live and Work In." July 16, 2017. https://www.thenational.ae/uae/abu-dhabi-named-second-best-city-to-live-and-work-in-1.609267.

"Excerpts from Khomeini Speeches." *New York Times*, August 4, 1987. www.nytimes.com/1987/08/04/world/excerpts-from-khomeini-speeches.html.

World Bank. "Public Data: Gross Domestic Product." April 17, 2015. https://

www.google.com/publicdata/explore?ds=d5bncppjof8f9_&met_y=ny
_gdp_mktp_cd&idim=country:QAT:ARE:KWT&hl=en&dl=en.

Zeineddine, Cornelia. "Employing Nation Branding in the Middle East-United
Arab Emirates (UAE) and Qatar." *Management & Marketing. Challenges for
the Knowledge Society* 12, no. 2 (2017): 208–221.

4

The Regionalization and Internationalization of Conflict

Robert Mason and Neil Partrick

Introduction

This chapter analyzes how regional and foreign intervention has created or exacerbated civil conflicts in the Middle East and North Africa, especially in the wake of the Arab Uprisings from 2011 onward. It shows how there is often little or no boundary between civil wars stemming from political repression and/or escalating intercommunal violence and foreign intervention. These foreign interventions have been conducted through unilateral or multilateral mechanisms, directly through state and/or state-affiliated commercial and military entities or indirectly through national or local proxy actors. The consequences of regionalization and/or internationalization of a conflict can lead to spillover effects, either for the states concerned or for neighboring states to the conflict.

This has clearly been evident in the Syria conflict and the instabilities brought about by arms transfers, military strikes, terrorism, and refugees, especially in Lebanon, Jordan, and Turkey. The conceptual frameworks associated with this chapter include regionalism, the regionalization or internationalization of conflict, transnationalism, security complexes advanced by Barry Buzan,[1] and other studies that deal with conflict spillover.[2] There is also a growing literature covering the many cases of foreign interference and proxy wars throughout history, including where the United States and emerging challengers are not able or willing to intervene directly or disengage in an overt manner.[3]

The chapter assesses how these conflicts are playing out and how temporary partnerships or longer-term alliances have been built between various local, national, and global actors according to specific national security and regional interests or objectives. It takes into consideration four case studies. First, Iraq, which in 2003 was set to become a staging post for US-led military intervention in the Middle East. The US and UK governments at the time put forward a mutable justification—from Saddam Hussein's supposed links to al-Qaeda, to the Iraqi government allegedly developing weapons of mass destruction (WMDs), and, later, to Iraq's human rights record. There was also a belief in the US administration that democracy was inevitable in Iraq and, therefore, that it may hold out hope for other nations in the Middle East. This has not been the case so far. After the drawdown of US forces, Iran has been the main beneficiary as Iraqi state politics continues to be driven by sectarian conflict and calculations, especially as happened during the Nouri al-Maliki administration from 2006 to 2014. Besides this, Iraqi politics remains dominated by other factors such as internally displaced people (IDP) and a diminished capacity to govern. The picture has been complicated by related factors such as the rise of ISIS and a three-year campaign to drive it out of Iraqi territory (2014–2017) and the vote for Kurdish statehood in September 2017.

Second, Libya, which is included because it experienced its first civil war following NATO-led intervention and the demise of Colonel Muammar Gaddafi. This has led to a political and security contest between the Libyan National Army (LNA) and militia forces led by Field Marshal Khalifa Haftar, supported by some members of the international community who are willing to break the UN arms embargo, and the UN-recognized Government of National Accord based in Tripoli. The inability of either side thus far to establish enhanced measures of national security has led to even broader consequences, from the rise of the Islamic State (IS) in North Africa to the north Libyan coast becoming a major departure point for refugees traversing the Mediterranean, often facilitated by local people traffickers.

Third, Syria, which, under the presidency of Bashar al-Assad, quickly deteriorated from peaceful protests to brutal government crackdown followed by regional and international involvement, notably from Iran, as well as Russia and Israel. The Syrian case is an important study due to the general ambivalence of the international community, especially the United Kingdom and the United States, in not establishing a no-fly zone or aerial supremacy, thereby allowing Russia a gateway into Syria and the wider Levant in 2015. The diverse interests of the external actors involved have only exacerbated and escalated the conflict, primarily by weakening opposition forces on the ground, especially the Free Syrian Army (FSA) in the early stages of the uprising.

Fourth, Yemen, which has a well-documented history of disunity and southern secession. After President Saleh resigned in 2011 and his former deputy Mansour Hadi took power in February 2012, Yemen appeared to be on a path of controlled transition. However, the territorial expansion of the Houthis from the northern mountains to the capital, Sana'a, in 2014 sparked a Saudi-led military intervention that, as of early 2020, still had not ended. The Yemeni conflict again illustrates the role of regional and international powers. In addition, it highlights the part played by the nonexecutive branches of government and nonstate actors in the United States and Europe, who have been able to effect significant, albeit perhaps only temporary, change in government policy concerning arms supplies to actors in this conflict.

Iraq

In the lead-up to the 2003 Iraq War there was much debate and protest, particularly among Western nations and in the Middle East too, about the legality of the war and the consequences of military intervention, while a strong antiwar coalition was formed but did not ultimately coalesce to stop the intervention. France, Russia, China, and Germany opposed the invasion. US secretary of state Colin Powell responded with a dossier about supposed WMDs in Iraq, which increased support for the US position in the UN Security Council when it was presented on February 5, 2003.

There are multiple questions about the 2003 Iraq War in terms of the internationalization of conflict. First, whether it had a permanent effect in creating divisions in the 'international community'. Scholars such as Buzan and Gonzalez-Pelaez suggest this is not the case.[4] Second, whether Iraq has had any agency in its external affairs since the intervention. This includes domestic complications arising from security challenges such as al-Qaeda and ISIS and social and ethnic cohesion up to and beyond the Kurdish vote for independence. Third, what have been the spillover effects from the conflict, and what are the longer-term prospects for Iraqi and neighborhood security?

The US-led intervention and occupation of Iraq began on March 20, 2003, based on dubious evidence concerning WMDs in Iraq with additional aims to rid Iraq of Saddam Hussein and expand the otherwise limited practice of democracy in the region. Paul Bremer, who headed the Coalition Provisional Authority, disbanded the Iraqi army and sent hundreds of thousands of well-armed men into the streets. He also purged Ba'athists from the government, a policy that was partially reversed in 2008. The intervention soon faced armed Shia Iraqi resistance, and in 2004 al-Qaeda mounted a wave of suicide bombings. The United States lost the moral high ground with evidence of torture inside Abu Ghraib prison. After the battle for Fallujah rooted out twelve hundred insurgents in September 2004, there were signs of democracy in the fact that an open parliamentary election was conducted in 2005. However, following Shiite control of parliament, Sunni Arab extremists attacked the gilded shrine in Samarra and Iraq descended into sectarian conflict. This was not helped by the early US effort to dismantle the Iraqi state apparatus and support an Iraqi constitution that embodied sectarian division: the presidency for the Kurds, the premiership for the Shia, and the vice presidency and parliament Speaker post for the Sunni Arabs. The human cost of the conflict has been immense although no reliable figures exist. Estimates put civilian deaths during this period at between one thousand and thirty-five hundred per month.[5]

In 2007 the G. W. Bush administration announced that General Petraeus would take command and implement a surge in an attempt to bring stability to Baghdad. There were allegations that Iran was supplying Iraqi Shia militants with roadside bombs to attack coalition forces.[6] General Petraeus went on to work with Sunni Arab tribal members through Awakening Councils to fight militants associated with al-Qaeda in Anbar province. The United Kingdom withdrew from Basra in 2007, and although Iraqi security forces filled the void, the city was still overrun with militants and criminal gangs. Forces loyal to Muqtada al-Sadr, a Shiite Muslim cleric, attacked US and Iraqi security forces in Baghdad and Basra in 2008. After the Status of Forces Agreement (SOFA) was agreed on by President G. W. Bush and Prime Minister Nouri al-Maliki, and approved by the Iraqi parliament in November 2008, drawdown of US forces in Iraq began in 2009 with combat operations terminated in 2010. The last uniformed US troops left Iraq in 2011. However, the re-election of Nouri al-Maliki, supported by Iranian Ayatollah Khamenei, did little to quell the situation. Al-Maliki went after Sunni Arab political leader Tariq al-Hashemi with an arrest warrant for allegedly plotting to kill prominent Shiites after he and the Iraqiyya party garnered more votes in the 2010 election.[7]

By 2010, many in the United States and Iraq believed that the SOFA should be extended to enhance security and signal a stronger US intention toward Iraq's neighbor, that is, Iran. The anti-American Muqtada al-Sadr faction in the Iraqi parliament refused to sign an extension amounting to five thousand US troops. Thus, while the troop withdrawal allowed President Obama to keep one of his campaign promises, their removal did nothing to maintain stability. There will always be questions whether five thousand US military 'advisers' could have prevented ISIS from growing and spreading in Iraq, but it could have improved intelligence gathering. Had the United States responded sooner and more robustly, it could have made a difference. Instead, Prime Minister Haider al-Abadi had ISIS rooted from Iraqi territory in 2017, signifying a fresh start and possibility to move on from a sectarian conflict. The remaining issues between Iraq and the United States continue to be around some of the militia that appear to operate with the Iraqi government's blessing and the lack of Sunni representation in government.[8]

After the US withdrawal, the Sunni provinces of Anbar, Diyala, Mosul, and Salahuddin asked for federalism. US-backed Iraqi government forces, Iran-backed paramilitaries, and Kurdish fighters fought alongside each other to defeat ISIS, but now that the threat has diminished, so too has the makeshift alliance. On September 25, 2017, the Kurdistan Regional Government in Erbil held an independence referendum in which 92.7 percent of more than three million voters favored secession from Iraq. The Kurdish leader Masoud Barzani was forced to quit after the vote triggered military and economic retaliation from the Iraqi central government, including an attack on Kirkuk. The referendum also facilitated a regional crisis, including rhetorical threats and military drills from Turkey and Iran, which have their own Kurdish populations and worry that the Kurdish vote in Iraq could set a precedent.

After many years of unprecedented Iranian influence in Iraq, Saudi Arabia stepped into the fold by opening a new consulate in Baghdad for thirty years and providing economic incentives, including a $500 million loan to Iraq to boost exports and $1 billion in real estate and development projects, in order to cooperate more fully with the government in Baghdad.[9] Mindful of Iranian and ISIS expansionism throughout the region following the 2003 Iraq War and the 2011 Arab Uprisings, particularly in Syria, Saudi Arabia has showed increasing pragmatism and flexibility. It has sought to limit pro-Iranian groups in Iraq by exploiting the growing intra-Shia rift and to strengthen trade with Iraq, which has until recently been dominated by Iran and Turkey. The potential to keep Iraq on course to develop is present, but sectarian violence is still common, state capacity limited, and the legacy of war and insurgency still apparent. A continued lack of clean water and electricity and persistent unemployment culminated in protests throughout 2018 and 2019, often by youngsters who were born after the Saddam Hussein era. While the Iraqi government assured the international community that lethal force would not be used against the protestors, that appears not to have been the case, and there have been multiple attacks on protestors linked to Iraqi security forces or the Iranian Quds Force operating in Iraq.

As tensions rose in the Gulf, President Trump ordered the partial evacuation of the US embassy in Baghdad in May 2019. Iranian activity was stepped up and Shia militias allegedly once again had US personnel in their sights. On August 20, 2019, Israel attacked Iranian targets inside Iraq: supposedly Iranian missile shipments and guidance systems for use against Israel. Alongside similar attacks on targets in Syria and against Hezbollah in Lebanon, the threats are broadening out across the region in places such as Iraq where the Quds Force has access. The Israeli strike in Iraq was reminiscent of the 1981 air strike on the Osirak nuclear reactor in Iraq, applying the 'Begin Doctrine': the Israeli government's counter-proliferation policy of eliminating a potential enemy's capacity to possess WMDs.

The belt of instability from unresolved conflicts and sectarian politics in Syria, Iraq, and down to Bahrain requires a new diplomatic effort. Iraq is still perceived by many in the Gulf as an unreliable ally due to the Iran-Iraq War in the 1980s and Saddam Hussein's invasion of Kuwait in 1990. As many diplomats and analysts have suggested, one way to address this and other issues is through a Conference and Organization for Security and Cooperation in the Gulf and Middle East, involving Iran, Iraq, Turkey, the Gulf Cooperation Council (GCC) states, the United States, and the United Nations.[10] This would at least bring the contentious and relevant parties together to negotiate on areas related to vital national and regional security concerns. Ideally, it would prove comprehensive enough to begin to unravel the Gordian knot of social, religious, political, security, and economic issues that have accumulated over time to create an environment of persistent insecurity and vulnerability to penetration by subnational, pan-regional, and international interests.

If past spoilers such as Muqtada al-Sadr can push for pragmatic solutions, including ending sectarian violence and supporting reconstruction and security sector reform along national lines through the Sadrist social base in slums of Baghdad, the city of Kufa, and the governorate of Maysan, then the future for Iraq looks much better than it did in the first decade of this century. In spite of his criticism of Iran's regional policies, his appearance with Iranian supreme leader Ali Khamenei and Quds commander Qasem Soleimani at a religious assembly in September 2019 indicates that his allegiance is still with Iran versus the wider Arab world, including Saudi Arabia.

Libya
When thinking about regionalization and internationalization of conflict concerning Libya, one may quickly jump to the failure of the Libyan rentier state to provide full employment, the underdevelopment of Cyrenaica

in the east of the country, or the effect of the wider Arab Uprisings in 2011.[11] However, this section argues that the reasons are broader, beginning with Muammar Gaddafi's 'revolutionary' foreign policies since 1969, which were interventionist in the region and internationally, especially against political dissidents, covering a period right up to the mid-1980s.

Pursuing a pan-Arab agenda similar to that of Egyptian president Gamal Abdel Nasser, Gaddafi attempted but failed to merge Libya with Egypt and Syria through a Federation of Arab Republics (FAR) in 1971. As early as 1974, Egypt was contemplating war with Libya due to the combination of reasons: Libyan hostility toward Egypt over President Sadat's peace policy with Israel, Libya possibly funding the Muslim Brotherhood's (MB) military wing in Egypt to stage attacks, and regular expulsions of Egyptian laborers from Libya. During this time, amid growing US influence in the region, Gaddafi brought in Soviet expertise to develop missile bases in Libya. In July 1977, a short border war erupted between Libya and Egypt after which both parties agreed to a ceasefire.

Gaddafi openly supported rebel movements such as Nelson Mandela's African National Congress, the Popular Front for the Liberation of Palestine (the second largest group forming the Palestine Liberation Organization), and the Polisario Front (Western Sahara). More troubling to many states in the international community was his support for terror groups such as the IRA (including large-scale small arms, ammunition, and explosives smuggling) in Ireland, Red Army Faction (Baader-Meinhof gang) in West Germany, ETA in Spain, and Farc in Colombia. Libya conducted sporadic military operations against Chad on four occasions in the 1970s, occupying the Aozou Strip on the border between Chad and Libya in 1973 until 1994, and during Chad's civil war in the 1980s.

Libyan foreign policy became even more confrontational from the mid-1970s onward, including OPEC oil ministers being taken hostage by Ilich Ramirez Sanchez, 'Carlos the Jackal,' at the 1975 meeting in Vienna. Gaddafi's personal pilot, Neville Atkinson, flew Carlos, four other hijackers, and hostages from Algiers to Mogadishu and then on to Baghdad.[12] Gaddafi also implemented operational and intelligence activities against Libyan dissidents living in the West. The first to be shot was Muhammad Ramadan outside Regent's Park Mosque in April 1980.[13] Throughout 1980 and 1984, they served as a warning to dissidents to cease their opposition and return to Libya. In April 1984, an unknown gunman shot dead British police officer Yvonne Fletcher from the Libyan embassy on St. James's Square. In 1986, Libya was implicated in the bombing of a Berlin disco that killed two US soldiers. Libya was then implicated through an intelligence investigation in the most deadly act of terrorism in the United Kingdom so far. In 1988, Pan Am flight 103 from Frankfurt to Detroit was brought down over Lockerbie, Scotland, by a bomb. This may have been a response to the United States having shot down two Libyan fighters that challenged its warplanes over the Gulf of Sirte in 1981, or the US bombing of Libyan military facilities in 1986 that was itself a response to alleged Libyan involvement in the Berlin disco bombing. The Lockerbie bombing killed 243 passengers, 16 crew, and 11 people on the ground. Libya remained a pariah state, and in 1992 UN sanctions were enforced against it until it handed over two suspects to face trial in 1999. Abdelbaset Ali Mohmed al-Megrahi, an alleged Libyan intelligence officer, was convicted but released in 2009 on compassionate grounds. He traveled back to Libya and died in 2012. In 1989, perhaps to break its international isolation, Libya, along with Algeria, Morocco, and Tunisia, formed the Arab Maghreb Union. The same year, Libyan agents were allegedly responsible for another terror attack when UTA flight 772 from Congo to Paris crashed in the Ténéré desert in Niger. The attack killed 156 passengers and 14 crew.

In 2002 Libya and the United States held talks to mend relations (they reestablished diplomatic relations in 2006). In 2003, the UN Security Council voted to lift sanctions, and Libya agreed to abandon its WMDs and compensate families of the victims of the Lockerbie bombing. The United States, the United Kingdom, Italy, and Russia all became major trading partners with Libya. In 2008, Vladimir Putin, then Russian prime minister, signed deals with Libya worth between $5 and $10 billion, including for arms, the provision of a high-speed railway line between Sirte and Benghazi worth $2.2 billion, and oil and gas exploration, while Russia dropped $4.5 billion in Libyan-Soviet debt.[14] Trade and investment has been buttressed by Russian mercenaries engaging through private military contractors, such as the Wagner Group, to support Haftar and Russian interests in Libya, as they have in Syria and other parts of Africa.[15] Russia did not veto UN Security Council Resolution 1973, which was the legal basis for NATO intervention, nor did it see this military intervention as explicitly legitimized or warranted. Moscow would respond to Western encroachment of its economic and strategic interests through a more assertive policy in Ukraine and Syria. Russian-NATO relations were already strained by the eastward NATO enlargement that helped spark the Russia-Georgia War in 2008.

The political economy and economic gains to be had in Libya, especially in its oil industry, which is expected to double capacity from 2019 to 2023, and in its infrastructure, have become increasingly entangled with state support for different factions. France, Russia, the UAE, Saudi

Arabia, and Egypt support Khalifa Haftar, who heads the LNA and who at the time of writing had attempted but failed to seize power from the UN-recognized Government of National Accord (GNA), which is supported by Italy, Turkey, and Qatar. In fact, Turkey appears to be using Libya as part of a new foreign policy strategy to increase its presence in the MENA region by combining actions in Syria, Libya, and a new naval and air base in northern Cyprus.[16] Turkey, which claims over 44 percent of Cyprus's Exclusive Economic Zone, used a drone in December 2019 to support two drill ships and a warship already in disputed Cypriot waters prospecting for oil and gas.[17] Russia has been both providing military contractors in support of the LNA activities, using its diplomatic clout in the UN Security Council to block criticism of it, and engaging with the GNA simultaneously. China meanwhile had a policy of nonalignment and pragmatic engagement with the Libyan energy sector. Such external rivalry made peaceful solutions more difficult to achieve.[18]

The international response to the Libyan case, and specifically President Sarkozy's demand that Gaddafi face an investigation by the International Criminal Court (ICC), made it impossible for other leaders such as Silvio Berlusconi, prime minister of Italy at the time, to negotiate a solution in favor of the status quo. This was surprising given the improving relations between Libya and the West up to the uprisings and the alleged payments that Gaddafi made to Sarkozy's presidential campaign in 2007.[19] The subsequent NATO intervention was under UN Security Council auspices to safeguard civilians, and the application of the 'responsibility to protect' doctrine amounted, in effect, to regime change. Qatar secured the Arab League's approval in support of UN Security Council Resolution (UNSCR) 1973. In Europe, Germany abstained from supporting UNSCR 1973. France was the only state to unilaterally recognize the National Transitional Council (NTC). The only common thread now appears to be in maintaining a deal with Libya on refugees to stem dangerous crossings across the Mediterranean, without much interest in evidence of mistreatment in detention centers and exposure to people traffickers.[20]

Ironically, the NATO intervention contributed to the implosion of the quasi-state apparatus in Libya and the new reliance on local councils and militias based on families, cities, and tribes. Qatar moved quickly to funnel hundreds of millions of dollars through a limited number of Islamists (generally viewed as the most hardened and effective fighters), such as Abdel Hakim Belhaj and cleric Ali Sallabi, who also acts as a guide for the MB in Libya.[21] Abdel Hakim Belhaj and Sami Al-Saadi were leaders of the Libyan Islamic Fighting Group (LIFG), which rejected al-Qaeda's agenda but sought the overthrow of Gaddafi. They, along with their families, were abducted from Bangkok and Hong Kong airports, respectively, and rendered back to Libya where they were interrogated and tortured in March 2004. Their rendition involved the MI6 and the CIA at a time when Prime Minister Tony Blair was conducting a rapprochement with Gaddafi. The pair has since sued the British government and pushed the current incarnation of the LIFG toward an anti-Western agenda.[22] Qatar also sent troops to support the rebels in 2011.[23] It was heavily involved in the NATO air campaign in Libya, and its activities on the ground led to Qatar's flag flying above the ruins of Gaddafi's Bab al-Aziziya compound during the political transition.

The NTC under Prime Minister Abdurrahim El-Keib never managed to bring together the militia and local councils or translate the participation of women in the revolution into a more pluralist society. But what became more consequential in post-Gaddafi Libya was the Western Military Council (WMC) dominated by ex-army officers and based in Zintan, and the Misrata Military Council. Ali Zeidan, prime minister from November 2012 to March 2014, also struggled and was eventually ousted by parliament through a no-confidence vote after militia seized the port of al-Sidra and then tried to sell oil to a North Korean flagged tanker that had docked without permission.[24] This led to Field Marshal Haftar suspending parliament in February 2014. He has since set about using his small forces and support from eastern Libya and from former Gaddafi loyalists to consolidate his control over the territory against Islamist fighters. The reintroduction of Gaddafi loyalists is a concern in itself. Meanwhile, Egypt and the UAE have provided Haftar with modern weapons to deal with terrorism and the MB.

Unusually, the United States 'led from behind' on Libya, having been less hesitant to commit to military intervention in Afghanistan and Iraq. The United States has had little political interest in Libya during the Trump administration beyond partisan accusations associated with the death of its ambassador J. Christopher Stevens on September 11, 2012, when the US Special Mission in Benghazi was attacked by violent Islamists. Efforts with the United Kingdom to set up a new government force came to nothing, and so there has been little disarmament, demobilization, and reintegration (DDR) of militia forces into broader society. The NTC has paid the militia without the strength and reliability of a traditional force. The May 2013 Political Isolation Law was also too broad in banning anyone associated with the Gaddafi regime from holding public office, which has further undermined unity.[25]

So far, the international split over how to exert influence on Libyan politics has played into the hands of Field Marshal Haftar and led to the reauthoritarianism of the Libyan political system. An alternative, the rebuilding of a state that never really existed, was highly unlikely. The local identities of Tripolitania, Cyrenaica, and Fezzan remained strong because Gaddafi focused almost exclusively on transnational issues. Keeping groups such as Ansar al-Sharia from expanding into an enlarged national security threat will be paramount. They have been linked to al-Qaeda in the Islamic Maghreb and are dominated by IS advisers and fighters. The victory of the GNA, backed by the United States, against ISIS in Misrata on August 1, 2016, was a step in the right direction.

Colonel Gaddafi's revolutionary politics in Libya led to contentions with Western states such as the United Kingdom and the United States and uneven development in this oil-rich country. The lack of state institutionalization meant that Libya was highly susceptible to collapse following NATO intervention in 2011. This has led to anarchy and conflict involving various militia groups: the Toubou militia on the border with Chad and Niger, the Libyan Dawn militia alliance in the northwest of the country, Ansar al-Sharia in the east, and the Tuareg militia on the border with Algeria. A lack of forward planning by NATO allowed ISIS to form a base in Sirte from 2014 up to its 'defeat' by US and allied MB forces in 2016, but which has since gained from the instabilities created by Haftar's military campaign to take Tripoli. Lawlessness has played into the hands of people smugglers and enabled precarious Mediterranean crossings made by desperate refugees. Similar to Iraq, a lack of coherent post-intervention planning has allowed a security vacuum to develop, a prerequisite for extremists to prosper and proxy warfare to continue. Disagreements over NATO intervention in Libya and the best way to influence facts on the ground have meant that the international response to Libya continues to be characterized by disunity, small state ambition, and hedging.

Syria

Regional and international involvement in Syrian affairs did not begin with the outbreak of the Syrian civil war in 2011. Forced out of the Ottoman Turkish Empire into what passed for an international state system after the First World War, Syria's existence was the product of Franco-British connivance. This was in part a determined Great Power breakup of Arab nationalist aspirations, an ideological factor never since absent from Syrian politics. Britain's direct interest in and manipulation of events in Syria did not end with the League of Nations' blessing for the creation of a French Mandate authority for Syria, the forerunner to modern Syrian statehood. Syria was to be a significant front line between British and

German interests in the Second World War. Vichy France imposed a pro-Nazi regime on French Mandate Syria, while in the immediate aftermath of the war Britain sought to secure a Damascus regime more to its liking. Israel's creation in 1948 led to Syria playing a leading role in the first and in all subsequent Arab-Israeli wars, including the 1967 conflict that led to Israeli occupation of the Golan Heights. In the immediate aftermath of the 1973 war, in which Egyptian and Syrian forces crossed into this and other Israeli-held territory, rival US and Soviet Cold War interests at one point threatened a direct superpower confrontation.

Syria was weak in military, economic, and political terms. A country blessed with ethno-religious diversity, it was a state weakened by communal loyalty that prioritized one community to the detriment of others.[26] From its inception in 1961, Syria's Ba'athist regime trumpeted pan-Arabism, disparaging petit-nationalism as *iqleemi* ('regional' or 'local') in its confinement to colonial-era territorial divisions. However, substate loyalties rendered the Syrian 'nation-state,' like many Arab states, not just impotent but a contradiction in terms.[27]

The Syrian government's crushing of its MB challenge in the early 1980s was in part related to Jordan's use of this Islamist card inside Syria to offset Syrian pressure in Jordan via the Palestinians. The subsequent massacre by the Syrian regime at Hama provided more Islamist exiles for Saudi Arabia's Cold War–related embrace.[28]

Syria's alignment with non-Arab Iran during the 1980s Gulf War broke supposed Arab national norms due to the strong motivator of Syria's national interest. Iran for Syria represented a bulwark against an Iraq preoccupied with events to its east. This was, and is, a pragmatic alliance overlain with a minority Shia Alawi Syrian regime's discomfort with Sunni Arab regimes' dominance in regional affairs.

In response to the Syrian state's internal and external vulnerabilities, the regime has long sought asymmetric weight via proxies: the Palestinians from the late 1960s through to the 1990s; and Kurdish guerrillas, the PKK, as a counterweight to Syria's historic rival and distrusted neighbor Turkey. In 1998, Turkish troops invaded northern Syria in pursuit of its PKK enemies. The resultant Adana Agreement, by which Syria agreed to not allow its territory to host PKK fighters, was cited by President Erdoğan as justifying the de facto buffer zone that Turkish troops created inside northern Syrian in the course of the conflict that began in 2011, a process that seemed to be reaching its apogee with Turkish military's 'clearance' of Syrian Kurds in northeast Syria following the departure of US troops in October 2019.

These regional and international actors have been a direct or indirect party to the Syrian war. However, unlike at the time of Syria's founding and early modern history, Western powers have largely taken a backseat in the contemporary conflict. In the early years of the civil war, the role of the United Kingdom and France was one of diplomatic support for those Syrian rebels professing democratic values, but their military supplies were limited due to an Iraq-War conditioned fear of being drawn in in support of fighters they didn't wholly trust. The United States had a similarly restrained approach, despite President Obama in 2012 infamously declaring a 'redline' against any Syrian regime using chemical weapons and opting to provide modest military training for rebel fighters across the border in neighboring Jordan.

This at least was the case until Syria became a focus of regional and international fear of IS. In 2014, the United States marshaled the United Kingdom, France, and other Western allies in the conduct of air strikes against IS, together with a small but symbolic role for some Saudi and Emirati pilots, and a supposedly reinvigorated US training program was offered to rebel groups from more distant facilities in Saudi Arabia.[29] The US administration's desire was to ensure that the all-important fight against IS on the ground in Syria and Iraq was not left to Iran to mobilize via its Lebanese Shia ally Hezbollah and Iran's own troops, including the Islamic Revolutionary Guards Corps (IRGC) Quds Force, and foreign fighters resident in Iran. This meant that the United States eventually put in two thousand of its troops to work in northeast Syria with a largely Syrian Kurdish group (which also included some Arab members) called the Syrian Democratic Forces (SDF). However, the strategic value of an imploding Syria was viewed very differently by both Presidents Obama and Trump from the Cold War perspective that had driven US calculations in the aftermath of the 1973 war when Secretary of State Kissinger argued that no nuclear armed superpower should deploy troops in the Middle East because of the risk of escalating superpower confrontation.[30]

In contrast, following the rise of IS Syria became an open area for US and Russian intervention. Whereas the US role has largely been confined to its perceived greater interest in countering IS than shaping the Syrian security situation, the fighting capacity of Syrian troops and of Iran-sponsored armed forces, coupled with Russian aerial and ground intervention since 2015, proved decisive in ensuring the maintenance of the Assad regime. In the process, the Russian state secured two things in the Middle East it could never boast of during its much more powerful Soviet incarnation: a naval base and an air base in Tartus and Hmeimem, respectively, both in western Syria. In 1973, the Soviet Union had declined an Iraqi offer of its own naval base at the Iraqi port of Um Qasr, wary of the shallow waters of the northern Gulf and of being politically embroiled in Iraq's provocative territorial incursions into Kuwait.[31]

While Russia and Iran had different attitudes to how imperative the survival of the Bashar al-Assad regime was, both saw their presence in Syria as at least a semipermanent state of affairs. Both can claim that their military involvement was invited by the internationally recognized Syrian regime, and neither is likely to want to give up their strategic footholds there. For Russia, its role in Syria gives it leverage over a range of other regional and international questions such as the conflicts in Libya and Yemen and the dispute over Iran.

Following President Trump's announcement in December 2018 that the United States was withdrawing its troops from Syria, Russia became the United States' and the Gulf Arabs' best hope for constraining both Turkey and Iran from exploiting a resultant vacuum in northeast Syria for their anti-Kurdish and greater regional ambitions and, it was hoped, to counter an Iranian interest in pressuring Israel from southern Syria. The continuation of Israeli military strikes in Syria belied this aspiration, although Israel's actions were often preemptive or simply opportunistic. The problem for Assad's residual regional opponents, and, separately, for hopes for a meaningful, Iraq-style, Kurdish entity serving as a bulwark of Western interests, was that logically this could only mean the Russia-assisted reassertion of Syrian state control in the area. Recognizing this, Syrian Kurds began negotiating with Damascus as soon as President Trump made his comments about withdrawal. The Russia-assisted reassertion of Assad's control was conducted with devastating effect in Idlib, the last major urban territorial holdout against government forces, over the spring and summer of 2019 (following a series of bloody sieges of other major Syrian cities by government forces from the early months of the war onward). The fact that some Russian and Iran-sponsored Syrian allies clashed in the process exemplified the tactical nature of their patrons' alignment and longer-term problems over how these external powers can best manage Syria's internal and external affairs. A similar situation arose from some of Turkey's attacks on Syrian Kurds, which occasionally caused Turkish tensions with Russia when the latter's troops were close to the firing line. However, following US acquiescence in Turkey's military operation in northeast Syria in October 2019, Russia and Turkey conducted joint border patrols. Russian troops also assisted the Assad regime's objective of directly absorbing its lost territory back into Syrian state control. Iran was and continues to be able to use its role in countering IS in Syria and Iraq as an ideational and practical assertion of its credibility among the region's Shia. This gives it kudos in these countries and among other Shia communities in Lebanon and the Gulf.

The de facto spheres of interest in Syria were given shape by the role of regional and international allies of both the regime and its adversaries. US forces were (until their departure or, in some cases, redeployment in October 2019) located on part of Syria's border with Iraq, while Jordan, broadly supported by the United States, the United Kingdom, the Gulf Arab states, and Israel, held sway in parts of the southeast. The additional presence in the southeast of Sunni Arab Syrian fighters, including Islamist rebels that had been supported by the United States, Saudi Arabia, and Qatar, was part of a broader anti-Iranian front. Iran brought fighters and arms across the Iraqi border with Syria and via Damascus airport. With Hezbollah as adept at defending Iranian strategic interests in Syria as in Lebanon, Iran's role in the Syrian civil war was to deploy 'semipermanently' to give it the strategic advantage of direct Mediterranean access. Preemptive Israeli military action, especially after the United States withdrew from the internationally backed Iranian nuclear deal, encouraged Iran to use the Syrian conflict to gain an added pressure point on Israel via the Syrian side of the Golan Heights. In March 2019, President Trump used the weakness of the Assad regime, and consequently the weakness of the Syrian state, to recognize the Golan as sovereign Israeli territory. This was simultaneously testament to both the Trump administration's powerful assertion of an overt alignment with Israel and the relative US incapacity to reduce threats to Israel on the northern side of the border. In reality, Russia and Iran will be the ones to determine whether the Golan Heights once again becomes a major regional confrontation zone, this time emanating directly from the Syrian civil war. The Assad regime had kept order at the border from the conclusion of the 1973 war right up until 2011.

Israel was more concerned about Hezbollah's presence on its northeastern border, and a related Iranian strategic advantage, than it was about the presence of largely Syrian Sunni jihadis proximate to Israel and Jordan (as well as in parts of the north where to some extent they had functioned at Turkey's behest). The close relationship of Sunni Islamist jihadi groups such as Ahrar Al-Sham to Al-Nusra (al-Qaeda in all but name) and to Saudi Arabia,[32] and of other Sunni Islamist militants to both Saudi Arabia and Qatar, exemplified the Gulf's role in the internationalization of the Syrian conflict. Such Syrian groups often fought each other or, when they tactically cooperated, tended to be outclassed by Al-Nusra in various 'front' groupings. However, they were (Al-Nusra included) essentially 'national' rebel groups[33] and as such did not threaten the coherence of Syria as a state as IS had done for several years. Saudi Arabia and Qatar did not have to justify to the United States their funding of militant Syrian Islamists that were nationally focused; in fact such sponsorship was in part coordinated with the United States via the military operation command (MOC) rooms. The MOCs sought to manage, as far as anything could reliably and durably hope to do so, foreign support for rebel groups. They had the additional input of Turkey or Jordan, depending on whether the MOC was located near the northern or southern border of Syria. The United States' involvement in training Syrian rebel groups meant that it was effectively supporting Sunni Islamist fighters.[34] These were of a very different type from the FSA, which in the first few years of the war was to receive Western, Turkish, and Gulf political, as well as their more discreet military, backing. In a measure of the external dependency created by battlefield weakness, and the related need for external military and political backing in the face of the Syrian regime and its powerful backers, the FSA (the self-styled 'Syrian National Army') was eventually reduced to being little more than a pro-Turkish mercenary force in opposition to the SDF in northern Syria.

The internationalization of a domestic Syrian conflict was an inevitable development in a country whose strategic and political alignment is, and has long been, of clear importance to its neighbors and to international actors, whether they have local allies or not. Ultimately, Assad leadership's ability to call on an existing regional ally, Iran, and to greatly deepen an old relationship with an international one, Russia, proved decisive in asserting state control over most of the country. While far from a stable state comfortably holding a 'monopoly of legitimate violence' in the Weberian model, Syria appears to be undergoing the last phases of its civil war. In some cases, 'mopping-up' operations in parts of northern Syria will most likely neutralize what remains of Syrian Islamist rebel groups. These groups more or less lost Gulf-US connivance in their fight, due to the US acceptance of the inevitability of Assad's survival as much as any direct impact of President Trump.

The distinct case of IS in Syria may not yet be an entirely closed chapter. However, any residual IS threat in northeastern Syria may be more a matter of management, dependent on the precise mechanics of the transition from what had been US-backed de facto Kurdish self-rule to, potentially, Russia-backed Syria state rule. In different pockets of the country, the Syrian civil conflict may continue to rumble on as distinct groups are unable to reconcile with the apparent state victor. In other words, the country's lack of internal cohesion continues to make it vulnerable to the interference of neighbors and of others seeking to enhance their national security or more ambitious regional interests.

Yemen

The latest phase of the Yemen War did not occur in a vacuum. In 2010, the Saudis concluded their brief, and disastrous, land invasion, itself reflecting an Al-Saud history of seeking to shape the political complexion of north Yemen and sometimes the whole country. The Al-Saud's intimate connection with Yemen included its incorporation of part of its northern territory into the nascent Saudi kingdom that was being established in the 1920s.

The internationalization of the conflict in Yemen is not anything new either. In 1962, Egypt, a major extra-regional actor, led the external Arab 'radicals' in trying to overthrow the Saudi (and Western)-backed monarchy, the Zaidi imamate. Egypt's defeat in the Arab-Israeli War of 1967, and the politics of the regional aftermath, saw it and 'colonial' Britain withdraw from Yemen later that year. More recently, the United States conducted drone strikes on al-Qaeda targets under Presidents G. W. Bush and Obama, while the United States and the United Kingdom facilitated, and continue to assist and arm, the Saudi-led coalition fighting there. Another international actor with a historic if more muted pedigree is Russia. Unlike in Syria, Russia is not a direct, military party to the Yemen conflict. However, the further dissolution of Yemen, and the de facto recreation of at least one South Yemen, has seen Moscow reemerge as a diplomatic player in its former Marxist South Yemen fiefdom. Russia never lost its Soviet connections to the surviving former leading Southern Yemen players and through them or their descendants retains some diplomatic weight. This is compounded by Russia's proven ability to determine the outcome of the conflict in Syria and its contributory role to events in Libya.

The Saudi land war in Yemen over 2009–2010 was largely a Saudi attempt to beef up its border security, motivated by the belief that an armed expression of Yemeni Zaidi identity, the Houthis, threatened Saudi security, in part because of the Saudis' perception of the Houthis as Iranian allies. The deploying of the limited capabilities of the Saudi army was partly the result of the Saudis having been 'played' by the then Yemeni president, Ali Abdullah Saleh, who had an interest in making money and political capital out of intra-Yemeni division and Saudi discomfiture. The circumstances in which a Houthi incursion across relatively lawless tribal country occurred, and the subsequent events, including evidence[35] of meetings between Saudi military and civilian officials and Houthi representatives to try to establish a modus vivendi on mutual security, suggested that the Houthis had little real interest (at that point at least) in taking on Saudi Arabia. Nor did the Saudis want to make the political descendants of their one-time royalist allies their indefinite foes. Following the Iranian Revolution, the Saudis, like their *salafi* 'allies' in Yemen and many others of Sunni political affiliation throughout the Peninsula, increasingly saw the Zaidi as confessional and political fellow travelers with Iran. However, this did not mean that the Saudis viewed Houthi fighters as 'solely' an Iranian threat temporarily on standby. Subsequent events changed even this slanted Saudi perception though.

Prior to their short war of 2009–2010 with the Saudis, the Houthis had been engaged, like many Yemeni actors, in armed contestation for authority inside their country, making them a force that Saleh was keen to literally steer in Saudi Arabia's direction. It is likely that the Al-Saud knew that in that war, they and the de facto Saudi defense minister Prince Khalid bin Sultan, who seemingly hoodwinked an increasingly ill-focused king (Abdullah), had misconceived what was only a limited territorial threat.

What Changed in 2011?

In 2011 the Saudis reordered a failed Yemeni popular movement. The Yemenis' attempted semi-institutionalizing of reform morphed into a Saudi-led GCC process that underwrote Saleh until his eventual removal in favor of his deputy, Abed Rabbo Mansour Al-Hadi. This did nothing to address the popular demands for change or to more effectively manage the struggle of armed interests in, around, and in parallel to the would-be institutions of state. The unsurprising failure of the National Dialogue Conference (NDC) and other Yemeni 'structures' to agree to a durable sharing of power led irrevocably to the Houthis' takeover in 2014, utilizing their greater armed commitment, in common with all key Yemeni actors, to their own militia over loyalty to the putative state. The Houthis' power-grab was in a long Yemeni tradition of utilizing force and tactical alliances to operate the ostensible machinery of state.

The Saudi reaction was to allow its Iran-fixated perspective to determine its response. An unprecedented air war from 2015 helped devastate a country that the Saudis and their allies supposedly want to be a functioning state able to uphold southwestern Arabian security and in particular the security of the Yemen-Saudi Arabia border. There was little Saudi strategy at work here. In the process, Iran went from being a country that had sought to utilize, if not exploit, the Zaidis' increased sense of themselves as having a distinct political identity, rather than a nonpolitical community within a Yemeni morass,[36] to directly aiding the Houthis' war effort. Claims and counterclaims proliferate as to whether the Houthis' internal expansion in 2014 to the Yemeni capital Sana'a was sought by Iran, or simply provided useful, after the fact, propaganda. In 2014, Iran might have seen southwest Arabia as a strategic front line comparable to the direct Mediterranean access afforded by Hezbollah and the conflict in Syria. Or perhaps Yemen was a way for Iran to engage in a low-cost (for itself) 'bleed' of its rival Saudi Arabia, in other words, akin to backing Hezbollah in Lebanon with a similar ideational benefit placing Iran and its allies in the political front line against 'Wahhabi-Zionist interests'. That would be in keeping with Iran's self-appointed Shia guardianship imperative as the 'defender' of Shia, Twelver or otherwise, and its befriending of Sunni Islamists able to hurt Iranian enemies without threatening Iranian interests.

The Yemen War became more than the proxy for the regional struggle between Saudi/UAE and Iran, with Egypt in a largely political rather than military role, and some minor Arab and non-Arab actors providing mercenaries to the Saudi/Emirati side. In fact, the claimed Islamic and Arab coalition against Iran, launched after the Saudis began their air war in 2015, saw the Yemen War affect northeast Africa and the Horn of Africa. A two-way military, political, and economic exchange between western Red Sea littoral states and western Arabia compounded the conflict in Yemen and raised tensions in those proximate East African countries hosting Gulf military bases (and often related infrastructure).

Sudan had become a closer Saudi ally as the latter wrested influence from Iran and then, at President Bashir's connivance, competed with Qatar. The 2019 change in a Sudanese leadership that sits atop an essentially military regime with an absorbed MB made the Sudanese attachment to Saudi/Emirati largesse even greater and confirmed that Sudanese troops,[37] and other African vigilantes, were prepared to continue to do the dirty work that the two Gulf states had largely avoided, namely fight a ground war on their allies' side. In 2016, Eritrea had granted the Saudis and Emiratis use of Assab port as a military base; the UAE were especially active in utilizing a facility proximate to the Bab Al-Mandab waterway that runs between the Horn of Africa and Yemen. Eritrea reportedly sent troops to aid the Emirati and Saudi war effort in Yemen. Djibouti hosted a Saudi military base south of the Bab Al-Mandab, although it fell out with the Emiratis over a DP World port development. Likewise, part of the federal republic of Somalia, Somaliland, engaged in a commercial spat with DP World over a port development that had a security component. However, the Emiratis were determined to hold on to their strategic foothold in this part of the Horn,[38] and another component of Somalia, Puntland, had UAE military assistance. Qatar's deepening conflict with Saudi Arabia and the Emirates from mid-2017 onward ended its modest military role in support of Hadi in Yemen, just as the intra-Gulf dispute obliged Qatar to withdraw its would-be peacekeeping troops from the Eritrea-Djibouti border. Qatar had helped to frustrate Emirati port ambitions in Somalia though, and it signed its own port development deal with the federal Somalian government in August 2019. The Gulf thirst for Red Sea strategic assets has also included the Saudis' surprising enthusiasm for the Egyptian-held, and formerly Israeli-occupied, Tiran islands, where the Strait meets the Red Sea.[39]

Qatar retained its residual interests in Yemen via a tribalized version of the MB, Islah, whose political orientation and financial dependence varied according to Yemeni region and personnel. The Saudis have had a mercurial approach to Islah, for example, improving relations when the Kingdom's leadership changed in 2015 and out of recognition that Saudi influence in Yemen had weakened. This Saudi unpredictability toward Islah, and the Emiratis' implacable hostility to any MB variant, helped Qatar retain its influence in Yemen even after its military role ended. Its aid role has included assistance to Houthi-controlled areas. Qatar also mediated in the internal Yemen fight, which meant that it regarded the Houthis as an equal player in the conflict. The contradiction of Qatar being sympathetic to the Iranian-allied Houthis (and respected as such by the latter) and to the local MB backed by Saudi Arabia is not any more inexplicable than the Saudis' own brand of foreign policy 'doublethink.'[40]

Something akin to a regional struggle, with the Saudis playing a lead but essentially cashier and propagandist role on one side, and the Iranians both mobilizing ideational brethren and shedding their blood on the other, has been going on since the Iranian Revolution in 1979. The latter was decisive, along with the British 'withdrawal'[41] from the Arabian Peninsula from 1967 to 1971, in spawning the struggle. It became a 'hot' war in the Gulf in the 1980s but still remained a proxy conflict across much of Arabia and the Levant until the Saudis launched the air war in Yemen in 2015. South Yemen was seen by Saudi Arabia as a danger before the British pullout occurred, while the replacement of a federation of UK-backed sheikhdoms by the pro-Soviet People's Republic of South Yemen (PRSY) would prove both a threat to Saudi Arabia and Oman and an opportunity for a Saudi regime able to play on Yemen's internal contradictions for its perceived national security advantage.

These tensions may have been manageable were it not for a vulnerable Iranian regime that in its early, revolutionary, phase saw its security as aided by 'exporting' Shia (and sometimes Sunni) militancy. Yemen, however, had not been a perceptible strategic Iranian bridgehead until the unnatural stapling back together of its two parts following the fissures and Saudi manipulations that drove the 1994 civil war. The poorly managed Yemeni attempt at reform in 2011 further exacerbated southern disillusion and helped cause the dissolution of a barely functioning state. De facto southern Yemeni independence then meant separate entities surviving on 'rent' accruing to local militias. Aden, the home of Hadi's would-be national government, attempted to disburse monies throughout the country and earned 'rent' from its port function.

In an environment where some southern militias are working with the UAE, which wants political influence in and over the south, independence is being encouraged by Abu Dhabi whether this is an overt UAE policy aim or not. The Southern Transitional Council (STC) is an Emirati creation that presents itself as *the* vehicle for southern independence. Southern secession may not be very neat or resemble the federation of sheikhdoms that became the PRSY. However, it is being encouraged by the UAE and is not being strongly opposed by Saudi Arabia. Ostensibly the Saudis support intra-Yemeni unity: their decision to launch the air war in 2015 was on the claimed basis that 'the legitimacy,' the internationally recognized national Yemeni government of Mansur Hadi, was under threat. The Saudi military has not been on the ground in any significant numbers since 2010, however. So their political preference for Yemen to somehow be a coherent entity does not count for much.

In 2018, Saudi (and allied) troops took up position in some strategic locations in Mahra, the Yemeni province that borders Oman, in part to offset alleged Omani connivance with the Houthis. Oman admits only to sending humanitarian aid to Mahra (in part to prevent Mahran refugees fleeing to Oman). Some Saudi forces were stationed at a few Mahra-Oman border crossings and at the Mahran airport and sea port on the Arabian Sea. The Saudis' Mahran role did not appear to be a Saudi land-grab or a marker for a Saudi-backed Mahran independent state, however. Independence sentiment is quite strong in Mahra precisely because of the Saudi and Emirati troop presence. An established UAE practice of meddling in Oman[42] was, as likely, extended to the tribes on the Omani side of the Sultanate's border with Mahra. The UAE was seemingly exploiting Oman's historic Dhofari susceptibility to events in South Yemen. Oman probably encouraged Mahran protests in 2019 against the presence of Saudi and allied troops.

The shared Saudi-Emirati interest in policing Mahra emphasized the need for the two ostensible allies to coordinate, not compete. In 2018, their respective Yemeni allies fought each other for control of Aden airport, and the two countries are still competing for Red Sea bases. Burgeoning Saudi allies in the Horn—Somalia (Federal Republic of) and Djibouti—are in dispute with the UAE over the latter's port developments.

It is notable that in the strategic Arabian Sea island of Socotra,[43] the Saudis reportedly 'mediated' between the UAE occupiers and defiant Socotrans rejecting interference by any Gulf Arabs. The UAE reduced its military presence but, for all the talk in July 2019 of a UAE 'pullout' from Yemen, they kept control over an island important to the UAE's desire to project naval capacity around the Arabian Peninsula and into the Horn of Africa.

In fact the UAE removed most of the Emirati forces stationed with southern secessionist militias, without ending the arms, advice, intelligence, and political commitment to some version of southern independence. Thus, the UAE 'pullout' from Aden and to its east, Mukalla, was a reduction, but not a wholesale abandonment, of prized strategic Arabian Sea assets (such as Socotra). The UAE's north Yemeni Red Sea naval bases—Hodeidah, Mokha, and Khokha—were not wholly abandoned either. That said, the UAE's decision emphasized that any resumed Yemeni militia push on northern territory, including the Red Sea port city of Hodeidah where UAE-allied southern militias' ambitions had been stalled by the UK-backed UN peace effort, would be mostly down to what Yemeni fighters could do and sustain. With this reality, and a reported UAE pullout from Mahra, the Saudis faced a future whereby their best hope seemed to be to rely exclusively on air power, including possibly subcontracting it to some Yemenis,[44] or for the Saudi leadership to try more seriously to talk its way out of the war. Indicative of this situation, and of ongoing Emirates-backed southern secessionism, was the Saudi and Emirati brokering in October 2019 of a joint government in Aden in which Hadi, many of whose allied fighters had little authority in the south, agreed to share power with the STC. While this was presented as a coalescing of their forces for a fight against the Houthis in the north, it looked a lot like a putative, if potentially highly fractious, South Yemen government.

The Saudis' traditional Machiavellian Yemen policy: betting on several sides and therefore supposedly never losing, in theory also including Hadhramawti independence (presumably including Mahra, long administered by Hadhramawt). However, even if an independent southern Yemeni-Saudi vassal state was a concerted objective, the Saudis could not deliver it given the local realities, their own refusal to endanger uniformed Saudis, and the Emiratis' territorial holdings.

At the time of writing, the Yemen conflict looked likely to carry on, despite the possibility that increased communication between Saudi Arabia and the Houthis might calm the Yemen-Saudi Arabia border. There also remained sufficient regional and international interest in backing armed Yemeni proxies for the fighting to continue. For the US administration (not withstanding some Congressional opposition), the Saudis and Emiratis are containing Iran. The United Kingdom shares this view, while its 'plug-in role' with the US Navy and post-Brexit global pretensions made dissent from the United States unlikely. The United Kingdom's 'Friends of Yemen' enthusiasms and the efforts of UN secretary general's envoys had not mattered much. Ultimately, international mediation would only work if the international, regional, and Yemeni parties genuinely needed and wanted to end the fighting.

For some regional players, Yemen was a platform for other concerns. For Iran, it was a way of telling Saudi Arabia and the United States to come to terms with it in other theatres, end sanctions, and accept an Iranian civil nuclear and ballistic missile program. For Saudi Arabia, Yemen became about border and even internal security, as well as an ideational struggle between it and Iran. For the UAE, it provided maritime real-estate, power projection, and international status. For Egypt, Yemen was still a 'Vietnam' that it would revisit only for paid-for naval policing. For Oman, it was a matter of resisting perceived Emirati interference in its national security. For Horn of Africa countries, Yemen was a conflict that spelled riyals and dirhams.

Yemen is an international struggle set to continue at the expense of a coherent Yemen state, thereby ensuring that even a nominal single state will not exist anymore.

Conclusion

The US intervention in Iraq is widely regarded as having let loose forces and sectarian rebalancing that favored Iraqi Shia and Iran and that, together with a US troop withdrawal in December 2011, helped spur the growth of al-Qaeda and ISIS into Syria and beyond. However, US military-led initiatives such as encouraging a Sunni 'awakening,' which involved Sunni tribesmen who may have fought US forces but realigned to help counter other insurgents such as ISIS, have contributed to a measure of stability. This has been aided by a belated realization that the United States' de-Ba'athification policy had done much damage to Iraqi state institutionalization efforts and has been partially reversed. A US–Iraqi security dialogue is ongoing, but by September 2020 the US military expected troop numbers to drop to around 3,000. The situation is still nowhere near stabilized and much more work needs to be done, as the October 2019 protests in Iraq showed. Stabilization is also needed in Libya where the French- and UK-led NATO intervention against Gaddafi failed to learn lessons from Iraq in the need to adequately plan for the day after intervention. While there may be merit in removing authoritarian leaders and supporting a Responsibility to Protect (R2P) doctrine, the fallout in terms of lawlessness, protracted proxy warfare, and the rolling humanitarian crises it engenders can be worse.

There are also geopolitical consequences such as the mistrust that backing opposing factions can create: in the case of Libya between France and Italy, and between Saudi Arabia and the UAE on the one hand, and Qatar on the other. As noted in the Libyan case, the internationalization of conflict means far more than the spillover effects of transnational militia and proxy warfare in the Maghreb. It also plays into worsening relations between NATO and Russia and other theatres of conflict such as Ukraine and Syria. The intervention is at the root of growing contentions and deadlock in the UN Security Council over issues such as sovereignty, R2P (including humanitarian concerns and upholding the Geneva Convention), and spheres of interest. The conflict in Syria has created a major refugee crisis in the Levant, especially in Lebanon and Jordan. Following the trillions of dollars spent in Afghanistan and Iraq, and aware of the potential for an escalation of the conflict that could draw in direct confrontation with Iran and Russia, the United States has shown restraint. Nonetheless, Iranian influence in Iraq and Syria has still attracted preemptive strikes by Israel against arms depots, and an emerging Israeli alliance with some Gulf Arab states is helping to draw these protagonists closer than before.

The Yemen conflict remains a civil conflict, including a secessionist southern movement, and a regional conflict between the Saudi-led coalition and the Houthis. Whether growing international opposition to the war, together with UN efforts to mediate, succeeds in drawing it to a close will partly depend on Saudi Arabia's ability to continue to frame the intervention as one aimed at countering an existential Iranian threat or, conversely, on Saudi exhaustion with a war that has weakened its national security not enhanced it. Regional and international interests have had a free hand in pariah, weak, or collapsing Middle Eastern and North African states where internal cohesion and state institutions are lacking or have been deconstructed, such as Iraq. This has coincided with a period in the international system when neoliberal norms and US leadership are perceived to be in retreat.

What do these cases have in common? Predominantly, neighborhood interference is aimed at enhancing national security, and either bolstering or undermining the prospect of the local MB being able to replicate their electoral success in Egypt in 2012. For regional and international stakeholders, the outcome in these theatres of conflict has significant balance of power implications. Without a greater alignment between states and societies, the prospects for positive change in the regional security complex, such as creating more free trade opportunities, establishing and enhancing cooperation through durable alliances, and developing commitments to a comprehensive regional security structure, remain poor. Questions about human development, geopolitical competition, and political economy in the Middle East are therefore vital to explore in this regard. How the United States, the United Kingdom, and the European Union and its allies choose to manage and engage with each other through NATO is already being questioned after the Trump administration policies concerning Turkey and the SDF. This is apart from tensions between the Trump administration and those NATO states paying less than 2 percent of GDP promised on defense by 2024. Future NATO interactions with Russia and China on issues related to conflict and security will have major consequences in these specific conflicts in the Middle East and North Africa, in international relations, and in upholding or eroding international humanitarin law more broadly.

Notes

1. Regional Security Complex Theory (RSCT) was advanced by Barry Buzan and Ole Waever in *Regions and Powers: The Structure of International Security* (Cambridge: Cambridge University Press, 2003). It posits that international security should be examined from a regional perspective and that international relations exhibit clustered patterns known as the regional security complex.

2. See, for example, William Young, David Stebbins, Bryan Frederick, and Omar Al-Shahery, *Spillover from the Conflict in Syria: An Assessment of the Factors That Aid in the Spread of Violence* (Santa Monica, CA: RAND, 2014).

3. See Tyrone L. Gron, *Proxy War: The Least Bad Option* (Palo Alto, CA: Stanford University Press, 2019); and Andrew Mumford, *Proxy Warfare* (Cambridge: Polity, 2013).

4. Barry Buzan and Ana Gonzalez-Pelaez, "'International Community' after Iraq," *International Affairs* 81, no. 1 (January 2005): 31–52.

5. Council on Foreign Relations, "The Iraq War," https://www.cfr.org/timeline/iraq-war.

6. Ibid.

7. Vali Nasr, "Iraq: The Signal Democracy," in *The Dispensable Nation: American Foreign Policy in Retreat* (New York: First Anchor Books, 2014), 142.

8. Council on Foreign Relations, "US Intervention in Iraqi Politics," March 30, 2006, https://www.cfr.org/backgrounder/us-intervention-iraqi-politics.

9. Abas Tanus Mafud, "Iraq's Pragmatism: Between Iran's Sanctions and Saudi Grand Designs," *International Policy Digest*, April 22, 2019, https://intpolicy digest.org/2019/04/22/iraq-s-pragmatism-between-iran-s-sanctions-and -saudi-grand-designs/.

10. See, for example, Robert E. Hunter, "The Core Challenges for a New Security Structure," in *Building Security in the Persian Gulf* (Santa Monica, CA: RAND, 2010), 31.

11. Karim Mezran, "Libya in Transition: From Jamahiriya to Jumhūriyyah?," in *The New Middle East: Protest and Revolution in the Arab World*, ed. Fawaz Gerges (Cambridge: Cambridge University Press, 2014), 309–332.

12. Christopher Andrew, "British Official Perceptions of Muammar Gaddafi," in *Scripting Middle East Leaders: The Impact of Leadership Perceptions on US and UK Foreign Policy*, ed. Lawrence Freedman and Jeffrey H. Michaels (New York: Bloomsbury, 2013), 202.

13. Ibid., 203.

14. Federica Saini Fasanotti, "Russia and Libya: A Brief History of an On-Again and Off-Again Friendship," *Brookings*, September 1, 2016, https://www.brookings.edu/blog/order-from-chaos/2016/09/01/ russia-and-libya-a-brief-history-of-an-on-again-off-again-friendship/.

15. Alec Luhn and Dominic Nicholls, "Russian Mercenaries Back Libya Rebel Leader as Moscow Seeks Influence in Africa," *Telegraph*, March 3, 2019, https://www.telegraph.co.uk/news/2019/03/03/russian-mercenaries-back -libyan-rebel-leader-moscow-seeks-influence/.

16. Middle East Monitor, "Turkey to Establish Naval and Air Bases in Northern Cyprus," June 19, 2019, https://www.middleeastmonitor.com/20190619 -turkey-to-establish-naval-and-air-bases-in-northern-cyprus/.

17. Nick Squires, "Turkey Sends Drone to Turkish Northern Cyprus to Back Up Disputed Oil and Gas Exploration," *Telegraph*, December 16, 2019, https://www.telegraph.co.uk/news/2019/12/16/turkey-sends-drone -turkish-northern-cyprus-back-disputed-oil/.

18. Samuel Ramani, "Outsiders' Battle to Rebuild Libya is Fueling the Civil War There," *Foreign Policy*, August 22, 2019, https://foreignpolicy. com/2019/08/22/outsiders-battle-to-rebuild-libya-is-fueling-the-civil -war-there/.

19. Vivienne Walt, "Did Libya's Dictator Bankroll Sarkozy? Gaddafi's Son Hinted at Dirt in 2011," *Time*, March 21, 2018, https://time.com/5208822/ gaddafi-son-dirt-sarkozy-libya-regime/.

20. Sally Hayden, "The EU's Deal with Libya Is Sentencing Refugees to Death," *Guardian*, February 5, 2019, https://www.theguardian.com/

commentisfree/2019/feb/05/eu-deal-libya-refugees-libyan-detention
-centres.

21. Anthony Shadid, "Qatar Wields an Outsize Influence in Arab Politics," *New York Times*, November 14, 2011, https://www.nytimes.com/2011/11/15/world/middleeast/qatar-presses-decisive-shift-in-arab-politics.html.

22. Ian Cobain, "Libyan Rendition: How UK's Role in Kidnap of Families Came to Light," *Guardian*, May 10, 2018, https://www.theguardian.com/world/2018/may/10/libyan-rendition-how-uks-role-in-kidnap-of-two-families-unravelled.

23. Ian Black, "Qatar Admits Sending Hundreds of Troops to Support Libya Rebels," *Guardian*, October 26, 2011, https://www.theguardian.com/world/2011/oct/26/qatar-troops-libya-rebels-support.

24. Associated Press, "Libyan Prime Minister Ousted by Parliament," *Guardian*, March 11, 2014, https://www.theguardian.com/world/2014/mar/11/libya-prime-minister-ousted.

25. Frederic Wehrey, "The Revolution Devours Its Own," in *The Burning Shores: Inside the Battle for the New Libya* (New York: Farrar, Straus and Giroux, 2018), 150.

26. Or, as Hassan Abbas puts it, from a "cultural affiliation with sect" to a "culture of sectarian affiliation"; from "diverse forms of belonging" to a "culture of belonging." Hassan Abbas, "Between the Cultures of Sectarianism and Citizenship," in *Syria Speaks: Art and Culture from the Frontline*, ed. Malu Halasa, Zaher Omareen, and Nawara Mahfoud (London: Saqi, 2014), 51.

27. See discussion of the 'nation-state' in Neil Partrick, "Nationhood and Citizenship in the UAE and Wider Region," on www.neilpartrick.com/publications. The paper is directly accessible here: https://storage.googleapis.com/wzukusers/user-22594618/documents/5bcf0d71f2bd8X4iUq3j/Nationhood%20and%20Citizenship%20in%20UAE%20and%20Gulf%20N%20Partrick%2012%20Oct%202018%20Edit%203.pdf.

28. Just as the Nasser-led coup in Egypt in the 1950s had created Islamist exiles welcomed by the Saudis for their educational and juridical skills and their related utility in the pan-Islamist front that King Faisal bin Abdulaziz promoted, so too were Syria's exiled Brotherhood supporters in the 1980s hosted as part of Saudi Arabia's regional outreach.

29. Neil Partrick, *Saudi Arabian Foreign Policy: Conflict and Cooperation* (London: I.B. Tauris, 2016; 2nd ed. 2018), 218–219.

30. Henry Kissinger, *Years of Upheaval* (Boston, MA: Little, Brown, 1982), 594–595.

31. Neil Partrick, "Kuwait's Foreign Policy" (PhD thesis), http://etheses.lse.ac.uk/3164/, 204–205.

32. Partrick, *Saudi Arabian Foreign Policy*, 216–217.

33. Ibid.
34. Ibid., 214–217 and 370.
35. See Neil Partrick, "Saudi-Yemeni Relations," in Partrick, *Saudi Arabian Foreign Policy*, 242–261.
36. For detailed analysis 'solely' about the 'Yemeni' aspect of the transformation in Zaidi self-perception, see Abdullah Hamidaddin, "From Social Category to Social Identity; The Emergence of a New Zaydism," in *Precarious Belongings: Being Shi'i in Non-Shi'i Worlds*, ed. Charles Tripp and Gabriele vom Bruck (London: Centre for Academic Shi'a Studies, 2017), 232–235.
37. Under the Sudanese leadership that took power in mid-2019, the number of Sudanese soldiers serving in Yemen reportedly went up, having previously fallen from its 2016–2017 height. As of October 2019, however, it was being reported that Sudan was reducing its troop numbers by several thousand.
38. An informed Emirati told the author in June 2019 that conflict over the development saw UAE intelligence officers face down Somaliland officers—in other words the Emirati foothold there is not over.
39. Neil Partrick, "Saudi-Egyptian Relations," in Partrick, *Saudi Arabian Foreign Policy*, 55–75.
40. 'Doublethink' is one of the main themes running through *Saudi Foreign Policy*. George Orwell's term, deployed to great effect in *1984*, means to simultaneously hold two contradictory ideas at the same time.
41. However, the oft-referred to UK 'withdrawal' from the Gulf in particular is a terminological inexactitude. See my article "'East of Suez': Therese May Re-opens Harold Wilson's Imperial Closure," March 2, 2019, https://historyatkingston.wordpress.com/2019/03/02/east-of-suez-theresa-may-re-opens-harold-wilsons-imperial-closure/.
42. In 2011 and 2019 Oman accused the UAE of having spy networks in the Sultanate; for Emirati co-option of Omani tribal elements, Neil Partrick, *Nationalism in the Gulf States* (London: LSE, 2009), 11; http://eprints.lse.ac.uk/55257/.
43. Socotra has, formally speaking, been in the southern province of Hadhramawt since unification in 1990, when, in addition, Mahra was given its own administration separate from Hadhramawt. However, Socotra remains Mahra-identifying.
44. See Neil Partrick, "Saudi Arabia's Elusive Defense Reform" (Washington, DC: Sada, November 2019), https://carnegie-mec.org/sada/80354.

Bibliography

Abbas, Hassan. "Between the Cultures of Sectarianism and Citizenship." In *Syria Speaks: Art and Culture from the Frontline*, edited by Malu Halasa, Zaher Omareen, and Nawara Mahfoud, 48–60 .London: Saqi, 2014.

Andrew, Christopher. "British Official Perceptions of Muammar Gaddafi." In *Scripting Middle East Leaders: The Impact of Leadership Perceptions on US and UK Foreign Policy*, edited by Lawrence Freedman and Jeffrey H. Michaels. New York: Bloomsbury, 2013.

Associated Press. "Libyan Prime Minister Ousted by Parliament." *Guardian*, March 11, 2014. https://www.theguardian.com/world/2014/mar/11/libya-prime-minister-ousted.

Black, Ian. "Qatar Admits Sending Hundreds of Troops to Support Libya Rebels." *Guardian*, October 26, 2011. https://www.theguardian.com/world/2011/oct/26/qatar-troops-libya-rebels-support.

Buzan, Barry, and Ana Gonzalez-Pelaez. "'International Community' after Iraq." *International Affairs* 81, no. 1 (January 2005): 31–52.

Buzan, Barry, and Ole Waever. *Regions and Powers: The Structure of International Security*. Cambridge: Cambridge University Press, 2003.

Cobain, Ian. "Libyan Rendition: How UK's Role in Kidnap of Families Came to Light." *Guardian*, May 10, 2018. https://www.theguardian.com/world/2018/may/10/libyan-rendition-how-uks-role-in-kidnap-of-two-families-unravelled.

Council on Foreign Relations. "The Iraq War." https://www.cfr.org/timeline/iraq-war.

———. "US Intervention in Iraqi Politics." March 30, 2006. https://www.cfr.org/backgrounder/us-intervention-iraqi-politics.

Fasanotti, Federica Saini. "Russia and Libya: A Brief History of an On-Again and Off-Again Friendship." *Brookings*, September 1, 2016. https://www.brookings.edu/blog/order-from-chaos/2016/09/01/russia-and-libya-a-brief-history-of-an-on-again-off-again-friendship/.

Gron, Tyrone L. *Proxy War: The Least Bad Option*. Palo Alto, CA: Stanford University Press, 2019.

Hamidaddin, Abdullah. "From Social Category to Social Identity: The Emergence of a New Zaydism." In *Precarious Belongings: Being Shi'i in Non-Shi'i Worlds*, edited by Charles Tripp and Gabriele vom Bruck, 232–235. London: Centre for Academic Shi'a Studies, 2017.

Hayden, Sally. "The EU's Deal with Libya Is Sentencing Refugees to Death." *Guardian*, February 5, 2019. https://www.theguardian.com/commentisfree/2019/feb/05/eu-deal-libya-refugees-libyan-detention-centres.

Hunter, Robert E. "The Core Challenges for a New Security Structure." In *Building Security in the Persian Gulf*. Santa Monica, CA: RAND, 2010.

Kissinger, Henry. *Years of Upheaval*. Boston, MA: Little, Brown, 1982.

Luhn, Alec, and Dominic Nicholls. "Russian Mercenaries Back Libya Rebel Leader as Moscow Seeks Influence in Africa." *Telegraph*, March 3, 2019.

https://www.telegraph.co.uk/news/2019/03/03/russian-mercenaries
-back-libyan-rebel-leader-moscow-seeks-influence/.

Mafud, Abas Tanus. "Iraq's Pragmatism: Between Iran's Sanctions and Saudi
Grand Designs." *International Policy Digest*, April 22, 2019. https://intpoli
cydigest.org/2019/04/22/iraq-s-pragmatism-between-iran-s-sanctions-and
-saudi-grand-designs/.

Mezran, Karim. "Libya in Transition: From Jamahiriya to Jumhüriyyah?" In *The
New Middle East: Protest and Revolution in the Arab World*, edited by Fawaz
Gerges. Cambridge: Cambridge University Press, 2014.

Middle East Monitor. "Turkey to Establish Naval and Air Bases in
Northern Cyprus." June 19, 2019. https://www.middleeastmonitor.
com/20190619-turkey-to-establish-naval-and-air-bases-in-northern-cyprus/.

Mumford, Andrew. *Proxy Warfare*. Cambridge: Polity, 2013.

Nasr, Vali. "Iraq: The Signal Democracy." In *The Dispensable Nation: American
Foreign Policy in Retreat*. New York: First Anchor Books, 2014.

Partrick, Neil. "'East of Suez': Therese May Re-opens Harold Wilson's Imperial
Closure." March 2, 2019. https://historyatkingston.wordpress.com/
2019/03/02/east-of-suez-theresa-may-re-opens-harold-wilsons-imperial
-closure/.

———. "Kuwait's Foreign Policy." PhD thesis. http://etheses.lse.ac.uk/3164/.

———. *Nationalism in the Gulf States*. London: LSE, 2009. http://eprints.lse
.ac.uk/55257/.

———. "Nationhood and Citizenship in the UAE and Wider Region." www
.neilpartrick.com/publications.

———. "Saudi Arabia's Elusive Defense Reform." Washington, DC: Sada, November 2019. https://carnegie-mec.org/sada/80354.

———. *Saudi Arabian Foreign Policy: Conflict and Cooperation*. London: I.B. Tauris,
2016; 2nd ed. 2018.

Ramani, Samuel. "Outsiders' Battle to Rebuild Libya Is Fueling the Civil War
There." *Foreign Policy*, August 22, 2019. https://foreignpolicy
.com/2019/08/22/outsiders-battle-to-rebuild-libya-is-fueling-the-civil
-war-there/.

Shadid, Anthony. "Qatar Wields an Outsize Influence in Arab Politics." *New York
Times*, November 14, 2011. https://www.nytimes.com/2011/11/15/world/
middleeast/qatar-presses-decisive-shift-in-arab-politics.html.

Squires, Nick. "Turkey Sends Drone to Turkish Northern Cyprus to Back Up
Disputed Oil and Gas Exploration." *Telegraph*, December 16, 2019. https://
www.telegraph.co.uk/news/2019/12/16/turkey-sends-drone-turkish
-northern-cyprus-back-disputed-oil/.

Walt, Vivienne. "Did Libya's Dictator Bankroll Sarkozy? Gaddafi's Son Hinted

at Dirt in 2011." *Time*, March 21, 2018. https://time.com/5208822/
gaddafi-son-dirt-sarkozy-libya-regime/.

Wehrey, Frederic. "The Revolution Devours Its Own." In *The Burning Shores: Inside the Battle for the New Libya*. New York: Farrar, Straus and Giroux, 2018.

Young, William, David Stebbins, Bryan Frederick, and Omar Al-Shahery. *Spillover from the Conflict in Syria: An Assessment of the Factors That Aid in the Spread of Violence*. Santa Monica, CA: RAND, 2014.

5

The Middle-Oil Country Curse of the Middle East

Ishac Diwan

Introduction

To start exploring seriously the possible modalities for the reconstruction of war-damaged Iraq, Syria, Libya, and Yemen, one cannot avoid the necessity of considering the evolving political settlements in these countries, asking whether they can ensure a modicum of peace and stability and how they would be affected by 'reconstruction' interventions. In doing so, one is thus pushed to ponder on the deeper causes of instability in these countries, which have been afflicted by violence and insecurity more than the rest of the Middle East after the postcolonial constitution of the modern state. The ultimate goal of such thinking should be to help domestic actors better deal with the specific challenges facing their countries and inspire potential donors to think harder about the risk of their intervention ending up doing harm. These challenges center on finding ways to build workable new political settlements that can insulate these countries from future crises.

The goal of this chapter is to contribute to this debate, as I focus principally on characterizing the various dimensions of state fragility in these countries and on discussing several possible root causes of past and current instability. While country studies exist for each of these cases, these countries have not been studied seriously as a group before, in an investigation of joint structural or historical reasons behind their state weakness. I then conclude with some thoughts of what these considerations might imply for reconstruction efforts, with the understanding that more effort needs to go into this line of thinking.

The chapter is organized as follows. In its first, more descriptive part, I look at the economic, institutional, and governance performance of the countries of the MENA region. To do so, I use a typology of countries

according to their oil per capita endowment. Our countries of interest—
Iraq, Syria, Yemen, and Libya—all belong to the group of countries with
middle levels of oil. Other countries that belong to this group are Algeria,
Sudan, and Iran. I begin by showing that the countries with a middle level
of oil grew slowest over the past fifty years as compared with countries
with low oil per capita and those with high oil per capita. Then, I show
that the middle-oil countries also had worse governance indicators, as if
they were hit hardest by the oil curse. This includes indicators of the rule
of law, state capacity, state repression, corruption, and voice and accountability. In the second half of the chapter, I start by examining the evolution of political settlements in the three subgroups in Section 4. Like
the other countries of the region, the middle-oil countries went through
four main phases of development, post independence, and the effect of oil
prices was more marked in each phase than in the other two subgroups.
The third 'neoliberal' phase is characterized by the rollback of the state
and a rise in social discontent, and this happened with a greater intensity in the middle-oil countries than in the other two groupings. The last
phase, post-2011 uprisings, led to various political adjustments in most
of the region, but its effects in terms of rising insecurity and civil wars
were more marked in the middle-oil countries. Finally, I discuss three
possible reasons (which may be interconnected in complicated ways) that
can explain the ways in which these countries resemble each other and
are distinct from the other countries of the region. The first reason is the
classical oil curse, which I argue applies more to this group than to the
very rich oil countries. A second reason is that the countries of this group
are also republics with a populist past. A third reason (connected to the
first two) is that these countries were hit hardest by the oil bust of the
1990s and had already started to unravel then. In the concluding section,
I outline several broad ways in which reconstruction effort can interact,
positively or negatively, with the central goal of rebuilding a stable and efficient national settlement in the middle-oil countries of the region, given
the structural and historical specificities of the countries of that group.

Long-Term Economic Performance

The average long-term rate of GDP growth of the region over the past
fifty years stands at 4.9 percent a year, a seemingly reasonably solid performance by historical and international standards (Figure 5.1).[1] This rate of
growth is a bit higher than the average of the world middle-income countries (4.7 percent). When comparing the MENA to other regions of the
world, it grew at about the same average rate as South Asia (5 percent), at
a faster rate than Africa (3.5 percent) and Latin America (3.8 percent), but

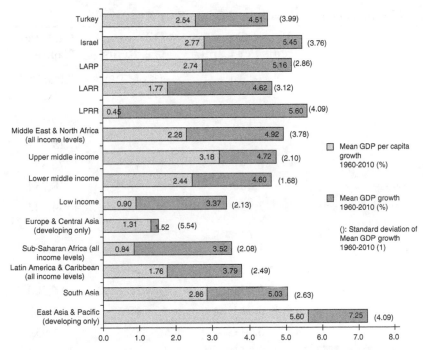

Figure 5.1 Regional/international economic growth performance, 1960–2010.
Source: World Bank Institute (WBI).

at a much slower rate than East Asia (7.3 percent). It is not surprisingly that, on average, the MENA region grew more rapidly than the Least Developed Countries (LDCs), given the impact of the oil boom and fast population growth. But averages often hide more than they reveal, and the reality is gloomier in parts of the region when we look at economic performance in greater detail. Moreover, growth has been highly variable overall, with booms and busts complicating economic management.

The dimension of variability of greater interest to us is the different countries in the region. In this regard, we will find it useful to classify the countries of the region according to their oil endowment, relative to the size of their population. The region has about two-thirds of the world's oil. As there are important differences, both political and economic, among oil-rich countries between those with large and those with relatively small populations, we divide our countries into three groups, depending on their level of oil per capita, with the threshold picked somewhat arbitrarily at $450 and $7,000. We get the following groups (Table 5.1):

Table 5.1 Political economies of the Middle East (2010)

	Oil and Gas Rents Per Capita	Oil and Gas Rents	GDP Per Capita
	(USD)	(% of GDP)	(2010 USD)
HOCs			
Kuwait	21,192	56	37,725
Oman	7,822	39	19,921
Qatar	30,191	43	70,870
Saudi Arabia	8,800	47	18,754
United Arab Emirates	7,956	23	34,342
MOCs			
Algeria	1,411	32	4,473
Bahrain	4,963	24	20,386
Iran	1,464	23	6,300
Iraq	2,012	45	4,487
Libya	6,543	55	11,934
Sudan	243	17	1,422
Syria	505	24	2,080
Yemen	329	25	1,310
LOCs			
Egypt	304	11	2,668
Jordan	142	3	4,371
Lebanon	13	0	8,764
Morocco	0	0	2,858
Tunisia	235	6	4,177
Palestine	0	0	2,339

Note: HOCs: high oil per capita countries; LOCs: low oil per capita countries; MOC: middle oil per capita countries.

- high oil per capita countries (HOCs)—the Gulf Cooperation Council (GCC) countries, with Saudi Arabia, at $23,000 per capita, being the lowest in the group;
- middle oil per capita countries (MOCs)—Algeria, Iran, Iraq, Libya, Sudan, Syria, and Yemen; and

- low oil per capita countries (LOCs)—Egypt, Jordan, Lebanon, Morocco, Tunisia, and West Bank/Gaza (WBG).

This taxonomy has porous boundaries. Syria, Yemen, and Sudan are placed in the MOC group, but not Egypt and Tunisia, although their oil per capita figures are not largely different ($250/330 for the first group vs. about $170 for the second). However, these countries are more clearly different when one looks at the relative importance of oil in the economy, as reflected by the oil/GDP ratio; for example, the first group has levels of oil/GDP in the range of 20 percent, while for Egypt and Tunisia, the ratio is well below 10 percent of GDP. Syria used to derive sizable revenues from oil, and while this has fallen, it remains relatively large and has played important roles in initially stabilizing the Ba'ath regime, and after 2012, in the dynamics of the civil war. Unless important new discoveries are made soon, dwindling oil reserves in Syria and Algeria will turn these countries into LOCs in a generation. Sudan's and Yemen's oil wealth is recent. Libya is the limiting case of an MOC, although a lower threshold could have classified it as an HOC.

Going back to Figure 5.1, we can see that economic performance varied quite a lot among the three groups of countries. The HOC group did best, growing at 5.6 percent a year, a remarkable average over this long stretch of time, and the fastest growth rate for any single region besides East Asia. Given the huge contribution of oil wealth to this growth, this performance is perhaps not too surprising, but it does stand in sharp contrast with the notion of a 'resource curse.' More surprisingly, it is the LOC group that comes second, with a good growth performance by global standards of 5.3 percent. The MOC region came a distant third at 4.4 percent average growth per year (and at only 1.3 percent on a per capita basis). It thus seems that the MOC group of countries is the most hit by the oil curse. The countries that exhibit the lowest performance are those that were believed in the past to show the greatest promise, as they could combine oil wealth with a large population to develop into industrial giants. Iraq, Iran, and Algeria all had such dreams and plans. However, they all got mired in internal and external conflicts that ended up undermining their economic potential. Syria, Libya, and Yemen have just entered such a destructive phase more recently.

This brings us to the variability of growth over time. Looking at the growth rate of each of the three groups over time in Figure 5.2, it is apparent that these vary much more in our three MENA groups than in the Middle Income Countries (MICs), being much higher during some

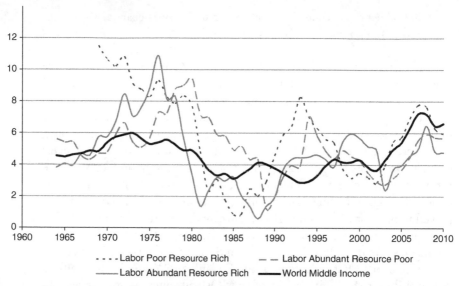

Figure 5.2 Annual GDP growth rates, 1960–2010, for the three MENA subgroups and MICs (% 5 years average). *Source*: WBI and World Economic Outlook (WEO).

periods (especially the 1970s and mid-1990s) and much lower at others (especially the 1980s and after 2005).

These variations over time were due in part to oil prices and in part to policy responses. One can discern four distinct phases. In the first phase, the first two decades after 1960, economic growth and structural change proceeded briskly in the region—initially because statist policies worked for a while before running into contradictions and later because the first oil boom in 1973 allowed states to continue with such policies after they had run their course. The second phase, during the 1980s and parts of the 1990s, was marked by the collapse of oil prices, which forced policy adjustment and resulted in a 'lost decade' that started earlier and lasted longer in the MOCs. The lost decade depressed the long-term performance of the region in important ways. Moreover, what happened then on the economic, social, and political fronts, including the massive rollback of the state and the shift to market economies, initiated social and economic processes that ultimately led to the political upheavals of 2011. In the third phase, which encompasses the past fifteen years until the uprisings of 2011, growth had resumed in most countries, and when it seemed to start to taper off, it was boosted by the second oil boom after 1998. Post the 2011 uprisings, countries' political and economic performance diverged, with some investing in the restoration of auto-cratic governance while others moved toward a more competitive po-litical system. Importantly, most MOCs either collapsed or teetered on the brink of failure. In the case of Algeria and Sudan, the breakdown of governance came later, in 2019. The collapse of oil prices in 2014 marked the beginning of a new phase of forced adjustment whose consequences are yet to be fully felt.

The course of oil prices and oil revenues is shown in Figure 5.3. Oil prices experienced two main periods of boom: 1973–1979 and 1998–2014. The figure also depicts the regional oil revenues over time. The first oil boom had spectacular effects: as oil prices quadrupled between 1972 and 1979, reaching nearly $100 per barrel (in 2010 dollars) in 1979, oil revenues in the region jumped from less than $100 billion in 1972 to over $700 billion (in 2010 dollars) in 1979—this represented nearly 50 percent and 90 percent of the GDP of the oil-rich countries, respectively, then. The second and more recent boom is equally, if not more, spectacu-lar, bringing the region over $900 billion in direct oil revenues in 2010—nearly 40 percent of GDP in both MOCs and HOCs. In between though, there was a long period where oil prices oscillated between $20 and $40 (again in 2010 dollars) and revenues were only around $200 billion a

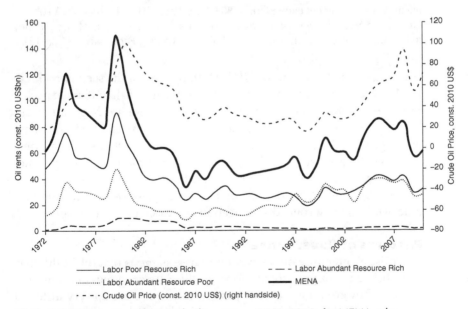

Figure 5.3 Oil prices and regional oil revenues, 1960–2010, for MENA sub-groups. *Source*: WBI and WEO.

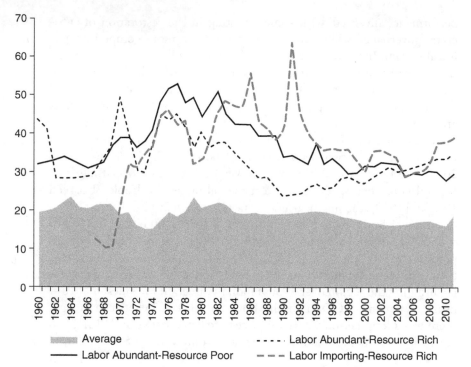

70
60
50
40
30
20
10
0

1960 1962 1964 1966 1968 1970 1972 1974 1976 1978 1980 1982 1984 1986 1988 1990 1992 1994 1996 1998 2000 2002 2004 2006 2008 2010

▨▨▨ Average   - - - - Labor Abundant-Resource Rich
——— Labor Abundant-Resource Poor   — — — Labor Importing-Resource Rich

Figure 5.4 Government expenditures (% GDP), 1960–2020, in the MENA sub-groups and MICs. *Source*: Ishac Diwan and Tarik Akin, "Fifty Years of Fiscal Policy in the Arab Region," *Economic Research Forum Working Paper.* No. 914 (2015).

year—less than 20 percent of GDP. With the end of the second boom in 2014, oil revenues to the region were nearly cut in half and are expected to remain at this level in the medium term. These are huge variations with equally huge effects. Oil production represents an important share of the gross national product in both MOCs and HOCs, but while on a per capita basis oil revenues grew much faster in the HOCs, oil production as a share of GDP grew higher in the MOCs during the second oil boom, reflecting the fact that the first group increased diversification over time, while in the second, diversification decreased over time (Figure 5.4).

Patterns of Governance

The existing literature on the resource curse suggests that oil wealth may be associated with poor institutional quality.[2] As we discuss in more detail later, however, the extent of per capita oil rents set up very different contexts for political exchanges between rulers and the ruled, resulting in varied governance environments, but where again MOCs seem to fare worse. We examine empirically where there is a distinct governance dimension across the different types of economies in the region by looking at governance indicators—both longitudinally across the aggregate types of political economies and cross-sectionally for the individual countries within these groupings.

Figure 5.5A provides measures of the 'rule of law' over time in the three country groupings. The rule of law indicator, which is drawn from the World Bank governance database, represents a broad measure of the respect of law and private property in a country, and as such, it is often taken as an overall measure of the growth potential of a country. As the figure shows, the subregions exhibit distinct governance patterns, especially across the two types of political economies with high natural resource endowments. Among our three groups, the MOCs have the lowest scores for the rule of law. Figure 5.5B plots the rule-of-law estimates and per capita oil rents by country, using data from 1998 to 2010, a period that captures a stretch of high oil prices and culminates on the eve of the Arab Uprisings. The figure shows that most countries within each resource grouping conformed to the trends depicted in the figure. The Gulf countries in the HOC group stand out for their high rule-of-law estimates. In contrast, within the MOC group, the rule-of-law values are uniformly low, with all country estimates below zero.[3]

Much ink has been spilled on corruption and rising cronyism in the Middle Eastern countries.[4] Scholars have linked the region's economic underperformance to corruption in politics and everyday social transactions and have suggested that privileged access to economic opportunities has disproportionately rewarded regime cronies, who may not run the most efficient firms. What trends and patterns do we see in 'perceptions of corruption' within the region? Figure 5.6A depicts perceived corruption in the three country groupings over the past decade (lower scores denote higher perceived corruption or less control of corruption). Again, similar patterns hold: the MOCs collectively have by far the highest reported levels of corruption. At the country level, as shown in Figure 5.6B, the most corrupt countries are found in the MOC grouping, with Iraq scoring the lowest (and therefore being perceived as most corrupt) of all countries in the region, a pattern that accords with those seen with respect to the rule of law as well.

Another vital dimension of governance with implications for development trajectories is the degree to which states perpetrate violence and physically repress their populations. Figure 5.7A depicts country scores on the Cingranelli-Richards (CIRI) Physical Integrity Rights Index, which measures physical repression of populations at the country level

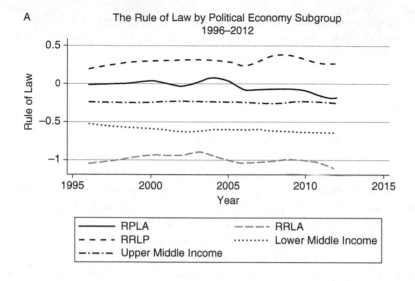

A

The Rule of Law by Political Economy Subgroup 1996–2012

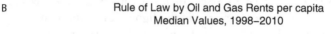

RPLA —— RRLA ———
RRLP – – – Lower Middle Income ……
Upper Middle Income –·–·–

B

Rule of Law by Oil and Gas Rents per capita Median Values, 1998–2010

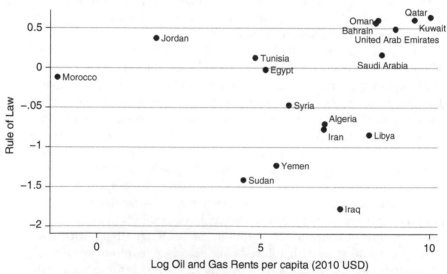

Figure 5.5 (A) The rule of law in the MENA political economy groups, median values of 1996–2012. (B) Rule-of-law estimates and oil rents per capita by country, average over time.

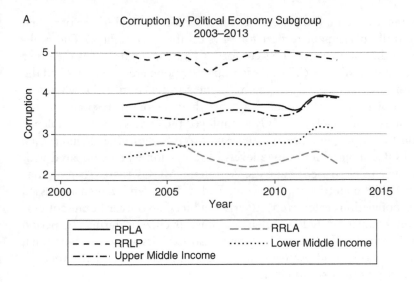

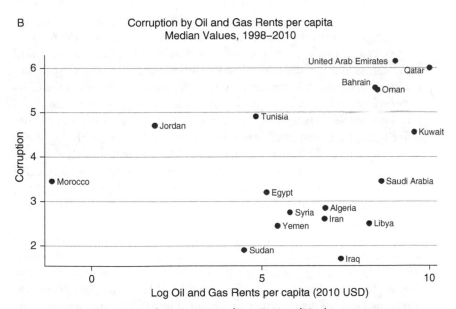

Figure 5.6 (A) Perceptions of corruption in the MENA political economy groups, 2003–2013. (B) Perceived corruption estimates and oil rents per capita by country, average over time.

and ranges from 0 (no government respect for physical integrity rights) to 8 (full government respect for physical integrity rights).[5] The rankings of the country groupings conform to the same patterns as the other governance indicators. The oil-rich, sparsely populated countries had the lowest levels of physical repression (highest scores) until 2011, when several HOCs employed violence against their people in response to the uprisings. Conversely, the MOCs employed the highest levels of violence against their people. As seen with respect to other governance indicators, the LOCs adopted mid-range levels of repression when compared with both groups of oil-rich countries. Within the MOCs, there is some variation. While countries such as Iran, Sudan, Syria, and Yemen repressed their populations extensively, Algeria is a bit of an outlier because it employed comparatively less violence against its citizens during the period (see Figure 5.7B). The HOC group also exhibits some cross-national variation, with Saudi Arabia employing more repression than other regimes in its category (and in a rising fashion).

The Middle East stands out in global perspective for its low levels of 'political freedoms,' irrespective of political economy type.[6] While repression has either remained constant or increased in most MENA countries since the 1980s, voice and participation have exhibited a downward trend across much of the region, and all subregions fall below the middle-income average on this measure. Figure 5.8A shows the trends in the CIRI Empowerment Rights Index in the three main groupings of regional political economies. Here, the relative rankings of political economy types differ from those seen in all other governance indicators, with the LOCs exhibiting the highest levels of freedom. On average, the MOCs once again exhibit the worst scores of all three groups, although the HOCs also have a low score rank on this indicator.[7] Figure 5.8B depicts levels of political freedoms and rights across the countries of the region on the eve of the uprisings. Within each grouping, there is considerable variation with respect to levels of political and civil liberties, calling for greater attention to over-time trends within individual countries. Among the MOC countries, Syria and Yemen displayed the lowest levels of political freedoms. The slight upward trend in freedoms in the MOCs in the late 2000s was driven by political development in Sudan. The HOC countries are characterized by the most variation in political and civil freedoms, with Saudi Arabia being the most restrictive in the region.

Finally, the ability of governments to provide the basis of development, whether in terms of social services or in their capacity to support private sector growth, defend property rights, regulate markets, and provide the infrastructure needed for growth, all depend directly on 'state

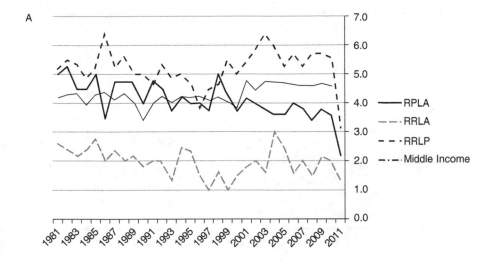

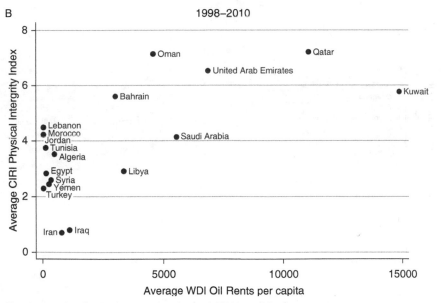

Figure 5.7 (A) Physical repression in the MENA political economy groups, 2003–2013. (B) Physical repression in the MENA political economy groups by country, average over time.

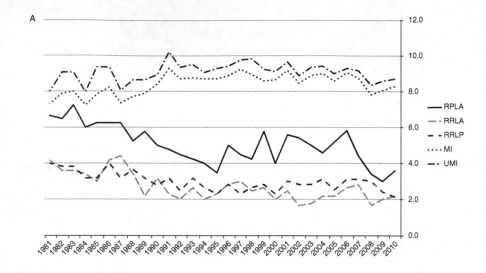

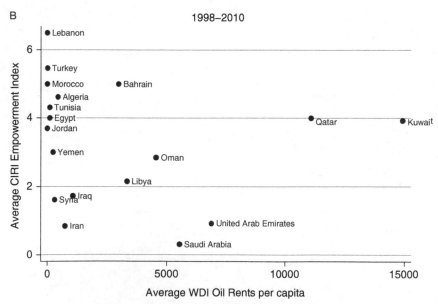

Figure 5.8 (A) Political rights in the MENA political economy groups, over time.
(B) Political rights in the MENA political economy groups by country, average
over time.

capacity.' While capacity is to some extent endogenous, being built when there is demand for it, it also directly constrains what the state can or cannot do, when political circumstances change. Figure 5.9A illustrates the average level of state capacity in our three groups of countries, as measured by World Bank data. It is apparent that state capacity is actually relatively high in both HOCs and LOCs. It is however extremely low in the MOCs, as it is close to the worse outcomes observed in the rest of the world. Figure 5.9B allows us to get a better feel for the differences across countries in the MOC group. Algeria and Iraq fare worse across the whole period. The HOCs tend to be on the top of state capacity index, with Saudi Arabia lagging the group.

In sum, an array of governance indicators, including measures of the rule of law, perceived corruption, repression, and civic and political freedoms, points to a fairly consistent pattern: all the MOCs exhibit inferior outcomes vis-à-vis the other country groupings in the Middle East. These findings contradict, or at least qualify, a core tenet of the resource curse argument and, more generally, an aggregated depiction of the region as a case of failed development. At a minimum, the alleged oil curse does not apply as a blanket rule across the region bur rather appears to afflict the MOCs far more than the other groups with less or more oil per capita. This relatively consistent picture of divergence across MENA political economies calls for greater analysis, in order to get a better appreciation of the conditions required to reverse the negative performances of these countries. What factors might explain the patterns and trends of the governance indicators in the MOCs relative to those of the two other types of political economies in the region?

The Evolution of Political Settlements

The economic and governance indicators discussed earlier clearly show that it is the MOCs of the Middle East that have largely been affected by an oil curse. But they do not add up easily to an account of how economic, institutional, and political circumstances interacted and influenced each other and, in so doing, influenced the dynamics of the political economy system. To try to build up a coherent and dynamic account, I will use a helpful political-economy framework that integrates governance and growth, as provided in the analysis of the evolution of 'political settlements' developed by Mushtaq Khan[8] and Douglas North[9] in particular.

The notion of 'political settlements' is associated with the relative distribution of power among different groups and organizations contesting the distribution of resources. A political settlement is the depiction of the institutional arrangements that emerge from conflicts over resources,

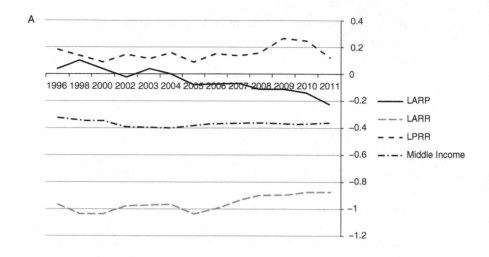

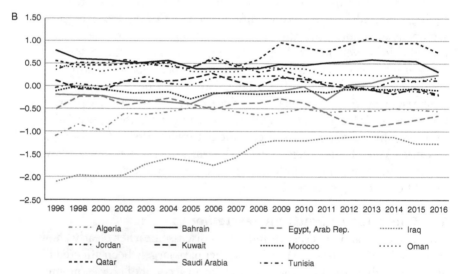

Figure 5.9 (A) State capacity by MENA subgroups. (B) State capacity by country.

most proximately among political and economic elites. The coalition of rulers and societal actors at the core of political settlements ensures the security of the regime by using the threat of force and extracting and distributing rents in order to maintain some popular support. The quality of a settlement can be judged by how costly it is for the economy to allow the coalition sufficient finance to sustain peace.[10] Depending on the breadth of the coalition and the nature of its underlying bargains, these coalitions may result in policies and practices that are more or less 'efficient' economically and that use varied levels of repression. In other words, the political settlements that encapsulate distinct patterns of state-society relations generate varied trends in the rule of law, government effectiveness, corruption, and other institutional factors that potentially shape development trajectories. At the same time, resource endowments affect the nature of political settlements: These arrangements arise out of struggles among actors with varied levels of power and may influence the nature of the bargains forged out of conflicts and bargaining processes among the key protagonists.

We are interested in the ways in which political settlements change and evolve. In this type of analysis, once countries manage to ensure a basic level of security, they evolve in a political space characterized by either a dominant party or a competitive political regime (the vertical axis in Table 5.2). We thus get, besides the initial settlement, four idealized types

Table 5.2 A typology of political regimes and regime dynamics

Founding Settlement:		Quality of Governance		
		Myopic/ Personalized	**Institutionalized**	
From conflict to a political settlement ⟶ that binds elites in a rent/power-sharing coalition, and society with a workable social ⟶ contract	**Dominant**	Dominant discretionary Oil importers in MENA after SAP (II) ↓	Rule by law dominant-developmental state ⟵ MENA states before regimes narrowed (I)	Sustainable democracy (V) ⟶
	Competitive	Personalized/ fragmented competitive Arab 'transition' countries after 2011 (III)	Rule of law competitive Goal post-AS for democratizing countries (IV)	⟶

Sources: Inspired by Brian Levy, *Working with the Grain* (Oxford: Oxford University Press, 2014); and Mushtaq H. Khan, "Political Settlements and the Governance of Growth Enhancing Institutions," unpublished manuscript, School of Oriental and African Studies (SOAS), London, United Kingdom, 2010.

of regimes, which fall short of a sustainable democracy. Movements along the map horizontally represent instances where the quality of governance improves or slides back, and vertical movements represent passages from autocratic to competitive systems. This is summarized in Table 5.2.

A 'founding' political settlement is a bargain among elites that ends violent conflict and forms a base for a country to begin its development history. The character of a 'founding' settlement sets a country along one of two broad trajectories.[11] The resulting political order could be organized around a dominant political party or leader and top-down nationalistic movements, as happened in much of the decolonized world in the 1950s and 1960s and in the Arab region. Alternatively, it could be more competitive, as in India and Bangladesh after their independence and in much of Latin America, Eastern Europe, and Africa after they moved to a new, more competitive settlement in the 1980s and 1990s. Within each trajectory the main developmental challenges are very different for countries in an early stage than in the later stages—making for four idealized categories.

In this classification, all Arab regimes (save Lebanon) were characterized by a dominant ruler or party in the past fifty years or so and belong to the upper part of the graph. Democratic/competitive and autocratic/dominant party regimes develop different types of institutions, with different strengths and weaknesses.[12] The second dimension of the table relates to the quality of governance in each of these distinct political paths, from basic settlements that deliver security to a low quality and then higher regimes. Various analysts have characterized 'quality' differently. The duality between 'myopic' and 'long horizon' rule dates back to Olson.[13] Khan focuses more on the degree of centralization, with territorial and intra-elite fragmentation found to weaken power.[14] Levy and Fukuyama, Khan, and North also emphasize a distinction between formal/informal and personalized/institutionalized relations. In these various meanings then, the 'good' governance regime would be associated with a development state that is more institutionalized, long-lived, and centralized, while a 'good' competitive system would be close to a rule-based sustainable democracy.

Let us now consider the relative place and evolution of the MENA countries in this governance space. There are no precise methods for measuring where countries fit in this space. But various heuristic claims can be argued.

First, all Arab countries approached type I after the modernist state push postindependence. These regimes were in some cases led by a king (Jordan, Morocco, Saudi Arabia) and in others by the military and/or unique parties (Iraq, Libya, Syria, Algeria, Lebanon); moreover, they were organized around charismatic individuals who became presidents for life after having successfully consolidated their grip on power.[15] In all cases, state building was pushed along the Attaturkian model of a modernist and secular state, with state-owned industries, large armies, a big focus on education, health, and infrastructure expansion all needing a large and sprawling bureaucracy that built up over time a new state-connected middle class. In this, they were similar to other state-dominant post-independence countries, such as Korea in the 1960s and early 1970s, or contemporary Ethiopia and Rwanda, countries where a flush of authority sets a country on the move after its leadership has embraced a coherent and mobilizing strategy for development

Second, the failure of the state-led modernization of the economy by the 1970s and 1980s pushed all countries to implement economic reforms. But importantly, no country undertook political liberalization. Rulers resorted to divide-and-rule strategies to stay in place, leading to a weakening of the quality of governance (and in particular in the rule of law and state capacity). So after the structural adjustment period (SAP) reforms of the 1980s and 1990s, these countries tended to move to the left toward type II, as governance became more myopic and oriented to short-term survival in some countries and more fragmented in others. Two developments are noteworthy during this period as drivers of change: the massive rollback of the state and the growth of crony capitalism, which were arguably more marked in MOCs.

After skyrocketing in the 1970s, government expenditures fell precipitously in Arab countries in the 1980s before stabilizing at much lower levels in the 1990s (see Figure 5.4).[16] By the early 1990s, state expenditures had been cut dramatically. Such a deep rollback had a dramatic impact on some of the key services offered by the state, especially where the cuts were large and public institutions declined steadily. It is noteworthy that the rollback occurred earlier in MOCs and resulted by 1990 in the lowest levels observed in the region (around 25 percent GDP), still larger than the average 20 percent observed in MICs around the world but much lower than in the rest of the region (which stabilized at about 35 percent around 1990).

The stated governments' plans were to move toward a market-based economy. However, market liberalization was done selectively to ensure that the private sector did not grow in ways that would create a political threat to regime stability. In the mid-1980s, the Arab regimes were nearly all in a state of crisis—autocrats faced rising social and political opposition at the very same time they were losing the levers of ideology and the ownership of state enterprises, flush investment budgets, large civil services, and generous military and security spending. Political stability required that the emerging private sector be managed to ensure that it did not offer support to the opposition, if not its neutrality. Control over the private sector was achieved by erecting barriers to entry that excluded political opponents and providing privileges to a small group of trusted allies. While networks of privilege existed in the private sector prior to the SAP of the 1980s and 1990s, the private sector was secondary in importance to state-owned enterprises (SOEs) and operated as a complement to the public sector. After the SAP period, however, these networks became more important in terms of their control of the economy, and they also became narrower in some countries, especially in the MOCs.[17] These narrow networks of privilege were reflected in low levels of the rule of law, particularly in the MOCs. Moreover, the lack of dynamism of markets must have taxed growth everywhere, but especially in the MOCs (Diwan et al., 2018).

Third, the social inheritance of concentrated capitalism has been highly problematic. Cronyism has made capitalism exclusive and unpopular; it has led to the emergence of a very rich '1 percent,' which has unbalanced politics by considerably strengthening the voice of the elite at the expense of the population at large. The slow growth of the formal private sector has exacerbated labor market dualism, increasing the inequality of opportunity faced by large cohorts of young graduates seeking their first job. For all these reasons, large swaths of the population increasingly came to see cronyism and corruption, both petty and grand, as the hallmark of failed economic policies and the source of many ills, including the job deficit and the rise in inequality. Popular frustrations with low-quality governance, rising repression, and unmet social aspirations by an increasingly educated population produced a political shock in 2011 when mass movements throughout the Middle East attempted to shift the course of politics toward more competitive systems.

Jumps from autocratic to more competitive systems have also occurred elsewhere in the past. Most political scientists seem to believe that as countries get richer, they will end up in a competitive polity with more space for 'voice.' This case is powerfully developed by Acemoglu and Robinson who argue that without political and economic inclusion, societies are unlikely to be able to become prosperous.[18] While the rise of China (or the GCC for that matter) puts such general statements in question, it is undeniable that countries that successfully traverse the earlier stages of the 'dominant state' trajectory have over time increasingly confronted governance-related challenges that push them to either restore lost power or open up their polity. Such pressures can arise from both failure and success.

Failures have often been associated with leadership that ends up using its authority for narrow, self-seeking ends, thus breaking the 'autocratic bargain' by losing legitimacy. In much of the Arab world of the 2000s, there was no ideological foundation left to ruling regimes, in sharp contrast to the widely legitimate and mobilizing ideologies of the 1960s. This was especially the case in the MOCs. These are all countries where postindependence regimes had built their legitimacy on a populist republican message, as they tended to expropriate the old economic elite, but where the failure of the statist model led to a dramatic shift in political alliances, with the regime dropping its support to the 'masses' and aligning its interest instead with those of a narrow crony capitalistic new elite base.[19]

Fourth, the countries of the region diverged in important ways in the reaction of political elites to these mass movements, setting the countries on widely different courses and in the extent to which the sudden political opening that followed decades of dominant state polities has unleashed previously suppressed conflicts, making the governance challenges post uprisings more complex and profound.

All political strategies during political transitions present challenges and risks. 'Jumps' from dominant to competitive trajectories could proceed relatively smoothly—as in Korea, where 'later stage state dominance' evolved fairly seamlessly into a competitive polity. But it could also unfold more discontinuously—as happened during Eastern Europe's color revolutions or in Indonesia and Thailand. Newly formed competitive democracies face challenges related to the lack of adaptation of their institutions to their new circumstances. The peculiarities of the MENA region in these respects are several. Unlike Eastern Europe, the delegitimized institutions of the past could not be replaced by ready-made new rules. Unlike the transition in Latin America, there was little in terms of historical traditions to come back to, since autocratic nationalism came right after independence and decolonization. Unlike the recent transition in Korea, Indonesia, or Mexico, the autocratic rulers had not prepared the institutional ground for a more inclusive future. Political parties to aggregate preferences did not exist at the outset of the 'jump,' and institutions that could generate cooperative solutions were also lacking.

MENA countries have reacted to the new situation in different ways, breaking the uniformity of politics that characterized the Middle East in the past.[20] At one extreme, the GCC countries remained stable as they reacted to the uprisings by increased patronage. In the transition countries, the two polar cases are those of Egypt and Tunisia. Egypt is seeking to adapt to the new circumstances through a 'reformation' of the old system—moving back from III to II and ideally to I.[21] Tunisia has chosen to try to move to a competitive political system (box IV).[22] Jordan and Morocco have chosen an intermediate path, with important political reforms initiated in order to preserve and gradually change the existing political settlement, but without major power loss in the short term. One can depict such a strategy as a gradual diagonal movement from regimes II to IV. The cases of interest to us, Syria, Iraq, Yemen, and Libya, illustrate extreme cases, where a move away from autocracy has led to the explosion of the past settlements (i.e., a move back to the extreme left box in the table). Why this is so (and also, why they turned to hard authoritarianism after SAP) is the subject we investigate in the next section.

Exploring the Causes of the Specificity of the MOCs

In this section, I ask whether the massive state failure of the MOCs was preordained or instead simply circumstantial. The MOCs all had a more hopeful period, and one would not have necessarily predicted that as a group, they would end up at the bottom rung of the MENA governance ladder. Indeed, Syria was reforming and growing in 2000–2010 under the youthful reign of Bashar al-Assad, with an early period of political opening (the Damascus Spring). Iraq was one of the first countries of the region to engage in reforming its economy in the early 1980s, before being adversely affected by wars.[23] At independence, Algeria was considered a paragon of a 'big push' state and was a leader in the nonaligned movement. Sudan was expected to become the bread basket of the Middle East, especially after its first revolution in 1964 when the street displaced a hard autocrat for the first time in the Arab world. Yemen managed to develop its oil resources after its political unification in 1990, which was followed by two decades of modest but positive developmental outcomes. Even Libya had reengaged and started reforms in the 2000s, as Gaddafi reduced his Arab and then African ambitions and tried to integrate into the world order.

We are therefore led to explore two questions of interest: (1) Why did all the MOCs end up moving into systems of narrow and repressive autocracy? (2) Why was their political settlement destroyed after the Arab Spring (and a bit later in the case of Algeria and Sudan)? I argue in this chapter that an explanation for this divergent governance must focus on both per capita resource endowments and variation in political settlements dating to the history of the regimes in place. In other words, institutional forms and coalitions that predate the discovery and exploitation of oil affect subsequent governance patterns. But at the same time, per capita resource wealth constrains the behavior of economic and political elites, reshaping or reinforcing political settlements to result in distinct governance patterns in different political economy types.

One of the main ideas in the literature on authoritarianism in general and on the Middle East in particular is that autocrats use a mix of repression and co-optation to stay in power.[24] A few analysts of Middle Eastern authoritarianism have explored how the type of regime in place affects the choice between these two strategies.[25] In essence, two main strategies are available to autocrats with access to oil rents: (1) developing a distributive state and building clientelistic relations to stabilize their rule; and (2) using oil rents to develop a coercive apparatus, turning their country into what Clement Henry and Robert Springborg[26] call a 'bunker state' (also see the work of Bellin).[27]

If authoritarian rulers deploy a combination of carrots and sticks to buttress their rule, then governments with higher per capita resource wealth at their disposal can afford to invest in more benefits for their populations. As shown in the previous section, however, the MOCs employed more repression than the LOCs, despite the fact that they had more resources to co-opt their people through material benefits than their resource-poor, populous cousins, and the HOCs employed less repression than the MOCs, even though they could certainly afford to do so.

This leads us to ask whether a co-optation strategy becomes more attractive only after a threshold of wealth is reached. The relative dependence of regime survival on one strategy over the other must be based (at least in part) on a cost-benefit calculus. Recent research claims that when oil earnings per capita are very high, as in HOCs, regimes tend to prefer survival strategies that rely more on the allocation of rentier earnings than on sheer repression, whereas if oil per capita is modest, as in the resource-rich labor abundant (RRLA) countries, a strategy of repression is preferred. In particular, Cammett et al. argue that in MOCs, oil tends to be a double curse.[28] Not only is it more tempting for autocrats to invest oil rents in a security apparatus, and to rely on repressing people as a central strategy to stay in power, but in addition, they also tend to distrust autonomous private firms, and thus, also repress markets. The very narrowness of the pool of beneficiaries, however, can incite popular dissatisfaction. Quelling real and potential opposition from an angered, deprived population in turn compels rulers to invest in their coercive apparatuses in order to maintain control. By this logic, when resources are more constrained, ruling coalitions would tend to be narrower both politically and economically. The pursuit of growth and development would have required rulers to foster or at least tolerate the rise of a relatively independent private sector, which may generate a key foothold for the rise of opposition. Deterring the rise of a powerful private sector is however a more attractive approach to ensuring regime survival, despite the loss in potential output.

The empirical record of the countries of the region seems to fit closely the expectations sketched earlier. First, the rulers of the GCC states concentrate their efforts on distributing wealth to the population to buy social peace and preempt greater societal demands for accountability. Thanks to relatively high per capita resource wealth, these regimes can place tight restrictions on political voice and generally do not resort to high levels of repression. In contrast, all regimes in all the MOCs, including Saddam's Iraq, Assad's Syria, Saleh's Yemen, or Gaddafi's Libya, conform to the contrasting high repression scenario. Algeria, Sudan, and Iran also resemble this model. No MOC has been unable to bring tangible and sustainable gains to their population since the 1980s, despite their resource wealth. The recent histories of the MOCs reveal track records of failed industrialization, bankrupt ideological programs, and growing indifference of state elites to society. These countries did not have the luxury of distributing rents broadly and, instead, were forced to make choices about whom to favor, generating potential grievances and at times calling for repression to maintain order. The main mechanisms for power preservation in the MOCs came to include the development of large state policing and security apparatuses and minimal reliance on private sector, save for formal private firms closely associated with the governing clan, and a sprawling but inefficient informal economy. In all cases, the MOCs have exhibited declining state capacity, contributing to poor economic and social performance, despite greater availability of resources than in the poorer labor-abundant countries.[29]

The story privileging resource endowments is compelling, but more deeply rooted political explanations are critical to account for variation in governance patterns both across and within the clusters of MENA political economies. Natural resources clearly do not, by themselves, automatically condemn political regimes to be autocratic or contribute to patterns of governance that deter long-term development. Indeed, there are many MOCs around the world that have been more successful at development efforts, such as Malaysia, Mexico, or Brazil. In the same vein, it was not inevitable that the Gulf states would be able to extract such high volumes of oil. The ability to do so was contingent on the construction of a social order and sufficient infrastructural capacity prior to the oil boom, and so even their high level of per capita rents must have grown somewhat endogenous. The same argument plays out in reverse in the MOCs, underlying the pernicious effect of middle levels of oil in countries with unfavorable initial circumstances. Algeria, Iran, or Iraq could have been high rent per capita countries, given the size of their proven reserves. Indeed, the prospect of constructing a developmental state was then seen as more realistic than in the GCC countries, given their access to high natural *and* human resources. Up to the 1970s, their statist development paradigms were consistent with their autocratic mode of governance. Their second, more violent and repressive phase emerged later, after the failed industrialization drives of the 1960s and 1970s.[30] It is thus when their ambitious development plans failed that they reversed course, becoming repressive states less willing than other countries to open up to the private sector, because of their inherent unwillingness to trust autonomous private sector actors.[31] The situation in these countries thus increasingly came to resemble the violence trap equilibrium.[32]

But there are historical patterns that are also coherent with this divergence of governance. The emergence of the modern Gulf states—generally around the same time as the twilight of colonial empires worldwide—coincides with the discovery of oil reserves in the Gulf. The initial development of an oil production industry occurred at a nascent stage of statehood—and, in some cases, before states gained formal independence—which was founded on bargains between rulers and key tribal families that had already been forged. This timing and set of historical developments permitted old structures of patrimonial and monarchical governance in the Gulf not only to endure but also to prosper—a relationship that continues into the present. *All* the MOCs, however, built postindependence republican regimes that were born out of more violent political processes. The revolutionary breaks from the past that gave rise to the new regimes put at the helm groups that espoused radical departures, embodied in Ba'ath ideology in Iraq and Syria, Islamism in Iran and Sudan after the 1980s, and socialism in Algeria. All of the MOCs adopted populist policies at independence. Such policies strengthened the hold on power of previously marginalized groups (such as lower level military and particular ethnic or tribal groups), and this was further achieved by expropriating the existing economic elite, in the several waves of nationalizations that took place in Iraq, Syria, and Libya (and also in Iran and Algeria). Initially, the support from the 'masses' ensured legitimacy for the new rulers. The failure of this economic model exposed the weaknesses of their political structure, pushing these regimes to increasingly resort to sheer repression to survive (given their inherent opposition to the growth of autonomous private actors).

One can go further and ask about the influence of colonial history. In the Gulf states, ruling families had largely centralized their authority prior to the discovery of oil.[33] This was generally with support from British colonial officials.[34] With a relatively secure hold on power, rulers could build on preexisting patronage networks to secure their rule. Arguably, this enabled them to develop longer time horizons, generating incentives to deliver benefits to the population. The political and institutional contexts differed markedly in the newly independent republics— Algeria, Iraq, Syria, Sudan, Yemen, Sudan, and Libya. In these countries, postindependence rulers constructed state institutions on the foundations of colonial institutions, which in many cases left legacies of economic and institutional destruction. Indeed, colonialism in its varied guises had important legacies for subsequent state-building process and development trajectories in the Middle East.[35] The GCC states were only lightly incorporated into both the Ottoman Empire and the European empires, compared with the rest of the MENA region. Prime examples of the deleterious effects of colonial exploitation on the construction of postindependence state institutions are Iraq and Algeria, both MOCs. The colonial legacy and Ottoman history in Iraq or Syria through the early twentieth century can also partly account for how relatively slowly state institutions became stable in these countries, as compared with the largely uncolonized Gulf region.

This leaves the issue of why the MOCs were unable to preserve their harsh political settlement after 2011. In this discussion, it is useful to recall Eva Bellin's prescient analysis of what makes a successful MENA autocrat.[36] Her analysis came down to four conditions required to support the 'will to repress': (1) the existence of some rents to pay for security services; (2) the organization of the security apparatus in ways that ensure that top officials would be 'ruined by reforms'; (3) the ability to resist international pressure to change; and (4) low degree of popular mobilization. Oil resources allowed the MOCs to satisfy conditions (1) and (3) and have large armies and security forces. They also allowed these countries to remain somewhat independent of foreign patrons. This independence is an important difference from other countries, such as Jordan and Egypt, which received large external rents, not from oil but from foreign donors; the dependence of these countries on donors restricted the extent of the repression they could use. Condition (2) was also met as these countries moved toward patrimonial forms of organization, especially of their security forces, but also of their economies.

The last condition was not satisfied post 2011. But in the absence of foreign interventions, it is likely that the MOCs could have preserved their hard autocracies, at least in the short term (this is also true of Iraq under Saddam before the US invasion). Most Arab countries, including our countries of interest, witnessed large public demonstrations and protests. In the face of massive social mobilization, relatively peaceful political change occurred in Tunisia and Egypt, countries where the army defected from the contested autocrat. In Yemen, the army split and each faction sought an alliance with different groups vying for power, which was later exacerbated into a full-fledged war after the GCC armed intervention. In Syria and Libya, the army did not defect, but regime brutality and foreign interventions in support of a myriad of groups led to proxy civil wars of high intensity. In Iraq, state collapse dates to the 2002 US invasion. In Sudan and Algeria, the army replaced a contested autocrat and is trying to remain in power (in the case of Sudan, with help from the GCC, and in the case of Algeria, with the tacit approval of the West).

Conclusions

I have argued in this chapter that the MOCs of the Middle East have evolved over time—from being the countries of the region with the greatest potential to failing or failed states. Their economic performance also ended up being the worst in the MENA region, and by 2010, they had the poorest governance indicators, high on repression of their population's voice, and of markets, and low on state capacity and the rule of law. I then argued that factors that pushed the MOCs to become 'bunker states' after their rising modernist phase were related to their level of oil endowment, but also to their historical inheritance and the circumstances of the international world order. While this analysis was shown to apply quite well to Iraq, Syria, Yemen, and Libya, it is also arguably relevant to the other MOCs, and especially to Iran, Algeria, and Sudan, who while still enjoying a level of stability, seem to have deep sources of weaknesses in their current political economy equilibrium.

What does this analysis tell us about these countries that is relevant when considering how to enter into a postconflict reconstruction phase? I focus here on three aspects of the issue: the challenge of building a workable political settlement; the ways the negative effect of oil may be neutralized; and the ways in which reconstruction effort can have a negative bearing on both factors, if not carefully planned.

First, ending a civil war and rebuilding a ruling coalition is a notoriously tricky and difficult task in the best of circumstances. Challenges focus largely on finding ways to overcome problems created by lack of coordination among various groups vying for power. This includes asymmetric information about the power of each group and the lack of commitment mechanisms, which keep civil wars from stopping, especially when some groups are perceived to lack the legitimacy needed to enter into long-term commitments.[37] In the region, these problems were compounded by the fact that our four countries did not have a workable political settlement since the demise of the state-led growth model in the 1980s, in the sense of a political economy system that allows for private sector growth while preserving a modicum of political stability.

One extra layer of complexity relates to the ongoing proxy-war logic introduced by the fierce competition between Saudi Arabia and Iran for regional dominance, and the complex changes taking place in the foreign policies of the superpowers most influential in the region, the United States, Russia, and the European Union. In the current context, the emergence of a national pact that can ensure security and get reconstruction and growth going is at the mercy of incentives of foreign powers. As a result, spoilers abound, although geopolitical and oil rents are too low to allow for large coalitions. In this respect, Iraq represents an iconic case, where the power vacuum left by the demise of the Ba'ath regime has fostered the profusion of groups competing for power, including the Islamic State of Iraq and Syria (ISIS), but has not resulted yet in a comprehensive wealth- and power-sharing agreement that includes all major and popular forces.

Second, the question arises as to how (and indeed whether) reconstruction efforts can be structured to help, rather than hinder, the constitution of a workable political settlement in these countries. One can imagine that such efforts can aid at best to cement a new order, giving it oxygen to traverse the first most perilous years and setting the country on a virtuous path. The experience of reconstruction in the region, however, does not inspire confidence in this possibility, as it has tended to support—probably unwillingly—efforts by particular factions to dominate others, thereby weakening their ability to constitute coalitions that can ensure peace and stability. In South Sudan, oil revenue was monopolized by the dominant faction of the Sudan People's Liberation Army (SPLA), leading to the current situation of civil war. In Lebanon, reconstruction efforts consolidated a sectarian division of the country among the protagonists of the civil war, to the exclusion of other groups with economic power but no violence potential. In 1990 in Yemen and in 2000 in Iraq, important groups with violence potential were left out of the governing coalition, leading to instability down the line. These considerations suggest that an important role and responsibility for externally funded reconstruction efforts is to have a clear vision of the minimum conditions required for a political settlement to be stable enough to warrant engaging in such efforts that can stabilize the situation, as opposed to investing wrongly in a settlement that is doomed to failure, with potentially enormously destructive potential.

Third, the analysis in the chapter suggests several considerations in asking whether a political settlement is 'good enough' to engage in. This includes elements that ensure that oil revenues are less at risk of being monopolized by one group to oppress others. Thus, conditions for positive involvement are likely to include centrally whether the recipient governing coalition is broad enough to ensure security. This involves looking at arrangements in the security sector, as well as the existence of wealth- and power-sharing agreements among the main groups with violence potential. These considerations can thus involve technical assistance in the design of decentralized intergovernmental arrangements, or of institutions that can represent the various groups, while keeping in mind the risk of national disintegration. Unfortunately, it would also be necessary to ask whether the recipient coalition is not too broad to be manageable financially, especially given that donor funding is likely to remain limited in the current international context.

Notes

1. The averages are computed as unweighted averages over time and over countries, since the goal here is to illustrate the performance of an average country.

2. Kiren Aziz Chaudhry, *The Price of Wealth: Economies and Institutions in the Middle East* (Ithaca, NY: Cornell University Press, 1997).

3. In general, the rule of law is higher in the monarchies than in the authoritarian republics. But given the overlap between monarchies and high per capita natural resource endowments, this association may not arise from the effects of the regime type but rather may result from resource levels. Furthermore, the two monarchies without oil wealth have markedly lower rule-of-law estimates.

4. Ishac Diwan, Philip Keefer, and Marc Schiffbauer, "On Top of the Pyramids: Cronyism and Private Sector Growth in Egypt," Working Paper, World Bank, Washington, DC, 2014; Clement Moore Henry and Robert Springborg, *Globalization and the Politics of Development in the Middle East*, vol. 1 (Cambridge: Cambridge University Press, 2010); Steven

Heydemann, ed., *Networks of Privilege in the Middle East: The Politics of Economic Reform Revisited* (New York: Palgrave Macmillan, 2004); Oliver Schlumberger, "Structural Reform, Economic Order, and Development: Patrimonial Capitalism," *Review of International Political Economy* 15, no. 4 (2008): 622–649.

5. David L. Cingranelli and David L. Richards, "The Cingranelli and Richards (CIRI) Human Rights Data Project," *Human Rights Quarterly* 32, no. 2 (2010): 401–424.

6. Eva Bellin, "Reconsidering the Robustness of Authoritarianism in the Middle East: Lessons from the Arab Spring," *Comparative Politics* 44, no. 2 (2011): 127–149; Marsha Pripstein Posusney and Michele Penner Agrist, eds., *Authoritarianism in the Middle East: Regimes and Resistance* (Boulder, CO: Lynne Rienner, 2005).

7. Furthermore, in contrast to the patterns seen in other governance indicators, all three types of MENA political economies scored well below middle-income and upper-middle-income averages on political freedoms.

8. Mushtaq H. Khan, "Political Settlements and the Governance of Growth Enhancing Institutions," unpublished manuscript, School of Oriental and African Studies (SOAS), London, United Kingdom, 2010.

9. Douglass C. North, *Institutions, Institutional Change, and Economic Performance* (Cambridge: Cambridge University Press, 1990).

10. Douglass C. North, John Joseph Wallis, and Barry R Weingast, *Violence and Social Orders: A Conceptual Framework for Interpreting Recorded Human History* (Cambridge: Cambridge University Press, 2009).

11. Brian Levy and Francis Fukuyama, "Development Strategies: Integrating Governance and Growth," World Bank Policy Research Working Paper Series, no. 5196, 2010.

12. But their economies do not fare very differently on average. The accepted wisdom until recently was that economic growth under autocratic and democratic systems has similar means, but larger variance under autocracy. Timothy J. Besley and Masayuki Kudamatsu, "Making Autocracy Work," LSE STICERD Research Paper No. DEDPS48, May 2007. More recently, Acemoglu, Naidu, Restrepo, and Robinson, "Democracy Does Cause Growth," NBER Working Paper 20004, National Bureau of Economic Research, March 2014, argue that democratic countries grow slightly faster than autocracies.

13. Mancur Olson, "Dictatorship, Democracy, and Development," *American Political Science Review* 87, no. 3 (1993): 567–576.

14. Khan, "Political Settlements and the Governance of Growth Enhancing Institutions."

15. Roger Owen, *The Rise and Fall of Arab Presidents for Life: With a New Afterword* (Cambridge, MA: Harvard University Press, 2014). In Yemen's case, 'progressive' South Yemen fits into this description, and after 1990, unified Yemen under Abdallah Saleh. Libya under Gaddafi is exceptional in the low level of development of its institutions.

16. Expenditures only started to rise again, in oil-exporting countries, in 2005, with many ramping up energy subsidies and state employment. The movement accelerated after 2011, but slowed down in 2014, when oil prices collapsed.

17. Roger Owen, *State, Power and Politics in the Making of the Modern Middle East* (Abingdon: Routledge, 2004); Owen, *The Rise and Fall of Arab Presidents for Life*.

18. Daron Acemoglu and James A. Robinson, *Why Nations Fail: The Origins of Power, Prosperity, and Poverty* (New York: Crown, 2012).

19. But pressures arise equally from success. Success in accelerating economic growth, as happened in the LOCs in the 2000s, resulted in a more sophisticated private sector, a growing middle class, and an emerging network of civil society organizations. This enhanced social and economic complexity tends to come into increasing conflict with control-oriented political and state institutions. One can argue that this was especially the case in LOCs, where growth was large before 2011, even if not inclusive, and where as a result, middle-income educated youth came to have increasingly modernist aspirations, which gradually clashed with the mode of economic and political governance that controlled their lives.

20. Roger Owen, *Power and Politics in the Making of the Modern Middle East* (Abingdon: Routledge, 2004); Owen, *The Rise and Fall of Arab Presidents for Life*; Heydemann, *Networks of Privilege in the Middle East*.

21. Autocratic restorations, as in Egypt, face steep challenges, albeit of a different type from those experienced by a young and fragile democracy such as Tunisia. Examples from the former Soviet Union's failed reformation to Pakistan's unstable equilibrium point to the dangers ahead in Egypt. The 2011 revolts have unleashed social activism to a level unseen in the past, and while the fear of chaos may have cooled down those impulses in the short term, it has become much harder for regimes to stay in place if a minimum level of satisfaction is not insured for important constituencies in a reformulated political bargain.

22. Political scientists have examined the reasons for this political divergence, attributing it variably to the existence of a large army in Egypt, the leadership of Tunisia's main parties and the active role of civil society in mediating dispute, and the moderating qualities of Tunisia's Islamic opposition

and its ability to find compromises. See Eva Bellin, "The Puzzle of Democratic Divergence in the Arab World: Theory Meets Experience in Tunisia and Egypt," *Political Science Quarterly* 133, no. 3 (Fall 2018).

23. Kiren Aziz Chaudhry, "Economic Liberalization and the Lineages of the Rentier State," *Comparative Politics* 27, no. 1 (October 1994): 1–25.

24. See, for example, Eva Bellin, "The Robustness of Authoritarianism in the Middle East: Exceptionalism in Comparative Perspective," *Comparative Politics* 36, no. 2 (2004): 139–157; Bruce Bueno de Mesquita, Alastair Smith, Randolph M. Siverson, and James D. Morrow, *The Logic of Political Survival* (Cambridge, MA: MIT Press, 2004); Marsha Pripstein Posusney, "Enduring Authoritarianism: Middle East Lessons for Comparative Theory," *Comparative Politics* 36, no. 2 (2004): 127–138.

25. Omer Ali and Ibrahim Elbadawi, "The Political Economy of Public Sector Employment in Resource Dependent Countries," Economic Research Forum, 2012; Adeel Malik and Bassem Awadallah, "The Economics of the Arab Spring," *World Development* 45, no. C (2013): 296–313; Melani Cammett and Ishac Diwan, "Resource Wealth, Political Settlements and the Rule of Law in the Middle East," unpublished manuscript, Cambridge, MA, 2018.

26. Henry and Springborg, *Globalization and the Politics of Development in the Middle East*.

27. Bellin, "The Robustness of Authoritarianism in the Middle East," 139–157.

28. Melani Cammett, Ishac Diwan, and Andrew Leber, "Is Oil Wealth Good or Bad for Private Sector Development?," ERF Working Paper Series, no. 1299, http://erf.org.eg/wp-content/uploads/2019/03/1299.pdf.

29. Both scenarios contrast with the situation in the LOCs, in which governing elites had few or no resource rents at their disposal. Rulers in the LOCs were compelled to tolerate greater competition in society because they lacked sufficient rents to repress or buy the loyalty of all. If they were unable to deliver important economic improvements, they were equally unable to maintain power by sheer repression. In general, political regimes in the LOCs had adopted by necessity mixed political and economic survival strategies aimed at the same time at buying the allegiance of the middle class (while repressing the poor) but with production structure based on a relatively narrow elite base.

30. For the frontline states, especially Egypt, Iraq, and Syria, this was coupled with the humiliating defeat in the 1967 Arab-Israeli War that put the core legitimacy of these regimes into question.

31. Dominated by security apparatuses, many countries of this group sought risky outside adventures to prop up their grip on power, including Saddam's Kuwait invasion, Syria's occupation of Lebanon, Bachir's war on east

and south Sudan, Saleh's takeover of South Yemen, Gaddafi's involvement in many countries' internal politics in Sub-Saharan Africa, Algeria's support for the Polisario, and after 2011, Iran's expansionist efforts in the region.

32. Gary W. Cox, Douglass C. North, and Barry R. Weingast, "The Violence Trap: A Political-Economic Approach to the Problems of Development," Available at SSRN 2370622, 2015.

33. Jill Crystal, *Oil and Politics in the Gulf* (New York: Cambridge University Press, 1995); Michael Herb, *All in the Family: Absolutism, Revolution, and Democracy in Middle Eastern Monarchies* (Albany: State University of New York Press, 1999); Steffen Hertog, *Princes, Brokers, and Bureaucrats: Oil and the State in Saudi Arabia* (Ithaca, NY: Cornell University Press, 2010).

34. Sami Atallah, "The Gulf Region: Beyond Oil and Wars—the Role of History and Geopolitics in Explaining Autocracy," in *Democracy in the Arab World; Explaining the Deficit*, ed. Ibrahim Elbadawi and Samir Makdisi (Abingdon: Routledge, 2011), 166–196.

35. Roger Owen, "Introduction," in *State, Power and Politics in the Making of the Modern Middle East*. As Acemoglu, Johnson, and Robinson (2002) and Mahoney (2010) argue, the legacy of colonial-era extraction economies correlates with the weakness of postindependence state institutions. Daron Acemoglu, Simon Johnson, and James A. Robinson, "Reversal of Fortune: Geography and Institutions in the Making of the Modern World Income Distribution," *Quarterly Journal of Economics* 117, no. 4 (2002): 1231–1294; James Mahoney, *Colonialism and Postcolonial Development: Spanish America in Comparative Perspective* (Cambridge: Cambridge University Press, 2010).

36. Bellin, "Reconsidering the Robustness of Authoritarianism in the Middle East."

37. James D. Fearon, "Primary Commodity Exports and Civil War," *Journal of Conflict Resolution* 49, no. 4 (2005): 483–507.

Bibliography

Acemoglu, Daron, Simon Johnson, and James A. Robinson. "Reversal of Fortune: Geography and Institutions in the Making of the Modern World Income Distribution." *Quarterly Journal of Economics* 117, no. 4 (2002): 1231–1294.

Acemoglu, Daron, and James A. Robinson. *Why Nations Fail: The Origins of Power, Prosperity, and Poverty*. New York: Crown, 2012.

Acemoglu, Daron, Suresh Naidu, Pascual Restrepo, and James A. Robinson. "Democracy Does Cause Growth." National Bureau of Economic Research Working Paper no. 20004, March 2014.

Adly, Amr. "Triumph of the Bureaucracy: A Decade of Aborted Social and Political Change in Egypt." Jadaliyya, January 31, 2015.

Ali, Omer, and Ibrahim Elbadawi. "The Political Economy of Public Sector Employment in Resource Dependent Countries." Economic Research Forum, 2012.

Atallah, Sami. "The Gulf Region: Beyond Oil and Wars—the Role of History and Geopolitics in Explaining Autocracy." In *Democracy in the Arab World; Explaining the Deficit*, 166–196. Abingdon: Routledge, 2011.

Auty, Richard, and Alan Gelb. "Oil Windfalls in a Small Parliamentary Democracy: Their Impact on Trinidad and Tobago." *World Development* 14, no. 9 (1986): 1161–1175.

Ayubi, Nazih. *The State and Public Policies in Egypt since Sadat*. Reading, UK: Ithaca, 1991.

Beblawi, Hazem. "The Rentier State in the Arab World." In *The Rentier State*, edited by Hazem Beblawi and Giacomo Luciani, 85–98. London: Croom Helm, 1987.

Bellin, Eva. "Drivers of Democracy: Lessons from Tunisia." *Middle East Brief* 75 (2013): 1–8.

———. "Reconsidering the Robustness of Authoritarianism in the Middle East: Lessons from the Arab Spring." *Comparative Politics* 44, no. 2 (2011): 127–149.

———. "The Robustness of Authoritarianism in the Middle East: Exceptionalism in Comparative Perspective." *Comparative Politics* 36, no. 2 (2004): 139–157.

Besley, Timothy J., and Masayuki Kudamatsu. "Making Autocracy Work." LSE STICERD Research Paper No. DEDPS48, May 2007.

Brownlee, Jason, Tarek Masoud, and Andrew Reynolds. "Why the Modest Harvest?" *Journal of Democracy* 24, no. 4 (2013): 29–44.

Bueno de Mesquita, Bruce, Alastair Smith, Randolph M. Siverson, and James D. Morrow. *The Logic of Political Survival*. Cambridge, MA: MIT Press, 2004.

Cammett, Melani Claire. *Globalization and Business Politics in Arab North Africa: A Comparative Perspective*. Cambridge: Cambridge University Press, 2007.

Cammett, Melani, and Ishac Diwan. "Resource Wealth, Political Settlements and the Rule of Law in the Middle East." Unpublished manuscript, Cambridge, MA, 2018.

Cammett, Melani, Ishac Diwan, Allan Richards, and John Waterbury. *The Political Economy of the Arab Uprisings*, 4th ed. New York: Perseus Books, 2015.

Chaudhry, Kiren Aziz. "Economic Liberalization and the Lineages of the Rentier State." *Comparative Politics* 27, no. 1 (October 1994): 1–25.

———. *The Price of Wealth: Economies and Institutions in the Middle East*. Ithaca, NY: Cornell University Press, 1997.

Cingranelli, David L., and David L. Richards. "The Cingranelli and Richards

(CIRI) Human Rights Data Project." *Human Rights Quarterly* 32, no. 2 (2010): 401–424.

Collier, Paul. *Breaking the Conflict Trap: Civil War and Development Policy.* Washington, DC: World Bank Publications, 2003.

Cox, Gary W., Douglass C. North, and Barry R. Weingast. "The Violence Trap: A Political-Economic Approach to the Problems of Development." *Journal of Public Finance and Public Choice* 34, no. 1 (April 2019): 3–19.

Crystal, Jill. *Oil and Politics in the Gulf.* New York: Cambridge University Press, 1995.

Davenport, Christian, Hank Johnston, and Carol McClurg Mueller. *Repression and Mobilization*, vol. 21. Minneapolis: University of Minnesota Press, 2005.

Desai, Raj M., Anders Olofsgård, and Tarik M. Yousef. "The Logic of Authoritarian Bargains." *Economics & Politics* 21, no. 1 (2009): 93–125.

Diwan, Ishac. "Understanding Revolution in the Middle East: The Central Role of the Middle Class." *Middle East Development Journal* 5, no. 1 (2013): 1350004.

Diwan, Ishac, and Tarek Akin. "Fifty Years of Fiscal Policy in the MENA Region." ERF Working Paper, 2015.

Diwan, Ishac, Philip Keefer, and Marc Schiffbauer. "On Top of the Pyramids: Cronyism and Private Sector Growth in Egypt." Working Paper, World Bank, Washington, DC, 2014.

Diwan, Ishac, Adeel Malik, and Izak Atiyas. "Crony Capitalism in the Middle East—What Do We Know and Why Does It Matter?" In *Crony Capitalism in the Middle East*, edited by Diwan Ishac, Adeel Malik, and Izak Atiyas. Oxford: Oxford University Press, 2019.

Dunning, Thad. *Crude Democracy: Natural Resource Wealth and Political Regimes.* Cambridge: Cambridge University Press, 2008.

Elbadawi, Ibrahim, and Raimundo Soto. "Resource Rents, Political Institutions and Economic Growth." *ERF Working Paper no. 678*, 2012.

European Bank for Reconstruction and Development (EBRD). The Transition Report, 2013.

Evans, P. B. *Embedded Autonomy: States and Industrial Transformation*, vol. 25. Princeton, NJ: Princeton University Press, 1995.

Fearon, James D. "Primary Commodity Exports and Civil War." *Journal of Conflict Resolution* 49, no. 4 (2005): 483–507.

Gandhi, Jennifer, and Adam Przeworski. "Authoritarian Institutions and the Survival of Autocrats." *Comparative Political Studies* 40, no. 11 (2007): 1279–1301.

Haber, Stephen, and Victor Menaldo. "Do Natural Resources Fuel Authoritarianism? A Reappraisal of the Resource Curse." *American Political Science Review* 105, no. 1 (2011): 1–26.

Haddad, Bassam. *Business Networks in Syria: The Political Economy of Authoritarian Resilience.* Stanford, CA: Stanford University Press, 2012.

Harris, Kevan. "The Rise of the Subcontractor State: Politics of Pseudo-privatization in the Islamic Republic of Iran." *International Journal of Middle East Studies* 45, no. 1 (2013): 45–70.

Henry, Clement Moore, and Robert Springborg. *Globalization and the Politics of Development in the Middle East*, vol. 1. Cambridge: Cambridge University Press, 2010.

Herb, Michael. *All in the Family: Absolutism, Revolution, and Democracy in Middle Eastern Monarchies*. Albany: State University of New York Press, 1999.

———. *The Wages of Oil: Parliaments and Economic Development in Kuwait and the UAE*. Ithaca, NY: Cornell University Press, 2015.

Hertog, Steffen. "Defying the Resource Curse: Explaining Successful State-Owned Enterprises in Rentier States." *World Politics* 62, no. 2 (2010): 261–301.

———. *Princes, Brokers, and Bureaucrats: Oil and the State in Saudi Arabic*. Ithaca, NY: Cornell University Press, 2010.

———. "Shaping the Saudi State: Human Agency's Shifting Role in Rentier-State Formation." *International Journal of Middle East Studies* 39, no. 4 (2007): 539–563.

Heydemann, Steven, ed. *Networks of Privilege in the Middle East: The Politics of Economic Reform Revisited*. New York: Palgrave Macmillan, 2004.

Kaufmann, Daniel, Aart Kraay, and Massimo Mastruzzi. "The Worldwide Governance Indicators: Methodology and Analytical Issues." Policy Research Working Paper 5430, World Bank, Washington, DC, 2010.

Khan, Mushtaq H. "Political Settlements and the Governance of Growth Enhancing Institutions." Unpublished manuscript, School of Oriental and African Studies (SOAS), London, United Kingdom, 2010.

Kienle, Eberhard. *A Grand Delusion: Democracy and Economic Reform in Egypt*. London: I.B. Tauris, 2001.

King, Stephen Juan. *The New Authoritarianism in the Middle East and North Africa*. Bloomington: Indiana University Press, 2009.

Kuran, Timur. *The Long Divergence: How Islamic Law Held Back the Middle East*. Princeton, NJ: Princeton University Press, 2011.

Levy, Brian, and Francis Fukuyama. "Development Strategies: Integrating Governance and Growth." World Bank Policy Research Working Paper Series, WPS5196, 1, 2010.

Levy, Brian. *Working with the Grain*. Oxford: Oxford University Press, 2014.

Lowi, Miriam R. *Oil Wealth and the Poverty of Politics*. Cambridge: Cambridge University Press, 2009.

Luciani, Giacomo. "Allocation v. Production States: A Theoretical Framework." In *The Rentier State*, edited by Hazem Beblawi and Giacomo Luciani, 63–82. London: Croom Helm, 1987.

Mahdavy, H. "The Patterns and Problems of Economic Development in Rentier

State: The Case of Iran." In *Studies in the Economic History of the Middle East*, edited by Michael Cook, 428–467. London: Oxford University Press, 1970.

Malik, Adeel, and Bassem Awadallah. "The Economics of the Arab Spring." *World Development* 45 (May 2013): 296–313.

Menaldo, Victor. "The Middle East and North Africa's Resilient Monarchs." *Journal of Politics* 74, no. 3 (2012): 707–722.

Moore, Barrington, Jr. *Social Origins of Dictatorship and Democracy: Lord and Peasant in the Making of the Modern World*. Boston, MA: Beacon, [1966] 1993.

Noland, Marcus, and Howard Pack. *The Arab Economies in a Changing World*. Washington, DC: Peterson Institute for International Economics, 2007.

North, Douglass C. *Institutions, Institutional Change, and Economic Performance*. Cambridge: Cambridge University Press, 1990.

North, Douglass C., John Joseph Wallis, and Barry R. Weingast. *Violence and Social Orders: A Conceptual Framework for Interpreting Recorded Human History*. Cambridge: Cambridge University Press, 2009.

Olson, M. "Dictatorship, Democracy, and Development." *American Political Science Review* 87, no. 3 (1993): 567–576.

Osman, Tarek. *Egypt on the Brink: From Nasser to Mubarak*. New York: Yale University Press, 2010.

Owen, Roger. *The Rise and Fall of Arab Presidents for Life: With a New Afterword*. Cambridge, MA: Harvard University Press, 2014.

Owen, Roger, and Şevket Pamuk. *A History of Middle East Economies in the Twentieth Century*. London: I.B. Tauris, 1998.

Polanyi, Karl. *The Great Transformation: The Political and Economic Origins of Our Time*, 2nd ed. Boston, MA: Beacon, 2001.

Posusney, Marsha Pripstein. "Enduring Authoritarianism: Middle East Lessons for Comparative Theory." *Comparative Politics* 36, no. 2 (2004): 127–138.

Robinson, James A., Ragnar Torvik, and Thierry Verdier. "Political Foundations of the Resource Curse." *Journal of Development Economics* 79, no. 2 (2006): 447–468.

Ross, Michael. *The Oil Curse: How Petroleum Wealth Shapes the Development of Nations*. Princeton, NJ: Princeton University Press, 2010.

Schlumberger, Oliver, ed. *Debating Arab Authoritarianism: Dynamics and Durability in Nondemocratic Regimes*. Stanford, CA: Stanford University Press, 2007.

———. "Structural Reform, Economic Order, and Development: Patrimonial Capitalism." *Review of International Political Economy* 15, no. 4 (2008): 622–649.

Smith, Benjamin. *Hard Times in the Lands of Plenty: Oil Politics in Iran and Indonesia*. Ithaca, NY: Cornell University Press, 2007.

Vandewalle, Dirk. *A History of Modern Libya*. Cambridge: Cambridge University Press, 2012.

Waldner, David, and Benjamin Smith. "Rentier States and State Transforma-
   tions." In *Oxford Handbook on Transformations of the State*, edited by Stephan
   Leibfried, Evelyne Huber, Matthew Lange, Jonah D. Levy, Frank Nullmeier,
   and John D. Stephens, 714–730. Oxford: Oxford University Press, 2015.
World Bank. "Jobs or Privileges: Unleashing the Employment Potential of the
   Middle East and North Africa." Washington, DC: World Bank, 2014.

6

The Fall and Rise of Extra-Regional Actors

Robert Mason and Philipp Casula

This chapter provides an overview of the historic role of great powers in the Middle East (France, Britain, the United States, and the Soviet Union/Russia). It charts growing US engagement following the demise of the Soviet Union in 1991, symbolized by the Gulf War and a new US security architecture in the Gulf. By the 2000s, 9/11, the second intifada, and the Global War on Terror (GWOT), including the 2001 US-led war in Afghanistan and the 2003 US-led intervention in Iraq, had raised questions about US Middle East policy. The chapter goes on to discuss the consolidation of a unified EU foreign policy following the fall of the Berlin Wall in 1989 and the return of Russia to the Middle East, especially following military intervention in Syria in 2015. Finally, it assesses the growing Chinese presence in the region and the potential for a realignment of alliances in the age of growing multipolarity within the international community.

France

French Middle East policy stretches back to Napoleon Bonaparte's three-year occupation of Egypt starting in 1798 and the occupation of Algeria in 1830. The campaign in Egypt was a combination of military adventurism and intellectuals who attempted to modernize the Egyptian system. These scholars and engineers were linked to the work of Saint Simon and were responsible for initiating grand projects such as the Suez Canal, which opened to international navigation in 1869. The French intervention in Egypt moved the British to protect its interests in India by establishing dominance in the Gulf from 1820 onward. The French would also notably protect Lebanese Christians in 1860 and extend aid to religious orders across the Ottoman Empire, Iran, and Egypt.[1] After the Berber tribal revolt against French colonialism in Morocco and the subsequent bombardment of Casablanca in 1907, the 1912 Treaty of Fez established a French protectorate in Morocco until 1956.

The transition to a modern French Middle East policy was informed by broader changes in French foreign policy in the 1960s, notably de Gaulle's speech in 1963 against US intervention in Vietnam and the French decision to withdraw troops from NATO in 1966 in order to pursue a nuclear deterrent. It coincided with the end of the Algerian War, culminating in Algerian independence in 1962. The French occupation of Tunisia in 1882 further imbedded French culture and language in the Ottoman Empire, which was experiencing pressure on many fronts. However, it became quite difficult to reconcile the population transfers to places such as Algeria (*colons* or *Pied Noir*) with the principle of equality for the Arab and Berber populations, especially concerning land rights and suffrage. Indeed, their presence was simply used as an excuse to exert harsh repressive measures against rioters calling for independence, as took place in Setif on May 8, 1945. The Evian Accords managed transitional relations after Algerian independence, pivoting around choice of citizenship for the *colons*, oil, and temporary nuclear arms testing.

Competition between France and Britain in the Middle East would become more of an entente in Europe during the First World War and after the breakup of the Ottoman Empire, leading to the Sykes-Picot agreement in 1916 and the Balfour Declaration in 1917.[2] However, during the Second World War, Britain sent the army into Syria and Lebanon in June and July 1941 for fear that Vichy France was not strong enough to withstand pressure from Nazi Germany efforts to take control of the region. This aided the independence movement from the beginning and led to success in gaining independence in November 1943 (although French troops stayed on until 1946). In response, the French Secret Service covertly supported Jewish nationalist movements that began attacking British interests in Palestine after 1945. Only during episodes such as attempts to take back control of the Suez Canal in 1956 did Britain and France work closely together. French relations with Egypt never recovered their full potential even after a balanced response to the 1967 conflict, mainly due to Egyptian nationalism and the continued demise of French influence abroad following the Second World War.

Modern French foreign policy is discernable by France's status as a permanent UN Security Council member with nuclear weapons and leverage of political relations based on former colonial ties evident with regard to Lebanon, Algeria, and Tunisia. Indeed, postcolonial ties appear to have dominated in the way France interacted with Libya, Tunisia, and, more recently, Algeria, at first preferring to maintain elite relations and then being forced to make a series of policy U-turns.[3] In security terms, France has been a major player in wider operations against Islamic State of Iraq and Syria (ISIS) in Syria and in the Maghreb. It has some military installations in the region, such as Camp de la Paix (Peace Camp) set up in Abu Dhabi in 2009, and extensive cultural programs in operation, ranging from the Sorbonne University to the Louvre Museum, both in Abu Dhabi. President Macron's diplomacy managed to secure the release of Lebanese prime minister Hariri from Saudi Arabia in November 2017 and enabled him to rescind his resignation as prime minister, which he made on November 4, 2017, in the kingdom, blaming Hezbollah. France is also an important normative actor unilaterally, having hosted the climate conference in 2015, which led to an agreement in 2016, and through core membership of the European Union. This is particularly the case regarding EU decision-making on Russia and the Middle East.[4]

Britain

By the end of the Second World War, Britain had influence across the Middle East and North Africa, from Libya to the enclave associated with the Anglo-Iranian Oil Company in Iran. It was active from Iraq in the north to Sudan in the south. The precipitous decline of British imperial interests in the Middle East over the following two decades shows how Iranian and Arab nationalism, the latter promulgated by Egyptian president Gamal Abdel Nasser, impacted its regional ambitions. The Iranian coup in 1953 was orchestrated by the CIA and British intelligence to maintain their company's access to Iranian oil supplies and revenues, and support the pro-Western shah in power. The 1955 Baghdad Pact[5] was a military alliance formed by Turkey, Iraq, Britain, Pakistan, and Iran, supported by the United States, and similar to NATO in attempting to prevent communist incursions into their Western spheres of influence.[6] However, it was never afforded means to guarantee collective defense and was compromised by a series of regional developments such as the Egyptian-Syrian union (the United Arab Republic (1958–1961)), an Iraqi revolution (July 1958), and civil unrest in Lebanon (1958). Continued regional instability, which favored Soviet encroachments, meant that the United States became more interventionist in Middle East affairs through the 1957 Eisenhower Doctrine. If there is a key date of British and French decline in the Middle East, it is 1956, which simultaneously enhanced American influence, partly through American willingness to use sanctions to secure a resolution to the crisis, and partly through Britain then being marginalized and criticized in all aspects of Arab-Israeli peacemaking efforts and in Middle East alliances. The 1958 Iraqi Revolution also posed a threat to British interests, part of a series of coups led by Arab nationalists across the region from Egypt in 1952 to Yemen in 1962.

A policy of nonintervention during the Labour government under Prime Minister Clement Atlee from 1945 to 1951 contributed to decolonization up to the 1960s, and the anticolonial policies of President Nasser also facilitated Western caution and calculations. Prime Minister Anthony Eden would continue with a policy of nonintervention from 1955 to 1957, apart from the notable exception of the Suez crisis. He was also focused on maintaining a global footprint through various 'Gibraltars,' including Diego Garcia (leased to the Americans in 1966) and Cyprus to secure oil supplies from the Middle East, forming part of British interests after Cypriot independence in 1960.[7]

By 1967, British troops had withdrawn from its garrison in Aden after being pushed out by the National Liberation Front (NLF) and Front for the Liberation of Occupied South Yemen (FLOSY), who sought to expel Britain from what they saw as South Yemen through a sustained insurgency and successful infiltration into the local security services, supported by Egypt and the Soviet Union. A communist-supported rebellion quickly spread to the Dhofar region of Oman and was only arrested by the covert introduction of a few Special Air Service (SAS) forces.

Then, under Prime Minister Harold Macmillan, Britain would focus on managed decline by concentrating foreign policy toward key alliances and shrewd diplomacy. Nevertheless, it would not be enough to stop Britain withdrawing its forces from east of Suez in 1967 and the Gulf in 1971 (although political influence was not challenged by other external forces until the United States responded to the Iraqi invasion of Kuwait in 1990). British withdrawal from the Middle East was primarily due to a lack of military and economic resources and an insurrection in Northern Ireland to address during the 1970s. Economic dependence on the United States after the Second World War contributed to the end of British imperial ambition, and the United Kingdom has been allied to US policy in the Middle East and internationally ever since.

The Eisenhower Doctrine from 1957 would also create new direct defense linkages between the United States and its Middle Eastern allies during the Cold War. British defense reviews, especially since the end of the Cold War, have reduced its military resources further and challenged its global footprint. Still, active engagement and leadership from Margaret Thatcher to Tony Blair, who focused on Europe, the United States, and the Commonwealth (including the Middle East), has helped the United Kingdom punch above its weight for better or worse (namely UK association with President G. W. Bush's decision to invade Iraq in 2003). From 1985 to 2006, the United Kingdom has engaged Saudi Arabia in a multibillion-pound arms sales program, Al-Yamama, which is the United Kingdom's largest ever export agreement. In 2018, the United Kingdom marked a return to the Gulf with a new naval base, HMS *Juffair*, in Bahrain to help ease concerns about undue Iranian influence in the country and insecurity in the Gulf. A new joint defense agreement was signed with Oman in 2019, with Duqm port capable of accommodating HMS Queen Elisabeth and HMS Prince of Wales aircraft carriers. The 2019 tanker crisis with Iran and attack on Saudi oil installations illustrate the threat to the Arab Gulf states but also the limits of UK power over shipping and security. The United Kingdom remains to a large extent reliant on US military, in contrast to its domination of the Persian Gulf waterway during the eighteenth and early nineteenth centuries.

United States

The United States did not support the Sykes-Picot agreement between France and Britain, which carved their respective spheres of influence across the northern Levant around Beirut and the corridor to Damascus and Aleppo; and Mesopotamia, including the incongruous provinces of Baghdad, Mosul, and Basra. In contrast, President Woodrow Wilson outlined his famous 'fourteen points,' including open treaties, freedom of navigation on the seas, removal of economic barriers, arms reductions to the safest lowest levels, and self-determination. It was presented in January 1918, nine months after the United States entered the First World War. The Paris Peace Conference and Treaty of Versailles in 1919 went on to favor the victors but excluded Germany, Austria-Hungary, Turkey, and Bulgaria. The terms of the peace would come to dominate the politics and insecurity of Europe and the Middle East for the next century.

The United States has generally been adept at protecting its national interests in the Middle East throughout the twentieth century through a succession of presidents and secretaries of state and through changes to foreign policy. Since the creation of Israel in 1948, each US administration has attempted to broker solutions to various regional challenges, including the peace process. US diplomacy in the region has included the Tripartite Declaration in 1950 to regulate arms transfers. President Eisenhower and his secretary of state, John Foster Dulles, initiated secret political initiatives from 1953 to 1956, including the Jordan Valley Unified Water Plan (the Johnston Plan), brokered secret contact between the Egyptian and Israeli leaders (the Alpha and Omega projects), and warned Israel about expanding its territory by force.

The US special relationship with Israel is at the center of US Mideast policy, and this has been particularly the case since 1967, based largely on domestic US political calculations related to the disproportionate influence of the Jewish lobby.[8] However, every US administration has also recognized the need to maintain contacts with Arab governments across the region. The core US objective post 1945 was to prevent Soviet expansionism into the Middle East and maintain the steady flow and stable price of international oil, which it has generally managed to do (barring the 1973 oil crisis).

The 1970s was the turning point for US engagement in the Gulf, having reluctantly assumed responsibility for Gulf security after the United Kingdom withdrew from the east of Suez. The United States was then deeply engaged in the Middle East to counter Soviet influence, known as the Truman Doctrine. This included opposing Soviet influence in Iran and Turkey by encouraging the latter to join NATO in 1952 and sponsoring a CIA-led coup in 1953 to oust nationalist leader Mohammad Mossaddegh in Iran in order to secure the shah's rule and his alliance with the United States. President Nixon's 'twin pillars' policy of the 1970s put Saudi Arabia and Iran at the center of US strategic ties in the region. These were two major oil exporters, able to influence other states and purchase US weapons with their high state revenues. The 1973 Arab-Israeli War surprised the United States but meant that Egyptian-Soviet ties were undermined and led to a new pathway for diplomacy between the United States, Egypt, and Israel. The result was the 1978 Camp David Accords, which led to the Egypt-Israel Peace Treaty in March 1979. Further diplomatic breakthroughs followed with the Madrid Conference (cosponsored by the Soviet Union) in October–November 1991, the Oslo Accords in 1993 and 1995, and the Israel-Jordan peace treaty in July 1994.

The combination of the 1979 Iranian Revolution and the US hostage crisis specifically impacted on the failed reelection bid of President Carter (more than fifty US hostages would be released on the first day of the Reagan administration). This was one of many US policy mishaps along with the failure to end Hezbollah's actions in kidnapping US nationals in Lebanon during the Iran-Iraq War, and the Iran-Contra Affair, as well as the unresolved Arab-Israeli conflict. But unlike Southeast Asia, the United States had not engaged in costly military interventions in the Middle East in the twentieth century. The Soviet invasion of Afghanistan led to more robust attempts to bolster US capabilities in the region. But the importance of the US role as a security guarantor for the Gulf states would not become fully apparent until tested during the Iraqi invasion of Kuwait in 1990, after which its role in regional diplomacy bloomed, including more cooperative US-Syrian relations up to 2000. Under the Clinton administration, an Israel-Palestine peace agreement was close to conclusion in 1993 and again in 1995–1996. In the 1990s, as Walt notes in *The Hell of Good Intentions*, the United States was on good terms with most of the major powers and defense budgets the size of the next twenty or more countries combined.[9] Iraq and Iran had been contained and globalization was spreading, and a sense of optimism was apparent in US foreign policy. Even the debacle of the Battle for Mogadishu in Somalia in which eighteen Americans and hundreds of Somalis died in an eighteen-hour urban firefight did not detract from the overwhelming force and omnipotence of the US military.

Soviet Union

The USSR was founded with a strong internationalist posture. It firmly believed in the spread of socialism around the world. Through the Comintern, it followed events in the Middle East, such as the Great Syrian Revolt in 1925.[10] The Soviet Union believed that socialism could be brought to underdeveloped parts of the world by revolutionary means or by development aid. Soviet experiences in Uzbekistan or Kazakhstan, its 'own Orient,'[11] would later influence Soviet perceptions in the Middle East. However, during Stalin's tenure, under the slogan of 'socialism in one country,' the USSR turned inward looking and largely forgot about its internationalist mission.

This stance changed dramatically after the Second World War. Moscow's postwar relationship with the Middle East can be roughly divided into two phases. The first one, lasting until 1964, can be dubbed 'romantic and revolutionary,' while the second one, after 1964, can be termed as 'realist and conservative.' This timeline reflects the domestic developments of 'Thaw' and 'Stagnation.' Another timeline of Soviet-Middle East relations is identifiable between the phase before 1978 and afterward, reflecting more international developments, as will be shown in this chapter.

The USSR emerged out of the Second World War as a major power in need of new allies in the Cold War against the United States. In this phase, the USSR witnessed with keen interest the decolonization processes taking place in Asia and Africa, and massively expanded its institutions of regional expertise as well as its foreign presence (competing at times with China in its support for liberation movements).[12] The Communist Party had its own International Department that expanded relations with revolutionary movements in the Middle East. Under Nikita

Khrushchev, particularly close ties developed with Egypt. Gamal Abdel Nasser fascinated Khrushchev politically and personally, without Moscow ever fully grasping Egyptian political dynamics.[13] Soviet policymakers believed in Arab Socialism and underestimated the fact that nationalism and independence had priority for Egypt. The USSR supported Nasser politically, economically, and militarily throughout his tenure. In exchange, it received credibility as a reliable ally of the Arabs and could bolster its identity as a staunch supporter of decolonization. No other country in the Arab world at that time received as much unlimited support as Egypt. It continued to help Egypt even after Nasser's death in 1970. However, relations with Nasser's successor quickly deteriorated: Anwar Sadat's volte-face in the Yom-Kippur War of 1973 and the 'Cold peace' brokered with Israel in 1978 angered Soviet policymakers, and to this day, former Soviet diplomats write with dismay about Sadat, while praising Nasser.[14]

At the end of the 1970s, Soviet-Middle Eastern relations entered the second phase. Politically, the USSR had lost its revolutionary zeal domestically as well as its faith in the advancement of socialism in the Middle East. Neither Nasserism nor the two Ba'athist regimes in Syria and Iraq had moved in the direction of socialism, despite implementing some remotely socialist policies and paying lip-service to socialist values. In fact, all these regimes tended at some point or another to jail its communist activists. Only Khaled Bagdash, who led the Syrian Communist Party, fared well by entering into an alliance with Assad's Ba'ath party. The USSR sided with the Palestine Liberation Organization (PLO), while it deemed smaller left-wing Palestinian factions, such as the Popular Front for the Liberation of Palestine (PFLP) and the Democratic Front for the Liberation of Palestine (DFLP), to be too extremist. While some MENA countries might have conformed to the Soviet 'socialist orientation' theory, only in South Yemen did a Soviet-style regime come to power and receive substantial Soviet support.[15]

The most important Soviet partner in the Middle East became Syria. This alliance was based more on pragmatic and less on ideological considerations. After the loss of Egypt and the conclusion of the Egyptian-Israeli peace treaty under US auspices, the USSR sought a new foothold in the Middle East. Hafez al-Assad's Syria needed a strong ally to boost his claim to leadership in the Arab world. This created an interdependence between the two countries, in which Damascus could sometimes set the rhythm in relations, for example, in the 1976 Syrian invasion of Lebanon or in the Syrian demands for advanced weaponry.[16]

At times, the USSR also entertained good relations with Iraq, which was one of the most modern states in the region and had similar claims to the leadership in the Arab world as Syria. However, Moscow was unhappy about Saddam Hussein's domestic initiatives (against the Kurds and the Iraqi Communist Party) and foreign policies, including the war against Iran. Muammar Gaddafi's Libya was a regular customer of Soviet weaponry, too, but displeased Moscow by its intransigent policy. All in all, the Soviet position in the Arab world grew weaker after 1978. Following the onset of the Islamic Revolution in Iran in 1979, a new Islamist actor entered the MENA region and has shaped Arab Gulf responses and bilateral alliances with the United States since. In the same year, the USSR started its intervention in Afghanistan, which proved to be very costly and which shattered the Soviet anti-imperialist image in the Middle East.

With Mikhail Gorbachev initiating Perestroika, Soviet engagement with the Middle East reached a new low. His advisers, such as Anatolij Černjaev, pushed Gorbachev to cut loose regimes that endangered Soviet reputation and drained its economic resources.[17] The failure to persuade Saddam Hussein to retreat from Kuwait in the wake of the 1991 Gulf War is a telling example of the decay of Soviet clout and prestige in the region.[18]

The Failure of US Middle East Policy: 2000–2020

Since the United States suddenly became the sole superpower in 1991 (its 'unipolar moment') after the fall of the Soviet Union, it has continued to pursue a global policy in support of a liberal-capitalist world order, including values such as democracy, liberty, human rights, open markets, and the rule of law. Richard Haass, former director of the State Department's Policy Planning Staff, calls this "arrangements that will sustain a world consistent with US interests and values, and thereby promote peace, prosperity, and justice."[19]

In practice, the policy has failed on multiple counts. Somalia, Sudan, and Yemen stand out as states that have been sidelined by US efforts to bring about prosperity in the global environment. Economic benefits from globalization have been uneven, with many nations of the Middle East being bypassed by growing trade flows, especially if oil is taken out of the equation. The wars in Afghanistan and Iraq have been incredibly expensive in humanitarian, geostrategic/soft power (the Abu Ghraib debacle and extraordinary rendition, for example), and financial terms (more than $2.4 trillion spent). Afghanistan remains a war zone to which US presidents have committed troops, but they have been unable to secure peace with the Taliban for ten years (notwithstanding brief ceasefires).[20] Saddam Hussein is gone but Iraqi politics and the domestic security situation remain unresolved. The financial crisis of 2007–2008 put unprecedented economic pressure on the US budget but US foreign policy remained on the unwavering course of 'global leadership' and management. President Trump, like President Clinton, has focused on the economy, but foreign policy is an intrinsic part of that effort, whether through alliances or free trade agreements. Like previous presidents, President Trump has not innovated in the Middle East. He remains only marginally tied, on a quid pro quo basis, to traditional US allies such as Egypt, Saudi Arabia, Israel, and Jordan, leading to its own challenges as some regional states feel at greater liberty to trounce the peace process and human rights with impunity.

In summary, US Mideast policy is being eroded from above, below, and within. The changes in the global economic environment favor the growth and rise of China, which is investing in greater hard-power capabilities and a global presence. The US agenda of globalization, now being championed by others, its democratization efforts, as well as NATO expansion, in the case of Russia, have directly threatened the state security interests of authoritarian regimes that have reluctantly adapted or pushed back. Haass notes that in order to thwart the Thucydides trap, that is to say, when one great power threatens to displace another, war inevitably breaks out, the United States should accommodate other powers but push back against their acts of aggression. Walt notes that where the existing balance of power breaks down, the United States can engage in offshore balancing to shape events when needed.[21] However, to do that in the Middle East and globally will require a new and stronger coalition with other democracies, especially those with growing influence in the region. The United States should update its Mideast policy to better reflect its changing global power status, its national and international interests, including through multilateral mechanisms, concerning the Middle East. It should probably start with Syria, where it has lost all leverage, and enable Iran and Russia to gain more autonomy and leverage in regional affairs. The limits of US influence in the Gulf have been evident in the limited security terms of the thirty-three member nation Combined Maritime Taskforce (CMF). The CMF was established in 2004 and is commanded by the US Navy (Fifth Fleet), which has at least kept the Strait of Hormuz open at a time when insurance costs for shipping have increased tenfold in 2019. But it has no fixed political or military mandate beyond counterterrorism, counter-narcotics, and keeping energy export routes open. After US strikes against Iran-backed militia in Iraq and Syria in late December 2019, protestors quickly moved to attack the US embassy in Baghdad, making a proxy conflict between the United States and Iran more likely in 2020.

Finally, the role of President Trump, brought into office by rural white Republicans and a wave of support from Rust Belt states such as Michigan, Wisconsin, and Iowa, has been successful in upending a delicate Israel-Palestine status quo in explicit favor of the pro-Israel lobby. President Trump could be more damaging to multilateralism, treaties, and agreements than any state adversary, including his attempts to undermine NATO and the European Union, withdrawal from the Joint Comprehensive Plan of Action (JCPOA) and the Paris climate agreement, and pro-Russian stance while neglecting to negotiate a new strategic arms reduction treaty with Moscow. But as Nye notes, Trump's impact on state institutions, trust, and soft power depends largely on whether he is re-elected in 2020 and whether his successor can repair the damage.[22]

The European Union

The establishment of the European Union by the Maastricht Treaty in 1993 coincided with momentous changes in the international environment, such as the end of the Soviet empire, and created new concerns about unconventional challenges, such as organized crime, failed states, and refugees. The first major fissure with US policy was over the 2003 Iraq War when France and Germany, in agreement with Russia, coordinated their opposition against a US-led invasion. There have been internal issues besides, such as President Sarkozy's 2007 plan to create a Union of the Mediterranean, which excluded Germany. Germany's abstention during the passage of UN Security Council Resolution 1973, which arguably laid the way for NATO intervention in Libya in March 2011, was another indicator of a split foreign policy approach at the heart of Europe.

Thus, EU engagement with the Middle East, in contrast to some member states, has generally favored a soft-power approach and socioeconomic enhancement policies. This is based on the European Union being the number one destination for exports from the Middle East and North Africa (including Israel), although the trade balance is in Europe's favor. Many EU states remain heavily dependent on energy exports from the Gulf. Migration and security issues related to proximity tend to drive engagement, although major obstacles remain in the path to multilateral engagement with MENA states, which prefer bilateralism. Various dialogues exist, including the EU-GCC (Gulf Cooperation Council) dialogue from the 1990s; the European Neighborhood Policy (ENP) established in 2004 to drive multilateral relations beyond free trade provisions of the Euro-Mediterranean Partnership (EMP); and the United Kingdom, France, and Germany being parties to the JCPOA with Iran, which was signed in October 2015. The latter was one of the few European diplomatic success stories in the Middle East until President Trump withdrew the United States as a party to it on May 18, 2018.

On the Israel-Palestine conflict, the European Union was part of the Quartet, with the United States, Russia, and United Nations, to produce a road map toward a final agreement. Apart from a 2005 agreement on movement and access, the issue of settlements is not one that has been negotiated to a successful conclusion with the Israeli government.

Although there are great areas for complementary cooperation, and a meeting of the European Union and Arab League took place in February 2019 with various bilateral meetings on the margins, much work remains to be done to improve European interactions in the MENA region. Responses are still driven by the 2011 Arab Uprisings and the 2015 refugee crisis. In other words, current events drive policy. Systemic challenges such as societal disconnects and the rise of populist and right-wing groups in Europe also exist. The ENP principle of 'more for more' conditionality has not been well received in the southern neighborhood and some argue that a reset in relations is necessary. The local context of state-society relations cannot be ignored either, but what the European Union and Arab states need more of is an ongoing official and track II dialogue in which to find common ground and address a series of pressing socioeconomic issues. Their lack of engagement thus far has allowed other actors such as Russia as well as regional actors such as Saudi Arabia, Iran, Turkey, and the UAE to enhance their influence and alliances at the expense of the EU. Long-term progress beyond some limited cooperation on regional crises and conflicts is unlikely given that many political views have become narrow and polarized. The EU could enhance their collective positioning (including trade, investments, and arms sales) to be more effective.[23] However, fundamentally, divergence will continue to exist between the two blocks, based on the different priorities of developmental states and fears of mass migration in Europe, and the domestic regime security and survival imperative of authoritarian states in the MENA, as well as the (neo)patrimonial networks they create.[24]

A Resurgent Russia

Russian foreign policy in the Middle East is highly dependent on Russian relations with the West. In the post-Soviet period, it is marked by two turning points. The first turning point was the 2001/2003 juncture, that is, the rise of international terrorism including 9/11 and following the toppling of Saddam Hussein in 2003. Both events are linked and led to the first reengagement of Russia in the Middle East. The second turning point was the Arab Spring from 2011 that deeply reoriented the Russian presence in the MENA. Both cases contributed to Russia's return to an international role and to bolster its great power ambitions. On the cultural level, Russia reactivated a narrative of its relevance in the MENA and brushed the dust off its regional expertise.

Post-Soviet Russian foreign policy started accentuating the tenets of late Soviet foreign policy. Especially in its early phase, it sought to disentangle itself from the other former republics of the Union and its former Third World allies, while fully embracing the West, in order to gain membership in Western institutions. As this foreign policy trajectory increasingly ran into a dead end, Russia returned to a confrontational stance toward the West on key matters such as NATO enlargement in 1999 and 2004 as well as NATO's intervention in Kosovo in 1999. With Yevgeny Primakov at the helm of the Foreign Ministry, Russia engaged in great power balancing and increasingly sought to diversify its alliances.[25] Primakov, a former graduate of the Institute of Oriental Studies and a well-known broker across the MENA, especially eyed Asian countries, such as China or India, as potential partners. However, between 1991 and 2001, trade and economic cooperation agreements were stipulated with former client states.

The events of 9/11 posed a unique opportunity for Russia. Under Vladimir Putin, Russia offered a helping hand to Western countries in their fight against terrorism. It supported the US-led campaign against the Taliban and the NATO mission in Afghanistan by offering supply lines and transport capabilities. One consideration in this approach was to inscribe its own war in Chechnya into the narrative of the GWOT. Russian support for the West, however, stopped short in Iraq in 2003. Putin strongly opposed the coalition of the willing and found like-minded partners in France and Germany. The US invasion of Iraq confirmed to the Russian leadership that the United States was not to be trusted and that it was willing to adopt military means to expand its zone of influence. According to a former Russian diplomat in Iraq, the 2003 invasion represented a breach of normative principles in international relations. It risked setting a precedent according to which the United States could bypass the UN Security Council altogether, and thus Russia.[26]

By the 2000s, Russia had generally recovered from the post-Soviet economic turmoil and was in a position to flex its muscles at the international level. Recovering great power status and an obsession with 'sovereignty' became key elements of the Russian presidency. As in the past, the Middle East again developed into a place of competition with the West and a place where great power identities could be forged. After 2003, Russia intensified its economic and military cooperation in the MENA, including new long-term cooperation agreements with Syria. However, Russia and Saudi Arabia found themselves in disagreement on Iraq in 2003, as they would more seriously on Syria from 2011.[27] Still, Russia banned the Muslim Brotherhood in 2003, a move that was strengthened by the Chechen president Ramzan Kadyrov and the UAE's Tabah Foundation, which provides a platform for a renewed Islamic discourse.

The Russian regime has felt increasingly besieged by Western influence. Moscow blamed the West for the protests that erupted during the 2011/2012 election cycle, as it had blamed the West for the Color Revolutions across the former Soviet Union and the Balkans in the early 2000s. In Russian media and official discourse on the Arab Uprisings, a recurring narrative was employed, according to which the West was in breach of other countries' sovereignty, attempting to replace legitimate regimes, and allying themselves with Islamists. The uprising against Libya's Muammar Gaddafi set the basic tone in Moscow. While Russia had abstained in the UN Security Council regarding a no-fly zone over Libya, it firmly disagreed with regime change and felt betrayed after the international coalition went beyond its mandate.

The Syrian uprising in 2011/2012 thus started when the Russian government had experienced at least two recent negative experiences with what it took to be Western-led or Western-supported regime-change efforts. Russia, initially, honored its military agreements with Syria and continued to supply the regime, while it thwarted early UN Security Council resolutions against Syria. Russia also deployed unprecedented diplomatic efforts to negotiate a settlement to the conflict, engaging in multilateral negotiations with various Syrian and international stakeholders. The first effort included setting up an informal series of three 'consultative conferences' in Moscow in 2015.[28] By 2017, continuing negotiations had developed into the 'Astana format,' which included Turkey and Iran.[29] These initiatives were criticized for bypassing Western powers and ignoring key members of the Syrian opposition.

Russian military intervention in late 2015 was deemed necessary in Moscow due to several reasons. First, the diplomatic efforts had not yielded any results. In particular, Russia failed to get any concessions from the Gulf states. Second, on the ground, the Syrian regime forces were exhausted and overstretched. Third, Russia recognized and stressed the international entanglement of the conflict, with many foreign fighters coming from former Soviet republics and possibly posing a threat to the Russian homeland. Fourth, Russia recognized the power vacuum in Syria, the possibility for new alliances with Turkey and Iran, and thus the potential for gaining a renewed and enhanced foothold in the MENA.

Finally, the intervention came at a time of Russian isolation. In 2014, the Ukrainian president was deposed in a massive popular uprising, in yet another perceived maligned Western influence in the post-Soviet space. Moscow reacted by annexing Crimea and supporting separatist movements in Eastern Ukraine. The Syria intervention offered a possibility to divert attention from Crimea and for Russia to return to international negotiations. Increasingly, there are Russian private military contractors, such as the 'Wagner PMC' operating in the MENA, for example, in Syria and Libya, who bring expertise from waging hybrid wars in Crimea or in the Ukrainian breakaway republics. They further Russian state interests while allowing Moscow to deny involvement.

Russia's return to and resurgence in the Middle East is riddled with ambivalences. On the one hand, it rests on shaky foundations. Moscow succeeded in stabilizing the Assad regime partly through long-term deployments of troops to Syria and new or expanded military bases for additional leverage in Syrian and Middle Eastern affairs. On the other hand, in doing so, Moscow alienated parts of the Middle East, especially the influential Arab Gulf states. Russia has little soft power in the MENA, arguably less than the USSR had, although it did try to advance a Gulf security proposal at the UN in 2019.[30] The proposal is useful due to its inclusion of Iran and the BRICS, whose external support might make a difference to getting a regional dialogue on track. But it is hard to envision commitment to US-Russian cooperation in the Gulf similar to the period of the Madrid Conference of 1991, which aimed to end the Arab-Israel conflict. At a minimum, Russia would need to jettison its foreign policy agenda aimed at undermining NATO broadly and in states such as Libya, something which may be possible following changing facts on the ground. It will also take time for the next US president to re-commit to multilateral frameworks and institutions, after President Trump pulled out of major arms control treaties, and build trust with Iran after President Trump withdrew the United States from the Joint Comprehensive Plan of Action (JCPOA) and implemented a 'maximum pressure' campaign against Iran including the assassination of IRGC commander, Qasem Soleimani, on January 3, 2020.

Russia's influence is founded mainly on hard-power relations, including weapon deliveries. For example, that Turkey opted to buy the advanced S-400 air defense system instead of US F-35 fighter jets was a major coup for Russia. Moscow also managed to reenter the Egyptian market by delivering a batch of MiG-29 fighters. Older but still powerful S-300 surface-to-air missiles have now been delivered to Syria and Iran.[31] Finally, the Astana alliance with Turkey and Iran is based on a mid-term convergence of interests, especially a shared anti-Western stance, not yet on a common strategic vision.

China: A New Illiberal Alliance?

The Gulf states, and increasingly Saudi Arabia, Kuwait, and Oman, are a key driver for continued Chinese economic growth through oil imports. China overtook the United States as the world's top oil importer in 2013.[32] These energy flows have been sustained in part by the US security architecture, which has enabled China to enhance its regional presence at a low cost. Yet, the role of oil in China-Gulf relations should not be overstated; after all, China has access to oil on the international market and through the Russian pipeline to China. In a period of global economic recession, supply is likely to continue to outstrip demand and maintain a period of low oil prices.

China opened its first regional base in Djibouti, alongside US naval expeditionary base, Camp Lemmonier, and French, Italian, and Japanese bases, to help combat piracy in 2015. Beijing has conducted numerous and sometimes extended naval visits in the region and is the second largest financial contributor to UN peacekeeping operations worldwide after the United States. The growing soft or nontraditional military footprint is thus far not aimed at competing with the United States but rather on mission-specific tasks.[33] External powers such as China have been satisfied with the stability that a US security presence brings, content to allegedly free ride while continuing to build up their economic and military capabilities. It has also enhanced its economic role, notably through 'comprehensive strategic partnerships' with Iran, the UAE, Saudi Arabia, and Egypt. Some key visits include President Xi's visits to the region in 2016 and 2019, and Saudi king Salman's 2017 visit to Beijing, where a memorandum of understanding was signed to explore $65 billion in joint ventures.[34] Chinese non-oil trade with the UAE grew to $43 billion in 2018.[35]

There are already further economic opportunities available beyond oil, through the diversification strategies underway in the Gulf, such as New Kuwait 2035, Saudi Vision 2030, and Abu Dhabi 2030, as well as major reconstruction and infrastructure projects. China's Belt and Road Initiative (BRI), including neighboring Muslim-majority Pakistan, could also be significant in enhancing some of the close bonds that already exist between Middle Eastern and Asian allies. Asian states such as Japan, South Korea, and India are already looking to create new regional synergies with West Asia. So we could see further Asian engagement on a par with Chinese trade and investment in Africa if state resources match the growing interest.[36] With deepening economic relations comes potential to broaden out into other forms of cooperation.

The Middle East does not yet represent a high foreign policy priority as China continues to focus on other major global players such as the United States, Russia, and the European Union. China's growing relationship with Israel represents a high priority target in terms of access to its high-tech sector. The Shanghai International Port Group (SIPG), a multibillion-dollar deal with Israel's transportation ministry to operate Haifa port from 2021, could scupper US naval visits to the port.[37] This following the 2017 US National Security Strategy, which identifies China and Russia as strategic threats.[38] China-US tensions have risen during the Trump administration over trade, the response to COVID-19, race relations in the United States, and the new security law being proposed by Beijing in Hong Kong in 2020, all in the context of US presidential election year. So Israel could become a pivot point for China-US relations in the Middle East going forward. China has made similar port deals in Greece and Italy after the 2008/9 economic crisis has undermined US and EU influence. Thus China could continue to be at the center of a cleavage in Europe over economic cooperation, coordination, and, ultimately, alliance choices. The European Union has responded to the shifting balance of challenges and opportunities presented by China through the publication *EU-China: A Strategic Outlook* in 2019.[39]

China's economic weight makes it a priority and partner for most MENA states. However, for the Gulf states to benefit from regional development initiatives in the Belt and Road Initiative such as major infrastructure projects, it would require not only the de-escalation of current tensions but also the resolution of conflicts that compromise regional and interregional cooperation.[40] The Chinese focus continues to be on development, respect for sovereignty and equality which has been met in the MENA region with great enthusiasm and reciprocity.

Few MENA states apart from Turkey have voiced any concern about Chinese Uyghurs (Turkic speaking) that have experienced constraints on their freedoms and detention in the Xinjiang Uyghur Autonomous Region of China due to allegations of terrorism and separatism.[41] Instead, more than thirty-five countries have defended China in a riposte letter to the UN Human Rights Council over mass detentions in July 2019. Signatories included MENA states such as Algeria, Bahrain, Egypt, Kuwait, Oman, Qatar, Saudi Arabia, Sudan, Syria, and the UAE.[42]

If the United States should pull back from the Middle East and prefer an all-out offshore balancing strategy, further Chinese endeavors to build military-military partnerships could be possible. This is likely to include higher arms exports to the region, which represents a small but significant fraction of its total arms sales output.[43] Given American and Russian superior weapons systems, as well as options from eastern Europe, China's arms supply penetration into the Middle East could be slow. But it is still a worldwide leading supplier of low-cost weapons and ammunition, and unlike many states that refuse to buy Chinese arms for political reasons, such as India, South Korea, and Vietnam, this is not usually an issue in the Middle East.[44] China's continuing move into surveillance and facial recognition technology is attractive to export clients in the region, including the UAE, Egypt, and Saudi Arabia.[45] Much depends on the existing US security umbrella and confidence in US Mideast policy, which for some states such as Saudi Arabia reached a nadir in 2013 when President Obama decided on the JCPOA and no major military commitment to the Syria conflict.[46] The future for China in the MENA region also depends on state threat perception, the dynamics of any regional arms race, the state of political relations, and threats of sanctions or incentives from the United States.

Conclusion

This chapter shows how the domestic context of great power policymaking has been evident in each case, involving global and regional role conception, domestic constraints (including economic turmoil and limits imposed by the legislative branch of government), threat perception, as well as hard- and soft-power capabilities. These powers have interacted with the MENA region based on available partnership and alliance opportunities, driven by considerations such as converging state and nonstate interests. The premise for external engagement is usually linked to domestic political considerations, economic considerations (such as hydrocarbons and arms), and extending influence.

Extra-regional approaches to the MENA reflect changes in the international order, from the demise of the USSR in 1991 to NATO expansionism and intervention, notably in Libya. Resurgent Russian interests have been a function of this, especially in attempts to secure the homeland, achieve great power status, ensure a seat at the negotiating table, and limit further NATO encroachment. Russian relations in the MENA region, while apparently economic and security in nature, also hinge to some extent on ideational and historic influences and convergences. Although power certainly lies with a growing multitude of extra-regional actors, this very trend has led to increasing opportunities for MENA regimes to balance with Russia for greater relative autonomy rather than bandwagon with the United States in their international relations. Negotiations over missile defense systems is just one example.

The MENA region is often viewed through the prism of a global approach, whether as forward bases for the projection of power, represented for US Central Command by Al Udeid Air Base in Qatar, or vital in executing the GWOT in Afghanistan and Iraq. President Assad in particular has been fortunate to have Russia onside, at least in the short term, with Iranian and Hezbollah's interests convergent with his own. What made the most difference were early UK and US policies that were hesitant to arm the Free Syrian Army (FSA) and avoid direct military confrontation. Although offshore balancing with Kurdish fighters tipped the balance against ISIS in Syria, it did not tip the balance against the Assad regime.

China remains tied to energy and trade priorities, but there are clear signs that its approach to governance is also highly attractive to MENA regimes following the Arab Uprisings. Interestingly, the British 'Gibraltars' policy of the 1960s appears to have been replicated in the contemporary Chinese 'string of pearls' theory—a network of military and commercial facilities operating from the Chinese mainland to Port Sudan in the Horn of Africa. Whether the US and EU pushback with soft-power capabilities, a focus on multilateralism, and people-to-people engagement will be successful in reestablishing the postwar international order remains to be seen.

These powers have each experienced shifting foreign policies, from the 'twin pillars' and 'dual containment' policies of the United States reflecting changes in the region, notably the Iranian Revolution, and carried to unprecedented lengths through the Trump administration's 'maximum pressure' policy on Iran. Much depends on economic engagement, diplomacy, and accommodation. Whether NATO, Russia, China, and regional powers can agree on a set of more effective stabilization and conflict-resolution measures across a range of weak and failed MENA states is a question that is likely to resonate through the rest of the twenty-first century.

Notes

1. For more on France's historic policies in the Arab world, see: Rémy Leveau, "France's Arab Policy," in *Diplomacy in the Middle East: The International Relations of Regional and Outside Powers*, ed. L. Carl Brown (London: I.B. Tauris, 2001), 3–21.

2. On this topic, see: James R. Fichter, *British and French Colonialism in Africa, Asia and the Middle East: Connected Empires across the Eighteenth to the*

Twentieth Centuries (Cambridge: Cambridge University Press, 2019); James Barr, *The Anglo-French Struggle for the Middle East, 1914–48* (New York: W. W. Norton, 2012).

3. See, for example, Laura-Theresa Kruger, "The French Foreign Policy U-Turn in the Arab Spring—the Case of Tunisia," *Mediterranean Politics* 23, no. 2 (2018): 197–222.

4. For more on French foreign policy since 1945, see: Frederic Bozo, *French Foreign Policy since 1945: An Introduction*, trans. Jonathan Hensher (New York: Berghahn, 2016).

5. Following the Iranian Revolution in 1979 and changes to threat perception in states such as Pakistan, the organization was disbanded in 1979.

6. It was renamed Central Treaty Organization (CENTO) after Iraq pulled out in 1959.

7. Wm Roger Lewis, "Britain and the Middle East after 1945," in *Diplomacy in the Middle East: The International Relations of Regional and Outside Powers*, ed. L. Carl Brown (London: I.B. Tauris, 2001), 38.

8. For details, see Stephen M. Walt and John Mearsheimer, *The Israel Lobby and US Foreign Policy* (New York: Farrar, Straus and Giroux, 2008).

9. Stephen M. Walt, *The Hell of Good Intentions: America's Foreign Policy Elite and the Decline of US Primacy* (New York: Farrar, Straus and Giroux, 2018).

10. Grigorij G. Kosač, "Komintern i Kommunističeskie Partii Arabskich Stran v 20-30-ch godach," *Komintern: Kritika i Kritiki* (Moscow: Nauka, 1978), 296–344.

11. Vera Tolz, *Russia's Own Orient: The Politics of Identity and Oriental Studies in the Late Imperial and Early Soviet Periods* (New York: Oxford University Press, 2011).

12. Jeremy Friedman, *Shadow Cold War* (Chapel Hill: University of North Carolina Press, 2015).

13. Mohamed Heikal, *The Sphinx and the Commissar: The Rise and Fall of Soviet Influence in the Middle East* (New York: Harper & Row, 1978).

14. Oleg Grinevskij, *Tajny Sovetskoj Diplomatii* (Moscow: Vagrius, 2000); Yevgeny Primakov, *Russia and the Arabs* (New York: Basic Books, 2009).

15. Miriam K. Müller, *How the Germans Brought Their Communism to Yemen* (Bielefeld: transcript, 2018); Alexei Vasil'ev, *Russia's Middle East Policy: From Lenin to Putin* (London: Routledge, 2018).

16. Galia Golan, *Yom Kippur and After* (Cambridge: Cambridge University Press, 1979); Efraim Karsh, *The Soviet Union and Syria: The Asad Years* (New York: Routledge, 1988), 49, 78. "Assad ... had grown accustomed to milking the Soviet Union for support," according to Aron Lund, "From Cold War to Civil War: 75 Years of Russian-Syrian Relations," https://www.ui.se/

globalassets/ui.se-eng/publications/ui-publications/2019/ui-paper-no.-7
-2019.pdf.

17. Anatolij S. Černjaev, "Analitičeskaja zapiska A.S. Černjaeva," Gorbačev
Fund Archives, f.5, op.1, d. 20674, April 15, 1987.

18. Evgenij Maksimovič Primakov, Fabienne Mariengof, and François Olivier,
Missions à Bagdad: histoire d'une négociation secrète (Paris: Éd. du Seuil, 1991).

19. Richard Haass, *Defining US Foreign Policy in a Post-Post-Cold War World*, The
2002 Arthur Ross Lecture, Remarks to Foreign Policy Association, New
York, April 22, 2002.

20. Peter Baker, Michael Crowley, and Mujib Mashal, "How Trump's Plan to
Secretly Meet with the Taliban Came Together, and Fell Apart," *New York
Times*, September 9, 2019.

21. Stephen M. Walt, "Deep Dish: Stephen Walt's Guide to Realism," Chicago
Council on Global Affairs, November 22, 2018, https://www.thechicago
council.org/blog/global-insight/deep-dish-stephen-walts-guide-realism.

22. Joseph S. Nye Jr, "Trump's Effect on US Foreign Policy," Project Syndicate, September 4, 2019, https://www.project-syndicate.org/comment
ary/trump-long-term-effect-on-american-foreign-policy-by-joseph-s
-nye-2019-09.

23. See European Council on Foreign Relations, "Mapping European Leverage in the MENA Region," https://www.ecfr.eu/specials/mapping_eu
_leverage_mena.

24. See, for example, Marc Lynch, ed., *The Arab Thermidor: The Resurgence of
the Security State* (Washington, DC: POMEPS, 2015).

25. Andrei P. Tsygankov, *Russia's Foreign Policy: Change and Continuity in National Identity*, 3rd ed. (Lanham, MD: Rowman & Littlefield, 2013), 95–131.

26. Viktor Viktorovič Posuvaljuk and Svetlana Nikolaevna Posuvaljuk, *Bagrovoe
nebo Bagdada* (St. Petersburg: Aletejja, 2012).

27. Philipp Casula and Mark Katz, "Russian Foreign Policy in the Middle
East," in *The Routledge Handbook on Russian Foreign Policy*, ed. Andrey Tsygankov (London: Routledge, 2018), 295–310.

28. Philipp Casula, "Russia between Diplomacy and Military Intervention: The
Syrian Conflict through Russian Eyes Revisited," *Russian Analytical Digest*
175 (2015): 6–10, http://www.css.ethz.ch/publications/pdfs/Russian
AnalyticalDigest175.pdf.

29. Alexey Khlebbnikov, "Is Astana Format on the Way to Be Reformatted?,"
https://www.institutfuersicherheit.at/is-astana-format-on-the-way-to
-be-reformatted/.

30. TASS, "Russia Presents to UN Its Concept of Collective Security in Persian Gulf," July 30, 2019, https://tass.com/world/1070933.

31. Alexey Khlebnikov, "Russia Looks to the Middle East to Boost Arms

Exports," *Middle East Institute*, April 8, 2019, https://www.mei.edu/publications/russia-looks-middle-east-boost-arms-exports.

32. Javier Blas, "China Overtakes US as World's Top Oil Importer," *Financial Times*, March 5, 2013, https://edition.cnn.com/2013/03/04/business/china-u-s-oil-importer/index.html.

33. Degang Sun, "China's Soft Military Presence in the Middle East," *Dirasat*, no. 30, January 2018, http://www.kfcris.com/pdf/07b46fba22562acf20bb92fb68f5ea5c5aaa11036d535.pdf.

34. Ben Blanchard, "China, Saudi Arabia Eye $65 Billion in Deals as King Visits," *Reuters*, March 16, 2017, https://www.reuters.com/article/us-saudi-asia-china/china-saudi-arabia-eye-65-billion-in-deals-as-king-visits-idUSKBN16N0G9.

35. Staff Report, "China Leading Trade Partner of UAE: Al Mansouri," *Gulf News*, July 22, 2019, https://gulfnews.com/uae/china-leading-trade-partner-of-uae-al-mansouri-1.65370898.

36. For a discussion on this, see Andrew Scobell, "China's Search for Security in the Greater Middle East," in *The Red Star and the Crescent: China and the Middle East*, ed. James Reardon-Anderson (Oxford: Oxford University Press, 2018), 13–37.

37. Michael Wilner, "US Navy May Stop Docking in Haifa after Chinese Take Over Port," *Jerusalem Post*, December 15, 2018, https://www.jpost.com/Israel-News/US-Navy-may-stop-docking-in-Haifa-after-Chinese-take-over-port-574414.

38. White House, "National Security Strategy of the United States," December 2017, https://www.whitehouse.gov/wp-content/uploads/2017/12/NSS-Final-12-18-2017-0905.pdf.

39. European Commission, "EU-China: A Strategic Outlook," March 12, 2019, https://ec.europa.eu/commission/sites/beta-political/files/communication-eu-china-a-strategic-outlook.pdf.

40. Tim Niblock, "Problems and Opportunities for China in Developing Its Role in the Gulf Region," *Asian Journal of Middle Eastern and Islamic Studies* 11, no. 3 (2017): 1–11.

41. Anna Hayes, "Explainer: Who Are the Uyghurs and Why Is the Chinese Government Detaining Them?," *Conversation*, https://theconversation.com/explainer-who-are-the-uyghurs-and-why-is-the-chinese-government-detaining-them-111843.

42. Catherine Putz, "Which Countries Are for or against China's Xinjiang Policies?," *Diplomat*, July 15, 2019, https://thediplomat.com/2019/07/which-countries-are-for-or-against-chinas-xinjiang-policies/.

43. Richard A. Bitzinger, "How China Weaponizes Overseas Arms Sales,"

Asia Times, April 16, 2016, https://www.asiatimes.com/2019/04/opinion/how-china-weaponizes-overseas-arms-sales/.

44. Grace Shao, "China, the World's Second Largest Defense Spender, Becomes a Major Arms Exporter," *CNBC*, September 26, 2019, https://www.cnbc.com/2019/09/27/china-a-top-defense-spender-becomes-major-arms-exporter.html.

45. Justin Sherman and Robert Morgus, "Authoritarians Are Exporting Surveillance Tech, and with It Their Vision for the Internet," *Council on Foreign Relations*, December 5, 2018, https://www.cfr.org/blog/authoritarians-are-exporting-surveillance-tech-and-it-their-vision-internet.

46. Robert F. Worth, "Saudi Arabia Rejects U.N. Security Council Seat in Protest Move," *New York Times*, October 18, 2013, https://www.nytimes.com/2013/10/19/world/middleeast/saudi-arabia-rejects-security-council-seat.html.

Bibliography

Baker, Peter, Michael Crowley, and Mujib Mashal. "How Trump's Plan to Secretly Meet with the Taliban Came Together, and Fell Apart." *New York Times*, September 9, 2019.

Barr, James. *The Anglo-French Struggle for the Middle East, 1914–48*. New York: W. W. Norton, 2012.

Bitzinger, Richard A. "How China Weaponizes Overseas Arms Sales." *Asia Times*, April 16, 2016. https://www.asiatimes.com/2019/04/opinion/how-china-weaponizes-overseas-arms-sales/.

Blanchard, Ben. "China, Saudi Arabia Eye $65 Billion in Deals as King Visits." *Reuters*, March 16, 2017. https://www.reuters.com/article/us-saudi-asia-china/china-saudi-arabia-eye-65-billion-in-deals-as-king-visits-idUSKBN16N0G9.

Blas, Javier. "China Overtakes US as World's Top Oil Importer." *Financial Times*, March 5, 2013. https://edition.cnn.com/2013/03/04/business/china-u-s-oil-importer/index.html.

Bozo, Frederic. *French Foreign Policy since 1945: An Introduction*. Translated by Jonathan Hensher. New York: Berghahn, 2016.

Brown, L. Carl, ed. *Diplomacy in the Middle East: The International Relations of Regional and Outside Powers*. London: I B. Tauris, 2001.

Casula, Philipp. "Russia between Diplomacy and Military Intervention: The Syrian Conflict through Russian Eyes revisited." *Russian Analytical Digest* 175 (2015): 6–10. http://www.css.ethz.ch/publications/pdfs/RussianAnalyticalDigest175.pdf.

Casula, Philipp, and Mark Katz. "Russian Foreign Policy in the Middle East." In

The Routledge Handbook on Russian Foreign Policy, edited by Andrey Tsygankov, 295–311. London: Routledge, 2018.

Černjaev, Anatolij S. "Analitičeskaja zapiska A.S. Černjaeva." Gorbačev Fund Archives, f.5, op.1, d. 20674, April 15, 1987.

European Commission. "EU-China: A Strategic Outlook," March 12, 2019. https://ec.europa.eu/commission/sites/beta-political/files/communication-eu-china-a-strategic-outlook.pdf.

European Council on Foreign Relations. "Mapping European Leverage in the MENA Region." https://www.ecfr.eu/specials/mapping_eu_leverage_mena.

Fichter, James R. *British and French Colonialism in Africa, Asia and the Middle East: Connected Empires across the Eighteenth to the Twentieth Centuries*. Cambridge: Cambridge University Press, 2019.

Friedman, Jeremy. *Shadow Cold War*. Chapel Hill: University of North Carolina Press, 2015.

Golan, Galia. *Yom Kippur and After*. Cambridge: Cambridge University Press, 1979.

Grinevskij, Oleg. *Tajny Sovetskoj Diplomatii*. Moscow: Vagrius, 2000.

Gulf News Staff Report. "China Leading Trade Partner of UAE: Al Mansouri." *Gulf News*, July 22, 2019. https://gulfnews.com/uae/china-leading-trade -partner-of-uae-al-mansouri-1.65370898.

Haass, Richard. *Defining US Foreign Policy in a Post-Post-Cold War World*. The 2002 Arthur Ross Lecture, Remarks to Foreign Policy Association, New York, April 22, 2002.

Hayes, Anna. "Explainer: Who Are the Uyghurs and Why Is the Chinese Government Detaining Them?" *Conversation*. https://theconversation.com/ explainer-who-are-the-uyghurs-and-why-is-the-chinese-government -detaining-them-111843.

Heikal, Mohamed. *The Sphinx and the Commissar: The Rise and Fall of Soviet Influence in the Middle East*. New York: Harper & Row, 1978.

Karsh, Efraim. *The Soviet Union and Syria: The Asad Years*. New York: Routledge, 1988.

Khlebbnikov, Alexey. "Is Astana Format on the Way to Be Reformatted?" https://www.institutfuersicherheit.at/is-astana-format-on-the-way-to -be-reformatted/.

———. "Russia Looks to the Middle East to Boost Arms Exports." Middle East Institute, April 8, 2019. https://www.mei.edu/publications/russia-looks -middle-east-boost-arms-exports.

Kosač, Grigorij G. "Komintern i Kommunističeskie Partii Arabskich Stran v 20- 30-ch godach." In *Komintern: Kritika i Kritiki*, 296–344. Moscow: Nauka, 1978.

Kruger, Laura-Theresa. "The French Foreign Policy U-Turn in the Arab

Spring—the Case of Tunisia." *Mediterranean Politics* 23, no. 2 (2018): 197–222.

Lund, Aron. "From Cold War to Civil War: 75 Years of Russian-Syrian Relations." https://www.ui.se/globalassets/ui.se-eng/publications/ui-publica tions/2019/ui-paper-no.-7-2019.pdf.

Lynch, Marc, ed. *The Arab Thermidor: The Resurgence of the Security State*. Washington, DC: POMEPS, 2015.

Müller, Miriam K. *How the Germans Brought Their Communism to Yemen*. Bielefeld: transcript, 2018.

Niblock, Tim. "Problems and Opportunities for China in Developing Its Role in the Gulf Region." *Asian Journal of Middle Eastern and Islamic Studies* 11, no. 3 (2017): 1–11.

Nye Jr., Joseph S. "Trump's Effect on US Foreign Policy." Project Syndicate, September 4, 2019. https://www.project-syndicate.org/commentary/trump -long-term-effect-on-american-foreign-policy-by-joseph-s-nye-2019-09.

Posuvaljuk, Viktor Viktorovič, and Svetlana Nikolaevna Posuvaljuk. *Bagrovoe nebo Bagdada*. St Petersburg: Aletejja, 2012.

Primakov, Evgenij Maksimovič, Fabienne Mariengof, and François Olivier. *Missions à Bagdad: histoire d'une négociation secrète*. Paris: Éd. du Seuil, 1991.

Primakov, Yevgeny. *Russia and the Arabs*. New York: Basic Books, 2009.

Putz, Catherine. "Which Countries Are for or against China's Xinjiang Policies?" *Diplomat*, July 15, 2019. https://thediplomat.com/2019/07/which -countries-are-for-or-against-chinas-xinjiang-policies/.

Scobell, Andrew. "China's Search for Security in the Greater Middle East." In *The Red Star and the Crescent: China and the Middle East*, edited by James Reardon-Anderson. Oxford: Oxford University Press, 2018.

Shao, Grace. "China, the World's Second Largest Defense Spender, Becomes a Major Arms Exporter." *CNBC*, September 26, 2019. https://www.cnbc .com/2019/09/27/china-a-top-defense-spender-becomes-major-arms -exporter.html.

Sherman, Justin, and Robert Morgus. "Authoritarians Are Exporting Surveillance Tech, and with It Their Vision for the Internet." *Council on Foreign Relations*, December 5, 2018. https://www.cfr.org/blog/authoritarians -are-exporting-surveillance-tech-and-it-their-vision-internet.

Sun, Degang. "China's Soft Military Presence in the Middle East." *Dirasat*, no. 30, January 2018. http://www.kfcris.com/pdf/07b46fba22562acf20bb92fb 68f5ea5c5aaa11036d535.pdf.

TASS. "Russian Presents to UN Its Concept of Collective Security in Persian Gulf," July 30, 2019, https://tass.com/world/1070933.

Tolz, Vera. *Russia's Own Orient: The Politics of Identity and Oriental Studies in the*

Late Imperial and Early Soviet Periods. New York: Oxford University Press, 2011.

Tsygankov, Andrei P. *Russia's Foreign Policy: Change and Continuity in National Identity*, 3rd ed. Lanham, MD: Rowman & Littlefield, 2013.

Vasil'ev, Alexei. *Russia's Middle East Policy: From Lenin to Putin*. London: Routledge, 2018.

Walt, Stephen M. "Deep Dish: Stephen Walt's Guide to Realism." Chicago Council on Global Affairs, November 22, 2018. https://www.thechicago council.org/blog/global-insight/deep-dish-stephen-walts-guide-realism.

———. *The Hell of Good Intentions: America's Foreign Policy Elite and the Decline of US Primacy*. New York: Farrar, Straus and Giroux, 2018.

Walt, Stephen M., and John Mearsheimer. *The Israel Lobby and US Foreign Policy*. New York: Farrar, Straus and Giroux, 2008.

White House. "National Security Strategy of the United States." December 2017. https://www.whitehouse.gov/wp-content/uploads/2017/12/NSS -Final-12-18-2017-0905.pdf.

Wilner, Michael. "US Navy May Stop Docking in Haifa after Chinese Take Over Port." *Jerusalem Post*, December 15, 2018. https://www.jpost.com/ Israel-News/US-Navy-may-stop-docking-in-Haifa-after-Chinese-take -over-port-574414.

Worth, Robert F. "Saudi Arabia Rejects U.N. Security Council Seat in Protest Move." *New York Times*, October 18, 2013. https://www.nytimes.com/2013/ 10/19/world/middleeast/saudi-arabia-rejects-security-council-seat.html.

7

Environmental Politics in the Middle East

Robert Mason and Mohamed Abdelraouf

Introduction

While much attention is paid to the region's political economy, far less is paid to the environment, political economy of the environment during periods of rapid economic growth, or environmental politics, including its effect on state-society relations and vice versa. Humankind has been influenced by environmental factors throughout history. Premodern environmental determinism is apparent in the capital cities located by rivers or the sea: Cairo on the Nile (on which Sudan and Ethiopia also depend); Baghdad on the Tigris (and the importance of the Tigris-Euphrates river system for Turkey, Syria, and Iraq); Abu Dhabi, Kuwait City, Muscat, and Manama next to the Gulf waters; Beirut, Algiers, Tunis, and Tripoli on the Mediterranean; and Rabat on the Atlantic coast. The MENA environment has also played a surprising role in justifications for colonialism, including colonial military misadventures and efforts at state building.[1] The rentier economies of the Gulf states and Algeria continue to affect state and nation (under)development even in the present.

This chapter covers the structural issues affecting the environment across the region. It pays particular attention to food and water insecurity and air pollution before covering in more detail the illustrative cases of Lebanon, Syria, Iraq, Yemen, and Egypt. The chapter shows how the Middle East is a part of transnational and global environmental trends and issues, but is often being disproportionately affected by them, including water scarcity, desertification, global climate change, and changing weather patterns and agrarian crises, thus blurring the borders of the region and connections to far-off cities and countries.

The Food and Agriculture Organization (FAO) of the United Nations says that effective management in the Arab World is key to future growth and stability.[2] Yet, this has been remarkably lacking within and between states despite the fact that Islamic teachings call for the protection of natural resources and environmental stewardship, even at times in wars and conflicts. It is even considered a religious duty to protect the environment and natural resources. Failing to do so, in Islam, is considered to be a sin. For example:

> *Do you not see that Allah sends down rain from the sky and makes it flow as springs [and rivers] in the earth; then He produces thereby crops of varying colours; then they dry and you see them turned yellow; then He makes them [scattered] debris. Indeed in that is a reminder for those of understanding.* (Qur'an 39:21)

Environmental concerns in the Middle East are often disassociated with what is perceived as the more urgent state politics and only come into full view through the lens of an environmental crisis, foreign investment opportunity, and/or public protest. Indeed, the uprising in Syria is often attributed to earlier years of crop failure from 2006 onward, along with other socioeconomic and political factors/mismanagement, although some scholars express caution about securitizing climate change.[3] The conflict in Yemen has also been viewed through a natural resource lens, namely the persistent water and food crises that have contributed to state failure prior to the Yemen uprising. The environment then, broadly conceived as issues ranging from water, food, air, heat, waste management, disease, as well as a more even distribution of wealth derived from natural resources and working conditions, could be considered to be a large part of the drivers toward the Arab Uprisings and social inequality that is still prevalent across the region.[4] Even Qatar, which has avoided the Arab Uprisings, has been accused of not investigating hundreds of migrant labor deaths associated with 'sudden death syndrome' after working in temperatures of up to 45°C for close to 10 hours a day.[5] When amplifying the causal link between heat exhaustion and potentially fatal heart attacks, the findings in Qatar should resonate with those responsible for working conditions in a number of countries across the region.

Environmental issues are usually a result of power politics within the state and at the local level, including the "complex re-regulation and restructuring of resources, roles, and authority."[6] While agricultural, water (irrigation), energy, urban (including real estate), and land policy may have an impact, the lack of implementation capacity or 'politics of neglect' tends to intrude, although some progress has been made with regard to sludge management in Morocco. These environmental problems act as a latent issue that can fuel unrest and conflict across the region. The environment contributes to a host of socioeconomic issues but also is a function of them. Without a (holistic) strategy, states often fall short of prescriptive measures to alleviate human suffering associated with environmental degradation, if that is in fact part of the overall brief for authoritarian regimes, which is highly disputable.

Violent conflicts have also had a major impact on the environment, including forest clearing, diversion or contamination of rivers, releases of oil, access issues, and use of contaminating materials by the military (such as depleted uranium from ammunition). At the end of the first Gulf War, Iraqi troops set fire to over seven hundred oil wells south of the Iraqi border, releasing 1.5 billion barrels of oil into the environment, which was the largest 'oil spill' in human history. Claims were made against Iraq by a number of state actors, but the difficulty of quantifying the degradation to groundwater, long-term consequences to the environment, and uncertainties about refugee human health meant many claims were unsuccessful.[7] The US military used as much as oil in Iraq in 2008 as the equivalent of putting 1.2 million extra cars on the road that year.[8] Cases of ill health from increased levels of dust and toxins have also been reported in Iraq.[9] During war and in cases of state fragility and collapse, it is extremely difficult to maintain the necessary infrastructure to protect the environment. In fact, environmental concerns may run entirely contrary to socioeconomic and political interests and objectives.

Environmental Status in the MENA Region

The majority of MENA countries are characterized by extreme arid climates, sparse natural vegetation, and fragile soil conditions. The region comprises mainly desert lands with the exception of coastal strips on the fringes and some high mountain ranges, including the Taurus Mountain range from southern Turkey to the Iraqi and Iranian borders, Iran's Elburz and Zagros Mountains, and the Atlas Mountains in Morocco.

The rapid economic growth mainly confined to the Gulf region since oil was discovered in the early years of the twentieth century led to a new state distributive model and a huge dependence on natural resource revenue. Despite a historic lack of environmental protection, the Gulf Cooperation Council (GCC) countries represented a unique case of development, where oil and gas revenues enabled an exceptional accelerated development process in all aspects of life. These countries have become a hub of intense geopolitical, military, economic, industrial, construction, tourism, and other anthropogenic activities. There is no doubt that the main drive for the transformation of the region came from hydrocarbon-related activities. The economies of the GCC countries are driven primarily by the oil and gas sectors, which contribute between 25 and 56 percent of their GDP. However, the scale of oil and gas production and use in the GCC countries and some countries in North Africa leads to severe environmental problems. The main concern continues to relate to oil spills and other discharges on land and offshore from large tankers, oil refineries, distribution stations, and the petrochemicals industry, with consequent impacts on natural resources, including biodiversity loss and air pollution. As a result, it appears that as economies grow, traffic, waste, greenhouse gas (GHG) emissions, and ecosystem destruction also increase. The management and use of natural resources as well as chemical, hazardous wastes, and GHG emissions has not kept pace with economic development in GCC countries. Even amid the Paris climate accord in 2015, Saudi Arabia and Iran, with US support, were still questioning the science on fulfilling the goals in 2019.[10]

The whole MENA region is facing many environmental challenges. Some are traditional, linked to water scarcity, land degradation and desertification, and a lack of capacity linked to resource allocation and mismanagement. Others are emerging, such as climate change, increased demand for energy, construction and demolition debris, and hazardous war remnants. The MENA region is in fact the most water-scarce region in the world. While it accounts for approximately 6 percent of the world's population and has a high birth rate, it only has 2 percent of the world's renewable water resources.[11] Water pollution is another problem due to contaminants from the oil industry, war remnants, untreated sewage, and salinization. Water resources depletion and quality deterioration have added to an unsustainable water consumption pattern and created undeclared state tensions over shared water sources, both surface and underground. Other environmental problems related to water are: the marine and coastal pollution from oil spills and the shipping trade, land-based sources of pollution, and the negative impacts of global climate change. Temperatures are increasing due to climate change with parts of the Gulf and Red Sea regions expected to become uninhabitable due to extreme heat waves caused by climate change. Qatar has already installed air conditioning outside.[12]

The rapid urbanization, population growth (rising from 100 million in 1950 to 380 million in 2000, growing faster than any other major world region), and unsustainable consumption patterns have built up considerable stress on the environment, raising water and energy demand in the region, which has been coupled with poor resource management that has resulted in widespread soil, land, and marine degradation. Even limited political changes aimed at improving environmental governance and social equality could lead to a virtuous cycle of year-on-year efficiencies and improvements, building national resilience to further resource shocks or shortages, and new social processes and norms that favor environmental conservation and protection.

A Slow and Measured Response to Food and Water Insecurity
There has been a politicization and even securitization of environmental challenges and climate change, and as a result a lack of 'rational' policies aimed at effectively dealing with it. Social engagement on environmental issues has the potential to unite people and mobilize them against the government or local decision-makers on other issues as well; therefore, it is generally discouraged. Historically, these groups have generally lacked the leverage required to change state behavior, including as far back as the 'bread riots' of the late 1970s, 1980s, and 1990s when World Bank and IMF reforms mandated the termination of state subsidies on basic food-stuffs, which disproportionately affected the poor. In 2008, food prices reached historic highs, blamed in part on supply-side dynamics such as slowing cereal cultivation, insufficient stockpiles worldwide, and more agricultural land being used for biofuel cultivation.[13] Other factors said to have had an effect on food prices were higher fertilizer and agricultural energy costs and commodity speculation.[14]

Food is conceptualized differently across nations and states, but vulnerability (especially vulnerable populations, i.e., the poor) to shocks and food sovereignty (people's rights to determine food access and choices) are often at the core.[15] In the smaller oil-rich states in the Gulf, food sovereignty often refers to land acquisitions abroad or, in the case of Qatar, which is experiencing an intra-GCC blockade, investments in agriculture and livestock at home and abroad. Heavy investments in sectors such as dairy have led to some self-sufficiency and aim toward self-reliance in other areas such as the availability of fresh juice. Generally though, food self-sufficiency has dropped across the region and imports have become the norm, which is creating upward pressure on the state import bill. Although the MENA countries are not the worst-affected regions to suffer from hunger, food insecurity (especially dependence on large-scale grain imports) could grow with increasing populations to feed. As incomes grow in the region, there are often many millions left behind in poverty, which leads to food insecurity. The differences between Qatar and Yemen are telling, where the poorest in Yemen are spending upward of 35 percent of household income on bread.[16] Arid conditions, conflict, and the lack of self-sufficiency suggest a regional or international policy aimed at stabilizing commodity prices that would best address the challenge. The prospects for prices over the next decade look better, with higher levels of cereal production (reaching highs in 2017) and weaker demand from China.[17] Nevertheless, the long-term prospects are still likely to remain challenging as demand grows in line with a global rise in population.

When it comes to environmental controls and access to water and food, MENA governments are often said to lack capacity. But some governments incorporate a range of opaque state institutions and divide regulatory capacities to fuel domestic uncertainty about state decision-making. Environmental expertise often does exist but is underutilized, land reform is uncertain, and a proliferation of donor projects in this area has not performed well.

Climate change is global and will affect the MENA region. Egypt (notably Alexandria) is vulnerable to rising sea levels, and when Islamic State of Iraq and Syria (ISIS) took control of dams in Iraq, it left Karbala and Najaf without water. Every country from Morocco to Iran shares water resources with a neighbor, highlighting the need for cooperation across the region. Syria, Tunisia, Libya, Jordan, Lebanon, and Yemen rank among those 'extremely' vulnerable to climate change negative impacts. Climate change affects almost all sectors of the economy, such as water, agriculture, energy, and tourism, and could therefore be catastrophic to humanitarian and economic development efforts. In the United Nations' 2014 report of the Intergovernmental Panel on Climate Change (IPCC), it was agreed that climate change could "indirectly increase risks of violent conflicts in the form of civil war and inter-group violence by amplifying well-documented drivers of these conflicts such as poverty and economic shocks."[18] In 2007, the ex-UN secretary general Ban Ki-moon described the conflict in Sudan's Darfur region as the world's first climate change conflict. The assumption was that water scarcity from changed rainfall patterns resulting from climate change had contributed to this conflict. His thinking reflects findings to date that the incidence of conflict is likely to be higher in years of lower precipitation, especially in arid or desert areas.

It could be assumed that if the MENA region was to expect a heavy impact from climate change and environmental change, it ought to be at least aware of the issues and take appropriate action to cushion the impact and mitigate its worst effects.

During the twenty-sixth session of the Council of Arab Ministers responsible for the Environment (CAMRE) in Jeddah, 2014, it was noted that there are a myriad of initiatives aimed at improving the green economy, including:

- the Green Economy Policy in Morocco;
- UAE's support to the global Partnership for Action on Green Economy (PAGE) and recent acceptance of the Cartagena Protocol on Biosafety;
- Saudi Arabia's work to set and enforce new energy efficiency codes for key sectors;
- Mauritania's remarkable efforts to promote renewable energy investments;
- Jordan's leadership on Eco-Cities and Sustainable Buildings;
- Egypt's ambitious wind farms expansion; and
- Kuwait's Green-Belt.[19]

However, many governments in the region have been slow to formulate solid national action plans for the environment and enhance their nationally determined contributions (NDCs) according to the 2015 Paris climate agreement. The environment continues to be the silent casualty of the civil unrest and from the various conflicts in the region.

Air the MENA Pollution
In the MENA region, people are dying not only from bombs, missiles, and bullets but also from preventable diseases, maladies, and complications arising from environmental pollution, including air pollution, which cost an estimated 125,000 lives in the Middle East in 2013 and $9 billion.[70] Egypt and Iran are listed as the worst affected.[21] But they are by no means the only states. Indeed, Onitsha in Nigeria and Zabol in Iran are stated as being the world's two most polluted cities.[22] Other notoriously polluted cities include Kabul, Lagos, Tehran, Beijing, and New Delhi (which measured over 1,000 AQI in November 2019[23]), mainly due to a combination of rapid urbanization without planning and public services creating pollution. Geography also plays a part, as does drought in wetlands and desertification, dust storms, burning low-quality diesel, burning waste in rubbish dumps, and discharges from industry. The conditions in which waste accumulates are also important, whether in difficult political and security contexts and mixed governance structures of the West Bank and Lebanon.[24]

On October 17, 2019, IQAir AirVisual measured 87 US AQI in Cairo (moderate air pollution), 76 US AQI in Baghdad (moderate), and 77 US AQI in Riyadh (moderate). They also measured 155 US AQI in Beijing (unhealthy), 19 US AQI in London (good), and 61 US AQI in Los Angeles (moderate).[25] While these measurements are not necessarily representative, they do give a limited window of readings across the region and globally and show there is room for air quality improvements across the Middle East. This is especially the case since the economic losses associated with air pollution are greater than the GDPs of Lebanon, Syria, Tunisia, and Yemen combined.[26]

In the following sections, we turn to a discussion on the relationship between conflict and the environment in selected countries in the MENA region (Lebanon, Syria and Iraq, Yemen, and Egypt). We highlight the role that environmental problems and natural resources play as cause and consequence of conflict and as a long-term development challenge.

Lebanon

The Lebanese environment is a function of the country's recent conflicts, including contamination of land, air, water, and biota from the most recent conflict, which lasted July–August 2006 in which 1,191 people were killed, 900,000 fled their homes, severe damage was caused to infrastructure, and 30,000 housing units were destroyed.[27] In August 2006, the Lebanese minister of environment requested that the UN Environment Program (UNEP) conduct a postconflict environmental assessment of Lebanon. In the subsequent report, the UNEP found that the bombing of fuel storage tanks at the Jiyeh thermal power plant resulted in 10,000–15,000 tons of heavy fuel being spilled into the sea.[28] The conflict exacerbated solid waste issues since there were vast amounts of rubble to be disposed of, along with hazardous healthcare waste, which was mixed in with normal waste and therefore threatened public health, and thousands of cubic meters of hydrocarbon-contaminated soil requiring treatment. Heavy metals remain in the air around heavily bombed sites and the clearing of unexploded ordinance remains a priority.[29]

Beyond conflict, a waste crisis began in 2015 when residents near the Naameh landfill site forced the government to shut it down, more than a decade after it was scheduled to close. The protest followed trash being left in the street from July 2015 to August 2016 and led to one of the first mass mobilizations in more than a decade, spurring the government to open a new landfill at Bourj Hammoud on the outskirts of Beirut.[30] Since the 1975–1990 wars, Lebanese militia forces have run the dump, accepted toxic waste from Italy, and the government has been unable to implement a functional national waste management plan.[31] Instead, a series of quick fixes have been implemented, including expanding the dump upward rather than outward. By August 2019, the dump was expected to be at capacity with the risk of trash once again being left in the street.[32] An alternative, such as an incinerator, could become a health hazard with the added potential for explosions. The infrastructure needs updating and law enforcement requires improvement in order to improve accountability. The Lebanese case suggests that with the right combination of political will, external support, and ongoing grassroots pressure, an environmental solution might present itself. That grassroots pressure built up in Beirut in October 2019 and was evident in the pan-sectarian protests that broke out against government corruption and with the aim of replacing the political elite. These protests have intensified following an economic crisis that has pushed tens of thousands into poverty and a fire that triggered an explosion of large quantities of ammonium nitrate in the port area on August 4, 2020. This incident killed more than two hundred people and caused widespread damage across parts of the city. It was followed by another fire in the city on September 10, 2020. It will be imperative for Lebanon to transition beyond its established sectarian fiefdoms in order to more adequatelty address environmental, economic, and other socio-economic concerns at the state level.

Syria and Iraq

In the case of Syria, political and security issues will be compounded in the future by decreasing annual precipitation. Many areas will become drier, damaging agriculture and contributing to urbanization during and after the conflict. The worst three-year drought in Syria's record began in the winter of 2006–2007. The River Barada, which provided water to villages near the capital city of Damascus, has almost dried up over recent years due to low levels of rainfall. Herds of livestock died and the prices of many crops more than doubled. Moreover, food subsidies on which many depended were cut. The widespread deterioration of agricultural harvests meant farmers moved off the land and became 'environmental refugees.' State instability was also a result of urban problems related to energy, water, sanitation, and waste management. Worsening environmental conditions were coupled with incoming refugees from Iraq after coalition forces took over the country and amid worsening sectarian violence and conflict.

The consequences of conflict in Syria are similar to those in Lebanon during the 2006 conflict with Israel, albeit on a greater scale. Syrian coalition and Russian forces have targeted oil installations and storage sites and bombarded populated areas and industrial facilities, especially in Aleppo.[33] ISIS repeated Saddam Hussein's technique of setting fire to entire oil fields during their retreat from Mosul in 2016.[34] Timely identification of health risks in a war zone is difficult but should be prioritized as soon as possible and form an important part of the reconstruction effort. More than half the residential areas have been destroyed, there are millions of tons of rubble to dispose of, and the reconstruction effort is expected to cost $1.2 trillion.[35] The likely platforms to connect these efforts include the World Humanitarian Summit and the UN Environmental Assembly.

Across Iraq and Syria, many churches, mosques, museums, and statues have either been destroyed or looted by ISIS. In addition, Assyrian monuments in Syria are being ruined. That is apart from the destruction of statues of musicians, poets, and thinkers because they represent a different ideology than that of ISIS. Sadly, all these treasures, many built more than five thousand years ago, are being looted or destroyed. This is a loss not only for Iraq, Syria, and the Arab region but also for human heritage and civilization.

In Iraq, environmental concerns stem from population growth, the impact of three wars, climate change, poor land-use planning, and encroachment on fragile ecosystems.[36] In terms of climate change, between 1970 and 2004, the country's mean temperature increased by 1–2°C.[37] Expectations are that Iraq will suffer from more intense heat waves with adverse effects on agriculture, water resources, human health, and infrastructure. Water resources are challenged by a combination of poor water management, conflict, lack of local policies, unstable relations with neighbors, and climate change. There are also various dams upstream on the Tigris and Euphrates rivers in Turkey, Iran, and Syria causing escalating levels of salinity in the Shatt al Arab river, which threatens local livelihoods. The Kurds maintain control over the Tigris water flow upstream from Baghdad, and therefore a national plan that includes negotiation and cooperation with the Kurdish Regional Government (KRG) is required. Biodiversity loss has followed from unregulated hunting, lack of protection of important sites, and trade in endangered species.

After the Iran-Iraq War in the 1980s, the Gulf War in 1990, and the US-led intervention in 2003, followed by internal sectarian conflict and an insurgency led by ISIS, Iraq is experiencing a legacy of war that makes the environmental issues more complex. Conflict has undermined the government's ability to manage contaminated sites, risks from oil fires and ammunition dumps, and deal with a vast quantity of waste. Water installations were already in a poor state before ISIS expansion, and therefore their reinstatement and upgrading to ensure they cannot be weaponized or affected in the future would help ensure water security in Iraq.[38] If the marshes can be rescued in the south, Basra port modernized to boost economic growth, and better cooperation achieved with regional neighbors on water management, it would help turn the situation around in Iraq. In 2018, Basra experienced a water crisis whereby sixty-two hundred people needed hospital treatment for intestinal infections after the Tigris and Euphrates rivers fell to low levels and the basin water sources became increasingly saline.[39] Desalination efforts have been stepped up, but it is not known whether these efforts will be sufficient to address the challenge.

Drops in nitrogen dioxide (NO_2) levels are not always indicators of progress. In Saudi Arabia, Kuwait, and the UAE, drops are usually to do with air quality controls. But in Syria, Iraq, and Egypt, as indeed in Greece, the trend is more to do with interrupted economic growth. In Syria, NO_2 levels in Damascus and Aleppo dropped by as much as 50 percent between 2011 and 2015 during the ISIS onslaught.[40] In Lebanon, NO_2 levels rose by 20–30 percent due to the knock-on effect of Syrian refugees entering the country.[41] While the effects of conflict are likely to be temporary, it shows that building in new environmental safeguards into reconstruction efforts and into future economic planning could sustain lower NO_2 levels without affecting economic output.

Yemen

Yemen is one of the most ancient cradles of civilization in the Middle East. In Arabic literature, Yemen used to be, and still is, called "the happy or fortunate Yemen." Sadly, there is no sign of happiness for this country in the near future in light of the ongoing conflict. Yemen might be the poorest country in the Middle East, but it is of great strategic importance to its neighbors. The country sits on the Bab al-Mandab Strait, a waterway linking the Red Sea with the Gulf of Aden, through which much of the world's oil shipments and goods trade passes.

Yemen is largely dependent on its agricultural sector, including production of khat, fruit, and vegetables, which supports 75 percent of the rural-based population.[42] Yet, it remains vulnerable to climate change impacts such as drought, flooding, pests, sudden disease outbreaks, severe storms, and rising sea levels. Yemen is among the most water-stressed countries in the world, brought on by regional drought, a naturally dry climate, and failed attempts at management. Some estimates say that Yemen will run out of fresh water by 2023.[43] There are very limited natural freshwater resources and inadequate supplies of potable water. Yemen has experienced long periods of water shortages due to the rapid growth of the market economy, government support for development, and groundwater extraction. The water quality is very poor due to a degraded water supply infrastructure. Poor central planning, wastage, and policies that encourage heavy water use—from cheap diesel pricing to funding surface or spate irrigation for water-heavy cash crops such as khat—are to blame for the current shortage.

Community water sources were overburdened or dysfunctional before the crisis and have been affected by conflict-related damage and further strain due to the influx of internally displaced persons (IDPs). In the context of a rising population, severe unemployment, political instability, active terrorist organizations (ISIS and al-Qaeda), external interests, and dwindling water and food resources, the impact of climate change will be much worse. Urban infrastructure has been destroyed, including water and desalination facilities, and only 45 percent of the healthcare facilities are operational.[44] Plans for development have had to be put on hold while the fighting continues. In 2015, 13 million Yemenis lacked reliable access to drinking water and conditions have worsened as supplies dry up and prices increase beyond what most people can afford.[45] Local water shortages have coincided with several other critical political, economic, and demographic factors to precipitate a full-scale civil war from 2015 and the mobilization again of a southern succession movement. Damage to the water and sanitation infrastructure and disruption of the public health system have contributed to many cholera outbreaks. From October 2016 to September 2017, cholera affected 797,772 Yemenis.[46] By 2018, there were about 3 million IDPs.

Agriculture lands continue to be threatened by droughts, desertification, wind, and water scarcity. Food security and economic income have been lost and affect many Yemenis. These issues continue to affect the shape of the conflict in Yemen, which, along with lost infrastructure, will take many years to rebuild. Yemen, like Syria and Iraq, shows how different threats can combine to form an apparently insurmountable developmental challenge. The best prospect for Yemen is to learn the lesson from Syria—that ending the conflict will give the country a better chance to address the other environmental and economic challenges it faces. If parties to the conflict continue to wait, it may be too late. Water will need to take its rightful place as a policy priority in whatever government(s) is formed after the conflict.

Egypt

The most obvious connection between the January 25 Revolution and the environment was the adverse impact on the man-made sphere and biosphere caused by the burning or destruction of a number of buildings, including the Interior Ministry and former president Mubarak's party headquarters on Tahrir Square. There were other less obvious but far more meaningful connections. For example, many signs displayed during the protests indicated that the ruling regime had come to be viewed as culpable for squandering the country's precious natural resources. The

April 8 demands included: the issue of land management, use of carcinogenic pesticides, allegedly corrupt practices in the private sector that affect the environment, and severe punishments for those who poison food or water. The issue was framed not so much in terms of sustainable development as social justice.[47]

During and after the public protests that brought down the regime, protesters included environmental and resources-related issues among their catalogue of grievances, loudly proclaiming 'no' to carcinogenic pesticides and fertilizers, 'no' to polluted water resources, and 'no' to the bulldozing of farmland. The linkage between the revolution and the environment can also be seen in the actions taken by demonstrators. Immediately after the regime was ousted from power, youth campaigns were launched to clean, paint, and plant in streets and cities across the country. These and other acts of collective 'environmental citizenship' were very important and stood in contrast to the small neglected green spaces across Cairo. Youth sent a clear signal to the authorities challenging the self-interested rational actor model that had pervaded official thinking and policies for decades and articulating the people's wider social interests and concerns.

It is estimated that 60 million tons of solid waste are generated each year in Egypt, including 29.4 million tons of sludge from canal dredging, 9.3 million tons of municipal waste from major cities, and 5.6 million tons of waste from rural areas.[48] Only 30–60 percent of waste is collected with much of the rest scattered in the environment without being treated.[49] At present, international enterprises under contract with governorates are disposing of waste in Cairo, Giza, and Alexandria but in many small cities, waste is often burned. Industrial waste is usually treated with municipal waste, and there is only one treatment plant in Alexandria for hazardous waste, although incinerators in hospitals are being increasingly used. As of January 2019, the European Bank for Reconstruction and Development is requesting proposals to develop a Hazardous Waste Management Programme—Phase 1.[50] This program will be particularly important as hazardous waste generated in Cairo has no route to proper disposal.[51] There are at least fifty-six composting plants in operation. More waste composting plants, transfer stations to feed the plants, and sanitary landfills will help Egypt achieve Goal 7 of the sustainable development goals (SDGs) on ensuring environmental sustainability.

One of the important lessons of the Egyptian experience is that the Arab world needs to carry out continuous greening projects that utilize individuals, especially youth, to serve and protect their countries. This is a lesson that is already in effect across large swathes of China and India.

More can be learnt from these and other states about sustainable tourism, development, and waste management. While there is progress on government subsidies and energy policies which have long driven wasteful consumption practices and habits, that at least is now being addressed through some reform of energy subsidies and pricing. However, in practice, it is unlikely that a significant change in usage will take place without an accompanying shift in social norms, especially as relatively cheap energy is still regarded as part of the remaining social contract between society and the state. It is the task of the international community, through international aid, investment, and other forms of cooperation, to support local efforts to pursue environmental concerns and sustainable development within the new authoritarian reality.

Conclusion

The state of the environment is a function of economic development, unrestrained population growth, conflict, and poor governance anywhere. In the Middle East, the environment has been hit hardest where these dynamics have continued to dominate and where the destruction of lives, physical infrastructure, and ecosystems has taken place and left a legacy of toxic pollution, displacement, and destroyed livelihoods. Security is a prerequisite for the implementation of environmental regulation and protection, so too is a concerned government attuned to the logic of the environment–humanitarian–prosperity nexus. Significant impediments remain in role conception (shifting elites from being proponents of narrowly defined often security interests to being public servants), the skills and capacity necessary to carry through environmental regulation, and it is assumed all spaces are governed by the central government, which may not reflect reality.

This chapter shows how important environmental expertise is to identifying the challenges to human security in all its forms, and quickly developing sustainable agricultural, health, and other public policy solutions to address national humanitarian and developmental needs. This is especially the case in states such as Iraq and Yemen, which are already experiencing water crises and water scarcity. It is also increasingly clear that many fragile and conflict-affected countries will fail to adopt any development plans unless the negative impacts of conflict on the environment are addressed. Furthermore, the consequences of not adopting stringent environmental plans in weak or failing states will be more humanitarian crises, displacement, and conflict.

The international community has a moral responsibility to enable diverse communities to unite and peacefully cooperate to enhance health prospects, establish stability, and build prosperity in their societies and across borders through 'environmental citizenship' programs. In this regard, supporting realistic, coherent, and national good environmental governance programs with significant stakeholder engagement will help reduce the probability of conflicts over scarce natural resources and unsustainable practices. While some of these programs already exist, information is still sparse and has only been collected in many cases in MENA since the 1990s. More can be done to improve air quality, encourage land reform and land use regulations, and support antidumping practices, desalination, and renewable energy projects. In some cases, leverage may be required to establish a deeper cooperation between neighboring states to ensure a more equitable use of shared resources. It is only by restoring the ecosystem that the region will be able to realistically achieve SDGs that feed into Vision 2030 and other economic development plans.

Notes

1. More on the philosophical theories on environmental issues and its impact in colonial narratives can be found in Harry Verhoeven, ed., "Introduction," in *Environmental Politics in the Middle East* (Oxford: Oxford University Press, 2018), 1–27.
2. Food and Agriculture Organization, "Effective Management of Water Resources in Arab World Key to Future Growth and Stability," August 28, 2018, http://www.fao.org/neareast/news/view/en/c/1150769/.
3. Jan Selby et al., "Climate Change and the Syrian Civil War Revisited," *Political Geography* 60 (September 2017): 232–244.
4. Mohammad Abdel Raouf, "Arab Spring: A Curse on Environment," *Gulf News*, September 24, 2014, https://gulfnews.com/opinion/op-eds/arab-spring-a-curse-on-environment-1.1389505.
5. Pete Pattison and Roshan Sedhai, "Sudden Deaths of Migrant Workers in Qatar not Investigated," October 7, 2019, https://www.theguardian.com/global-development/2019/oct/07/sudden-deaths-of-hundreds-of-migrant-workers-in-qatar-not-investigated.
6. See Jeannie Sowers, "Networks, Authority, and Environmental Politics in Egypt," in *Environmental Politics in Egypt* (Abingdon: Routledge, 2014), 3.
7. Laurence Menhinick, "What the Environmental Legacy of the Gulf War Should Teach Us," Oxford Research Group, March 18, 2016, https://www.oxfordresearchgroup.org.uk/blog/what-the-environmental-legacy-of-the-gulf-war-should-teach-us.
8. Watson Institute of International and Public Affairs, Brown University, "Costs of War: Environmental Costs," https://watson.brown.edu/costsofwar/costs/social/environment.

9. Ibid.

10. Die Welt, "Climate Groups Blast Saudi, US 'Science-Deniers' at UN Environment Meeting," June 27, 2019, https://www.dw.com/en/climate-groups -blast-saudi-us-science-deniers-at-un-environment-meeting/a-49381381.

11. Ghanimah Al-Otaibi, "By the Numbers: Facts about Water Crisis in the Arab World," March 19, 2015, https://blogs.worldbank.org/arabvoices/ numbers-facts-about-water-crisis-arab-world.

12. Jane Dalton, "Qatar Now So Hot It Has Started Air-Conditioning the Outdoors," *Independent*, October 19, 2019, https://www.independent.co.uk/ news/world/middle-east/qatar-air-conditioning-temperature-weather-heat -climate-change-athletics-world-cup-a9160751.html.

13. Zahra Babar and Mehran Kamrava, "Food Security and Food Sovereignty in the Middle East," in *Food Security in the Middle East*, ed. Zahra Babar and Mehran Kamrava (Oxford: Oxford University Press, 2014), 2.

14. Ibid.

15. Ibid., 2–4.

16. Tom Flinn and Nour Merza, "Political Unrest Deepens Plight of Yemen Children," *Reuters*, February 15, 2012, https://www.reuters.com/article/ uk-yemen-children-idUKTRE81E1EP20120215.

17. Food and Agriculture Organization of the United Nations, "OECD-FAO Agricultural Outlook 2008–2027: Special Focus: Middle East and North Africa," http://www.fao.org/publications/oecd-fao-agricultural-outlook/ 2018–2027/en/.

18. IPCC, "Assessing and Managing the Risks of Climate Change," https:// www.ipcc.ch/site/assets/uploads/2018/03/WGIIAR5_SPM_Top_Level _Findings-1.pdf.

19. Abulaziz Bin Omar Al-Jasser speech, "26th Session of the Council of Arab Ministers Responsible for the, Environment (CAMRE), Jeddah, Saudi Arabia," November 22, 2014, https://www.unenvironment.org/fr/node/19480.

20. World Bank, "Air Pollution Deaths Cost Economies in Middle East and North Africa More than $9 Billion," September 8, 2016, https://www .worldbank.org/en/news/press-release/2016/09/08/air-pollution-deaths -cost-economies-in-middle-east-and-north-africa-more-than-9-billion.

21. Ibid.

22. John Vidal and Saeed Kamali Dehghan, "Which Are the World's Two Most Polluted Cities—and Why?," *Guardian*, May 12, 2016, https://www .theguardian.com/environment/2016/may/12/which-are-the-worlds-two -most-polluted-cities-and-why.

23. Debjit Chakraborty and Rajesh Kumar Singh, "Air Pollution in Delhi Spikes as Deadly Smog Envelops City," *Bloomberg*, November 4, 2019, https://www.bloomberg.com/news/articles/2019-11-04/air-pollution-in

-new-delhi-spikes-as-deadly-smog-envelops-city#:~:targetText=The%20
air%20quality%20index%2C%20or,50%20is%20the%20safe%20level.

24. See, for example, Sophia Stamatopoulou-Robbins, *Waste Siege: The Life of Infrastructure in Palestine* (Stanford, CA: Stanford University Press, 2019).

25. Information on the AirVisual app is limited to users. US AQI stands for United States Air Quality Index, and the breakdown of what each value and classifications mean can be found at United States Environmental Protection Agency, "A Guide to Air Quality and Your Health," https://www3.epa.gov/airnow/aqi_brochure_02_14.pdf.

26. Mahmoud Abouelnaga, "Poor Air Quality and Lost Economic Opportunities," *Atlantic Council*, July 18, 2019, https://www.atlanticcouncil.org/blogs/menasource/poor-air-quality-and-lost-economic-opportunities/.

27. UNEP, "Lebanon: Post-Conflict Environmental Assessment," 2007, http://wedocs.unep.org/bitstream/handle/20.500.11822/16756/Lebanon_Post Conflict_Environmental_Assessment.pdf?sequence=1&isAllowed=y.

28. Ibid.

29. Ibid., 162–165.

30. Fiona Broom, "Fighting the Big Burn: Lebanon's Waste Dilemma," *New Internationalist*, November 27, 2018, https://newint.org/features/2018/11/01/lebanon-trash.

31. Ibid.

32. Timour Azhari, "Trash to Pile Higher at Burj Hammoud Landfill," *Daily Star*, May 17, 2019, http://www.dailystar.com.lb/News/Lebanon-News/2019/May-17/483379-trash-to-pile-higher-at-burj-hammoud-landfill.ashx.

33. Conflict and Environment Observatory, "Five Years On: Lessons Learned from the Environmental Legacy of Syria's War," March 16, 2016, https://ceobs.org/five-years-on-lessons-learned-from-the-environmental-legacy-of-syrias-war/.

34. Olivier Laurent, "The Fires of Qayyarah," *Time*, March 16, 2017, https://time.com/iraq-fires/.

35. Ibid.

36. Roz Price, "Environmental Risks in Iraq," Institute of Development Studies, June 8, 2018, https://assets.publishing.service.gov.uk/media/5b3b63a3e5274a6ff466faa5/Environmental_risks_in_Iraq.pdf.

37. Ibid.

38. Tobias von Lossow, "More than Infrastructures: Water Challenges in Iraq," Clingendael Policy Brief, July 2018, https://www.clingendael.org/sites/default/files/2018-07/PB_PSI_water_challenges_Iraq.pdf.

39. Mohammed Al-Khuzai, "Iraq: Red Crescent Responds to Water Crisis in Basra," International Federation of Red Cross and Red Crescent Societies,

September 10, 2018, https://reliefweb.int/report/iraq/iraq-red-crescent
-responds-water-crisis-basra.

40. Emma Howard, "Middle East Conflict 'Drastically Altered' Air Pollution
    Levels in Region—Study," August 21, 2015, https://www.theguardian.com/
    environment/2015/aug/21/middle-east-conflict-decrease-air-pollution
    -levels-iraq-baghdad-egypt-syria-study.
41. Ibid.
42. United Nations Development Program, "Yemen," n.d., https://www
    .adaptation-undp.org/explore/western-asia/yemen.
43. Austin Bodetti, "Yemen Is Running Out of Water," *Lobelog*, March 20, 2019,
    https://lobelog.com/yemen-is-running-out-of-water/.
44. Margaret Suter, "An Update on Yemen's Water Crisis and the Weaponiza-
    tion of Water," Atlantic Council, November 29, 2018, https://www.atlantic
    council.org/blogs/menasource/an-update-on-yemen-s-water-crisis-and-the
    -weaponization-of-water/.
45. Ibid.
46. Conflict and Environment Observatory, "Country Brief: Yemen,"
    March 26, 2018, https://ceobs.org/country-brief-yemen/.
47. Mohamed Abdel Raouf and Abdel Hamid, "Middle East Revolutions: An
    Environmental Perspective," Middle East Institute, June 1, 2011, https://
    www.mei.edu/publications/middle-east-revolutions-environmental
    -perspective.
48. Japanese Ministry of the Environment, "Waste Management—Egypt,"
    https://www.env.go.jp/earth/coop/coop/c_report/egypt_h16/english/
    pdf/021.pdf.
49. Ibid.
50. European Bank for Reconstruction and Development, "Egypt: Assistance
    in Developing Hazardous Waste Management Programme—Phase 1,"
    https://www.ebrd.com/cs/Satellite?c=Content&cid=1395279973559&d=M
    obile&pagename=EBRD%2FContent%2FContentLayout.
51. World Bank, "Egypt—Hazardous Waste Management," http://sitere
    sources.worldbank.org/EXTMETAP/Resources/HWM-EgyptP.pdf.

Bibliography

Abdel Raouf, Mohamed, and Abdel Hamid. "Middle East Revolutions: An Envi-
    ronmental Perspective." Middle East Institute, June 1, 2011. https://www
    .mei.edu/publications/middle-east-revolutions-environmental-perspective.
Abdel Raouf, Mohammad. "Arab Spring: A Curse on Environment." *Gulf
    News*, September 24, 2014. https://gulfnews.com/opinion/op-eds/
    arab-spring-a-curse-on-environment-1.1389505.
Abouelnaga, Mahmoud. "Poor Air Quality and Lost Economic Opportunities."

Atlantic Council, July 18, 2019. https://www.atlanticcouncil.org/blogs/
menasource/poor-air-quality-and-lost-economic-opportunities/.

Al-Jasser, Abulaziz Bin Omar. "26th Session of the Council of Arab Ministers
Responsible for the, Environment (CAMRE), Jeddah, Saudi Arabia." Speech,
November 22, 2014. https://www.unenvironment.org/fr/node/19480.

Al-Khuzai, Mohammed. "Iraq: Red Crescent Responds to Water Crisis in Basra." International Federation of Red Cross and Red Crescent Societies, September 10, 2018. https://reliefweb.int/report/iraq/
iraq-red-crescent-responds-water-crisis-basra.

Al-Otaibi, Ghanimah. "By the Numbers: Facts about Water Crisis in the
Arab World." March 19, 2015. https://blogs.worldbank.org/arabvoices/
numbers-facts-about-water-crisis-arab-world.

Azhari, Timour. "Trash to Pile Higher at Burj Hammoud Landfill." *Daily Star*,
May 17, 2019. http://www.dailystar.com.lb/News/Lebanon-News/2019/
May-17/483379-trash-to-pile-higher-at-burj-hammoud-landfill.ashx.

Babar, Zahra, and Mehran Kamrava. *Food Security in the Middle East*. Oxford:
Oxford University Press, 2014.

Bodetti, Austin. "Yemen Is Running out of Water." *Lobelog*, March 20, 2019.
https://lobelog.com/yemen-is-running-out-of-water/.

Broom, Fiona. "Fighting the Big Burn: Lebanon's Waste Dilemma." *New Internationalist*, November 27, 2018. https://newint.org/features/2018/11/01/
lebanon-trash.

Chakraborty, Debjit, and Rajesh Kumar Singh. "Air Pollution in Delhi Spikes as
Deadly Smog Envelops City." *Bloomberg*, November 4, 2019. https://www
.bloomberg.com/news/articles/2019-11-04/air-pollution-in-new-delhi
-spikes-as-deadly-smog-envelops-city#:~:targetText=The%20air%20
quality%20index%2C%20or,50%20is%20the%20safe%20level.

Conflict and Environment Observatory. "Country Brief: Yemen." March 26,
2018. https://ceobs.org/country-brief-yemen/.

———. "Five Years On: Lessons Learned from the Environmental Legacy of
Syria's War." March 16, 2016. https://ceobs.org/five-years-on-lessons
-learned-from-the-environmental-legacy-of-syrias-war/.

Dalton, Jane. "Qatar Now So Hot It Has Started Air-Conditioning the Outdoors." *Independent*, October 19, 2019. https://www.independent.co.uk/news/
world/middle-east/qatar-air-conditioning-temperature-weather-heat
-climate-change-athletics-world-cup-a9160751.html.

Die Welt. "Climate Groups Blast Saudi, US 'Science-Deniers' at UN Environment Meeting." June 27, 2019. https://www.dw.com/en/climate-groups
-blast-saudi-us-science-deniers-at-un-environment-meeting/a-49381381.

European Bank for Reconstruction and Development. "Egypt: Assistance in
Developing Hazardous Waste Management Programme—Phase 1." https://

www.ebrd.com/cs/Satellite?c=Content&cid=1395279973559&d=Mobile&pa
gename=EBRD%2FContent%2FContentLayout.

Flinn, Tom, and Nour Merza. "Political Unrest Deepens Plight of Yemen Children." *Reuters*, February 15, 2012. https://www.reuters.com/article/uk-yemen
-children-idUKTRE81E1EP20120215.

Food and Agriculture Organization. "Effective Management of Water Resources
in Arab World Key to Future Growth and Stability." August 28, 2018. http://
www.fao.org/neareast/news/view/en/c/1150769/.

———. "OECD-FAO Agricultural Outlook 2008–2027: Special Focus: Middle
East and North Africa." http://www.fao.org/publications/oecd-fao
-agricultural-outlook/2018–2027/en/.

Gulf News Staff Report. "Diabetes Cases in Middle East to Rise 110% by 2045,"
Gulf News, December 19, 2018.

Howard, Emma. "Middle East Conflict 'Drastically Altered' Air Pollution Levels
in Region—Study." August 21, 2015. https://www.theguardian.com/environ
ment/2015/aug/21/middle-east-conflict-decrease-air-pollution-levels-iraq
-baghdad-egypt-syria-study.

Intergovernmental Panel on Climate Change. "Assessing and Managing the
Risks of Climate Change." https://www.ipcc.ch/site/assets/uploads/2018/03/
WGIIAR5_SPM_Top_Level_Findings-1.pdf.

Japanese Ministry of the Environment. "Waste Management—Egypt." https://
www.env.go.jp/earth/coop/coop/c_report/egypt_h16/english/pdf/021.pdf.

Laurent, Olivier. "The Fires of Qayyarah." *Time*, March 16, 2017, https://time
.com/iraq-fires/.

Lossow, Tobias von. "More than Infrastructures: Water Challenges in Iraq."
Clingendael Policy Brief, July 2018. https://www.clingendael.org/sites/
default/files/2018-07/PB_PSI_water_challenges_Iraq.pdf.

Menhinick, Laurence. "What the Environmental Legacy of the Gulf War
Should Teach Us." Oxford Research Group, March 18, 2016. https://www
.oxfordresearchgroup.org.uk/blog/what-the-environmental-legacy-of-the
-gulf-war-should-teach-us.

Pattison, Pete, and Roshan Sedhai. "Sudden Deaths of Migrant Workers in
Qatar Not Investigated." October 7, 2019. https://www.theguardian.com/
global-development/2019/oct/07/sudden-deaths-of-hundreds-of-migrant
-workers-in-qatar-not-investigated.

Price, Roz. "Environmental Risks in Iraq." Institute of Development Studies,
June 8, 2018. https://assets.publishing.service.gov.uk/media/5b3b63a3e5274
a6ff466faa5/Environmental_risks_in_Iraq.pdf.

Selby, Jan, Omar S. Dahi, Christine Frohlich, and Mike Hulme. "Climate
Change and the Syrian Civil War Revisited." *Political Geography* 60 (September 2017): 232–244.

Sowers, Jeannie. *Environmental Politics in Egypt*. Abingdon: Routledge, 2014.

Stamatopoulou-Robbins, Sophia. *Waste Siege: The Life of Infrastructure in Palestine*. Stanford, CA: Stanford University Press, 2019.

Suter, Margaret. "An Update on Yemen's Water Crisis and the Weaponization of Water." Atlantic Council, November 29, 2018. https://www.atlanticcouncil.org/blogs/menasource/an-update-on-yemen-s-water-crisis-and-the-weaponization-of-water/.

The Editorial, "Food Security in the Middle East and North Africa." *Lancet*, July 14, 2018. https://www.thelancet.com/journals/lancet/article/PIIS0140-6736(18)31563-0/fulltext.

World Bank. "Air Pollution Deaths Cost Economies in Middle East and North Africa More than $9 Billion." September 8, 2016. https://www.worldbank.org/en/news/press-release/2016/09/08/air-pollution-deaths-cost-economies-in-middle-east-and-north-africa-more-than-9-billion.

———. "Hazardous Waste Management." http://siteresources.worldbank.org/EXTMETAP/Resources/HWM-EgyptP.pdf.

———. "In Middle East and North Africa, Health Challenges are Becoming Similar to Those in Western Countries." September 4, 2013. https://www.worldbank.org/en/news/press-release/2013/09/04/middle-east-north-Africa-health-challenges-similar-western-countries.

United Nations Development Program. "Yemen." https://www.adaptation-undp.org/explore/western-asia/yemen.

United Nations Environment Program. "Lebanon: Post-Conflict Environmental Assessment." http://wedocs.unep.org/bitstream/handle/20.500.11822/16756/Lebanon_PostConflict_Environmental_Assessment.pdf?sequence=1&isAllowed=y.

United States Environmental Protection Agency. "A Guide to Air Quality and Your Health." https://www3.epa.gov/airnow/aqi_brochure_02_14.pdf.

Verhoeven, Harry, ed. *Environmental Politics in the Middle East*. Oxford: Oxford University Press, 2018.

Vidal, John, and Saeed Kamali Dehghan. "Which Are the World's Two Most Polluted Cities—and Why?" *Guardian*, May 12, 2016. https://www.theguardian.com/environment/2016/may/12/which-are-the-worlds-two-most-polluted-cities-and-why.

Watson Institute of International and Public Affairs, Brown University. "Costs of War: Environmental Costs." https://watson.brown.edu/costsofwar/costs/social/environment.

8

The Israel-Palestine Conflict as a Shaping Factor in Regional Politics

Robert Mason

The Israel-Palestine conflict has roots in the question or problem of Palestine, the inalienable rights of the Palestinian people, including the right of self-determination without external influence, the right to national independence and sovereignty, and the right to return to their homes and property in cases of displacement. This chapter explores how the Israel-Palestine conflict has developed over time and the role it continues to play in regional politics. While the conflict has historically been important in regional and to some extent international politics, there is evidence to suggest a changing threat perception in the Middle East, particularly of Iran by some Arab Gulf states, which is more closely aligning their foreign policy interests with Israel than has previously been the case. This appears to support adjusted realism that suggests a preoccupation of decision-makers with threats, in this case Iran, as a driver of foreign policy decision-making.[1] Omnibalancing is also an appropriate concept in this case, as some of the Arab Gulf states seek to address their security needs through advancing a broader alliance at the regional level, which complements close security ties with the U.S.

Background to the Conflict

Britain had promised to recognize a single Arab state from Aleppo in Syria to Aden in Yemen following the Arab revolt against the Ottoman Empire from June 1916 to October 1918. However, it reneged on this policy when it published the Balfour Declaration in 1917, which publicly supported a home for the Jewish people in Palestine. From 1919, the sovereign possession of Palestine would be vested with the League of Nations. From 1936 to 1939, the Arab revolt in Palestine demanded Arab independence and a halt to open-ended Jewish immigration and land purchases with the objective of establishing a Jewish state. On July 7, 1937, the Peel Commission, or Palestine Royal Commission, stated that the League of Nations Mandate had become unworkable and recommended partition. In 1938, the Woodhead Commission came up with the partition plan. The London Conference from February 7 to March 17, 1939, planned the future governance of Palestine and an end to the Mandate.

The Arab delegation opposed partition, along with the idea of a Jewish state, and called for an independent state of Palestine. A Jewish insurgency against British rule in Mandatory Palestine was carried out from February 1, 1944, to May 14, 1948, and facilitated British withdrawal. The United Nations adopted a resolution to partition Palestine on November 29, 1947. The subsequent 'Palestine War' began in response to release of the Partition plan. The Arab-Israeli War was then the second stage of conflict, which began in 1948 when the state of Israel declared its independence. The 1947–1949 war, known as the War of Independence in Israel or the *Nakba* in Arabic (meaning catastrophe), included fighting in the Sinai Peninsula and in southern Lebanon. It involved Egypt, Jordan, Syria, and elements of the Iraqi and Lebanese armies. From then on, Israel controlled not only territory demarcated for its state but also 60 percent of the area proposed for the Palestinian state in the 1947 partition plan. The 1949 Armistice Agreements that followed the war created demilitarized zones on the Israel-Syria border and in the south, from the Sea of Galilee east to the Yarmouk River, where the borders of Israel, Jordan, and Syria converge. Water cooperation in this area was particularly fraught from 1948 when there were military clashes with Syria. Then, from 1948 to 1966, Palestinians in Israel were granted nominal citizenship but forced to live under Israeli military rule, which abrogated many of the rights that citizenship afforded, until the end of 1966.

The next crisis took place in October 1956. The so-called Suez Crisis, a full-fledged war, involved a British, French, and Israeli military response to the nationalization of the Suez Canal by Egyptian leader General Gamal Abdel Nasser in July 1956. It was incredibly counterproductive. It prevented the maintenance of free shipping through the canal as forty-seven ships were scuttled in the waterway. It diminished British influence in the Middle East and globally, put sterling under sustained attack, and placed the British and American bilateral relationship under undue strain. On January 9, 1957, British prime minister Anthony Eden resigned.

The 1967 Arab-Israeli War took place from June 5 to 10, 1967. There were multiple causes for this military confrontation; these included: tensions over Israel's National Water Carrier project, which was siphoning off water from the Sea of Galilee from 1964; the Arab response, which deprived Israel of 35 percent of its water by diverting the Jordan River headwaters to the Yarmouk River; border clashes with Syria in 1967; a Syria-Egypt military pact, which Jordan and Iraq joined later; the expulsion of the UN Emergency Force (UNEF) from the Sinai Peninsula and the buildup of Egyptian forces there; and the Egyptian closure of the Straits of Tiran to Israeli shipping. An Israeli preemptive strike took place on June 5, 1967, during the course of the war, which led to the capture of West Bank, East Jerusalem, and the Gaza Strip.

But according to historians such as Pappé, the Israelis had wanted to occupy the West Bank since 1948, and allegedly thought about doing so in 1958 and 1960; therefore, the 1967 war could be considered a continuation of Zionist colonization of Palestine evident since 1882.[2] However, there is evidence to suggest that West Bank status was on the negotiating table at several times under moderate Israeli politicians such as Rabin. The confrontation between the United Arab Republic (UAR) and Israel had already led to the Rotem Crisis in 1960,[3] when tensions along the Israel-Syria border prompted Nasser to deploy its armed forces on Israel's southern flank. But David Ben-Gurion avoided a military confrontation then. By 1966, the Israeli military rule was replaced by what some scholars refer to as a process or system of settler colonial consolidation.[4]

The 1973 October War took place from October 6 to 25 and was led by a coalition of Arab states, with Egypt and Syria at the forefront. Only following this conflict and with the Egypt-Israel peace treaty signed in 1979, which President Sadat would pay for with his life in 1981, was the Sinai Peninsula handed back to Egypt. In protest against the peace treaty, the Arab League moved its headquarters from Cairo to Tunis until 1989.

The Golan Heights were not returned to Syria. Furthermore, the West Bank (including East Jerusalem) and the Gaza Strip remained under Israeli control. The West Bank and Gaza Strip were never up for renegotiation from the point of Israeli government meetings held on June 19 and 20, 1973, which has largely been supported by successive administrations.[5] Palestinians still remain citizen-less. UN Security Council Resolutions 242 and 338 stipulate that Israel withdraw from 1967 territories in return for peace. Palestinian rights are also recognized in UN General Assembly Resolutions 3236 (1974) and 3376 (1975) after which a UN Committee on the Exercise of the Inalienable Rights of the Palestinian People was set up.[6]

Repeated attacks from the Palestine Liberation Organization (PLO) led to the Israel Defence Forces (IDF) invading southern Lebanon in 1982. Lebanese Christian militia called Falangists, then allied to Israel, entered the Shatila refugee camp with IDF authorization and massacred up to three thousand residents of Shatila and the adjacent Sabra neighborhood. The Israeli government's Kahan Commission found that the then defense minister, Ariel Sharon, bore personal responsibility and recommended he be removed from office.[7] Sharon resigned after this but remained in the cabinet as a minister without portfolio.

From the 1982 incursion into Lebanon came the birth of Hezbollah, a Shia militia allied to Iran, intent on destroying Israel and expelling Western influences from Lebanon and the wider Middle East.[8]

Due to a collision between an IDF truck and a civilian car, which killed four Palestinians, the first intifada (a period of intensified Israeli-Palestinian violence) began in 1987. It included civil disobedience in the West Bank and Gaza, general strikes, and boycott of Israeli administrations. After the 1990–1991 Gulf War, the United States recognized it needed to take action and launched the Madrid Conference, hosted by Spain, in 1991. It was cosponsored by the United States and USSR and looked like a chance to revive the peace process.

Yitzak Rabin returned to office in 1992 and his participation in what would become the Oslo Accords showed that Israel and the PLO could negotiate via Norway in this case without US guidance. The Oslo I Accord, or the Declaration of Principles, was signed in Washington, DC, in 1993. It set a timetable for the Middle East peace process and planned for an interim government, the Palestinian Authority (PA), in Gaza and Jericho in the West Bank. The PLO acknowledged Israel's right to exist, and Israel acknowledged the PLO as the sole representative of the Palestinian people and therefore its partner in the peace process. The League of Arab States was suddenly deprived of one of its main raison d'êtres—to support the Palestinian cause and coordinate policy and actions. Rabin's hope was to normalize relations not only with the Palestinians but also with all Arab states, beyond the existing peace treaties with Egypt and Jordan.

In 1994, Yitzak Rabin and Israeli foreign minister Shimon Peres attempted to use Oslo I as a way to bring Jordan back into negotiations. Peres and King Hussein of Jordan had met in England in secret in 1987 in an attempt to arrange a peace deal that would cede control of the West Bank to Jordan. But the talks were fruitless after Peres's coalition partner, Yitzak Shamir, refused to sign onto the deal.[9] This time, the West Bank was off the negotiating table, but following encouragement from Egyptian president Mubarak (not Hafez al-Assad) and President Clinton's promise of debt forgiveness, the Israel-Jordan peace treaty was signed on July 25, 1994. It included resolutions over land and water disputes, cooperation on tourism, as well as a nonaggression pact.

Oslo II Accord was signed in Taba, Egypt, on September 24, 1995. It included provisions to complete the withdrawal of Israeli troops from all West Bank towns except Hebron. It also set a timetable for Palestinian Legislative Council elections. But on November 4, 1995, Yitzak Rabin was assassinated in Kings of Israel Square (now named Rabin Square) by an ultranationalist radically opposed to the Oslo Accords. The first Palestinian elections were held in 1996, and the Hebron Protocol in 1997 meant a partial redeployment of Israeli military forces from the city. By 1998, the Wye River Memorandum meant that Israel and Palestine set out to resume the Oslo II Accord. Implementation was again hampered by each party accusing the other of not fulfilling its obligations.

The Camp David Summit from July 11 to 25, 2000, was an effort by US president Bill Clinton, Israeli prime minister Ehud Barak, and PA chairman Yasser Arafat to end the conflict. Although they got close, the oral proposals did not go far enough and were dashed by facts on the ground. There are also accusations that the United States was not an impartial intermediary but identified more with Israeli domestic concerns. The sense of optimism that such an opportunity presented and could have achieved cannot be overstated. The sense of pessimism and discontent that failure left spoke for itself. It at least led to the Clinton Parameters, which remain as the approximate guidelines for a permanent status agreement. They cover issues such as:

- territory (a viable state for the Palestinians);
- sovereignty over Jerusalem (Al-Haram Al-Sherif and a capital in the Arab section);
- refugees (a limited right of return, resettlement, and compensation); and
- security guarantees.

It was accepted with reservations on both sides. The two sides met in Taba, Egypt, in January 2001 to address areas of concern but no agreement was forthcoming.

With tensions already high, the second intifada from 2000 to 2005 was finally triggered by Ariel Sharon provocatively walking around Temple Mount/Al-Haram Al-Sherif, the holiest site in Judaism and also the third holiest site in Islam. He became prime minister in 2001 up to his death in 2006. In March 2002, Crown Prince Abdullah of Saudi Arabia put forward the Arab Peace Plan, which was endorsed by the Arab League, and asked Israel to withdraw to the 1949 borders and establish Jerusalem as Palestine's capital. In return, the Arab states would consider the conflict over and recognize Israel. The proposal had little effect, although in June 2002 President G. W. Bush became the first president to explicitly call for an independent Palestinian state. In June 2003, the Quartet (the United States, Russia, the European Union, and the United Nations) developed the so-called Roadmap, a set of proposals that included an end to Palestinian violence, Israeli settlement freeze and withdrawal from occupied territories, an independent Palestinian state in phase two, and an international conference to discuss permanent status issues in phase three.

The 2002 Nusseibeh-Ayalon Principles and the 2003 Geneva Accord recognized the reality of changing facts on the ground, especially settlements and refugees, and adjusted strategies to cope with both, including one-for-one land swap and resettlement only to Israel or Palestine subject to consent. In the Geneva Accord, Palestinian access to Haram Al-Sherif would be ensured by an international force.

Yasser Arafat, the head of the PLO since 1969, died in 2004. His successor to the PA was Mahmoud Abbas, who signed a ceasefire agreement on February 8, 2005, and led to Israeli military disengagement from Gaza. Tensions were building with Hezbollah to the north and in 2006 the IDF once again conducted a full-fledged war in southern Lebanon but were largely resisted, giving Hezbollah and Iran's then-president Ahmadinejad a boost to their image on the 'Arab street.' From 2008 to 2009, the Gaza War or Operation Cast Lead led to more than one thousand deaths from indiscriminate rocket fire, but mainly from Israeli attacks on Gaza, Khan Yunis, and Rafah in densely populated areas.

Locating the Conflict in Regional Politics
Peace Proposals and Contact
The Israel-Palestine conflict has been central in the politics of the Middle East, a cause of multiple wars and refugees, but also a festering wound that has compromised even a sense of regional integration and cooperation. In the MENA region, Algeria, Iraq, Kuwait, Lebanon, Libya, Saudi Arabia, Syria, and Yemen have never recognized Israel. There have been repeated attempts to negotiate a peace deal. The most recent was the 2002 Arab Peace Plan reached at the Arab League summit in Beirut, which promises recognition of Israel by fifty-seven Arab and Muslim states (including Iran, Pakistan, Sudan, and Libya as members of the Organization of Islamic Cooperation (OIC)) in exchange for a comprehensive peace agreement.

In the plan, terminology about full Israeli withdrawal has been dropped and replaced with text supporting land swaps, which takes better consideration of changed facts on the ground. The plan did not receive a very positive reception by the Israeli government, which sees security, particularly of border areas, as paramount, although further details could have been negotiated. The very nature of the plan incorporating the Muslim world and states, which maintain official policies of nonrecognition toward Israel, meant that the Israeli leadership has remained skeptical of any peace overtures at the macro level, no matter how sincere. The fact that the only negotiators from the Arab League side could be those states that already had peace agreements with Israel, that is, Jordan and Egypt, and lack of follow-up by the Arab League made it difficult to make progress.[10]

In 2006, Hamas won legislative elections held in the West Bank and Gaza Strip, and afterward, in 2007, it formed a coalition with Fatah.[11] (This quickly broke down, as did talks in Cairo in 2017 aimed at mending the rift.) The PA rejected Israeli prime minister Ehud Olmert's peace proposal in 2008 because it did not provide a contiguous Palestinian state with Jerusalem as the capital.[12] Changes to the 1967 border also appear to be an obstacle to Palestinian acceptance of the offer, which presupposes that the PA can reign in Hamas in Gaza.[13] Since then, Benjamin Netanyahu took office in 2009 with a right-wing coalition, and there have been multiple conflicts between the IDF and Hamas in Gaza, both leading to a stalled peace process. Most Arabs (two-thirds) still supported a two-state solution in 2013 as the only realistic option to securing peace.[14] Iran, Syria, Hezbollah, and Hamas (the latter of which had officially left the 'resistance axis' in 2012 over conflicting interests during the Syria conflict) all continue a resistance discourse and actions against Israel, such as rocket and mortar attacks.

Spillover Effects in Lebanon and Jordan

Palestinian refugees have been living in Lebanon since the Israeli War of Independence or *Nakba* when seven hundred and fifty thousand fled the newly formed Israeli state in 1948. The Palestinians in Lebanon refer to themselves as 'the forgotten people' since no political solution has been forthcoming for the past seventy years.[15] Palestinians lack Lebanese citizenship (the same is true for many in Jordan as well), excluding them from many professions, and are not eligible to receive government services such as education or healthcare. This makes them reliant on the United Nations Relief and Works Agency (UNRWA) for basic services. The lack of rights and integration is testament to the steadfastness on both sides of the Israel-Palestine conflict, including Lebanon, all of whom see the refugee issue as the other's responsibility. As many Palestinian refugees still live in unsanitary camps where unemployment and poverty remain high, the attractiveness of any right of return is perhaps greater here than in other states, although no reliable data yet exists for the four million refugees that UNRWA has registered.[16] There are also ideological and generational issues. For example, for those growing up in exile, the right of return might look somewhat different from those who still remember their homes and lives during the *Nakba*.[17] In 2005, Lebanon did eliminate a ban on Palestinians holding most clerical and technical positions. But the regulation of foreign labor following an influx of Syrian refugees has been rejected by Palestinian refugees who say it will affect their status as refugees.[18]

Lebanon has continued to suffer from conflicts and strategies that have played out on its territory, including the 1975–1990 Lebanese Civil War and the 1982 Lebanon War. In 2000, Israeli prime minister Ehud Barak withdrew Israeli forces from southern Lebanon, and in 2005, Syrian forces were expelled through protests and the popular peaceful movement of the Cedar Revolution. But by 2006, Israeli forces were once again committed to a Second Lebanon War against Hezbollah in southern Lebanon. Without a decisive Israeli victory, Hassan Nasrallah, Hezbollah's leader, Mahmoud Ahmadinejad, president of Iran at the time, and the asymmetric warfare methods employed by Hezbollah were all widely regarded to have won the war.[19]

In Jordan, more than half of the population of 6.3 million is of Palestinian origin, that is, originating from areas west of the River Jordan, including the West Bank and Gaza. Therefore, national identity and the politics of national identity, including maneuvering within the context of the Israel-Palestine conflict and addressing political Islam and radicalism, have become priority issues for the ruling Jordanian monarch, King Hussein. Most Palestinians entered Jordan between 1947 and 1967. Most were granted Jordanian citizenship. However, after Jordan lost control of the West Bank to Israel in 1967, Palestinian fighters (*fedayeen*) moved their bases to Jordan and stepped up their attacks on Israel-occupied territories. Israeli retaliation at the Battle of Karameh in 1968 helped to embolden the PLO, and by 1970, groups within it were calling for the overthrow of the Jordanian Hashemite monarchy. In what was to become known as 'Black September,' the Jordanian army routed the *fedayeen* from the cities and expelled them to Lebanon. Black September was founded as an organization afterward, and in 1971, it assassinated Jordanian prime minister Wasfi Tal, who led the military operation against them. The organization then shifted focus back to Israel and conducted the 1972 Munich Olympics massacre of Israeli athletes.

Although there are high levels of interfaith cohesion in Jordan, ethnic and nationalist loyalty dividing lines across society are apparent.[20] Since 1988, there is evidence presented by Human Rights Watch that the Jordanian government is arbitrarily withdrawing nationality from citizens of Palestinian origin.[21] The move was initially sparked by Jordan severing 'administrative and legal' ties to the West Bank following the first Palestinian intifada.[22] It may also be seen in the light of the Arab League decision to prohibit dual nationality in its member states, although Palestine has not been recognized as a member state yet. More likely is that the policy would force affected Palestinians to reregister their residency permit with the Israeli military's Civil Administration in order to qualify for the right of return should a political settlement be reached.

Jordan remains exposed to multiple negative regional influences, including conflict and crisis in neighboring Syria and Iraq, which are driving up refugee figures. The economic impact for a semi-rentier state (due to its reliance on labor remittances and foreign aid) is also apparent as health and education costs and interrupted trade routes are affecting Jordan's economy. Continued uncertainty and reduced external assistance all add pressure and have left long-term economic growth prospects stymied. Unemployment remained high at 19.2 percent in the second quarter of 2019.[23]

Israel and Syria

Syria and Israel have technically been in a state of war since 1948. The countries have fought three major wars, including the 1948 Arab-Israeli War, the 1967 Six-Day War from which point Israel occupied large parts of the Golan Heights, and the 1973 Yom Kippur/Ramadan War. Syria was also involved in the Lebanese Civil War and 1982 Lebanon War between the PLO and Israeli Defense Forces. On May 31, 1976, Syria occupied Lebanon with Palestinian units under its command and then used its own army in response to appeals from Christian Maronite villagers under attack from Leftists. In the Riyadh Summit of October 1976, the Arab League decided to rely almost exclusively on Syrian troops as its Arab Deterrent Force in Lebanon. After the Israeli-Egyptian peace treaty of 1979, Syria became Israel's number one foe. Thus, during the 1982 Lebanon War, the IDF were targeting Syria and the PLO in Lebanon in a response to the changing security situation at first and then in an attempt to shape its immediate security environment.[24]

In 1991, after Michel Aoun's rival administration in Lebanon was defeated, Syria and Lebanon signed a Treaty of 'Brotherhood, Cooperation, and Coordination,' which legitimized Syrian forces in Lebanon.

The 1990s heralded a golden era for Israeli and Syrian diplomacy in the United States on the Golan Heights. The offer made first by Israeli prime minister Yitzhak Rabin in 1993/1994, and then by Shimon Peres in November 1995 after the former was assassinated, was for Israel to withdraw to the 1967 boundary of the Golan Heights in exchange for its requirements on peace and security, which included open borders and diplomatic relations with a phased withdrawal over years. Some analysts such as Patrick Seale have said this may have been a ruse given the timing of the verbal offer coinciding with the conclusion of the Olso Accords, which Assad could have scuppered.[25] Mutual suspicion and uneven strategic advantage on the border appear to be the main reasons why the deal faltered.

Syrian occupation of Lebanon ended with the assassination of former Lebanese prime minister Rafic Hariri in 2005. The general perception has been that Hezbollah and Syria were behind the attack, even though the UN-backed Special Tribunal for Lebanon found just one member of Hezbollah guilty and without any evidence implicating the Hezbollah leadership or Syrian government.[26] The continued convergence of Iranian and Syrian interests in Lebanon has sustained their 'resistance axis' against Israeli and Western influence and has been labeled as both 'rational' and 'realist' when considering the regional balance of power and spheres of influence.[27] As the conflict in Syria has intensified, Israel has reportedly carried out thousands of strikes in Syria and in neighboring Iraq against their advanced air defense systems, surface-to-air missiles, and arms depots.[28] The list of targets also included the symbolic Quds Force headquarters in Syria, the 'Glass House' at Damascus International Airport.

Syria remains a land bridge between Iran and Hezbollah in Lebanon, which Israel is intent on disrupting. Air supremacy and controlling arms deployments also appear to be a major part of the strategic calculation. Even though Syrian government forces regained control of the eastern Golan Heights in July 2018, on March 25, 2019, President Trump announced that the Golan Heights are part of the state of Israel. The move ignores UN Security Council Resolution 242 and 497, supported by the United States, which state unilateral annexation of Syrian territory is in violation of international law. But, in the context of the Syria conflict and Israeli security concerns, it might be a temporary measure to alleviate Israeli fears of Syrian and Iranian sponsored forces amassing near the border, in addition to the 30-mile buffer zone that Israel was negotiating with the United States and Russia in 2017.

Israel and Iran

Israel had, since David Ben-Gurion's periphery doctrine of the 1950s, developed close relations with its non-Arab neighbors (including Iran, Turkey, and Ethiopia) to protect itself from hostile Arab countries and Nasser's growing voice in pan-Arabism from 1956.[29] From 1967 up to the 1979 Islamic Revolution, both Israel and Iran pursued quiet diplomacy in areas of mutual benefit, including attempts by the shah to influence US opinion of him through Israel. However, following the Israel-Egyptian peace treaty in 1980 and the Oslo peace process, Iran became relatively less important to Israel. Once the Islamic republic was operational, Tehran put Israel at the heart of its ideational role conception and propaganda as a way to gain leverage over the Arab masses in order to undermine the legitimacy of pro-American Arab rulers, especially in the Gulf. Any resolution of the Israel-Palestine conflict would, therefore, represent a threat not only to Iranian regional interests and influence but also to a core part of Iranian political philosophy. This has been apparent since the Iran-Iraq War when Ayatollah Khomeini declared that the liberation of Jerusalem would follow on from a liberated Baghdad.[30]

Iran's message of Islamic/Shia solidarity was heard most profoundly in Lebanon in the 1980s, during the 1982 IDF invasion of southern Lebanon, through the establishment and support of Hezbollah as an umbrella organization for violent Shia resistance groups, and through a process of mingling between Lebanese, Iranian, and Iraqi Shia clergy in the learning center of Najaf. The emerging Iran-Israel rivalry was only stifled by the Iranian necessity to use Israel as a countermeasure to Ba'athist Iraq. This is demonstrated by the period 1985–1987, when Israel participated in supplying arms to Iran through the covert American-sponsored Iran-Contra affair. However, tacit cooperation stalled in the 1990s, and by the 2000s, Iran's changing political system and the regional system more broadly spelled out a new phase of the rivalry. There is speculation that Israel assists Iranian opposition/antirevolutionary groups such as the Mujahedin Khalq Organization (MKO), which operates outside of Iran.[31] And since Israel has supported Kurdish groups in Iraq in the past, there is the constant belief in Tehran that it continues to do so to the present day.

Similarly, Iran-US relations have deteriorated over time on issues ranging from state-sponsored terrorism to transparency over its nuclear program. The United States did not, notably, engage Iran post 9/11 on Afghanistan or any other issue because it did not want to legitimize the regime. Diplomatic activity with the Europeans suggested cooperation could be the way forward, first through the critical dialogue following the 1992 European Council, a comprehensive dialogue after the election of Mohamed Khatami in 1997, and a Trade and Cooperation Agreement (TCA) in 2001.[32] But by 2002, the discovery that Iran had begun construction of a secret nuclear facility at Natanz and Arak could have derailed negotiations, but the need to support reformists in Iran and international attention on Iraq bought the EU time to negotiate the Paris Agreement in 2004, which entailed Iran voluntarily suspending uranium enrichment.

By 2003, the United States had intervened in Iraq and had thus become a neighboring power, regional challenger, and a potential existential threat aimed at regime change in Iran too. Thus, Iranian perceptions of Israel took on a new guise whereby it equated Israeli and US interests in the Middle East as synonymous. Iranian insecurity and Israeli concerns about Iranian nuclear enrichment spearheaded new insecurities and instabilities in the 2000s. It is unsurprising then that Iranian president Mahmoud Ahmadinejad denied the Holocaust in 2005 in order to put rhetorical pressure on Europe and Israel over the plight of the Palestinians.[33] However, Ahmadinejad's comments were not an aberration. The scale of Holocaust doubters in the Middle East and North Africa is large, with just 8 percent of respondents reporting that they had heard of the genocide and believed descriptions were accurate.[34]

Ahmadinejad was also erroneously reported to have said in 2005 that Israel would be 'wiped off the map.' In fact, the remarks were originally made by the Ayatollah and could be translated as saying Israel would collapse.[35] It does not really change the degree of animosity between Iran and Israel. Indeed, Ahmadinejad backed Hezbollah during an IDF invasion into southern Lebanon in 2006 and received widespread support in the Arab world as an independent leader who stood up to the United States and Israel.[36] He went on to step up uranium enrichment to 20 percent in 2010, sparking fears in the United States and Europe that Iran would get nuclear weapons. Iranian attempts at securing and extending its regional interests go hand in hand with US and Israeli countermeasures, especially in delaying the Iranian nuclear program through nuclear scientist assassinations and the Stuxnet virus. The degree of escalation has been all too clear through Iranian Revolutionary Guards Corps (IRGC) and Hezbollah involvement in the Syria conflict, which has brought Iran and Israel in close proximity, and where Israeli air strikes against their bases have raised the prospect of an all-out conflict. That prospect is enhanced by the Trump policy of 'maximum pressure' against Iran, associated largely with the former US national security adviser John Bolton, which has been equated by Iranians such as Foreign Minister Javad Zarif as akin to war.[37]

However, rationalizing Lebanon's secular political system after the protests there, continued international support for the nonpartisan Lebanese Armed Forces, and Russian attempts to distance Iran-backed forces from Syria's armistice line with Israel and halt Iran's construction of military infrastructure in Syria could aid in the de-escalation of tensions.

Israel and the Arab Gulf States

The Israeli government continues to assert that the global public is uninterested in the Israel-Palestine conflict, citing 2019 figures that show that many Arab nations wanted better relations with Israel.[38] Benjamin Netanyahu insists that Israel-Gulf relations have never been better following various visits and other trade relations, especially with Qatar and Oman, from the 1990s, when the peace process was still on track.[39] Other contacts, such as between Israeli prime minister Ehud Olmert and Saudi national security adviser Bandar bin Sultan, and separately with the head of Jordanian intelligence, following the 2006 Hezbollah-Israel conflict, remain a state secret.[40] Israel has for a long time pursued covert relations with Saudi Arabia, the UAE, and Bahrain to avoid pressure on the Israel-Palestine conflict and weaken the Palestinian side. There have been a number of changes taking place at various levels: security, trade, and people to people. Israel has been involved in fighting ISIS in Sinai since 2015, alongside Egypt, and Israel's security relations with Morocco are also close.

In October 2018, Benjamin Netanyahu visited Oman—the first trip there since 1996. Sultan Qaboos was a longtime mediator in the Middle East, and this visit was no different as he sought to advance the peace process while discussing concerns about Iran. President Obama antagonized Benjamin Netanyahu by attempting to put pressure on the Israeli government for settlement activity and the Al Saud due to his willingness to engage Iran in the JCPOA. Both states have become somewhat more cooperative in this context. Israel and Saudi Arabia share intelligence on Hezbollah, Hamas, the Muslim Brotherhood, and activities in the Red Sea to the benefit of both countries.[41] Israel has already targeted Iranian military assets in Lebanon, Syria, and Iraq, all congruent with Saudi security interests. Furthermore, the Warsaw Conference in February 2019 allowed Netanyahu to appear beside Saudi, Emirati, and Bahraini ministers to show a common collective interest against Iran. While trade between Israel and Arab League states through third countries amounts to around $1 billion, there is potential to reach $25 billion.[41] This would be comparable to Israeli trade with the European Union but, more importantly, could help normalize political relations, a far superior objective. This began in September 2020, when the UAE and Bahrain moved swiftly to sign The Abraham Accords Declaration with Israel to establish full diplomatic relations and cooperation across a wide range of economic sectors. With further U.S. support, it is conceivable that some other Arab Gulf states will follow suit. Qatar, an obvious choice, would need to balance its relations with Iran and Turkey.

Trump has reestablished close relations with both Israel and Saudi Arabia, so there may be chances for Israel to leverage that joint support and interest in pushing back Iranian influence through more security and intelligence cooperation. However, unofficial spokespeople for the Saudi position, such as Prince Turki al Faisal, continue to insist that there has been no change in policy concerning Palestine.[43] Saudi Arabia needs to keep allying itself with the United States for reasons of national security, but with Russia and China becoming more assertive in the region, Iran also has options concerning naval cooperation[44] and sanctions avoidance.[45] The issues for Israel and the United States, as well as Iran and the United States, continue to revolve around domestic politics and negative history, regional turmoil and disintegration, lack of a workable security architecture, and the diffusion of international power. Iranian interdicted shipping in the Gulf and the probable Houthi or Iranian drone attack against Aramco facilities in Abqaiq, Saudi Arabia, in September 2019 illustrate the risks of worsening relations in the Gulf and elsewhere. All parties must be keenly aware that any changes to Arab Gulf-Israel security relations carries a risk of further destabilization in already tense spaces, namely the Gulf and Levant. Nevertheless, after Iran has managed to embed Shia militia in Syria, in the face of Israeli annexation in the West Bank, and the need to support commercial and diversification objectives domestically, a normalization of relations has a clear rationale.

Trump Administration Policy on the Israel-Palestine Conflict

Since Benjamin Netanyahu became Israeli prime minister again in 2009, he has staked his political career on security, notably citing Iran as an existential threat and continuing with settlement expansion. President Obama tried to address this logic, but Netanyahu was able to ride out the Obama administration and appeal directly to the US Congress. The Trump administration has been an ideal partner for the right-wing Israeli government, and Netanyahu has continued to play on his close political relations with President Trump. Indeed, President Trump, cognizant of his appeal to the Christian right and their importance to his reelection in 2020, has implemented a number of startling policy choices. They include:

1. In December 2016, Trump decided to move the US embassy from Tel Aviv to Jerusalem, recognizing Jerusalem as the capital of Israel.
2. In August 2018, the US government stopped funding Palestinian refugees through UNRWA, equating to a $300 million shortfall.
3. In March 2019, Trump tweeted it was time for the United States to recognize Israel's sovereignty over the Golan Heights.[46]
4. In June 2019, Kushner's economic plan sidelined Israel and appealed to the Gulf states (it was launched in Bahrain) for leverage, but it is not enough to solve the conflict, at least not without a viable political plan, which is why the Palestinians boycotted it.[47]
5. In August 2019, President Trump urged Israel not to allow in two US House Representatives critical of Israeli policy.[48]
6. By late 2019, Israeli settlements have been treated by the Trump administration as a legal endeavor without any significant US response aimed at halting them as a prerequisite to further negotiations—the Israeli government's ability to thwart any previous attempts at settlement freezes lends weight to some analysts' opinions that the United States was never serious about halting Israeli settlements.[49]
7. In January 2020, President Trump launched the much anticipated Middle East peace plan alongside Benjamin Netanyahu in the White House—it effectively gives Israel sovereignty over territory it already has settlements on, eliminating the Palestinian right of return, and does not provide any clear details on achieving Palestinian statehood.[50]
8. In August 2020, Secretary of State Pompeo ended a trip to the Middle East to lobby for the normalization of relations with Israel. The timing of the visit suggested the urgent need for a foreign policy 'win' in the lead up to the presidential election.

Gaza: Movement and Access

Israel has occupied Gaza since 1967 but disengaged in 2005. Since Hamas won elections there in 2006, Gaza has been under a blockade and a strict Israeli border control regime, including along the coastline. On multiple occasions, Israel has conducted several military offenses in Gaza aimed at destroying rocket-launching units, but also homes since Gaza City in particular is so densely populated. Reconstruction is often slow as many products used for construction, such as cement, are found to be allegedly diverted from intended end users or are suspended following rocket attacks.[51] Military operations include one in 2008, known as the Gaza War or Operation Cast Lead, when approximately 1,400 Palestinians and 13 Israeli soldiers died; another in 2012, when 167 Palestinians died and 6 Israelis were killed; and one in 2014, when 2,200 people were killed and many more injured in over a month of violence. Ceasefires between Israel and Hamas have been agreed to after each incident. From July 10 to 22, 2018, Israeli patrol boats opened fire on Palestinian boats on fourteen occasions.[52]

The Rafah Crossing from Egypt into Gaza has been closed since June 2007. It was reopened again following the 2011 Uprising in Egypt, but after President Sisi took power in 2013, Egypt's military destroyed the tunnels used for smuggling food and weapons across the border. Egypt has occasionally allowed supplies through such as diesel fuel for Gaza's power plant in 2017 and gas in 2018. It has been estimated that 1.5 million Palestinians live in Gaza and unemployment remains very high due to strict border control, which makes manufacturing and trade difficult. The funding shortfall for UNRWA is likely to play into the resistance ideology of Hamas and make Palestinian unity and statehood that much more difficult to achieve. Qatar has sought to fill the emergency and humanitarian gap in Gaza with a $150 million aid package announced in early 2020.

Conclusion

The 1990s represented the golden era for US and Middle East diplomacy, encompassing the Madrid Conference, Oslo Accords, and peace treaty between Israel and Jordan. But progress required moderate leaders with courage and the political foresight to think about their legacies. If Lyndon B. Johnson had been as firm with Israel in 1967 as Dwight D. Eisenhower had been with Britain during the Suez Crisis, it is entirely possible that Israeli annexation may have been halted and reversed and a two-state solution realized. Instead, a drawn-out 'peace process' was implemented.

The asymmetry in this conflict is highlighted by Israel's 2020 annexation plans for much of the West Bank, it could not only harm relations with the Palestinian Authority but also security cooperation and ultimately its peace treaty with Jordan. Regional and international actors are likely to continue to play a role in restarting any diplomatic track aimed at implementing a version of the Road Map. During the Syria conflict in particular is not the ideal time to start new negotiations. But as in early attempts, where there is political will, progress can be made. Although the Israel-Palestine conflict can be viewed as the regionalization of a conflict, it also serves as a blueprint on how to narrow down the variables of a complex negotiation yet to take place, including: the final status of Jerusalem, Israeli settlements, territorial renegotiation of borders, and any right of return for Palestinian refugees. This could be done through a combination of peace treaties, protocols, memoranda, principles, accords, and plans. The conflict has become internationalized over time, as an issue of global leadership, a cause célèbre, and a function of Israeli and Palestinian Diaspora politics globally.[53]

Intrinsically, despite great interest from the United States, Europe, and Arab states, the conflict remains an issue for the Israeli government and PLO/PA to negotiate on themselves with external support and pressure for both sides to reengage. That pressure has largely been lost following moves toward Arab Gulf state normalization with Israel. Progress is still possible with a more politically centered or left-leaning and open-minded Israeli government willing to engage in settlement suspension and negotiation. It will also require a Palestinian leadership intent on Palestinian unity, willing to adopt good and transparent governance, and be flexible on the issues of refugees and borders without necessarily ceding further concessions through a bad deal.

A change of governance structures in Lebanon and of Iranian and Syrian foreign policy or regimes may also be constructive in removing resistance to a two-state solution. The Israel-Palestine conflict remains central and relevant in regional relations as a primary ideological input into grievance, resistance, and control; as a historic and current legitimizing tool used by various governments and militia; as a factor in social identity; and as an obstacle to pan-regional cooperation and community. Its effects continue to spill over into, and create new dynamics in, neighboring states. Along with the Syria conflict, the Gulf Crisis with Qatar (and more broadly on the question of political Islam with reference to Turkey), and tensions between Saudi Arabia and Iran/Yemen, the Israel-Palestine conflict forms a significant part of a tightening Gordian Knot of Middle East conflict that is yet to be cut.

Notes

1. Raymond Hinnebusch and Anoushiravan Ehteshami, "Foreign Policymaking in the Middle East: Complex Realism," in *International Relations of the Middle East*, edited by Louise Fawcett, 3rd ed. (Oxford: Oxford University Press, 2013), 225.
2. Ilan Pappé, "Myths of the Six-Day War," *Cairo Review of Global Affairs* (Spring 2017), https://www.thecairoreview.com/essays/myths-of-the-six -day-war/.
3. 'Rotem' was the code name used by the General Staff of the Israel Defence Forces for an emergency movement of forces.
4. Arnon Yehuda Degani, "The Decline and Fall of the Israeli Military

Government, 1948–1966: A Case of Settler-Colonial Consolidation," *Settler Colonial Studies* 5, no. 1 (2014): 84–99.

5. Pappé, "Myths of the Six-Day War."

6. United Nations, "Question of Palestine," https://www.un.org/unispal/.

7. Jewish Virtual Library, "First Lebanon War: The Kahan Commission of Inquiry," https://www.jewishvirtuallibrary.org/the-kahan-commission-of-inquiry.

8. Stanford Center for International Security and Cooperation, "Hezbollah," July 2019, https://cisac.fsi.stanford.edu/mappingmilitants/profiles/hezbollah#text_block_18070.

9. CBS News, "Israelis Remember King Hussein," February 10, 1999, https://www.cbsnews.com/news/israelis-remember-king-hussein/.

10. Raphael Ahren, "Why Is Israel So Afraid of the Arab Peace Initiative?" *Times of Israel*, June 18, 2013, https://www.timesofisrael.com/why-is-israel-so-afraid-of-the-arab-peace-initiative/.

11. There was also a brief unity deal in 2011 after Fatah and Hamas both felt the aftershocks from the Arab Uprisings—for the former, pressure coming from the alignment between the Morsi government in Egypt and Hamas; and for the latter, concerns about popular protests over governance issues.

12. Reuters, "Palestinians Reject Proposal by Israeli PM," August 12, 2012, https://www.reuters.com/article/us-palestinians-israel/palestinians-reject-proposal-by-israeli-pm-idUSLC6231820080812.

13. Ibid.

14. Shibley Telhami, "The Arab Prism of Pain," *The World through Arab Eyes: Arab Public Opinion and the Shaping of the Middle East* (Philadelphia: Basic Books, 2013), 83.

15. For details, see: Rebecca Roberts, *Palestinians in Lebanon: Refugees Living with Long-Term Displacement* (London: I.B. Tauris, 2010).

16. Robert Mason, "The Price of Peace: A Reevaluation of the Economic Dimension in the Middle East Peace Process," *Middle East Journal* 67, no. 3 (Summer 2013): 405–425.

17. Diana Allan, *Refugees of the Revolution: Experiences of Palestinian Exile* (Stanford, CA: Stanford University Press, 2013).

18. Hanan Hamden, "Palestinians Reject Lebanon's Move to Regulate Foreign Labor," *Al-Monitor*, August 14, 2019, https://www.al-monitor.com/pulse/originals/2019/08/lebanon-ministry-labor-foreign-workers-palestinian-refugees.html.

19. The Economist, "Nasrallah Wins the War," *Economist*, August 17, 2016, https://www.economist.com/leaders/2006/08/17/nasrallah-wins-the-war.

20. Luisa Gandolfo, *Palestinians in Jordan: The Politics of Identity* (London: I.B. Tauris, 2012).

21. Human Rights Watch, "Stateless Again: Palestinian-Origin Jordanians Deprived of their Nationality," February 1, 2010, https://www.hrw.org/report/2010/02/01/stateless-again/palestinian-origin-jordanians-deprived-their-nationality.

22. Ibid.

23. World Bank, "Jordan: Overview," https://www.worldbank.org/en/country/jordan/overview.

24. Charles D. Freilich, "Israel in Lebanon—Getting It Wrong: The 1982 Invasion, 2000 Withdrawal and 2006 War," *Israel Journal of Foreign Affairs* 6, no. 3 (2012): 43.

25. The Guardian Foreign Staff "Israel 'Agreed to Leave All of Golan Heights," *Guardian*, November 24, 1999, https://www.theguardian.com/world/1999/nov/24/israel2.

26. UN News, "Hariri Assassination: UN-backed tribunal finds one guilty, three acquitted," August 18, 2020, https://news.un.org/en/story/2020/08/1070482.

27. Anoushiravan Ehteshami and Raymond Hinnebusch, *Syria and Iran: Middle Powers in a Penetrated Regional System* (Abingdon: Routledge, 1997).

28. Eyal Tsir Cohen and Kevin Huggard, "What Can We Learn from the Escalating Israeli Raids in Syria?" *Brookings*, December 6, 2019, https://www.brookings.edu/blog/order-from-chaos/2019/12/06/what-can-we-learn-from-the-escalating-israeli-raids-in-syria/.

29. Dalia Dassa Kaye, Alireza Nader, and Parisa Roshan, "A Brief History of Israeli-Iranian Cooperation and Confrontation," *Israel and Iran: A Dangerous Rivalry* (Santa Monica, CA: RAND, 2011), 10.

30. Anoushiravan Ehteshami, "Iran's Post-Revolution Regional Policy," *After Khomeini* (London: Routledge, 1995), 132.

31. Anoushiravan Ehteshami, "Iranian Perceptions and Policies towards Israel," *After Khomeini* (London: Routledge, 1995), 61.

32. Robert Mason, "The Shaping Factors of Regional Insecurity," *Foreign Policy in Iran and Saudi Arabia: Economics and Diplomacy in the Middle East* (London: I.B. Tauris, 2015), 28–32.

33. Associated Press, "Holocaust a Myth, Says Iranian President," *Guardian*, December 14, 2005, https://www.theguardian.com/world/2005/dec/14/iran.secondworldwar.

34. Emma Green, "The World Is Full of Holocaust Deniers," *Atlantic*, May 14, 2014, https://www.theatlantic.com/international/archive/2014/05/the-world-is-full-of-holocaust-deniers/370870/.

35. Glenn Kessler, "Did Ahmadinejad Really Say Israel Should be 'Wiped off the Map?,'" *Washington Post*, October 5, 2011, https://www.washingtonpost.com/blogs/fact-checker/post/did-ahmadinejad-really-say-israel-should-be-wiped-off-the-map/2011/10/04/gIQABJIKML_blog.html.

36. Jeffrey Fleishman, "Arab Sees a Heroin Iran Leader," *Los Angeles Times*, September 24, 2007, https://www.latimes.com/archives/la-xpm-2007-sep-24-fg-ahmadinejad24-story.html.

37. Reuters, "Iran's Zarif Says US 'Thirst for War' Should Go with Bolton—Tweet," September 11, 2019, https://uk.reuters.com/article/uk-usa-trump-bolton-zarif/irans-zarif-says-u-s-thirst-for-war-should-go-with-bolton-tweet-idUKKCN1VW168.

38. Tom O'Connor, "Israel Says World No Longer 'Interested' in Palestinian Conflict, Publishes Poll Showing Arabs Suspicious of Iran," *Newsweek*, March 29, 2019, https://www.newsweek.com/israel-world-uninterested-palestinian-conflict-1380800.

39. Ian Black, "Just below the Surface: Israel, the Arab Gulf States and the Limits of Cooperation," LSE Middle East Centre Report, March 2019, 5.

40. Ibid.

41. Ibid., 10.

42. Tony Blair Institute for Global Change, "Assessing Israel's Trade with Its Arab Neighbours," August 14, 2018, https://institute.global/insight/middle-east/assessing-israels-trade-its-arab-neighbours.

43. Andrew Parasiliti, "Saudi Arabia Still Awaiting Signs of 'Goodwill' from Iran," *Al Monitor*, November 1, 2019, https://www.al-monitor.com/pulse/originals/2019/10/prince-turki-aramco-attack-saudi-arabia-iran-israel.html.

44. Minnie Chan, "China's Role in Joint Drill with Iran and Russia Limited to Anti-Piracy Forces, Analysts Say," *South China Morning Post*, September 23, 2019, https://www.scmp.com/news/china/diplomacy/article/3030032/china-expected-send-anti-piracy-fleet-not-navy-joint-drill.

45. Bloomberg, "China Turns to Iran for LPG, Ignoring Sanctions," *South China Morning Post*, June 19, 2019, https://www.scmp.com/news/china/diplomacy/article/3015172/china-turns-iran-fuel-its-lpg-habit-ignoring-sanctions.

46. France 24, "Trump Signs US Recognition of Israeli Sovereignty over Golan Heights," March 25, 2019, https://www.france24.com/en/20190325-trump-signs-us-recognition-israeli-sovereignty-over-golan-heights.

47. Stephen Kalin, Suleiman Al-Khalidi, and Mohamed Abdellah, "Kushner's Economic Plan for Mideast Peace Faces Broad Arab Rejection," *Reuters*, June 23, 2019, https://www.reuters.com/article/us-israel-palestinians-plan-arabs/kushners-economic-plan-for-mideast-peace-faces-broad-arab-rejection-idUSKCN1TN0RW.

48. Emma Green, "Trump Has Enabled Israel's Antidemocratic Tendencies at Every Turn," August 15, 2019, *Atlantic*, https://www.theatlantic.com/politics/archive/2019/08/israel-bans-omar-tlaib/596167/.

49. Aaron David Miller and Daniel Kurtzer, "Let's Not Pretend Washington

Ever Really Tried to Stop Israeli Settlements," *Hour*, November 22, 2019, https://www.thehour.com/opinion/article/Let-s-not-pretend-Washington-ever-really-tried-to-14854509.php?utm_campaign=CMS%20Sharing%20Tools%20(Desktop)&utm_source=share-by-email&utm_medium=email.

50. BBC News, "Trump Releases Long-Awaited Middle-East Peace Plan," January 28, 2020, https://www.bbc.com/news/world-middle-east-51288218.

51. UN Office for the Coordination of Humanitarian Affairs, "Intensified Restrictions on the Entry of Building Materials Delay the Completion of Housing Projects in Gaza," December 13, 2016, https://www.ochaopt.org/content/intensified-restrictions-entry-building-materials-delay-completion-housing-projects-gaza; TOI Staff and Judah Ari Gross, "Israel Strikes Gaza, Suspends Cement Imports after Rocket Fire," *Times of Israel*, February 10, 2020, https://www.timesofisrael.com/israel-reportedly-strikes-gaza-suspends-concrete-imports-after-rocket-fire/.

52. UNRWA, "Gaza Situation Report 228," July 28, 2018, https://www.unrwa.org/newsroom/emergency-reports/gaza-situation-report-228.

53. See, for example, John Mearsheimer and Stephen Walt, *The Israeli Lobby and US Foreign Policy* (New York: Farrar, Straus and Giroux, 2008); and Alejandra Galindo, Cecilia Baeza, and Elodie Brun, "Diversity behind Unity: Latin America's Response to the Arab Spring," in *International Politics of the Arab Spring: Popular Unrest and Foreign Policy*, ed. Robert Mason (New York: Palgrave, 2014), 125–153.

Bibliography

Ahren, Raphael. "Why Is Israel So Afraid of the Arab Peace Initiative?" *Times of Israel*, June 18, 2013. https://www.timesofisrael.com/why-is-israel-so-afraid-of-the-arab-peace-initiative/.

Allan, Diana. *Refugees of the Revolution: Experiences of Palestinian Exile*. Stanford, CA: Stanford University Press, 2013.

Associated Press. "Holocaust a Myth, Says Iranian President." *Guardian*, December 14, 2005. https://www.theguardian.com/world/2005/dec/14/iran.secondworldwar.

BBC News. "Trump Releases Long-Awaited Middle-East Peace Plan." January 28, 2020. https://www.bbc.com/news/world-middle-east-51288218.

Black, Ian. "Just below the Surface: Israel, the Arab Gulf States and the Limits of Cooperation." LSE Middle East Centre Report, March 2019.

Bloomberg. "China Turns to Iran for LPG, Ignoring Sanctions." *South China Morning Post*, June 19, 2019. https://www.scmp.com/news/china/diplomacy/article/3015172/china-turns-iran-fuel-its-lpg-habit-ignoring-sanctions.

CBS News. "Israelis Remember King Hussein." February 10, 1999. https://www.cbsnews.com/news/israelis-remember-king-hussein/

Chan, Minnie. "China's Role in Joint Drill with Iran and Russia Limited to Anti-Piracy Forces, Analysts Say." *South China Morning Post*, September 23, 2019. https://www.scmp.com/news/china/diplomacy/article/3030032/china-expected-send-anti-piracy-fleet-not-navy-joint-drill.

Cohen, Eyal Tsir, and Kevin Huggard. "What Can We Learn from the Escalating Israeli Raids in Syria?" *Brookings*, December 6, 2019. https://www.brookings.edu/blog/order-from-chaos/2019/12/06/what-can-we-learn-from-the-escalating-israeli-raids-in-syria/.

Degani, Arnon Yehuda. "The Decline and Fall of the Israeli Military Government, 1948–1966: A Case of Settler-Colonial Consolidation." *Settler Colonial Studies* 5, no. 1 (2014): 84–99.

Ehteshami, Anoushiravan, and Raymond Hinnebusch. *Syria and Iran: Middle Powers in a Penetrated Regional System*. Abingdon: Routledge, 1997.

Fleishman, Jeffrey. "Arab Sees a Heroin Iran Leader." *Los Angeles Times*, September 24, 2007. https://www.latimes.com/archives/la-xpm-2007-sep-24-fg-ahmadinejad24-story.html.

France 24. "Trump Signs US Recognition of Israeli Sovereignty over Golan Heights." March 25, 2019. https://www.france24.com/en/20190325-trump-signs-us-recognition-israeli-sovereignty-over-golan-heights.

Freilich, Charles D. "Israel in Lebanon—Getting It Wrong: The 1982 Invasion, 2000 Withdrawal and 2006 War." *Israel Journal of Foreign Affairs* 6, no. 3 (2012): 41–75.

Galindo, Alejandra, Cecilia Baeza, and Elodie Brun. "Diversity behind Unity: Latin America's Response to the Arab Spring." In *International Politics of the Arab Spring: Popular Unrest and Foreign Policy*, edited by Robert Mason, 125–153. New York: Palgrave, 2014.

Gandolfo, Luisa. *Palestinians in Jordan: The Politics of Identity*. London: I.B. Tauris, 2012.

Green, Emma. "Trump Has Enabled Israel's Antidemocratic Tendencies at Every Turn." *Atlantic*, August 15, 2019. https://www.theatlantic.com/politics/archive/2019/08/israel-bans-omar-tlaib/596167/.

———. "The World Is Full of Holocaust Deniers." *Atlantic*, May 14, 2014. https://www.theatlantic.com/international/archive/2014/05/the-world-is-full-of-holocaust-deniers/370870/.

Hamden, Hanan. "Palestinians Reject Lebanon's Move to Regulate Foreign Labor." *Al-Monitor*, August 14, 2019. https://www.al-monitor.com/pulse/originals/2019/08/lebanon-ministry-labor-foreign-workers-palestinian-refugees.html.

Hinnebusch, Raymond, and Anoushiravan Ehteshami, "Foreign Policymaking in the Middle East: Complex Realism." In International Relations of the

Middle East, 3rd ed., edited by Louise Fawcett, 225–245. Oxford: Oxford University Press, 2013.

Human Rights Watch. "Stateless Again: Palestinian-Origin Jordanians Deprived of their Nationality." February 1, 2010. https://www.hrw.org/report/2010/02/01/stateless-again/palestinian-origin-jordanians-deprived-their-nationality.

Jewish Virtual Library. "First Lebanon War: The Kahan Commission of Inquiry." https://www.jewishvirtuallibrary.org/the-kahan-commission-of-inquiry.

Kalin, Stephen, Suleiman Al-Khalidi, and Mohamed Abdellah. "Kushner's Economic Plan for Mideast Peace Faces Broad Arab Rejection." *Reuters*, June 23, 2019. https://www.reuters.com/article/us-israel-palestinians-plan-arabs/kushners-economic-plan-for-mideast-peace-faces-broad-arab-rejection-idUSKCN1TN0RW.

Kaye, Dalia Dassa, Alireza Nader, and Parisa Roshan. *Israel and Iran: A Dangerous Rivalry*. Santa Monica, CA: RAND, 2011.

Kessler, Glenn. "Did Ahmadinejad Really Say Israel Should be 'Wiped off the Map?'" *Washington Post*, October 5, 2011. https://www.washingtonpost.com/blogs/fact-checker/post/did-ahmadinejad-really-say-israel-should-be-wiped-off-the-map/2011/10/04/gIQABJIKML_blog.html.

Mason, Robert. "The Price of Peace: A Reevaluation of the Economic Dimension in the Middle East Peace Process." *Middle East Journal* 67, no. 3 (Summer 2013): 405–425.

———. *Foreign Policy in Iran and Saudi Arabia: Economics and Diplomacy in the Middle East*. London: I.B. Tauris, 2014.

Mearsheimer, John, and Stephen Walt. *The Israeli Lobby and US Foreign Policy*. New York: Farrar, Straus and Giroux, 2008.

Miller, Aaron David, and Daniel Kurtzer. "Let's Not Pretend Washington Ever Really Tried to Stop Israeli Settlements." *Hour*, November 22, 2019. https://www.thehour.com/opinion/article/Let-s-not-pretend-Washington-ever-really-tried-to-14854509.php?utm_campaign=CMS%20Sharing%20Tools%20(Desktop)&utm_source=share-by-email&utm_medium=email.

O'Connor, Tom. "Israel Says World No Longer 'Interested' in Palestinian Conflict, Publishes Poll Showing Arabs Suspicious of Iran." *Newsweek*, March 29, 2019. https://www.newsweek.com/israel-world-uninterested-palestinian-conflict-1380800.

Pappé, Ilan. "Myths of the Six-Day War." *Cairo Review of Global Affairs* (Spring 2017). https://www.thecairoreview.com/essays/myths-of-the-six-day-war/.

Parasiliti, Andrew. "Saudi Arabia Still Awaiting Signs of 'Goodwill' from Iran." *Al Monitor*, November 1, 2019. https://www.al-monitor.com/pulse/originals/2019/10/prince-turki-aramco-attack-saudi-arabia-iran-israel.html.

Reuters. "Iran's Zarif Says US 'Thirst for War' Should go with Bolton—Tweet." September 11, 2019. https://uk.reuters.com/article/uk-usa-trump-bolton -zarif/irans-zarif-says-u-s-thirst-for-war-should-go-with-bolton-tweet-id UKKCN1VW168.

———. "Palestinians Reject Proposal by Israeli PM." August 12, 2012. https:// www.reuters.com/article/us-palestinians-israel/palestinians-reject-proposal -by-israeli-pm-idUSLC6231820080812.

Roberts, Rebecca. *Palestinians in Lebanon: Refugees Living with Long-Term Displacement.* London: I.B. Tauris, 2010.

Stanford Center for International Security and Cooperation. "Hezbollah." July 2019, https://cisac.fsi.stanford.edu/mappingmilitants/profiles/ hezbollah#text_block_18070.

Telhami, Shibley. *The World through Arab Eyes: Arab Public Opinion and the Shaping of the Middle East,* 83. Philadelphia: Basic Books, 2013.

The Economist, "Nasrallah Wins the War." August 17, 2016. https://www .economist.com/leaders/2006/08/17/nasrallah-wins-the-war.

The Guardian Foreign Staff, "Israel 'Agreed to Leave All of Golan Heights.'" *Guardian,* November 24, 1999. https://www.theguardian.com/world/1999/ nov/24/israel2.

TOI Staff and Judah Ari Gross. "Israel Strikes Gaza, Suspends Cement Imports after Rocket Fire." *Times of Israel,* February 10, 2020. https://www.timesofis-rael.com/israel-reportedly-strikes-gaza-suspends-concrete-imports-after -rocket-fire/.

Tony Blair Institute for Global Change. "Assessing Israel's Trade with Its Arab Neighbours." August 14, 2018. https://institute.global/insight/middle-east/ assessing-israels-trade-its-arab-neighbours.

UN Office for the Coordination of Humanitarian Affairs. "Intensified Restrictions on the Entry of Building Materials Delay the Completion of Housing Projects in Gaza." December 13, 2016. https://www.ochaopt.org/content/ intensified-restrictions-entry-building-materials-delay-completion-housing -projects-gaza.

United Nations. "Question of Palestine." https://www.un.org/unispal/.

UN News. "Hariri Assassination: UN-backed tribunal finds one guilty, three acquitted." August 18, 2020. https://news.un.org/en/story/2020/08/1070482.

UNRWA. "Gaza Situation Report 228." July 28, 2018. https://www.unrwa.org/ newsroom/emergency-reports/gaza-situation-report-228.

World Bank. "Jordan: Overview." https://www.worldbank.org/en/country/ jordan/overview.

Postscript

Robert Mason

A t the time this volume was being submitted to the publisher, a global public health crisis was unfolding and beginning to threaten Middle Eastern states. While it is a challenge for most states, some of those in the Middle East and North Africa (MENA) region stand to be particularly affected.

The Immediate and Substantive Concerns

In terms of human security, COVID-19 will highlight public health provision and policies that generally differ across the Gulf states, developing economies in the Levant and North Africa, and those states experiencing conflict. Even before COVID-19 struck, many MENA states have been suffering from low health expenditures and a lack of human resources and equipment, even in comparison to other developing countries.[1] The World Health Organization (WHO) recommends 4.45 medical professionals per 1,000 head of population, but in Egypt and Morocco these figures appear much lower at 0.79 and 0.72, respectively.[2] However, many governments have built up hospital capacity for COVID-19 patients, and the UAE has built dedicated treatment facilities.

As Chapter 7 shows, the MENA region is already experiencing a number of complex public health issues such as diabetes and obesity, which have been reported as risk factors for the hospitalization and mortality of COVID-19 patients. UK prime minister Boris Johnson's admission to hospital and intensive care is testament to the role that being overweight or obese can play. In fact it has been a contributing factor in 70 percent of COVID-19 UK intensive care cases.[3] The health impacts of the virus are likely to be worse in areas under blockade such as Gaza or in states experiencing conflict such as in Syria, Libya, and Yemen. According to the

United Nations, Yemen's healthcare system is already said to have collapsed amid a rise in COVID-19 admissions.[4] Aid workers have reported that they are turning people away due to a lack of oxygen and other medical supplies.[5] A lack of medical expertise and diminished central government authority are also to blame.[6]

There are also fears that COVID-19 will affect the most vulnerable in society and quickly spread in refugee camps where social distancing is not possible in shared tents. Yet, many refugees face more immediate concerns than that such as food. Lockdown in host states means no school and no work as day laborers in construction, agriculture, or janitorial sectors, and therefore no income to purchase essentials. In Lebanon, Syrian refugees have also been stigmatized at the highest level of government when President Aoun stated that the country's crisis was due to COVID-19, the economy, and Syrian refugees.[7] The UN High Commission for Refugees (UNHCR) has reported that refugees who have been unable to work due to lockdown or curfew have been threatened with eviction by their landlords in Algeria, Egypt, Iraq, Lebanon, Libya, Mauritania, and Tunisia.[8]

Despite the risks from contracting COVID-19 in mass gatherings, protests have continued in Algeria, Lebanon, and Iraq. In Iraq they have been particularly effective at forcing out a president and two prime ministers. In other aspects of society, such as prisons, there have been some surprising developments. Scores of prisoners have been released from jails in Turkey, Egypt, Bahrain, Iran (many only temporarily), and Syria, but many thousands, especially journalists and activists, remain incarcerated.[9] The question for diplomats and NGOs involved in campaigning for their release is whether COVID-19 can be leveraged into a longer-term reevaluation of the judicial system and the elite's threat perception.

In terms of economics, COVID-19 follows on from a period of already low oil prices, which has affected economic ties between the Arab Gulf states and states reliant on labor remittances, including the Palestinian Authority, Lebanon, Yemen, Jordan, Egypt, Morocco, Tunisia, Algeria, and Iraq. COVID-19 has impacted global travel and tourism, which are often important foreign income earners, amounting to 15–20 percent of GDP for states such as Jordan, Lebanon, and Morocco, and close to 12 percent in Egypt.[10] But the impact of lockdown will be even greater in some regions. For example, tourist hotpots such as Luxor and Aswan have been disproportionately affected, as has Dubai. The Gulf Cooperation Council (GCC) states have not been immune from the economic impacts of COVID-19, with the Institute of International Finance (IIF) expecting a contraction of 4.4 percent in 2020.[11] The UAE's main equity index was down 30 percent in March 2020, which was consistent with G20 nations.[12]

Some Saudi tourism projects may be put on hold and Saudi Vision 2030 will probably have to be reevaluated in the context of COVID-19, low international oil prices, and an expensive military intervention in Yemen, which is coming to a close. We won't know the true impact on tourism until months down the line when the peak tourism season is taken into account and after states in North Africa experience the worst impact of COVID-19, which may be in the winter of 2020. However, there are already signs that some airlines are beginning operations again, such as *Emirates* running limited routes, and some resorts are opening up.

Disturbingly, COVID-19, like any international crisis, serves as a distraction to governments around the world and an opportunity for authoritarian states to step up their repression, which has been reported with special reference to the actions of Field Marshal Haftar in Libya, a state of emergency that could affect civil society over the long term in Morocco, and surveillance measures put in place in Tunisia. COVID-19 has also put democracies under further pressure. In the United States, a perceived lack of governance by President Trump, including a high COVID-19-related death toll, a pledge to sever US ties with the WHO, police brutality in the case of George Floyd who died on May 25, 2020, and the securitized response to the protests that followed, has eroded US soft power and normative influence. As Chapters 6 and 8 show, US foreign and security policy has been shown to be controversial at times. Any further deterioration in soft power status and global leadership can only serve to embolden Russia and China to aspire to and assume more influence and a global leadership role, respectively.

The MENA State Response to COVID-19

Many states have taken relatively slow and uncertain steps to fight the pandemic, including Iran that became a hotspot for virus transmission through the religious center of Qom to the rest of the country (including the deputy health minister[13]) and to many Shia communities in other parts of the Gulf. Indeed, Iran has the highest number of cases at 73 percent of more than 100,000 cases tested across the MENA region.[14] Denials and underreporting of cases and deaths, while not unique to Iran, have followed a series of incidents and public protests (covered in Chapter 2), which could enhance the influence of hard-liners and threaten further social unrest.

Surprisingly, Egypt has given more authority to key ministers and public health professionals to tackle COVID-19, which is unusual given the military's involvement in resolving medical supply crises and in complementing the public healthcare system.[15] Still, there may be limits to this. In South Korea and Taiwan, where COVID-19 has been most successfully suppressed, the military has only been used in niche support roles. South Korean personnel from the Chemical, Biological, Radiological, and Nuclear military command have disinfected frontline hospitals and other facilities in Daegu and collected personal protective equipment (PPE) from Myanmar. Military personnel have also been involved in the treatment of patients. In Taiwan, the military has also been involved in the decontamination of repatriation flights and participated in the production of surgical masks.[16]

Sayigh identifies that COVID-19 could still be an issue for Egypt and other states for different reasons such as being ill-equipped to respond, maybe lacking readiness, and possibly through transmission in the ranks.[17] This latter risk has been demonstrated by infection across six hundred US sailors on the *USS Theodore Roosevelt* aircraft carrier and the fired commander, Brett Crozier, who wrote to superiors seeking help to deal with the outbreak.[18] Evidence of the risk of possible transmission can also be found in the thirteen thousand members of the UK armed forces, almost 10 percent of those on active duty, who were absent from duty in mid-April 2020 due to infection (which was actually quite low), the need to self-isolate, care for relatives, or work from home.[19] Syria has demobilized thousands of reservists on March 29, 2020, to avoid spreading infection.

Groups of policymakers not wearing protective gear have been publicly broadcast on television in the Middle East, but again this is not exclusive to the region. Over time, perhaps by March 2020, the threat has become better understood. Public gestures such as disinfecting streets, offering free face masks, and using night-time curfews highlight the state narrative of being in control but do less to highlight personal and collective responsibility for flattening the curve of infection. Relatively high illiteracy rates and poverty are likely to be key challenges in this area, so too access to advice such as social distancing. In megacities such as Istanbul and Cairo, social distancing will be difficult due to population density.

Apart from some new health initiatives and additional hospital capacity, the main governmental response to COVID-19 has been economic. Most states have announced economic and fiscal measures such as a $3 billion special fund in Morocco drawn from the IMF,[20] postponement of business loan repayments in Algeria,[21] and a $860 million support fund to support businesses in Tunisia (although the IMF only loaned $400 million).[22] In Egypt, the government announced a cut in natural gas and electricity prices for industry and will provide a monthly payment of EGP 500 ($32) to one million informal workers across the construction, fishing, and plumbing sectors.[23] Jordan has increased liquidity by injecting $705 million into the economy through reducing commercial banks' compulsory reserves.[24] It has recently secured a $1.3 billion loan from the IMF, which has been adjusted to help the country reduce the spread of COVID-19. Lebanon announced $150 to support each low-income family and has also launched a $797 million stimulus package aimed at public workers, healthcare employees, and small- to medium-sized enterprises (SMEs).[25]

The Palestinian Authority (PA) declared a state of emergency over COVID-19, but rather than dealing with infections, the greatest fallout from the virus so far has been in the fifty-three thousand families who have fallen below the poverty line.[26] The United Nations Relief and Works Agency for Palestinian Refugees (UNRWA) that might ordinarily assist in this case is experiencing its own financial crisis (as outlined in Chapter 8). Local initiatives have therefore begun to distribute income locally to those most in need. In Saudi Arabia, an economic package targeting the private sector and worth $18.7 billion was announced on March 20, 2020.[27] This was followed by a royal decree issued on April 3, 2020, unlocking $2.4 billion to cover a portion of private sector salaries for those in the most affected industries.[28] In the UAE, a stimulus package was announced on April 5, 2020, worth $69.7 billion.[29] This was followed by a comprehensive package on March 24, 2020, worth $4.36 billion to support the business continuity.[30] There have also been local financial assistance measures such as reduced or suspended government fees and penalties in Abu Dhabi.

In Bahrain, the central bank increased its loan facilities to $9.8 billion.[31] The government then announced a stimulus package worth $11.4 billion.[32] It will also cover the private sector wage bill for one hundred thousand workers from April to June 2020, worth another $570 million.[33] Kuwait's stimulus package is worth $16.5 billion.[34] Qatar introduced the easing of bank lending conditions and an exemption of duties on food and medical supplies. An amount of $820 million, part of a wider stimulus package, has been invested to help employers ensure that all employees, including expatriates, receive their wages in full.[35] In Oman, additional liquidity of $20.78 billion has been found along with tax relief for businesses.[36] Low-income households have also benefited from an initiative to deliver grocery kits with essential goods.

All GCC states are members of the Global Influenza Surveillance and Response System, which enables information, testing kits, and PPE to be shared. There remains, however, a disparity in each state's preparedness: the UAE scored 5 out of 5 (5 being the highest level of preparedness), while Qatar scored only 3 out of 5.[37] But this masks the exposure that each country has to a range of different risk factors. For example, before lockdown the UAE had 111 weekly flights to China.[38] COVID-19 has not only affected locals in the GCC but also a large proportion of foreign workers employed there from countries such as India, Pakistan, and elsewhere in Asia. In the UAE alone, more than two hundred thousand Indian nationals registered to be repatriated.[39]

Iran has requested a $5 billion loan from the IMF to deal with COVID-19, which the United States is likely to veto as part of President Trump's 'maximum pressure' campaign against Iran's economy over its nuclear program and due to the Iranian government's alleged support for terrorism.[40] Some analysts cite that Tehran already has access to $700 million in its IMF 'reserve tranche' and $2.1 billion in Special Drawing Rights and so question the Iranian government motive in pursuing this request.[41] It is likely that the Iranian government understood well that the Trump administration would use its veto in the IMF. If so, it could hand Iran an easy public relations win. Already, Iranian foreign minister Javad Zarif has tweeted that "US has gone from sabotage & assassinations to waging an economic war & #EconomicTerrorism on Iranians—to #MedicalTerror amidst #covid19iran."[42] It may still backfire though as attention was also drawn to alleged lockdown delays and COVID-19 mismanagement in Iran.

Conclusion

The COVID-19 outbreak has been met with different responses in the MENA based on regime role conception, available resources, capacity, and in some cases foreign policy calculations. COVID-19 has drawn attention to the lack of health capacity in some states and the need for, and sometimes use of, technocrats and health specialists who are qualified to implement a coherent COVID-19 strategy without recourse to denial, recrimination, and propaganda. While this process has led to some unprecedented actions and improvements in spheres of public health, if sustained, it could contribute to a healthcare revolution in the region. Economic interventions in the short term have aided peoples' livelihoods. But the consequences of a prolonged pandemic without a vaccine will continue to threaten everyone at the human level, from presidents and princes to the vulnerable and poor. The effect on jobs, especially in the informal sector, and on poverty rates is likely to be devastating.

Further social strains or state-led disengagement from the global economy or at least cooperation on importing a vaccine as soon as it's available could be enough to spark the onset of another Arab Uprising. That outcome in itself is difficult to assess, with the promise of significant reform, political transition, and/or further conflict. Even assuming the status quo, it is clear that the post-Arab Uprisings social bargain will probably have to be rewritten once again, especially as the Arab Gulf states are likely to draw down *riyal politik*, navigate a more troubled period in business-state relations as they shore up balance sheets, and determine the role and timescale of the transition to a diversified and private sector-led economy. It's possible that more states will turn to repression against further social criticism and agitation and assume a bunker mentality and position. However, there is also a hope that COVID-19 will continue to generate more community-focused solutions where the state retreats or that COVID-19 generates new opportunities for political openness and a willingness to engage with civil society. At the regional level, COVID-19 might also facilitate dialogue and cooperation between states where little or none existed before, starting for example with the UAE shipment of medical supplies and PPE to Iran.[43]

Notes

1. Organisation for Economic Co-operation and Development, "Covid-19 Crisis Response in MENA Countries," April 29, 2020, http://www.oecd .org/coronavirus/policy-responses/covid-19-crisis-response-in-mena -countries-4b366396/.
2. World Health Organization, Global Health Observatory data, "Density of Physicians (Total Number Per 1000 Population, Latest Available Year)," https://www.who.int/gho/health_workforce/physicians_density/en/.
3. Aamna Mohdin, "Hospital Admission Puts New Focus on Boris Johnson's Health," *Guardian*, April 6, 2020, https://www.theguardian.com/politics/ 2020/apr/06/hospital-admission-puts-new-focus-on-boris-johnsons -health.
4. Thomson Reuters, "Yemen's Health System 'Has in Effect Collapsed' as Coronavirus Spreads, UN Says," CBC, May 22, 2020, https://www.cbc.ca/ news/world/yemen-coronavirus-health-system-1.5579982.
5. Ibid.
6. Vivian Yee, "Coronavirus Slams Broken, Embattled Yemen," *New York Times*, May 30, 2020, https://www.nytimes.com/2020/05/30/world/mid dleeast/virus-yemen.html.
7. Diana Hodali, "Syrian Refugees in Lebanon More Scared of Starvation Than Covid-19," *Die Welt*, June 6, 2020, https://www.dw.com/en/syrian -refugees-in-lebanon-more-scared-of-starvation-than-covid-19/a-53355378.

8. UNHCR Staff, "Refugees across Arab World Feel Economic Pain of Coronavirus," May 1, 2020, https://www.unhcr.org/news/latest/2020/5/5eabcf704/refugees-across-arab-world-feel-economic-pain-coronavirus.html.

9. Joseph Hincks, "The Coronavirus Is Prompting Middle East Regimes to Release Prisoners. But Journalists and Activists Remain behind Bars," March 27, 2020, https://time.com/5811237/coronavirus-middle-east-prisoners-released/.

10. Organisation for Economic Co-operation and Development, "Covid-19 Crisis Response in MENA Countries."

11. Reuters, "Gulf Countries to Experience Worst Economic Crisis in History: IIF," June 2, 2020, https://www.reuters.com/article/us-gulf-economy-iif/gulf-countries-to-experience-worst-economic-crisis-in-history-iif-idUSKBN2390M4.

12. Gulf Business, "UAE to Limit Daily Decline in Shares to 5% from March 18," March 18, 2020, https://gulfbusiness.com/uae-limit-daily-decline-shares-5-march-18/.

13. BBC News, "Coronavirus: Iran's Deputy Health Minister Tests Positive as Outbreak Worsens," February 25, 2020, https://www.bbc.com/news/world-middle-east-51628484.

14. Organisation for Economic Co-operation and Development, "Covid-19 Crisis Response in MENA Countries."

15. Yezid Sayigh, "Egypt's Military Has Allowed Civilians to Lead the Coronavirus Response, But Some Things Are Troubling," Carnegie Middle East Center, April 24, 2020, https://carnegie-mec.org/diwan/81613.

16. Euan Graham, "The Armed Forces and Covid-19," International Institute of Strategic Studies, April 8, 2020, https://www.iiss.org/blogs/analysis/2020/04/easia-armed-forces-and-covid-19?_cldee=eXNheWlnaEBjYXJuZWdpZS1tZWMub3Jn&recipientid=contact-71bfbc9a549be011b1d2005056be0013-7d47036c3e8448f4b6a107227e97e9dc&esid=f906a581-557b-ea11-911a-0050560310e7.

17. Yezid Sayigh, "Egypt's Military Has Allowed Civilians to Lead the Coronavirus Response, But Some Things Are Troubling."

18. Geoff Ziezulewicz, "Fired Theodore Roosevelt Commander Brett Crozier Reassigned to San Diego," *Navy Times*, May 5, 2020, https://www.navytimes.com/news/your-navy/2020/05/05/fired-tr-commander-reassigned-to-san-diego/.

19. Dan Sabbagh, "13,000 Absent from UK Armed Forces Due to Coronavirus," *Guardian*, April 16, 2020, https://www.theguardian.com/world/2020/apr/16/13000-absent-from-uk-armed-forces-due-to-coronavirus.

20. IMF, "Morocco Draws on Funds Available under the Precautionary and Liquidity Line to Address Covid-19 Pandemic," April 8, 2020, https://www

.imf.org/en/News/Articles/2020/04/08/pr20138-morocco-draws-funds
-available-under-precautionary-liquidity-line-covid19-pandemic.

21. Reuters, "Algerian Banks to Defer Loan Payments for Firms Affected by
Coronavirus," April 7, 2020, https://www.reuters.com/article/algeria
-economy/algerian-banks-to-defer-loan-payments-for-firms-affected-by
-coronavirus-idUSC6N2BA00I.

22. Elizia Volkmann, "Swift Government Measures Will Not Save Jobs, Businesses in Tunisia," *Al-Monitor*, March 30, 2020, https://www.al-monitor
.com/pulse/originals/2020/03/tunisia-economy-tourism-measures-corona
virus.html.

23. Egyptian Streets, "Sisi Announces Monthly EGP 500 Payment to Temporary Workers, Urges Private Sector to Pay Wages in Full," April 7, 2020,
https://egyptianstreets.com/2020/04/07/sisi-announces-monthly-egp
-500-payment-to-temporary-workers-urges-private-sector-to-pay-wages
-in-full/.

24. Reuters, "Jordan's Central Bank Cuts Bank Reserves to Inject Liquidity,"
March 15, 2020, https://www.reuters.com/article/us-health-coronavirus
-jordan-economy/jordans-central-bank-cuts-bank-reserves-to-inject
-liquidity-idUSKBN212102.

25. Arab News, "Lebanon Launches $797m Stimulus Package to Cover Costs
of Covid-19," April 17, 2020, https://www.arabnews.com/node/1660416/
middle-east.

26. Rasha Abou Jalal, "How Is Palestine Dealing with Added Hunger, Poverty
from Covid-19?," *Al-Monitor*, April 23, 2020, https://www.al-monitor.com/
pulse/originals/2020/04/palestinian-poor-families-government-plans
-coronavirus.html.

27. Khaleej Times, "Covid-19: Saudi Arabia's 120 Billion Riyals Stimulus Package to Benefit Expats, Private Sector," March 20, 2020, https://www
.khaleejtimes.com/coronavirus-outbreak/120-billion-riyals-saudi-arabia
-stimulus-package-to-benefit-expats-private-sector-covid19.

28. Al-Monitor Staff, "Saudi Arabia to Pay Some Private Sector Salaries Amid
Coronavirus Fallout," *Al-Monitor*, April 3, 2020, https://www.al-monitor
.com/pulse/originals/2020/04/saudi-arabia-pay-private-sector-coronavirus
-fallout.html.

29. Waheed Abbas, "UAE Central Bank Doubles Stimulus Package, Extends
Debt Relief to Customers till 2020-End," April 5, 2020, https://www
.khaleejtimes.com/coronavirus-pandemic/combating-covid-19-uae-central
-bank-announces-debt-relief-until-december-31.

30. PWC, "Middle East Tax and Other Measures in Response to Covid-19,"
May 30, 2020, https://www.pwc.com/m1/en/services/tax/me-tax-legal
-news/2020/middle-east-tax-other-measures-response-to-covid-19.html.

31. Anup Oommen, "Bahrain Issues $11.4bn Stimulus Package to Counter Covid-19 Economic Impact," *Construction Week*, March 18, 2020, https://www.constructionweekonline.com/business/263808-bahrain-issues-114bn-stimulus-to-counter-covid-19-economic-impact.

32. Ibid.

33. Deena Kamel, "Bahrain to Fund Private Sector Salaries with $570 Million Relief Initiative Due to Covid-19," *The National*, April 8, 2020, https://www.thenational.ae/business/economy/bahrain-to-fund-private-sector-salaries-with-570-million-relief-initiative-due-to-covid-19-1.1003542.

34. Arabian Business Staff, "Kuwait's Stimulus Package Offers $16.5 Billion in Additional Lending, KBA Chairman," April 5, 2020, https://www.arabianbusiness.com/banking-finance/444385-kuwaits-stimulus-package-offers-165bn-in-additional-lending-kba-chairman.

35. Simone Foxman, "Qatar to Pay Private Sector Salaries as Virus Cripples Business," *Bloomberg*, April 12, 2020, https://www.bloomberg.com/news/articles/2020-04-12/qatar-to-pay-private-sector-salaries-as-virus-cripples-business.

36. Saudi 24 News, "The Central Bank of Oman Provides $20 Billion in Additional Liquidity to Banks," March 18, 2020, https://www.saudi24.news/2020/03/the-central-bank-of-oman-provides-20-billion-in-additional-liquidity-to-banks-2.html.

37. Jonathan Gorvett, "How Prepared Is the Gulf for Covid-19?," Castlereagh Gulf Monitor, March 6, 2020, https://castlereagh.net/how-prepared-is-the-gulf-for-covid-19/.

38. Ibid.

39. Sameer Hashmi, "Coronavirus Leaves Gulf Migrant Workers Stranded," BBC News, May 16, 2020, https://www.bbc.com/news/world-middle-east-52655131.

40. BBC News, "Coronavirus: Iran Appeals for $5bn IMF Loan as Deaths Near 4,000," April 9, 2020, https://www.bbc.com/news/world-middle-east-52217600.

41. Patrick Clawson, "Opposing an IMF Loan to Iran: Not an Outlier, Not a Barrier to Aid," Washington Institute for Near East Policy, Policy Alert, April 14, 2020, https://www.washingtoninstitute.org/policy-analysis/view/opposing-an-imf-loan-to-iran-not-an-outlier-not-a-barrier-to-aid#utm_term=READ%20THIS%20ITEM%20ON%20OUR%20WEBSITE&utm_campaign=Iran%5Cu2019s%20Unnecessary%20IMF%20Loan%20%28Clawson%20%7C%20Policy%20Alert%29&utm_content=email&utm_source=Act-On+Software&utm_medium=email&cm_mmc=Act-On%20Software-_-email-_-Iran%5Cu2019s%20Unnecessary%20IMF%20Loan%20%28Clawson%20%7C%20

Policy%20Alert%29-_-READ%20THIS%20ITEM%20ON%20
OUR%20WEBSITE.

42. Javad Zarif, Twitter feed, March 29, 2020, https://twitter.com/JZarif/status/
1244229089772224512?s=20.

43. Amira Khan, "Amid Coronavirus Crisis, UAE Offers Iran a Surprising
Olive Branch," *Haaretz*, April 15, 2020, https://www.haaretz.com/middle
-east-news/.premium-uae-s-surprising-coronavirus-gesture-toward-iran
-may-signal-regional-shift-1.8768087.

Bibliography

Abbas, Waheed. "UAE Central Bank Doubles Stimulus Package, Extends Debt
Relief to Customers till 2020-End." April 5, 2020. https://www.khaleejtimes
.com/coronavirus-pandemic/combating-covid-19-uae-central-bank
-announces-debt-relief-until-december-31.

Abou Jalal, Rasha. "How Is Palestine Dealing with Added Hunger, Poverty from
Covid-19?." *Al-Monitor*, April 23, 2020. https://www.al-monitor.com/pulse/
originals/2020/04/palestinian-poor-families-government-plans-coronavirus
.html.

Al-Monitor Staff. "Saudi Arabia to Pay Some Private Sector Salaries Amid
Coronavirus Fallout." *Al-Monitor*, April 3, 2020. https://www.al-monitor
.com/pulse/originals/2020/04/saudi-arabia-pay-private-sector-coronavirus
-fallout.html.

Arab News. "Lebanon Launches $797m Stimulus Package to Cover Costs
of Covid-19." April 17, 2020. https://www.arabnews.com/node/1660416/
middle-east.

Arabian Business Staff. "Kuwait's Stimulus Package Offers $16.5 Billion in Ad-
ditional Lending, KBA Chairman." April 5, 2020. https://www.arabian
business.com/banking-finance/444385-kuwaits-stimulus-package-offers
-165bn-in-additional-lending-kba-chairman.

BBC News. "Coronavirus: Iran's Deputy Health Minister Tests Positive as Outbreak Worsens." February 25, 2020. https://www.bbc.com/news/world
-middle-east-51628484.

BBC News. "Coronavirus: Iran Appeals for $5bn IMF Loan as Deaths Near
4,000." April 9, 2020. https://www.bbc.com/news/world-middle-east
-52217600.

Clawson, Patrick. "Opposing an IMF Loan to Iran: Not an Outlier, Not a Barrier to Aid." Washington Institute for Near East Policy, Policy Alert, April
14, 2020. https://www.washingtoninstitute.org/policy-analysis/view/
opposing-an-imf-loan-to-iran-not-an-outlier-not-a-barrier-to-aid#utm
_term=READ%20THIS%20ITEM%20ON%20OUR%20WEBSITE
&utm_campaign=Iran%5Cu2019s%20Unnecessary%20IMF%20Loan%20

%28Clawson%20%7C%20Policy%20Alert%29&utm_content
=email&utm_source=Act-On+Software&utm_medium=email&cm_mmc
=Act-On%20Software-_-email-_-Iran%5Cu2019s%20Unnecessary%20
IMF%20Loan%20%28Clawson%20%7C%20Policy%20Alert%29
-_-READ%20THIS%20ITEM%20ON%20OUR%20WEBSITE.

Egyptian Streets. "Sisi Announces Monthly EGP 500 Payment to Temporary
Workers, Urges Private Sector to Pay Wages in Full." April 7, 2020. https://
egyptianstreets.com/2020/04/07/sisi-announces-monthly-egp-500-payment
-to-temporary-workers-urges-private-sector-to-pay-wages-in-full/.

Foxman, Simone. "Qatar to Pay Private Sector Salaries as Virus Cripples Business." *Bloomberg*, April 12, 2020. https://www.bloomberg.com/news/articles/
2020-04-12/qatar-to-pay-private-sector-salaries-as-virus-cripples-business.

Gorvett, Jonathan. "How Prepared Is the Gulf for Covid-19?" Castlereagh Gulf
Monitor, March 6, 2020. https://castlereagh.net/how-prepared-is-the-gulf
-for-covid-19/.

Graham, Euan. "The Armed Forces and Covid-19." International Institute of
Strategic Studies, April 8, 2020. https://www.iiss.org/blogs/analysis/2020/04/
easia-armed-forces-and-covid-19?_cldee=eXNheWlnaEBjYXJuZWdpZS1t
ZWMub3Jn&recipientid=contact-71bfbc9a549be011b1d2005056be0013-7d
47036c3e8448f4b6a107227e97e9dc&esid=f906a581-557b-ea11-911a-00505
60310e7.

Gulf Business. "UAE to Limit Daily Decline in Shares to 5% from March 18."
March 18, 2020. https://gulfbusiness.com/uae-limit-daily-decline-shares-5
-march-18/.

Hashmi, Sameer. "Coronavirus Leaves Gulf Migrant Workers Stranded." BBC
News, May 16, 2020. https://www.bbc.com/news/world-middle-east
-52655131.

Hincks, Joseph. "The Coronavirus Is Prompting Middle East Regimes to
Release Prisoners. But Journalists and Activists Remain behind Bars." March
27, 2020. https://time.com/5811237/coronavirus-middle-east-prisoners
-released/.

Hodali, Diana. "Syrian Refugees in Lebanon More Scared of Starvation Than
Covid-19." *Die Welt*, June 6, 2020. https://www.dw.com/en/syrian-refugees
-in-lebanon-more-scared-of-starvation-than-covid-19/a-53355378.

IMF. "Morocco Draws on Funds Available under the Precautionary and Liquidity Line to Address Covid-19 Pandemic." April 8, 2020. https://www.imf
.org/en/News/Articles/2020/04/08/pr20138-morocco-draws-funds
-available-under-precautionary-liquidity-line-covid19-pandemic.

Kamel, Deena. "Bahrain to Fund Private Sector Salaries with $570 Million Re-
lief Initiative Due to Covid-19. *National*, April 8, 2020. https://www

.thenational.ae/business/economy/bahrain-to-fund-private-sector-salaries
-with-570-million-relief-initiative-due-to-covid-19-1.1003542.

Khaleej Times. "Covid-19: Saudi Arabia's 120 Billion Riyals Stimulus Package to
Benefit Expats, Private Sector." March 20, 2020. https://www.khaleejtimes
.com/coronavirus-outbreak/120-billion-riyals-saudi-arabia-stimulus-pack
age-to-benefit-expats-private-sector-covid19.

Khan, Amira. "Amid Coronavirus Crisis, UAE Offers Iran a Surprising Olive
Branch." *Haaretz*, April 15, 2020. https://www.haaretz.com/middle-east
-news/.premium-uae-s-surprising-coronavirus-gesture-toward-iran-may
-signal-regional-shift-1.8768087.

Mohdin, Aamna. "Hospital Admission Puts New Focus on Boris Johnson's
Health." *Guardian*, April 6, 2020. https://www.theguardian.com/politics/
2020/apr/06/hospital-admission-puts-new-focus-on-boris-johnsons-health.

Oommen, Anup. "Bahrain Issues $11.4bn Stimulus Package to Counter Covid-
19 Economic Impact." *Construction Week*, March 18, 2020. https://www
.constructionweekonline.com/business/263808-bahrain-issues-114bn
-stimulus-to-counter-covid-19-economic-impact.

Organisation for Economic Co-operation and Development. "Covid-19 Crisis
Response in MENA Countries." April 29, 2020. http://www.oecd.org/corona
virus/policy-responses/covid-19-crisis-response-in-mena-countries
-4b366396/.

PWC. "Middle East Tax and Other Measures in Response to Covid-19."
May 30, 2020. https://www.pwc.com/m1/en/services/tax/me-tax-legal
-news/2020/middle-east-tax-other-measures-response-to-covid-19.html.

Reuters. "Jordan's Central Bank Cuts Bank Reserves to Inject Liquidity."
March 15, 2020. https://www.reuters.com/article/us-health-coronavirus
-jordan-economy/jordans-central-bank-cuts-bank-reserves-to-inject
-liquidity-idUSKBN212102.

Reuters. "Algerian Banks to Defer Loan Payments for Firms Affected by Coronavirus." April 7, 2020. https://www.reuters.com/article/algeria-economy/
algerian-banks-to-defer-loan-payments-for-firms-affected-by-coronaviru
s-idUSC6N2BA00I.

Reuters. "Gulf Countries to Experience Worst Economic Crisis in History: IIF."
June 2, 2020. https://www.reuters.com/article/us-gulf-economy-iif/gulf
-countries-to-experience-worst-economic-crisis-in-history-iif-idUS
KBN2390M4.

Reuters, Thomson. "Yemen's Health System 'Has in Effect Collapsed' as Coronavirus Spreads, UN Says." CBC, May 22, 2020, https://www.cbc.ca/news/
world/yemen-coronavirus-health-system-1.5579982.

Sabbagh, Dan. "13,000 Absent from UK Armed Forces Due to Coronavirus."

Guardian, April 16, 2020. https://www.theguardian.com/world/2020/apr/16/13000-absent-from-uk-armed-forces-due-to-coronavirus.

Saudi 24 News. "The Central Bank of Oman Provides $20 Billion in Additional Liquidity to Banks." March 18, 2020. https://www.saudi24.news/2020/03/the-central-bank-of-oman-provides-20-billion-in-additional-liquidity-to-banks-2.html.

Sayigh, Yezid. "Egypt's Military Has Allowed Civilians to Lead the Coronavirus Response, but Some Things Are Troubling." Carnegie Middle East Center, April 24, 2020. https://carnegie-mec.org/diwan/81613.

UNHCR Staff. "Refugees across Arab World Feel Economic Pain of Coronavirus." May 1, 2020. https://www.unhcr.org/news/latest/2020/5/5eabcf704/refugees-across-arab-world-feel-economic-pain-coronavirus.html.

Volkmann, Elizia. "Swift Government Measures Will Not Save Jobs, Businesses in Tunisia." *Al-Monitor*, March 30, 2020. https://www.al-monitor.com/pulse/originals/2020/03/tunisia-economy-tourism-measures-coronavirus.html.

World Health Organization, Global Health Observatory data. "Density of Physicians (Total Number Per 1000 Population, Latest Available Year)." 2019. https://www.who.int/gho/health_workforce/physicians_density/en/.

Yee, Vivian. "Coronavirus Slams Broken, Embattled Yemen." *New York Times*, May 30, 2020. https://www.nytimes.com/2020/05/30/world/middleeast/virus-yemen.html.

Zarif, Javad. Twitter feed, March 29, 2020. https://twitter.com/JZarif/status/1244229089772224512?s=20.

Ziezulewicz, Geoff. "Fired Theodore Roosevelt Commander Brett Crozier Reassigned to San Diego." *Navy Times*, May 5, 2020. https://www.navytimes.com/news/your-navy/2020/05/05/fired-tr-commander-reassigned-to-san-diego/.

Index

United States: 9/11 5; Afghanistan policy 172, 225; Arab–Israeli policy 171, 172, 219, 228–29, 230; foreign assistance to Egypt 41–42; Iran policy 53, 55, 177, 181, 184, 225, 227; Iraq policy 5, 36, 75, 98, 99–101, 119; Middle East policy 171–73, 175–77; relations with Russia 177, 179, 241; *see also* Abraham Accords Declaration; Bush, George W.; Clinton, Bill; Global War on Terrorism (GWOT); Joint Comprehensive Plan of Action (JCPOA); Obama, Barack; NATO; Trump, Donald

Velayat-e faqih see Iran

Wagner Group 104, 181
weapons of mass destruction (WMDs) xvi, 98, 99, 102, 104
West Asia 3, 182
West Bank 9, 133, 199, 217–219, 222–23, 228, 230; *see also* Arab–Israel conflict; Fatah; Gaza Strip
Wilson, Woodrow 171; 'fourteen points' 171

Woodhead Commission 216
World Bank 15, 197
Wye River Memorandum 219

Yemen xxiix; activism in 25; Arab uprising 75; British policy 170; conflict 113–19; divided society 75–76;Egyptian intervention (1962) 113; employment 20; environment 194, 198, 203–204, 206; governance 35, 113; health and education 16, 17, 197, 240; Horn of Africa states 115–16, 118; Houthi movement 76, 114, 115; Iranian influence and policy 76, 116–17, 119; al-Islah 116; National Dialogue Conference (NDC) 114; political economy 130, 132, 133, 138–42, 150, 152, 154, 155, 156; Qatari influence 116; reform 117; Russian policy 113; Saudi policy 114, 115, 116, 117, 118; Socotra 118; Soviet relations 174; southern secession 98; Southern Transitional Council (STC) 117; Sudan involvement in 115; UAE policy 117, 118, 119; US drone strikes 113; *see also* Saleh, Ali Abdullah; Hadi, Mansour